THE POLITICS OF THE PEOPLE
IN EIGHTEENTH-CENTURY BRITAIN

Also by H. T. Dickinson

BOLINGBROKE
BRITAIN AND THE FRENCH REVOLUTION 1789–1815
BRITISH RADICALISM AND THE FRENCH REVOLUTION
  1789–1815
CARICATURES AND THE CONSTITUTION 1760–1832
LIBERTY AND PROPERTY: Political Ideology in Eighteenth-
  Century Britain
POLITICS AND LITERATURE IN THE EIGHTEENTH
  CENTURY
THE CORRESPONDENCE OF SIR JAMES CLAVERING
THE POLITICAL WORKS OF THOMAS SPENCE
WALPOLE AND THE WHIG SUPREMACY

The Politics of the People in Eighteenth-Century Britain

H. T. Dickinson
Professor of British History
University of Edinburgh

First published 1994 by
MACMILLAN PRESS LTD
Houndmills, Basingstoke, Hampshire RG21 6XS
and London
Companies and representatives
throughout the world

ISBN 0–333–52171–4 hardcover
ISBN 0–333–65733–0 paperback

A catalogue record for this book is available
from the British Library.

10   9   8   7   6   5   4   3   2
04   03   02   01   00   99   98   97   96

Printed and bound in Great Britain by
Antony Rowe Ltd, Chippenham, Witshire

Published in the United States of America 1994 by
ST. MARTIN'S PRESS, INC.,
Scholarly and Reference Division
175 Fifth Avenue, New York, N.Y. 10010

ISBN 0–312–12456–2 (cloth)
ISBN 0–312–16033–X (paper)

For Frances Dow

Contents

Preface

The researching and writing of this book has taken much longer than I had expected or hoped. I first began to take a serious interest in popular politics in eighteenth-century Britain after I had finished my book on *Liberty and Property* (1977), but various other writing commitments, some heavy administrative duties and the sheer scale of the subject and the amount of work being produced in the general field by other scholars have defeated my attempts to complete the task earlier. I must particularly apologise for this to those who invited me to give the Anstey Memorial Lectures at the University of Kent in 1989 because the general topic of those lectures was the same as that for this book. I am grateful to the organisers of this series of lectures for inviting me to give them, to the family of the late Roger Anstey and to Professor David Birmingham who were so kind to me when I visited Canterbury, and to the University of Kent who made my stay there such a pleasant one. I am only sorry that they have had to wait so long for this book to appear.

Only four of the chapters in the book (Chapters 2, 3, 5 and 8) were delivered as lectures in the series and these have been revised and expanded. Some of the arguments and material in Chapters 6, 7 and 8 have appeared in other publications of mine: 'The Precursors of Political Radicalism in Augustan Britain', in Clyve Jones (ed.), *Britain in the First Age of Party 1680–1750* (Hambledon Press; London, 1987); 'Popular Politics in the Age of Walpole', in Jeremy Black (ed.), *Britain in the Age of Walpole* (Macmillan; London, 1984); 'Radicals and Reformers in the Age of Wilkes and Wyvill', in Jeremy Black (ed.), *British Politics and Society from Walpole to Pitt 1742–1789* (Macmillan; London, 1990); 'Popular Conservatism and Militant Loyalism 1789–1815', in H.T. Dickinson (ed.), *Britain and the French Revolution 1789–1815* (Macmillan; London, 1989); and *British Radicalism and the French Revolution 1789–1815* (Blackwell; Oxford, 1985). I am grateful to the foregoing publishers for allowing me to incorporate some elements of these works into parts of this volume.

This book is both a work of original research and a work of synthesis. I have researched deeply in some of these areas for many years. In other areas I have relied heavily for ideas and details on the work of a whole range of historians, though the overall argument presented here is my own. I have tried to acknowledge this debt in the notes at the end of this book. I also owe much to the University of Edinburgh for granting me sabbatical leave, the Leverhulme Trust for allowing me to take extra leave, and the University of California, Los Angeles, for awarding me the Ahmanson Foundation Fellowship which I held for a term at the William Andrews Clark Memorial Library in Los Angeles. I am grateful to the staff there and to the staff of the British Library, the National Library of Scotland and the Library of Edinburgh University for years of excellent service.

My greatest debt, however, is to my friend and colleague Dr F.D. Dow. She has read and commented upon the drafts of almost everything I have written for nearly twenty-five years. We also taught a course together at Edinburgh University on Radical Ideas, Popular Politics and Social Protest that helped to shape my ideas. Her advice has always been intelligent, perceptive and generous. I have benefited greatly from it and I have acknowledged this in the dedication as well as here in the preface.

HARRY DICKINSON

Introduction

Several very different interpretations of eighteenth-century British politics have been put forward by historians during my academic career and yet each has added something important to our understanding of the subject. Together these interpretations have provided us with a greater understanding of the political culture of both the governing elite and the non-elite and, most importantly of all, of the relationship between the two. None the less, the way in which elite politics and popular politics inform, influence, and interact with each other has been imperfectly realised. This book is a study of some of the most important aspects of popular political culture in eighteenth-century Britain, but it is also an attempt to show how that political culture related to that of the political elite. In my view we cannot fully understand the politics of the governing elite unless we also attempt to appreciate the political actions, beliefs and organisations of the people at large.

When I was an undergraduate the work of Sir Lewis Namier and his disciples still dominated the scholarly debate and the voice of a critic such as Herbert Butterfield was rarely heeded. Both Namier's interpretation and his historical method were almost universally accepted. Indeed, to this day Namier's conclusions on the politics of the early years of George III's reign still command considerable respect: he rejected the old claim that George III was trying to restore the prerogative powers of the crown; he proved that political disputes in parliament did not revolve around two organised parties, Whig and Tory; he played down the extent of political corruption and stressed the significance of the independent MP; and he emphasised the role of personal ambition and vested interests in determining men's political actions. Namier's historical method proved even more influential than his particular conclusions. In attempting to understand the political motivation of groups rather than individuals, Namier helped to develop a new method of historical enquiry, namely prosopography or collective biography. By collecting evidence on the personal life, public career, connections, and behaviour of every single MP, Namier was able to test more stringently than

1

ever before the factors which may have motivated the political actions of an individual or group. This approach led eventually to a vast scholarly enterprise in which dozens of historians have collaborated in producing many volumes on the history of parliament since the sixteenth century. Namier himself helped to edit the later eighteenth-century volumes.[1] He and his disciples taught us much about MPs and their efforts to secure election to the House of Commons.

During his lifetime Namier's influence was huge, generally beneficial, but, in some ways, pernicious. Only after his death in 1960 did a significant number of historians begin to argue that Namier's interpretation of eighteenth-century British politics was too restricted in time, place, method of enquiry and type of political activity. The Namierite view was increasingly challenged in the 1960s and 1970s on three broad fronts. The first attack was on Namier's chosen ground of parliamentary politics. Historians such as Geoffrey Holmes, J.H. Plumb, W.A. Speck, Linda Colley and Frank O'Gorman[2] all argued persuasively that, while Namier was justified in rejecting organised political parties as a major feature of parliamentary politics in the 1760s, his conclusions could not be extended to cover either the earlier or the later decades of the eighteenth century. Far from being typical of the whole eighteenth century the politics of the early 1760s were in fact highly unusual. The second attack on the Namierite approach has been waged by historians such as Edward Thompson, George Rudé, John Cannon and Albert Goodwin,[3] who looked well beyond the restricted political world of court and parliament and sought to discover the political culture of radical activists and plebeian protesters. The third broad assault on Namierism came from those historians who came to acknowledge the validity of Herbert Butterfield's old charge that Namier was almost wilfully blind to the role of ideas, principles and prejudices. Historians such as J. G. A. Pocock, J. P. Kenyon, John Brewer, Isaac Kramnick and myself,[4] attempted to demonstrate the influence of political ideas and the impact of ideological controversy on the political actors of eighteenth-century Britain. These three attacks on Namierism have taught us about conflict and change in both parliamentary and extra-parliamentary politics.

By the end of the 1970s it looked as if historians influenced by these three approaches to the study of eighteenth-century British politics were integrating them into a new consensus.

There was widespread agreement about the sharp divisions within the parliamentary elite in the earlier and later eighteenth century, the growing challenge to aristocratic hegemony by radicals and reformers in the last decades of the eighteenth century, and the vital role of political discourse during most of the century on such issues as authority, sovereignty, obedience and resistance. Eighteenth-century Britain was seen as experiencing political change rather than political continuity, with political stability confined to a short period in the 1740s and 1750s when the old party rivalry had waned, new divisions within the elite had not yet emerged and extra-parliamentary radicalism had not yet developed. In the 1980s, however, what seemed to be becoming a new orthodoxy was vigorously challenged by self-proclaimed revisionists. Influenced by revisionist historians re-interpreting early Stuart politics and led by Jonathan Clark and Eveline Cruickshanks in particular,[5] these scholars began to shift the emphasis of research from change to continuity, from radical and plebeian protest to patrician power, and from the impact of secular ideology to the pervasive influence of orthodox religion and the established church. In the most important and influential work produced by these revisionists – Jonathan Clark's *English Society 1688–1832* – much was done to stress the surviving power of the monarchy, the aristocracy and the Church of England. According to Clark the firm alliance of church and state, and the pervasive influence of a conservative ideology stressing order and obedience, were not seriously challenged by the small, if vociferous, group of religious and political radicals of the later eighteenth century. While avoiding Dr Clark's aggressive style and his iconoclastic tone, other historians have agreed that these three traditional pillars of the political establishment were crucial to the upholding of an aristocratic political and social order.[6]

Not all historians of eighteenth-century British politics agree with Dr Clark that Britain was then an overwhelmingly aristocratic society, a confessional state and an *ancien regime* broadly similar to those in Europe. Some of those historians who previously criticised Namierism have also rejected the more extreme claims of Clark and the revisionists. In doing so they have been forced to revive and revise the socio-political approach to eighteenth-century Britain. Whereas the revisionists have stressed continuity

in eighteenth-century politics, their critics have emphasised the
extent of change in some aspects of British life at this time. They
deny that the governing elite was simply a tiny landowning oligarchy sustaining the narrow, conservative ideology of high-church
Anglicanism. They stress that Britain was experiencing significant
social and economic changes that were making her more of a
commercial and urban society than she had ever been. And,
crucial to the purpose of this particular book, they have insisted
that the political culture of Britain cannot be fully understood if
historians concentrate almost exclusively on the politics of the
governing elite.

It is now recognised that it was not easy to enter the ranks of
the aristocracy, but these men did not form a distinct feudal or
military caste and they were heavily involved in a whole variety
of ways with other men of property. Financiers provided them
with loans and mortgages, substantial farmers were their
tenants and neighbours, professional men provided them with
valuable services, and commercial and manufacturing men
supplied their desire for a vast range of products. When they
wanted to exploit the mineral resources under their estates
they usually sought alliances with commercial interests. They
themselves were quite convinced that they lived in a commercial society and that this brought them many benefits and
advantages. The governments of the eighteenth century were
heavily dependent upon loans raised from the financial
interest, while the taxes raised by parliament were increasingly
customs and excise duties on items and services produced by a
commercial society. The many wars fought by Britain were
almost invariably about colonies and commerce. A high proportion of the legislation passed by parliament was concerned
with property rights, commercial transactions, and improvements to a commercial economy and an urban society. Despite
their fondness for their estates, the landed elite often spent
much of their political life in London and some of their leisure
time in spas and the local market town.

The aristocratic elite were very conscious that they had a
natural right to rule their social inferiors and that the poor
could not be trusted to govern. They were convinced that
democracy was inherently unstable and would inevitably
degenerate into anarchy. To preserve order and to protect
property they recognised the need for an absolute and

irresistible authority in the state. On the other hand, they insisted on placing this authority in the hands of the king-in-parliament and not in the hands of a single magistrate. In their view men of substance (however they derived their wealth) could not be expected to put their property at the mercy of an absolute monarch but only under the ultimate control of a benign parliament composed of substantial men of property. More liberal still was their acknowledgement that all men had the right to their life, liberty and property. They did not concede active political rights to all men, but they did believe they should all enjoy certain civil liberties. These included the right to freedom of movement, liberty of conscience, freedom of expression, personal and private property, and the fruits of their enterprise and their labour. They themselves had struggled to limit the power of the crown, abolish prerogative courts, establish an independent judiciary, render all subjects equal in the eyes of the law, and end torture and arbitrary imprisonment. Liberty of conscience and freedom of worship were gradually extended in the eighteenth century to all those who were not a threat to the state even though civil disabilities were placed upon those who did not belong to the established church. All subjects were allowed to petition crown and parliament for the redress of grievances, while the freedom of the press was widely and increasingly regarded as one of the greatest safeguards of British liberty.[7]

Religion might well be used to sustain authority and to inculcate submission to the powers that be, and religious minorities might be denied the full civil rights accorded to Anglicans. On the other hand, Hanoverian governments were anxious to avoid religious conflicts and showed no desire to interfere in the spiritual life of the ordinary citizen. Religious freedom in Britain was extensive by continental standards. In theory church courts still retained considerable powers, but it proved increasingly difficult to exercise them. The Church of England might enjoy various privileges, but Convocation ceased to have any active role after 1717, indemnity acts and the practice of occasional conformity undermined the restrictions imposed on Dissenters by the Test and Corporation Acts, and even the laws against Catholics were rarely executed except at times of extreme political tension. The Church of England might, in theory, be a massive pillar of the establishment, but it almost always felt itself in danger. In the early eighteenth century it feared the rising threat from Dissent. In the 1720s and 1730s it was alarmed by the growth of the many-headed hydra of heterodoxy: Socinianism, Arianism, Deism, Freemasonry and even atheism. The mid-eighteenth century saw the Anglican clergy worried by the Methodist revival, while in the later eighteenth century they feared the activities of the Rational Dissenters, they found the Evangelicals uncomfortable bed-fellows and they saw an increasing percentage of the urban poor failing to attend their churches. Despite being the established church, the Church of England was always divided within itself and never held the allegiance of all English·subjects (still less, of course, all British subjects). In religious terms eighteenth-century Britain was already a pluralist society.[8]

Despite revisionist attempts to represent Britain as a traditional hierarchical agrarian society dominated by the landed aristocratic elite, many historians would stress that what distinguished Britain from most continental states was the breadth of her manufacturing base, the extent of her commercial activity, the size of the middling classes and the proportion of the population living in towns. Even by the mid-eighteenth century a very significant number of British people were involved in manufacturing a vast range of products. Most contemporary commentators were conscious that Britain was a commercial society and that her wealth and strength depended on making and selling all kinds of consumer products. The men who organised commerce, manufacturing and the distribution of goods, the middling farmers, and the professional men who serviced a commercial society were a larger proportion of British society than the equivalent ranks were in most continental societies. Their expansion and the rapid increase of the total population from the mid-1740s (the population of Britain doubled in the eighteenth century) helps to explain the rapid growth of towns that were such a marked feature of the eighteenth century. Again, by continental standards, Britain (and especially England) was quite exceptionally urbanised and she possessed a particularly large and economically vibrant capital city. The large number of growing towns were the engines of economic growth and they helped to produce a distinctive urban culture that appealed not only to their inhabitants, but to those who lived in the rural areas nearby. Towns were the centres of information, education and communication in eighteenth-century Britain. Literacy rates were generally higher in towns and were particularly high among urban middle-class males, most of whom lived in a world increasingly flooded with printed material. The eighteenth century witnessed a remarkable growth in the printed word – in newspapers, magazines, pamphlets, books, etc. – and these were circulated with increasing facility. Towns also experienced an astonishing proliferation of clubs, societies and voluntary associations. These varied enormously from box clubs providing primitive forms of social insurance through literary, debating, philosophical and conversation clubs to the radical political societies of the later eighteenth century.[9]

These features of eighteenth-century Britain that have been dismissed, neglected, or underplayed by recent revisionist historians are precisely those which are vital to an underpinning of a book such as this on the popular politics of the period – the relationships between the landed elite and other men of property; the acceptance by them of the rule of law, a wider role for parliament and civil liberties for all subjects; the acceptance of a genuine if fragile degree of religious tolerance; the importance of the commercial sectors of the economy; the expansion of the middling orders; and the growth of towns and a vibrant urban culture. All of these features of British society were contributing to a lively political culture that involved very large numbers of the non-aristocratic elite in consciously influencing the decisions which affected the public at large and which shaped the political environment in which many people lived. This emphatically does not mean, however ,that this book seeks to challenge the view that a narrow aristocratic elite dominated court and parliament and exercised an inordinate influence on the major institutions of the state and the most important decisions taken by that state. Indeed, this study helps to explain why this aristocratic domination was so remarkably durable and effective and why it was so widely accepted. It seeks to do so, however, by emphasising that it is impossible to understand the true basis of aristocratic hegemony unless we examine the full political context in which it operated and until we appreciate how well the governing elite were able to satisfy the demands and needs of so many ordinary British citizens. Thus, while this book concentrates on the political aims and activities of those outside the landed elite and it explores the political world beyond court and parliament, it does so in the conscious recognition that the aristocratic elite governed so effectively for much of the eighteenth century because they were fully apprised of the need to take cognizance of these activities and to respond to this wider political world. The political culture described in this book was populated by the middling and lower orders of British society, but it was a political world to which the governing elite was forced to relate and to which it wisely accommodated itself.

The first half of this book examines the four principal ways in which the British people could influence existing political institutions or could exploit their existing powers. The first chapter looks at the role of the people in parliamentary elections and it shows how the propertied elite could expect to control the membership of the House of Commons only because they expended considerable time, money and energy in trying to influence how the electorate cast their votes. The second chapter maintains that parliament was not simply an institution to raise taxes for the government or to pass laws for the benefit of the governing elite, but was a body which could be used or appealed to by a wide variety of pressure groups anxious to promote the interests and welfare of those who did not exercise a direct influence over those who sat in the legislature. The focus in the third chapter shifts away from parliament and national affairs to local government and the politics of the urban communities of eighteenth-century Britain. In the growing towns the commercial and professional middle classes created their own distinctive political culture and could contest with the landed elite for control over these communities. In their relations with the poorer inhabitants of these towns the urban elite sought to govern by consensus and compromise rather than by confrontation and conflict. Whereas Chapter 3 establishes that the middling orders were the most important political agents in the larger towns, Chapter 4 explores the influence of the poor sections of society who participated in the many hundreds of riots, crowd demonstrations and popular disturbances that were such a marked feature of urban life in eighteenth-century Britain. In responding to these numerous popular protests the governing elite very rarely resorted to brute force in order to suppress disorder and restore social control. Without an adequate police force and reluctant to concede too much independent authority to the army (which in any case was small and generally overstretched whenever there was a wave of protests), the governing elite believed that arbitration and conciliation rather than repression were the best remedies for the grievances of the poor.

The second part of this book explores the ways by which the British people became increasingly politicised and the efforts they made to shape the political world in which they lived. Chapter 5 explores the sustained and profound ideological debate on the rights of man in general and on the liberties of British subjects in particular. It shows how some men rejected the ideological fetters made for them by conservative propagandists and instead adopted increasingly radical notions of the political rights which ordinary men might enjoy. Chapters 6 and 7 look at the practical efforts made in the earlier and later eighteenth century respectively to educate public opinion 'out-of-doors', to increase participation in public affairs and to make government and parliament more accountable to the people at large. In the earlier eighteenth century the people out-of-doors tended to react to issues which divided the governing elite, they adopted much of the ideology of the parliamentary opposition, and they mainly sought to purify the existing constitution. In the later eighteenth century a much more sophisticated and organised extra-parliamentary reform movement was created, and a radical ideology and a political programme were promoted, which sought to reform the constitution and to extend the political power of ordinary British subjects. The last chapter explores the political attitudes and the political activities of the many ordinary British subjects who wished to defend the existing political order when it was under threat. Paradoxically, however, these humble men who rushed to the defence of the aristocratic constitution of eighteenth-century Britain were never the servile creatures of the propertied elite. Their views were not simply provided for them by their social superiors but were deeply held. They did not act solely at the instigation or behest of the governing elite but were prepared to act independently to preserve a political and social order which they believed, whether unwisely or not, provided them and the country at large with so many benefits and advantages.

Part One
The People in Politics

1 The People and Parliamentary Elections

For the great majority of people in Britain politics existed and was experienced not at Westminster but at the local level. The exercise of political and social control occurred primarily at the local level and often within the framework of parliamentary constituencies. Hundreds of thousands of individuals – voters and non-voters alike – experienced politics at this level. In looking at the role of politics in the parliamentary constituencies, however, historians have too often concentrated on the control exercised by the propertied elite. Not enough attention has been paid to the voters themselves, even though there were several hundred thousand of them and their actions frequently excited the interest of leading politicians and were reported in both the London and the provincial press. It has been too readily assumed that the vast majority of the electorate could not vote as they wished, but had to vote as they were instructed by their superiors. Historians have too often focused their attention on how the propertied elite exploited this patronage in order to gain control of parliamentary constituencies and too many of them have ignored the behaviour of the voters. Even the small minority of voters who have been perceived as having some measure of control over how they cast their suffrage have generally been seen as primarily concerned to dispose of their vote at a profit to one of the elite candidates canvassing for support in a contested seat. What preoccupied them, it has been alleged, was what any candidate could actually do to serve the interests of the voters or of the local community in which they lived. The electors as a whole have been seen as largely ignorant of national affairs and as unconcerned about major political issues when they came to cast their votes. Their participation in elections is perceived as being at the behest or largely under the control of their social superiors.[1]

It is true, of course, that the propertied elite made determined and largely successful efforts to dominate constituency politics and that general elections did not provide the people as a whole with an opportunity freely to express their views on national issues or to give their impartial verdict on a particular administration. The evidence that a majority of parliamentary constituencies had small electorates and that these voters were very much under the influence and patronage of men of substantial property is irrefutable. It cannot be denied, for example, that in Cornwall a mere 1400 or so voters elected 42 borough MPs, while in Scotland the total electorate returning all 45 Scottish MPs was three to four thousand voters. It is also possible to cite many rotten boroughs, such as Banbury with about eighteen voters, Marlborough with twelve, Old Sarum with a mere seven and Gatton with but two. In very small constituencies such as these the electors had no real opportunity to exercise their vote in any meaningful sense because the seats were rarely contested and there was therefore no actual poll. Furthermore, in any general election in the eighteenth century only a minority of constituencies, large or small, went to the polls and so gave the voters a chance to exercise their suffrage. The early eighteenth century did see more frequent general elections, a higher proportion of seats going to an actual contest, and only a minority of seats (perhaps 100 in all) under the clear control of the local landed elite. After the Septennial Act of 1716 and after a number of decisions taken in parliament to adopt a restricted interpretation of who had the right to vote in a particular constituency, however, there was a growing trend towards oligarchy in constituency politics.[2] With general elections held less frequently the value of a seat in parliament increased and so did the cost of electioneering. The result of this trend was that fewer constituencies went to an actual poll and more seats came under the influence of the propertied elite. A decline in party strife in parliament, an increase in social stability, a fear of popular tumult and a reluctance to give way to popular opinion, all encouraged the propertied elite to spend time, effort and money to gain control of the smaller constituencies that returned a majority of MPs to parliament.

In a growing number of the smaller constituencies the successful candidates were not freely elected by the voters, but were either nominated by a wealthy local landowner or their election was largely decided by the actions of a few leading families in the area. Parliamentary seats were expensive to win and the costs were such that only rich patrons or rich candidates could foot the bill. It often cost several thousand pounds to win a seat, even in the smaller boroughs. Some electoral costs were astronomical. The Oxfordshire election of 1754 cost around £80 000, while it has been claimed that some £100 000 was spent at Shrewsbury in the election of 1790.[3] Moreover, seats had to be nurtured all the time and money had to be spent maintaining an interest even when no contest was anticipated in the near future. Not surprisingly, therefore, all patrons and most candidates were men of wealth and substance. Money and status undoubtedly played a major part in deciding election results. To avoid expensive and divisive contests, especially in the counties, the propertied elite often arranged compromises among themselves in order to share the representation. This gave the voters no real chance to affect the decision. Even in some of the constituencies where a poll was taken the free exercise of the suffrage could be undermined by a partial returning officer or, if the result was disputed and a petition was sent to parliament challenging the declared return, by a partial majority in the House of Commons.[4]

None the less, while there is indeed a wealth of evidence to show how well the propertied elite were able to influence election results, historians are not justified in concluding that the electoral system was an entirely closed one and that the actions of the voters can therefore be ignored. The number of MPs chosen by the nomination or influence of patrons has usually been exaggerated. Only about one hundred MPs were so chosen in the earlier eighteenth century. While this number had doubled by the middle of the century and had tripled by the end of the century,[5] the actions of the voters in many of these constituencies could rarely be taken entirely for granted and a measure of independence could still be expressed. Moreover, in the larger and more important constituencies, patronage was very rarely enough to win the seat. In most seats therefore the opinions of the voters could not be totally ignored. Even in those smaller boroughs where patrons exercised considerable influence, they only succeeded in doing so because they spent considerable time, energy and money on the task of influencing the voters. In most constituencies the local elite had to consider the local reactions to their behaviour and so the influence they could exert depended on their reputation with the voters and indeed with the local community as a whole. The electorate, and, as we shall see, this was larger than many historians have supposed, always needed to be courted and wooed. The elections themselves were more often an active and participatory experience for the voters than the relative infrequency of contested polls might indicate. Voters were canvassed and courted, treated and flattered, even when the local elite hoped and expected to avoid an actual contest. At times, chiefly but not exclusively in the larger constituencies, the electorate displayed their independence and revolted against the propertied elite who hoped to influence their votes. When they did so, and even when they more often accepted the guidance of their social superiors, they showed a concern for local and sometimes national issues. Few voters were, in fact, entirely ignorant or totally unconcerned about what happened in their local communities or even about what occurred on the national stage. Their relations with the propertied elite, and their willingness to cast their votes as the elite desired, depended on their own estimate of the candidates and on their perception of the issues which needed to be addressed at the local or national level.

To understand the involvement of tens of thousands of people in constituency politics we need to look closely at the various types of constituency, the relations between patrons and candidates on the one hand and voters on the other, the nature and behaviour of the electorate, the organisation and actual conduct of elections, and the response of voters to both local and national issues.

I PARLIAMENTARY CONSTITUENCIES

There were broadly three kinds of parliamentary constituency in eighteenth-century Britain: those where a patron could largely ignore the opinions of the voters and could virtually nominate the members; those where the propertied elite had to exploit their influence to the full in order to persuade the voters to elect the candidates favoured by the elite; and those, particularly the large counties and the open boroughs, where none of the competing interests and influences could be certain that its electoral efforts would result in victory at the polls. Thus, while there were no democratic constituencies and not many constituencies in which the voters were free to exercise their votes in an entirely independent way, there were also few constituencies in which the views of the voters could be completely ignored. In most constituencies the propertied elite had to expend time, money and energy to influence the electorate; the extent to which they had to do this depended on many factors.

Patronage and influence played a significant role in most boroughs, but only a tiny minority of constituencies – perhaps twenty in all – were thoroughly venal. The most venal boroughs, such as Cricklade, Shaftesbury and Stockbridge, were the exceptions and not the norm in the eighteenth century. In such boroughs as these sufficient electoral support could be purchased in order to decide the outcome and political issues played little or no part in influencing the choice of the voters. Even in these constituencies, however, the electoral control of the patron could be precarious because a rival might appear with a larger purse and offer the electors a better return for their votes. Moreover, the electors themselves recognised that their material reward might be greater if there were a contested election and so they were sometimes prepared to combine in order to bid up the value of their votes. In Grampound the corrupt electors repudiated the Edgecumbe interest in favour of Edward Eliot in 1758, but later turned out Eliot in 1796.[6] Another 46 boroughs were proprietorial or closed constituencies where elections were rarely contested and the result was usually decided by those patrons who possessed the particular properties which conferred the franchise on their owners. When a single patron owned sufficient property of this kind there could no serious contest, but if patrons were in competition for control (as at Cockermouth between 1722 and 1756)[7] contests were possible. Even in boroughs such as these the voters expected to be canvassed and treated, but they had little room for independent action.[8] It was rare for any patron however to have an uninterrupted and unchallenged control of a borough's representation and even the most entrenched patron could be overthrown when the interests of the constituents were sufficiently threatened.[9] In some 38 boroughs in England and Wales, and in the royal burghs of Scotland, the members of the local town corporations controlled the representation even if the franchise extended beyond their membership. In most of these constituencies electoral contests were rare and the return of members was usually controlled by a handful of rich, propertied families. Where the corporation was dominated by a powerful patron, the members of it expected to be rewarded for casting their votes for the patron's candidates.[10] Not all of these boroughs, however, were easy to control. At least three English boroughs of this type – Bath, Devizes and Salisbury[11]– remained independent, while, in Banbury, Lord North had to spend a lot of time and effort to control the mere eighteen voters and in Tiverton, with only 25 votes exercised by the corporation, there were several efforts by non-voters to agitate for an extension of the franchise to all those paying local taxes.[12] Even in the normally venal royal burghs of Scotland the small number of voters sometimes rebelled against the propertied elite. At Ayr in 1761 the town council forced the aristocratic patrons to apologise for ignoring the interests of the voters. The town councillors of Dingwall also refused to be mere ciphers commanded by the landed elite.

> Their greed, ambitions, vanities, hopes and fears had all to be catered for.... Nor was it merely a question of money and places. Constant attention had to be paid to the magistrates and councillors of the burghs by the parliamentary politicians.... Far from being servile the magistrates and councillors were apt to take the huff at any slight or injury.[13]

In over eighty boroughs (largely freeman or scot and lot boroughs) a settled, natural interest predominated. Patrons in these constituencies usually owned considerable land in the area, but their influence also rested on their willingness to show goodwill towards the electors and their readiness to perform services for the constituency. A patron's power and status within the constituency carried obligations and responsibilities towards the local community. The voters were expected to show electoral loyalty towards him, but only so long as he fulfilled his paternalistic obligations towards them. Rarely was such a borough controlled by a single patron. In some the electors were quite numerous and therefore difficult to control and, in some, contests were quite frequent. In a few, such as Chester and Plymouth, there was regular conflict between the corporation interest and an independent party. Outright bribery was quite rare because few patrons had sufficient wealth to control relatively large electorates of this kind. Considerable expenditure did have to be lavished on these constituencies, but much of it went on improving local amenities, providing charity for the poor, or treating the electors, not on outright bribery. Even more time, money and effort had to be devoted to promoting the wider interests of the borough and its inhabitants than in putting money directly into the pockets of the voters.[14]

In all the constituencies so far noted the candidate returned was either nominated by a local landlord or his election was heavily influenced by the leading families in the area. While the number of MPs elected in either of these ways did increase significantly during the eighteenth century it is important to distinguish between those constituencies under 'nomination' and those subject to 'influence'. Only a minority of all seats were so far under the control of a patron that he could nominate, without fear of challenge, the candidates to represent the constituency. Perhaps 121 out of 558 MPs were nominated in the general election of 1747 and at no stage during the eighteenth century were there as many as a third of all MPs chosen without any real reference at all to the opinions of the actual voters themselves.[15] The city of Chester, for example, was strongly influenced by the patronage exercised by the Grosvenor family, but, as a freeman borough with over one thousand electors, the voters were at times able to express their independence. In 1732 Sir Richard Grosvenor almost forfeited his family's electoral interest because of his opposition to a proposal to widen the River Dee in order to revive the borough's declining trade. The situation was only saved by Grosvenor's death and the new candidate's decision to promote his own River Dee Navigation Bill.[16]

A significant number of constituencies, mainly the larger boroughs and counties, can be regarded as relatively free of patronage control. In these constituencies there was a sufficient number of independent voters, free to cast their vote as they wished, to render the result uncertain. The political elite could not be certain of the result of any election well ahead of the event, even if some of these constituencies did not in the end go so far as a poll. There is some disagreement among historians about how many such open constituencies there were. All agree that in most of the counties (including the Welsh and Scottish counties)[17] control by a single family was rare. Even though compromises were often reached among the landed elite and contests were not very frequent, few patrons or candidates could take the electorate for granted. This was particularly the case in the larger English counties. The landed elite could obviously exercise considerable influence over their own tenants, but they could never guarantee the votes of all of them. Even the tenants of the most ruthless electoral magnates, such as the Duke of Bedford and Lord Lonsdale, are known to have rejected the express dictates of their landlords.[18] Frank O'Gorman has estimated that as many as a quarter of tenants refused to follow the political lead given by their landlord.[19] Moreover, many among the county electorate were wealthy, propertied and respectable men who regarded themselves as independent agents. The ordinary forty-shilling freeholders in the counties also included significant numbers of artisans and tradesmen who lived in the unrepresented towns in the counties and who were not subject to pressure from the great landlords. Many counties had several thousand voters (Yorkshire, the largest of them, had between 15 000 and 20 000 voters in the eighteenth century) and they were not easily managed even when electoral contests were averted. Leading politicians were always concerned about the results in the larger counties. In the run-up to the 1754 general election the Duke of Newcastle took a great interest in what was happening in Yorkshire because he feared a damaging contest 'in the first and most zealous county in England'. Even George II was much concerned, as Earl Fitzwilliam recorded:

> I am this moment come from the King who has been talking to me about the Yorkshire election. . . . He is as anxious about it as about the election of a King of the Romans, and as solicitous for peace and unanimity as is possible. . . . You can have no conception how earnest he is about this affair and how much he interests himself in it. I can't conceive he could be more earnest about the Westminster election.[20]

The precise number of open borough constituencies is difficult to calculate. The number of boroughs with a fairly wide franchise and several hundred or more electors varied between nearly one hundred and just over 140 constituencies during the eighteenth century. The vast majority of the borough electorate lived in these constituencies. Most of these boroughs had a politically active electorate, though political influence was exerted by local patrons in a significant number of them. John Phillips claims that there were some 33 large boroughs. With over 1000 voters each they included some two-thirds of the total borough electorate. In these constituencies the voters were independent, contests were quite frequent, and the results uncertain.[21] Frank O'Gorman lists over twenty of the larger freeman and scot and lot boroughs as open constituencies which could not be controlled by patrons.[22] Both Phillips and O'Gorman include among the main open boroughs such constituencies as Westminster, London, Southwark, Liverpool, Bristol, Norwich, Exeter, Nottingham, Newcastle upon Tyne, Northampton, Coventry, Leicester, Colchester, Hereford, Lincoln, Gloucester, Worcester and Canterbury. Westminster had between 8000 and 12 000 voters during the eighteenth century, London had 7–8000 voters, Bristol had 4–5000, Canterbury, Warwick and the others between 1000 and 3000 voters. In a dozen or so boroughs, including Northampton, Leicester, Taunton, Preston and Minehead nearly every resident male householder possessed the vote, and so perhaps 25–50 per cent of all adult males in those towns possessed the franchise. In quite a few other boroughs 20–25 per cent of adult males could vote.[23] In such constituencies the electorate had a considerable measure of independence. They were more frequently contested than other seats and even more frequently canvassed. Many of them were divided between a corporation party and an independent party. No MP could feel confident of retaining his seat if he blatantly flouted the interests of his constituents. Supporters of Walpole's Excise Bill of 1733, for example, fell foul of their constituents in the general election of 1734 in such towns as Bristol, Coventry, Worcester and Newcastle, while no government candidate was even prepared to contest one of London's four seats in that election because of the unpopularity of this measure.[24] It was widely acknowledged that the results in the

large open boroughs could influence the voters elsewhere and
that together the decisions in these open seats could give a
clear verdict on the popularity of a particular government. The
political elite and informed public opinion were not preoccupied at election time with the results in the tiny boroughs of
the south-west of England, but with the decisions taken by the
voters in the large counties and the more open boroughs.

II PATRONAGE AND CONSTITUENCY MANAGEMENT

Those members of the landed elite with political ambitions
spent a great deal of their wealth in building up an electoral
influence, mainly in the boroughs with a small electorate and a
restricted franchise, but the mere possession of property was
only one ingredient in the recipe for establishing an interest in
a patronage borough. Those with ambitions to be borough
patrons were expected to place their economic resource and
their political influence at the service of the voters, and even at
the service of the whole local community. As landlords and
employers they could act in ways which would benefit their
tenants and servants. As wealthy purchasers and ample
consumers they were expected to spend money with local
craftsmen, shopkeepers, innkeepers and purveyors of services.
In the late 1730s Sir John Hynde Cotton lost influence with the
voters in Cambridge, who 'wanted their Members to be more
free with their money among them than they found Sir John
Cotton was, who they gave out, never traded with them for the
necessaries of his house at Madingly, but sent to London or
anywhere else he could purchase the cheapest.'[25] Patrons were
also expected to contribute substantially to the erection of
public buildings or the establishment of local amenities within
the constituency, including town halls, exchanges, schools,
hospitals, libraries and even gaols. Successful patrons, such as
the Grosvenors of Chester and the Bute family in Glamorgan,
gave annual donations to assist the poor of the borough and
they provided additional charity during periods of dearth or
trade depression.[26] Whenever possible, patrons also had to
help their constituents enjoy a share of those offices at the
disposal of the crown, government or town corporation.
Clearly, patrons with influence at court or in the cabinet could

help their constituents gain posts in the customs and excise, the post office, the army and navy, the church and the judiciary, the East India Company and the colonial service, etc. Patrons might also help constituents secure government contracts, leases of land, commercial advantages of various kinds, access to charities and local amenities, or even intervention in the legal process or release from a debtors' prison. In 1710 Sir John Verney was even persuaded to continue sending regular copies of the London newspapers to the poor woman running a coffee house in Stony Stratford because a rival coffee house was so supplied by Verney's political rival.[27]

Effective management of an electoral interest required the patron to do much more than strike a bargain in which votes were given in return for the exercise of patronage. The widespread exercise of electoral patronage did not reduce the voters even in the smaller constituencies into servile and completely submissive dependants of the elite. When a patron assisted a voter, he rarely made it obvious that he did so in the expectation that he had gained the voter's support at the next election. He would almost always give it in the guise of an act of friendship and it was the friendly relationship which he was seeking to build that was the truly significant factor. The intention of the politician was of course to create a feeling of obligation, which he undoubtedly hoped would stand him in good stead at the next election, but the shrewd patron did not act as if he had bribed the voter. He knew that acts of seemingly disinterested friendship were the best way to build a strong electoral interest. When William Hay, the Duke of Newcastle's chief election agent in Sussex in 1734, discovered that a voter feared to go out because he was in debt, he paid the debt in order to secure the man's gratitude. He also sought out the man's chief creditor:

> I told him that in paying him I did not only intend to do a kindness to Mr Bristed, but to him too, in procuring him a debt that might otherwise have been desperate, and that I did not believe the report that he intended to be against my friends in the election ... after a good deal of flattery and civil treatment, paying his money, and promising to buy some malt of him, I left him in a very good humour, and

well-disposed to receive any favourable impression; so that he may be struck out of the class of enemies, and placed among the uncertain, if not in a better rank.[28]

Thus, even after devoting time and money, he could not be certain he had won over the creditor to the Duke's interest.

Many voters were quite prepared to be deferential to men of wealth, status and power, but they were also sufficiently free as political actors to render deference not only a voluntary but a political act. Deference was certainly widespread, and it undoubtedly precluded many voters from being fully autonomous or exercising independent political leadership, but it did not prevent them from holding an intelligently critical attitude towards the elite who were in a position to give a political lead. The ideal of deference was not to reduce a man to helpless and imbecilic servility, but to treat him in such a manner as to acknowledge his essential independence and self-respect. Most voters acted in a manner which both preserved their integrity and showed a due regard for the opinions of their social superiors. Deference was usually given only when the voter believed that it had been earned by the patron who sought it.[29]

There was undoubtedly a great deal more to constituency management, even in the smaller boroughs, than the giving of orders by the patrons and the obeying of them by a grateful electorate. Voters often expected a material reward for their deference, but they also believed that patrons had obligations to perform and that they had to reciprocate in a whole variety of ways for the votes cast for the candidates. The patron was expected to earn the gratitude of the voters and this required not only wealth and power, but also tact and good sense. There was enormous pressure on patrons to serve the particular interests of the electorate and indeed of the local community as a whole. Material rewards were rarely enough in themselves. After all, there were always more applicants for patronage than rewards to be distributed. What also mattered was the personality and character of the patron. A successful patron needed to possess a good knowledge of the borough and its interests, and he was expected to give his personal attention to matters of concern to his constituents. Resident patrons almost always had greater influence over the voters than non-residents. It helped considerably when a patron lived in the neighbourhood of the constituency, involved himself in local affairs and was personally accessible to the electors. He was expected not only to bestow patronage, favours and charity, but to join in local celebrations and to promote the peace and prosperity of the whole constituency.[30] Even Namier admitted of a small corporation borough such as Harwich that 'close acquaintance with the men and their circumstances and much attention was required: the management had to be local and personal.'[31]

In all local affairs successful patrons preferred cooperation to coercion and so they set about influencing voters with enormous diplomacy and infinite care. To ignore the sensibilities of voters was the quickest route to electoral suicide. Even some of the most powerful families in the land lost electoral support simply because they failed to consult the voters or to take an interest in local affairs. The prodigiously wealthy Duke of Chandos spent lavishly to build up an electoral interest in Bridgwater in the early 1720s, but he failed because he never made himself familiar with the needs and desires of his constituents. Sir John Rogers had some success in Plymouth in the years 1713–22, but he squandered his electoral interest when he began to interfere too much in the town's internal affairs. George Treby, on the other hand, had greater success at Dartmouth and Totnes because he showed a greater respect for the independence of the voters. He left most political decisions to local men, while he himself made no unreasonable demands and did not intervene too actively in local affairs.[32]

Which individuals were chosen to represent them was hardly ever a matter of indifference to the voters. Even powerful and successful patrons needed good candidates to represent their boroughs if they were to maintain their interest in the constituency and the loyalty of the voters. In constituencies where there was no strong patron the personal qualities of the candidate were vital. Candidates for election were expected to be accessible, approachable and sensitive to the wishes of the constituency. The electorate preferred a local landed man, of wealth, honour and reputation, who, like any electoral patron, would devote his wealth and influence to the service of his constituency. Most voters were concerned with the candidate's ability to promote their interests and with his readiness to assist them with favours, custom, employment, donations and a personal attention to their needs. MPs were expected to lavish a great deal of time and money on their constituencies. Sir William Robinson, MP for York, wearying of such efforts, complained in 1710 that there was

> a vast trouble in discharging the duty of a parliament man, so many different interests to please while in the place I serve for, so much expected to be done for the citizens or their friends during the sessions of Parliament that one's never quiet, scarce [even] to attend their own affairs.[33]

The powerful Marchmont interest destroyed itself by making the wrong choice of candidate for the election in Berwickshire in 1780. Sir John Paterson, who regularly squabbled with his tenants and dependants and was often in dispute with local tradesmen and shopkeepers, was so unpopular that not even the support of the Earl of Marchmont could save his seat.[34] David Scott was another candidate who lost his seat in the county of Angus, despite the powerful backing of Henry Dundas, because he had lost touch with his constituents.[35] When Lord Monson, whose family had a strong interest in Lincoln, decided to put up a new candidate (his own brother), in 1747, he met with resistance from the freemen of the town, who did not think that he was an appropriate choice. Lord Monson admitted on 24 June:

> the common people grumbled that I should impose a man upon them whom they did not know, who had never been among them, who had not taken his freedom, who they understood did not design to be at the election, and whom perhaps they might never see.[36]

The classic example of a candidate being rejected primarily because he failed to convince the voters that he was serving the particular interests of his constituency is that of Edmund Burke in Bristol in 1780. Burke, who had been elected for the city in 1774, had accepted that he should keep in close touch with his constituents and he had spent a great deal of time in the House of Commons promoting the commercial interests of individual merchants.[37] On the other hand, Burke never visited Bristol between 1776 and the general election of 1780.[38]

He was surprised at how much he was expected to do for his constituents. In June 1777 he confessed, 'I could not have believed how very little the local constituents attend to the general public line of conduct observed by their member. They judge him solely by his merits as their special agent.'[39] Burke was disappointed that his constituents were not sufficiently impressed by his criticisms of the government's disastrous conduct of the American crisis, but were resentful of his support for trade concessions to Ireland that might prove injurious to the commerce of the Bristol Merchant Venturers and his attempt to reform the law on the imprisonment of debtors. Burke's efforts to defend this, and other actions disapproved of by most of his constituents, were to no avail. Recognising that he had no chance of retaining his seat, Burke withdrew from the contest.[40] Whatever the merits of his stance on national and international issues, he had clearly failed to convince his Bristol constituents that he was serving their particular interests.

If, as we shall see below, patrons and candidates had to devote time, energy and money to influencing the voters during the actual election campaign, it was just as necessary to devote resources to nursing and managing a constituency before any election was in the offing. Intense canvassing and campaigning could go on in a constituency prior to an election, even if the polls were not opened thereafter. Considerable political activity might well precede an election in an effort to test the response of the voters, but positive indications of success were needed before any patron or candidate risked opening the polls. Patrons generally exercised their electoral influence circumspectly and in accordance with established custom and practice. They engaged in a complex and long-term dialogue with the electorate. Insensitive and autocratic patrons could soon find that their behaviour was counter-productive. A few landlords did force those tenants who had opposed their candidate in an election to quit their farms, as Lord Clare did at Aldborough in 1713,[41] but most landlords did not expect and rarely attempted to dragoon their submissive tenantry to the polls. Even James Lowther, 'the tyrant of the north', did not evict tenants who refused to vote for him at Whitehaven in 1780, while the Earl of Nottingham even went so far as to reassure the freeholders of Rutland in 1710 that threats of turning tenants out of their

farms were very unlikely to be fulfilled.[42] Much more common
was for the patron or landlord to ask his tenants respectfully for
their support at a forthcoming election. Thus, Lord Ashburnham acted in the traditional manner when he told his election
agent in Bedfordshire in 1701:

> I would have you go round to such of my tenants as are free-
> holders, acquainting them that I shall take it very well if they
> all appear and vote for my Lord Edward Russell and Sir
> William Grostwick on the election day as they all were so
> kind to do the last parliament.[43]

Lord Ashburnham was hoping for greater loyalty from his
tenants than most landlords could expect. Most would have
expected to receive only one of their tenant's votes. In the
Cheshire election of 1710, for example, eight out of forty-one
tenants of Lord Bulkeley refused to give even one vote as he
desired.[44]

Canvassing was used initially to test whether it was worth
bothering to contest a poll. Poor early results might well
persuade a prospective candidate that it was not worth
proceeding to an election. Lavish gestures of respect were paid
to the electors, who rarely refused point-blank to give their
vote when asked for it in such a manner. A promise once given,
however, was not lightly broken. For this reason it was essential
to impress the voters and so the canvassing was often done by
local men of substance. In the counties and in the more open
or more closely contested boroughs, it was essential for men of
genuine standing in the area to approach the voters personally
and directly. In April 1754 Sir James Lowther and Sir George
Dalston canvassed the small borough of Appleby 'attended by
a great number of gentlemen, [who] went round the town, to
every house public and private, friend and foe'.[45] Twenty years
later Sir Walter Blackett canvassed Newcastle upon Tyne
attended by 'about five hundred gentlemen, tradesmen, and
others, some of whom had weight with almost every
freeman.'[46] William Hay, the Duke of Newcastle's indefatigable
electoral agent in Sussex, advised his master that the voters
were not sufficiently impressed by approaches from hired
agents like himself: 'People would not promise your Grace's
servants, but expected to be waited on by persons of a superior
rank; [saying] that on their side gentlemen of fashion had

asked votes in all places throughout the county.'[47] In Huntingdon the Earl of Sandwich had a very considerable interest, but he only narrowly carried both seats in 1741 by his personal relations with the voters: 'He gained his point by mere good management. I never saw anyone so engaging and affable towards the common people.'[48]

Whenever possible, canvassers or political agents sent personal letters to the voters or sought personal meetings with them. The canvassing was often accompanied by social festivities and the open treating of voters. This cost considerable time and money. Several agents or canvassers were needed in any sizeable borough and several dozen might be needed in a large county. While canvassing a county in 1734 Sir John Bland complained that 'There are vast numbers of independent freeholders who have always expected the civility of a pot of ale', while Robert Burnett, working as an election agent for the Duke of Newcastle in Sussex, canvassed six days a week for nine months before the county election in 1734.[49] Philip Yorke complained to the Earl of Hardwicke of one unsatisfactory agent in Cambridgeshire in 1780:

> It is said, ... that he has been about with a bottle in one hand and a guinea in the other, and will part with neither. The truth is, he has been too economical for a contested election; it proceeded from a good intention, but has answered ill, and I wish your Lordship would give him a hint about it, for some of your own tenants have been offended and are refractory.[50]

Once there were candidates in the field ready to contest an election, they too had to make every effort to meet the voters and to earn their respect or at least their support. In Buckinghamshire, in 1705, John Fleetwood and Richard Grenville employed clerks to copy six hundred letters addressed to the freeholders.[51] While campaigning in Preston in 1715, John Chetwynd protested, 'I am half dead already what with drinking, smoking and walking the streets at all hours.'[52] As early as November 1740 two potential candidates started a week's canvass of York to test whether they might have any chance in the 1741 general election. Initially, they were received enthusiastically, but one candidate recorded:

I soon found that without money, all this was but mere noise and shew, on which there wd be no dependance. Accordingly we were attended every night, after going about the City, to the publick house where we were to sup, by a great crowd of people, who were lavish in our praise, but more so of our money, the night's expenses generally amounting to near £50.[53]

In Newton in Lancashire, in 1701, Peter Legh of Lyme, the borough patron, did not anticipate a contest, but he still urged his nominees to solicit votes, in person if they could, 'to prevent some sort of censures that formerly has been made ... that Newton members seldom was known to the voters.'[54] Successful canvassing was an art that not all candidates could successfully master. David Hartley was critical of the abilities of Sir William Milner, who campaigned at York in 1784:

He has, I fear, too cold and ungracious a manner to make great or lasting conquests over the affections of a populace, that must be at least treated as equals – and *pro hac vice* as superiors. The hearty shake, and the familiar bit of conversation must be attended to.[55]

Whether a candidate was blessed with particular skills or not, it was nearly always vital for him to make the effort to ask for the support of voters in person. In 1705 Sir Justinian Isham, who had a very high standing in Northamptonshire, was nevertheless warned that his interest with the freeholders around Peterborough 'suffers much for want of your appearing amongst them. For your adversaries having been there and made their application to everybody of note the freeholders think themselves entitled to the same respect from the Old Candidates, which has been expressed to them by the new, especially since many keep themselves upon the reserve and would make no promises to the new ones in expectation of seeing the old ones.'[56] In Lewes, in 1733, the Duke of Newcastle's chief election agent, William Hay, warned him that his candidate might well lose the forthcoming election if he continued his unaccountable behaviour of neglecting, and hence insulting, the voters:

It is with the greatest concern I tell your Grace that things grow worse & worse, & if some speedy remedy is not found out the election will be in great danger. If it is lost, the loss of it must be imputed to Mr Pelham's inactivity. ... He has not been around the Town since he went with your Grace, nor I believe asked a single man for his vote: & I am firmly persuaded that half the voters that have been lost have been lost by this unpardonable negligence: the people are affronted at it; & indeed he has no reason to expect their votes if he does not think them worth asking; when the other side are perpetually courting them.[57]

III THE ELECTORATE

The right to vote in the eighteenth century was restricted to adult males who possessed certain property qualifications. In the counties the franchise was uniform. It was possessed by all freeholders owning land valued for tax purposes at forty shillings per annum, though those who held leaseholds for life of the same value were sometimes accepted as qualified voters. The voters in the counties made up about 60 per cent of the total electorate. In the boroughs, where about 40 per cent of the electorate might hope to exercise their right to vote, there was no such uniformity of franchise, but rather a great diversity of qualifications. It is possible however to distinguish four main types of borough representation. In the largest group of boroughs (nearly half the English borough representation in fact) it was the freemen of the borough who were allowed to vote. In the next group of boroughs the franchise was possessed by an even higher proportion of the adult males: by the resident or inhabitant householders, by the freeholders or by those who were assessed to pay the local assessments of 'scot and lot'. More restrictive than these two groups of boroughs were the burgage boroughs, where the franchise had long been attached to specific properties, and the corporation boroughs, where the franchise was exercised by the members of a self-perpetuating oligarchy. In some of the larger boroughs the voters might be qualified by possessing different kinds of franchises. In Bristol both freemen and freeholders could vote, whereas in Nottingham and Leicester both freemen and householders paying scot and lot possessed the franchise.

The total electorate had increased significantly during the seventeenth century.[58] By the eighteenth century it was larger than has often been supposed and it was a higher proportion of the adult male population than has usually been imagined. Since not all electors would choose or be able to cast their votes, even in a fiercely contested election, we need to increase the number of actual voters by at least 20 per cent in order to get a more realistic estimate of the size of the total number of men qualified to vote. When this calculation is made, it appears that the total electorate in England and Wales was about 240 000 in 1689, around 20.6 per cent of the adult male population. By 1715 these figures had risen to a total of about 300 000 voters and 23.4 per cent of adult males. By the late eighteenth century the total electorate in England and Wales had increased by nearly another 40 000, but, because the population as a whole was growing at an even faster rate, the proportion of adult males who could vote had declined to 17.2 per cent.[59] The proportion of adult males qualified to vote in a particular borough constituency varied according to the peculiar franchise operating in that borough and according to the social composition of that constituency. In many of the larger freeman boroughs about 25 per cent of all adult males possessed the vote. In Nottingham, Newcastle and Warwick the proportion was as high as 40 per cent. In smaller boroughs which had very wide franchises the proportion could be much higher. In Northampton 50–60 per cent of adult males had the vote, while in Honiton and Cirencester the totals were over 75 per cent and in Minehead the proportion was over 80 per cent.[60] Around a dozen boroughs had a resident householder franchise and a large proportion of adult males could therefore vote in those constituencies. The 'pool' of electors however was very much wider than the numbers voting in any particular election. There was a very large number of occasional voters who might abstain from voting, leave the constituency or lose the qualification for the franchise. Others could come of age, improve their status or gain the franchise by being given the freedom of the town they lived in or even of the town they had been born in but had long abandoned.[61] The number of voters in freeman boroughs could be suddenly increased prior to an election by the mass creation of new freemen. At various times hundreds of new freemen were created just before general elections in such towns as Liverpool, Bristol, Newcastle and Leicester. In boroughs with a higher than average proportion of voters there was usually a high turn-out, occasionally reaching over 90 per cent of voters, in contested elections.[62]

In general, the voters were largely drawn from the middling ranks of society, rather than from the propertied elite or the labouring poor, though there were some voters from all the significant social groups in the country. According to Frank O'Gorman only about 15–20 per cent of voters were drawn from the richest sectors of society (including landed gentlemen, professional men, merchants and manufacturers). About 60 per cent of voters were retailers, traders and craftsmen, men who prided themselves on belonging to the respectable classes of society and who often cherished their independence. Perhaps surprisingly, O'Gorman estimates that nearly 15 per cent of voters were semi or unskilled workers and common labourers (many of them engaged in transport work), while the rest of the voters were attached to agricultural work.[63] John Phillips's calculations, based on a smaller sample, are broadly similar. He estimated that nearly 80 per cent of the voters in Norwich and Liverpool were craftsmen, artisans and retailers. Perhaps, in general, 25–30 per cent of urban voters were drawn from the fairly prosperous middling sort and 50–60 per cent were craftsmen and those even lower in the social scale.[64] Although the electorate in most constituencies changed quite rapidly, and did so very considerably over time, the proportions in particular social groups remained fairly constant.

Clearly, the unreformed electorate was dominated by men from the broad middling ranks of society (the freeholders, retailers and craftsmen), but it reached quite far down the social scale. In most urban constituencies it went below the artisan level into the labouring classes. Few of these electors were in a totally dependent or vulnerable position, where they simply had to accept the dictates of their superiors and had no room for electoral manoeuvre. Few of them, of course, would be entirely free of the influence exerted by those above (and even those below) them in the social hierarchy. As we have seen, the wealth, status and power of their social superiors could influence them in a variety of ways; always provided

patrons exploited their advantages in a sensitive and
sophisticated manner. The electors possessed two votes in
nearly all constituencies. Even in the smallest boroughs the
patron normally expected to be able to command only one of
these votes and the voter was left free to dispose of the other.
Buckingham, a small borough of about 13 electors, was
regarded as under the control of the Grenville family, but the
Marquis of Buckingham admitted that it was 'necessary for me
to abide by the rule which I have always steadily observed of
never interfering, directly or indirectly, in the choice of a
second member.'[65] Lord Moira was afraid that, if he bullied his
tenants, 'I should revolt those who on other occasions gave me
real weight by following my influence.'[66] Electors were known
to refuse to accept instructions from their patrons or to offer
only one vote. A tenant of the Duke of Bedford explained
regretfully, but in detail, why he and his son could not support
one of the Duke's candidates in the general election of 1768.[67]
While very few electors repudiated the prevailing social order,
few servilely or meekly submitted to the wishes of their
landlords. They often supported their patrons, but only on
terms, and at times, which suited them. While they recognised
the existence of hierarchy and subordination, they were also
prepared to defend their own interests within the existing
social order. The majority of voters – the retailers and the
craftsmen – were locked into a complicated social and
economic relationship with patrons and clients, but they were
not entirely imprisoned within it. They possessed some room
for manoeuvre and some ability to adjust their relations with
their superiors. They were aware of the leverage that they
could exert over patrons at election time and they could
ensure that they made a material profit when there was the
prospect of a contested election. Economic advantages and
favours were gained, for example, by the voters of Minehead in
1767, Middlesex in 1770, Hull in 1784, and Stafford in 1788.[68]
Many voters, moreover, actually prided themselves on being
independent agents with political awareness and powers of
judgement. They even absorbed and subscribed to the rhetoric
of popular independence and they demonstrated that they
had ideas and opinions of their own. At times they could be
very assertive and they could revolt even against candidates
who enjoyed the backing of powerful patrons. In the smaller

boroughs the voters could be assertive and demanding, ready to involve themselves in contentious issues at the slightest provocation. In the more open constituencies electors frequently campaigned in opposition to the influence of oligarchy and rebelled against the domination of the constituency by a single patron or even a coalition of interests.

There were many factors which could influence how electors cast their vote and yet the evidence does not suggest that they voted in a casual or random fashion. They clearly took their duties seriously and their action was usually the result of premeditated, even partisan, choice. Most electors were surprisingly consistent in how they used their votes. There was a very high level of consistency in the way votes were cast by individual electors at all periods of the century, not merely in those decades when party alignments were stronger. A half or more of the electors voted in a similar fashion in more than one election. Floating voters who changed their allegiance from one election to another were always a small minority, though their change of mind could, of course, have a significant effect on the election result. In four-cornered contests (where four candidates standing as two pairs competed for the two vacant seats and each elector could cast two votes) there was little cross or split voting between these two pairs. In three-cornered contests the electors might have to consider splitting their vote or using only one of them to plump for the single candidate they favoured. Plumping was usually rare, because it meant throwing away a vote, and yet, on average, fewer than a third of voters in three-cornered contests chose to split their votes. Electors cherished their votes and desired to exercise some control over how they were cast. Even in parishes clearly owned by a single landlord they were not herded to the polls like sheep and unanimous voting patterns were rare. Local communities, even those as small as individual parishes or small villages, were usually split when elections were contested. Clearly, the voters (or at least some of them) were exercising independent judgement. When swings in electoral opinion did occur, it was not just the aristocratic elite and constituency patrons who changed their views, but many ordinary voters too.[69] The electorate could be highly volatile and 'The switches in the allegiances of the voters took place on such a scale,... that it is inconceivable that some at least did not change sides out of personal choice.'[70]

Throughout the eighteenth century many thousands of electors demonstrated that they expected their MPs to serve their interests or even, at times, to obey their instructions. Even in some of the smaller constituencies they were able to impress upon patrons that they cast their votes only on condition that their representative took cognizance of their interests. In the larger and more open constituencies they were even ready to insist that their MPs should follow a particular line of conduct in parliament or risk losing their votes at the next election. In some of these constituencies the electorate began to establish their own electoral clubs and societies in order to exercise greater control over who should actually represent them in parliament. Resistance to oligarchy and a desire to demonstrate their independence persuaded the voters in some constituencies to stress the liberties of the electorate and the right of the people to choose MPs who would be accountable to them. By the later eighteenth century thirty to forty constituencies were ready to support radical or independent candidates who were much more responsive to the opinions of their voters than those MPs who had no reason to fear a revolt by their narrow electorates.

There are many examples throughout the eighteenth century of normally docile voters asserting their independence because they resented the way the patron or their representative showed little concern for their interests. In the 1730s and 1740s voters rebelled against insensitive patrons in Chester, Lewes, Lincoln and Derby.[71] In 1733 Thomas Winford lost the support of the electors of Hereford and forfeited his seat the next year because of his support for an unpopular local turnpike trust. At Newcastle under Lyme, in the 1734 general election, Lord Gower had to placate the voters by announcing his opposition to any plan to enclose any common land in the town.[72] In Wallingford in 1727 and in Nottingham in 1774 the electors protested vigorously because the propertied elite sought to choose the candidates who would stand without even bothering to consult the voters about the choice being made.[73] In 1774 the voters of Bedford successfully rebelled against the Duke of Bedford because they did not like his choice of candidates and they returned two members of their own choice.[74] In the same general election the candidate put forward by the corporation of Coventry was badly defeated by an independent candidate, who praised the freemen after the poll:

> Permit me to congratulate you on the noble stand you have made in support of the liberty, freedom and independency of this great city. Your children's children – nay, lasting posterity, will from this great example learn to know that no *body corporate* has a right to exercise *undue* power, or trample with impunity on the privileges, franchises and freedom of the people.[75]

In Glamorgan in 1789 the voters rebelled against an oligarchy that had been entrenched for forty years and they won a hard-fought election. A greater volume of propaganda was distributed than in any previous election, with pamphlets in English and Welsh protesting at all manner of grievances against local landlords, including enclosures, tithes and the operation of the game laws.[76]

Sometimes the opposition to oligarchy led to more coordinated action within the larger constituencies in order to ensure that the voters themselves had the greater influence over the choice of candidate and the outcome of any contest. As early as 1724 there is evidence of a club of middle-class independent electors in London, which met at the Half Moon Tavern in Cheapside. By the late 1730s this tavern was the base for a political society that coordinated the opposition to the policies of Sir Robert Walpole in the city of London.[77] By then there was also a similar club of independent electors in Westminster and a second, more plebeian, group which met at the Crown and Anchor Tavern. These two societies supported opposition Whig candidates in 1741 and they swept the polls against Walpole's candidates in a very violent contest.[78] By the late 1730s Bristol also possessed two electoral clubs established by the local voters, the Steadfast Society established by the Tories and the Union Club founded by the Whigs.[79] Soon there were similar clubs at Coventry, Grantham, Birmingham and Colchester. These clubs monitored the parliamentary conduct of their MPs and orchestrated the popular resistance to aristocratic control.[80] In the 1760s these were joined by such organised constituency groups as the Patriotic Club in Berwick, the Blue Club in St Albans and the Market House

Society in Taunton.[81] Similar clubs proliferated in the last decades of the century with the growth of radicalism and reform at constituency level. The White Lion Club was set up in Nottingham, the Revolution Club in Leicester and the Rockingham Club in York, while Ipswich, Worcester, Shrewsbury and Lewes all had rival electoral clubs.[82] In Newcastle upon Tyne there were several clubs, such as the Lumber Troop, the Independents and the Sydney.[83] In Bristol, as well as the Steadfast Society and the Union, there were the Independent Society and the Constitutional Club.[84] Norwich probably had more of these independent constituency societies than any provincial city in the kingdom.[85]

Many of those electors who wished to stress their independence were not just resentful of the insensitive behaviour of local patrons or critical of the abuse of power within the constituency. They also took an interest in national affairs and they demonstrated a readiness to oppose the policies supported by government and parliament. In times of crisis they were prepared to instruct their MPs about how to vote in parliament and they were even prepared to demand pledges from their parliamentary candidates before agreeing to vote for them. In Scotland, where there was a different tradition, MPs were expected not only to receive instructions from their candidates, but to give pledges at their election to obey such instructions.[86] In England there was a long-running debate as to whether MPs were representatives, who were entirely free to vote as they saw fit, or delegates, who ought to accept instructions from their constituents on matters of great importance to the voters.[87] Although Edmund Burke was, in fact, frequently ready to support his constituents' interests, he was one of those who insisted that MPs were chosen to exercise their independent judgement for the benefit of the whole nation and therefore could not be expected to vote at the behest of their particular constituents.[88] His fellow member for Bristol, however, took the opposite view. After his election in 1774 he congratulated the free and independent spirit of his constituents:

> It has ever been my opinion that the electors have a right to instruct their members. – For my part, I shall always think it my duty in Parliament to be guided by your counsels and instructions. – I shall consider myself the servant of my

constituents, not their master, – subservient to their will, not superior to it. – And let me add, I hold myself accountable to you for every action of my life which respects the public. By your upright judgement, I desire to stand or fall.[89]

Many voters were indeed convinced that they possessed the right to instruct their representatives and, on a number of occasions, they exercised this privilege in considerable numbers. In 1701, for example, some nineteen constituencies instructed their newly-elected MPs in terms which implied that they were delegates rather than representatives.[90] During the Excise crisis of 1733 some 54 constituencies sent instructions to their MPs, asking them to oppose this measure.[91] Several MPs, including John Scrope, the secretary to the Treasury who represented Bristol, lost their seats in the 1734 general election because of their support for this highly unpopular measure.[92] In 1739 the electors of the city of London instructed their representatives to support a Place Bill, and this action was supported by similar instructions from five counties and twelve boroughs. In 1741–2 even more constituencies instructed their representatives to oppose Walpole's policies at home and abroad. In Scotland, not famous for its independent electors, instructions were sent from nine constituencies. The instructions to Edinburgh's MP were drawn up by the merchant companies and such tradesmen's corporations as the surgeons, goldsmiths, skinners and weavers.[93] In 1753 some fifteen constituencies instructed their MPs to oppose the Jewish Naturalisation Act. The instructions sent from Cirencester insisted:

> The voice of the People has fully declared itself; that voice, which is in some sense the voice of God... It is with the greatest pleasure and zeal that we have joined it. Your regard, gentlemen, to it or to us, we cannot doubt of.[94]

When Humphrey Sydenham did reject the instructions against the Jew Bill sent by his Exeter constituents, he paid for his independence with the loss of his seat in the 1754 general election.[95] Similar instruction campaigns were waged after the loss of Minorca in 1756, in support of John Wilkes in 1769, in favour of reconciliation with the American colonies in 1775, and in opposition to the policies of Charles James Fox in 1783–4.

In mounting Instruction campaigns of this kind the voters were making it clear that they thought MPs should be responsible to the electorate as a whole and not just to the narrow ruling oligarchy. When they were unable to persuade MPs to support their demands for opposition to government policies they began to campaign for constitutional measures which would either reduce the crown's influence over MPs or increase the voters' influence over their representatives. In the general election of 1722 several constituencies demanded pledges from their candidates that they would work to restore triennial parliaments.[96] In a by-election at Bristol in 1739 the Steadfast Society agreed to campaign for an independent candidate, Edward Southwell, on condition that he supported triennial elections and a Place Bill.[97] In 1742 over forty constituencies urged their MPs to support similar measures of constitutional reform.[98] In 1769 the voters in several constituencies, including Bristol and Newcastle upon Tyne, instructed their MPs to support John Wilkes over the Middlesex election case and to press for shorter parliaments and an effective Place Bill.[99]

When groups of independent voters began to campaign to wrest control of their constituencies out of the hands of the propertied elite, they urged the rights of the electorate (and even of *non-voters*) over the entrenched influence of aristocratic patrons. As early as 1761 it was the pressure applied by the non-voting craftsmen, servants and customers of those who did possess the vote that accounted for the rejection of the Duke of Argyll's candidate for the Edinburgh seat.[100] When the independents at Pontefract ran their own candidate in 1768 he actually topped the poll, but the violence which marred the election led to the return being voided. In the subsequent by-election the independent candidate stood on the principle of an inhabitant householder franchise. After a series of contests and petitions the House of Commons finally confirmed the wider franchise in 1783.[101] When the independent electors attacked the Duke of Devonshire's control of Knaresborough in 1784, they also demanded an extension of the franchise to all resident householders.[102] Before the 1774 election in Worcester the supporters of William Kelly described themselves as 'labouring freemen of this city, who, though poor, are determined to vote for no man but what shall act independent, and use his utmost interest to obtain triennial parliaments.'[103] In Newcastle upon Tyne the independent freemen put up two candidates in the 1774 general election who were pledged to support shorter parliaments, Place and Pension Bills and a more equal representation. Although these two candidates were defeated, the independent freemen ran another candidate in the by-election of 1777. They referred to the established oligarchies in the town as 'a combination of wealth and power to suppress the free election of the people.' They urged the voters 'O break the *closet-combinations* of the magistrates and gentry, whose glory it seems to be to treat their inferiors as slaves.' Though defeated in 1777, their candidate was successful in the general election of 1780.[104] In Lewes, in 1796, a group of independent electors unsuccessfully ran a radical candidate, William Green, who proclaimed his support for peace, parliamentary reform, the repeal of the Test Act, the abolition of the slave trade and the restoration of civil liberties.[105] When John Crewe unsuccessfully challenged the powerful Grosvenor interest in Chester in 1784, he protested to the voters:

> The plain truth is, the citizens of Chester are thoroughly convinced that there is an all-controlling power which disposes of the representation, pulling down one, and setting up another as it pleases. This power has been so long exercised, and so long submitted to, that any opposition to it, is now considered as little less than a rebellion by the citizens against a lawful authority.[106]

John Crewe's defeat showed how difficult it was for the electors to combat aristocratic influence without the benefits of money, a major issue and an effective organisation. On occasions, however, electors determined to be independent and ready to coordinate their activities were able to mount an effective challenge to the propertied elite. In thirty to forty constituencies, including such counties as Middlesex, Northumberland and Warwickshire and such boroughs as Lincoln, Nottingham, Newcastle upon Tyne, Hull, Oxford, Gloucester, Leicester, Coventry, Worcester, Cambridge, Reading, Shrewsbury and Taunton, independent electors were a force to be reckoned with.[107] They actually won seats in a number of these constituencies and put up a good contest in many more in the later eighteenth century. When they had a major issue on which to focus, radical candidates, who were outspoken supporters of constitutional reform and the rights of the voters, won at least four seats in 1768 and a dozen or so in 1774 and 1780.[108] Although their numbers declined thereafter, independent candidates were still able to triumph in a number of constituencies, including Glamorgan in 1789, Chichester in 1790 and Minehead in 1796.[109]

IV ELECTIONS

General elections were held more frequently in the early and late eighteenth century than in the decades in between. In the period from 1701 to 1715 there were eight general elections. Thereafter, largely as a consequence of the Septennial Act of 1716, parliaments usually lasted six years or so between general elections. From the 1780s, however, the duration of parliaments was reduced as general elections gradually increased in frequency. Much the same occurred in the pattern of electoral contests. In the early eighteenth century a higher proportion of seats was contested than at any other period in the eighteenth century. Between 30 and 50 per cent of all constituencies went to the polls in any general election and only thirty constituencies were never contested, nine of them being small Cornish boroughs.[110] The number of contests was reduced to only one-fifth of all constituencies by the years 1747–61, but the figure then slowly advanced to nearly one-third of all constituencies by the later eighteenth century. Not surprisingly, most contests regularly occurred in the constituencies with the largest electorates and the recovery in the number of contests in the later eighteenth century was fastest in the large freeman boroughs.[111] More than half of the largest boroughs in the country were contested in every election in the later eighteenth century.

Electoral activity was by no means confined to those constituencies which actually went to a contest. There was considerable activity, including much discussion over which candidates to nominate, and much canvassing to test the waters even in those constituencies where no contest finally took place. Canvassing did more than discover the political inclinations of the voters. It was an active effort to secure friends, express opinions and win over the uncommitted. In 1784, for example, only seven counties were contested, but in another eight there was considerable electoral activity. In the largest constituency in the country the Yorkshire Association helped to mount a highly sophisticated and systematic canvass. It built up accurate lists of the county's freeholders and canvassed 13 570 of them. This revealed overwhelming support for the Association's two favoured candidates, Wilberforce and Duncombe. These two candidates set up 19 district committees and canvassed seven West Riding manufacturing towns in four days. The two sitting MPs, who had employed no fewer than 167 election agents to canvass for them, recognised that the tide of public opinion was against them and they retired from the contest without going to the polls. Clearly, however, the voters had been involved in considerable electoral activity even though no formal contest had taken place.[112] Contests which did take place might be generated by the disputes, failings and ambitions of the political elite, but, even when the electorate did not initiate the contest, voters were given an opportunity to express a preference between rival candidates. In other cases, however, the voters did initiate a contest because they wished to repudiate a sitting MP or they were divided among themselves as to who would be the best person to represent them. The circumstances in the larger boroughs in particular gave many voters the chance to act independently. Whatever the final result of such contests the voters were able to involve themselves more fully in the electoral process. On occasions, as we have seen, the voters nominated their own independent candidate and fully organised the campaign to secure his return. Electoral activity of almost every kind, however, did much to involve the middling orders in the political life of the nation and they greatly encouraged the growth of political consciousness in the nation at large.

The whole electoral process undoubtedly demonstrated the political influence of the propertied elite, but it also showed that the voters had a definite role to play and there is no doubt that they jealously guarded their privilege. They cherished their relative independence and they exploited every available opportunity to bargain and negotiate with their social superiors. The enormous effort, in time, energy and money, devoted by patrons and candidates to achieve electoral success constantly reminded the political elite that there were definite limits to their authority. It also gave the voters a chance to promote their own interests, often in material and practical ways. Despite the oft-repeated claims that electoral bribery and corruption were widespread in the eighteenth century, there are in fact very few validated cases of direct bribery. Votes were very rarely put up for sale to the highest bidder and most voters would have been insulted by the offer of a direct bribe. On the other hand, electoral costs were often very high because the voters did expect to be complimented, flattered and rewarded for their loyalty. Payments were rarely offered to corrupt the voter or his conscience, but the electorate did expect benefits and favours in return for the obvious political service which they were performing for the propertied elite. Crude attempts at bribery might be criticised and condemned, but voters anticipated receiving a variety of rewards for their electoral support.[113] In the months before an election voters and even non-voters expected treats and entertainments. In a contested by-election at Bedford, in 1731, the Duke of Bedford provided meat and coals for the poor, while 'agents on both sides are come to a great degree of extravagance in their expenses; the common people are not content with ale as they had at first, but will have wine and punch at their meals, and bring their wifes and children to partake with them.'[114] Voters also expected to be compensated for the loss of wages and income and for the cost of travel, accommodation and refreshment when they took the trouble to go to the polls to serve their superiors. Election agents had to go to considerable lengths to make these arrangements. In the contested election for Norfolk, in 1784, the rival candidates had to meet bills at nearly one hundred inns and public houses where their supporters were accommodated.[115] Furthermore, the whole community expected patrons and successful candidates to spend lavishly on services, amenities and charities within the constituency as evidence of their concern for the people they were claiming to lead and represent.

Few patrons and candidates could be confident that a constituency was fully under control and so electoral expenses were incurred even in normally safe seats because the voters expected to be canvassed, treated and compensated for their support. When a contest was feared, or when one did occur, there was an even greater need to ensure that the voters were complimented, flattered and rewarded. Patrons and candidates needed to establish a formal electoral organisation and to employ election agents. The former included local men of landed wealth and status, while the latter were frequently lawyers or other professional men. Together, these men had to organise the canvass which brought as many voters as possible into the electoral process.[116] It was vital for them to know who was qualified to vote and, if possible, how these electors had last cast their vote. In a contested election the votes of a relatively small number of voters might decide the final outcome. Getting out this marginal vote was a matter requiring time, organisation and knowledge. It was to facilitate this task that manuscript and printed poll books were produced and distributed.[117] The election committees and agents were forever appealing to the independence of the electors. They stressed that the right to vote was held in trust for the whole nation and that it was a civic duty to use it wisely. While the elite demonstrated their status in contacts with the voters, they none the less regularly mixed with the latter and entreated their support. Canvassing needed to be undertaken early, conducted thoroughly and, in a close contest, even repeated a second or third time. The canvassers needed to look to the needs of each voter and to make all the necessary arrangements to get him to the poll. They chose party colours and favours, and distributed propaganda of all kinds, including broadsheets, handbills, election addresses, and circular letters. The press was also used to advertise meetings and to print speeches and addresses and was sometimes used on an astonishingly lavish scale. In the Westminster by-election of 1749 a single candidate issued no fewer than 227 500 electoral letters, advertisements and broadsheets in a constituency with around 10 000 voters. During the general election of 1768 one of the contestants in Essex circulated 33 700 pamphlets, broadsides, squibs and songs, while in the first Middlesex election of 1768 John Wilkes distributed 40 000 handbills in a constituency with around 3500 voters.[118] Clearly, in such constituencies as these, there were many independent voters and the result of a contest was never a foregone conclusion, and so the electors needed to be persuaded by propaganda and not simply influenced by material rewards.

Before any contested poll occurred, rival candidates had to be nominated. On nomination day the candidates sought a large turn-out, of non-voters as well as voters, and of women as well as men, because a good showing of popular support was an essential start to any successful campaign. The virtues of the rival candidates were put before the whole populace and a show of hands would be called for. Non-voters frequently demonstrated their views on such occasions, but, when the decision went to a formal poll, only the qualified electors were supposed to cast their votes. In fact, votes from unqualified electors were frequently accepted by the returning officer and this led to many petitions against the returns announced at the end of contested parliamentary elections. In contested elections voting could extend over several days, even occasionally over several weeks as in the Westminster election of 1784. On the first day of polling in a contested election the rival candidates were expected to make a splendid entry into the polling town, accompanied by a grand retinue, in order to impress everyone with the number, wealth and status of their supporters.[119] Charles Caesar was accompanied by 600 supporters at the Hertford election of 1715, though a Whig critic claimed that many of them were labouring men paid for their services. At the opening of the Kent election in 1790 Filmer Honeywood led a procession half a mile long, while, in the same year, Lord Sheffield was met by his supporters two miles outside Bristol and his carriage was drawn into the town by the populace.[120] One of the grandest entries was made by the supporters of John Wilkes at the by-election for Middlesex in April 1769, when three parties converged on the county town of Brentford from different parts of London:

At a little after ten o'clock 200 of Mr Wilkes's friends, preceded by music, and a flag with the words – FREEDOM. LIBERTY! entered Brentford. This procession was closed by Mr John Swan, carrying a white wand. Five minutes after this came a coach and six, the horses sumptuously adorned with blue ribbons; and persons were on the roof, bearing flags, inscribed BILL OF RIGHTS. MAGNA CARTA. At half past ten 300 sons of liberty entered Brentford on horseback, preceded by six French horns, and four silk flags, with the above inscription in letters of gold....Many ladies (freeholders) were among the friends of freedom, and [were] distinguished by breastknots of blue and silver, with the motto above mentioned.[121]

Throughout the days of polling the candidates were expected to make themselves visible and accessible at the hustings. They and their leading supporters would watch the polling and encourage the voters. Electoral propaganda would continue to be distributed and speeches would be made on every day of the poll. Large public meetings were sometimes organised by the electors themselves, as occurred in such constituencies as Bristol, Coventry and Bedford in 1784, when opposition was expressed to those candidates who had supported the Fox-North coalition.[122] Money continued to be spent getting the voters to the poll and in providing food and drink to voters and non-voters alike.[123] Money was also spent making the election a spectacle and an emotionally charged theatrical event. Rosettes, ribbons, and flags would be provided for supporters of the rival candidates; processions would be organised, often with bands, effigies and other symbols; and excitement would be heightened with gun salutes, firework displays, bonfires and bell-ringing; while entertainment and festivities would continue throughout the poll. At the Norwich election in 1784 William Windham's agents distributed 7369 cockades in a constituency with about 3000 voters.[124] Quite obviously, many non-voters were drawn by and into the political excitement generated by a hotly contested election. The poll was usually carefully managed by the respective agents and election committees, but it was done in a manner which demonstrated not only their influence, but the important participatory role played by the voters themselves. The voters often breakfasted together and marched in procession to the hustings in batches of ten or twenty men attached to the same interest, and led by a band and flying banners. At the end of the polling, loyal supporters would be given a final treat, the successful candidates would be chaired around the constituency accompanied by a boisterous crowd, including many non-voters, and the victors would generally organise a celebration dinner. After Charles James Fox's famous victory at Westminster in 1784 his campaign managers organised no fewer than five celebration dinners, each attended by between 700 and 1000 of his supporters.[125] It was an opportunity for the

ordinary voters to rub shoulders with the great and for the political elite to give thanks to their humble supporters.

Elections were clearly a form of street theatre and many non-
voters as well as voters were enlisted into crowds, audiences,
processions, and celebrations. Great excitement would be
generated in close contests as many of the local populace were
drawn into all the spectacle and ritual of the electoral process.
The great mass of ordinary people were able, indeed they were
even encouraged by the rival candidates, to involve themselves
in all the public spectacles of the election. In boisterous
elections the population cheered and jeered the candidates.
There was public merriment, an almost carnival atmosphere, a
sense of occasion, and an opportunity to demonstrate civic
pride and popular feelings. Candidates might be openly
ridiculed and the non-voters might deliver mock election
speeches and support their own mock-candidates. The social
order was occasionally inverted in some unofficial proceedings
and 'mock' elections were held in several places which were
not even qualified to return MPs.[126] After John Wilkes's first
Middlesex election victory in 1768 excited crowds ran through
the streets chalking the number 45 on almost every door and
forcing householders to recognise Wilkes's triumph by
illuminating their houses.[127]

Election crowds could be rowdy and boisterous even when
there was no contest. When there was a contest, large, excited
and partisan crowds, often inflamed with alcohol, could
threaten the peace of the town. Spontaneous small-scale
disturbances were very common and sometimes this spilled
over into rioting of a quite deliberate nature with attacks on a
particular candidate's supporters. To avoid such an occurrence
at the Norwich by-election in 1786 Henry Hobart's election
committee hired 2000 stavemen at ten shillings each to patrol
the streets and keep the peace during polling.[128] In the more
open constituencies violent demonstrations of popular
opinion were fairly common. There was significant rioting at
elections in Coventry in 1705, Hull in 1723, Norwich in 1727,
Great Yarmouth in 1734, Westminster in 1741, Pontefract in
1768, Liverpool in 1784, York and Leicester in 1790, and
Grantham in 1796. The election at Coventry in 1722 had to be
declared void because of the severity of the rioting. Over 2000
men, on horse and foot, with green twigs and leaves in their

hats, and with colours flying, drums beating and trumpets sounding, marched to the polls. They violently attacked their political opponents, damaged property and shouted virulent anti-Whig slogans.[129] In Leicester, in 1754, the anti-corporation voters pulled down fences which had been put up around common town land by the corporation. The corporation responded by hiring 300 non-voting colliers to intimidate their opponents.[130] In 1761 Thomas Scrope

> came to Lincoln attended by a great many people, many not freemen, and giving out that he came to support the liberties of the free and independent voters, occasioned a great riot, and the mob broke into the Town Hall and drove everybody out, broke all the windows and did other mischief.[131]

In most cases these election disturbances were not the work of thugs specially hired for the occasion. More often they were genuine expressions of opinions, principles and prejudices strongly-held and publicly vented by the local populace, voters and non-voters alike.

V ISSUES, LOCAL AND NATIONAL

In most constituencies during the eighteenth century the voters were primarily concerned with local issues. Local loyalties and local concerns remained paramount for most voters and most of the political elite had no wish to bring national divisions into the constituencies. The local elite usually chose the candidates for their constituency and they were often returned unopposed. As we have seen, this does not mean that the voters in these uncontested constituencies were ignored. Patrons, candidates and the local elite could only sustain their interest in all but a handful of the really venal boroughs by canvassing, flattering and rewarding the voters and by demonstrating that they were serving the best interests of the electorate and indeed of the constituency as a whole. The voters themselves represented much local property, wealth and influence. Most of them were directly affected, in an emotional and a material way, by local issues rather than by the great affairs of state. They therefore took a particular interest in local affairs, in the leadership of their local community, in the exercise of power and authority over them, and in their own future prospects in the constituency. Most of the parliamentary legislation which interested them was that which was enacted to satisfy local demands. Private and local bills involved such issues as enclosures, improvements to roads and navigation, street cleaning, lighting and policing, the building of town amenities, and the provision of charity to the poor, the dependent and the disturbed. These measures often provoked local controversy and inspired the calling of public meetings because they often materially benefited some local men at the expense of others. The local MPs were therefore expected to listen to the views of their constituents and to be active in the relevant committees set up by parliament to discuss the detailed terms of the required legislation.

When local patrons or MPs acted in a negligent, insensitive or high-handed fashion, they risked alienating even the normally docile and deferential voters. If they seemed to be betraying the interests of the local community, they could find themselves facing an electoral revolt. To overcome this, they would need to increase their expenditure of time, money and energy. Whenever possible, patrons and MPs sought to avoid this and so they concentrated on carefully nursing their constituencies and sensitively handling those local issues which interested the voters. Serious mistakes, misjudgements and mismanagement by the local political elite could lead to an outright revolt by the voters. Disputes within the local elite could also provoke a contest in which voters could choose between the rival candidates put forward by their social superiors. In most of these contests, however, it was local and personal issues that dominated the election.[132]

National issues did sometimes affect politics at the constituency level, especially in the more open constituencies where contests were quite common. National issues could be introduced to the voters because the parliamentary elite was sharply divided over ideology and political programmes or because the voters themselves were aroused by a particularly serious national crisis. In the early decades of the eighteenth century and, to a lesser extent, in its closing decades, the disputes between rival parliamentary parties or groupings encouraged political divisions among the ordinary voters. Most contested elections between 1701 and 1715, for example, took

the form of straight party fights and the electorate was faced
with the choice of supporting Whig or Tory candidates. There
were very few contests between candidates in the same party.
These parliamentary parties were divided on issues of
principle and on questions of national importance. The
ordinary voters were often drawn into these disputes and they
clearly voiced their opinion of them in petitions, addresses and
contested elections. Many voters, of course, deferentially
followed the political lead offered by their social superiors, but
others were more independent. They were influenced more by
the mass of political propaganda directed at them from press
and pulpit and they made up their own mind on how to
respond to what they had read or heard.[133] Thus, when
canvassed for his support prior to the first general election of
1701, Allan Chambre, recorder of Kendal, assured James
Grahme of his personal goodwill towards the latter's family,
but he added, 'as to voting for any them ... all I shall say is that
as occasion shall offer ... I shall vote for those who shall have
the same sentiments with me in relation to our national
concerns in church and state.'[134]

Whig and Tory interests existed in many localities and party
issues often dominated general election campaigns in the contested constituencies – the succession issue and the prospect of
war in 1701–2, the 'tack' and the cry of 'the Church in Danger'
in 1705, the Sacheverell affair and the unpopularity of the war
in 1710, the successful peace negotiations in 1713, and the succession issue again in 1715.[135] In 1710, in particular, there was
widespread and intense interest in many constituencies in what
had happened to the high Tory cleric, Dr Henry Sacheverell,
who was impeached before parliament. In the general election
that followed only ten of the twenty Whigs who had managed
the trial were returned to parliament (Robert Walpole finished
bottom of the poll in Norfolk) and only 144 of the 304 MPs who
had voted for Sacheverell's impeachment were re-elected. In
many constituencies there were spontaneous and virulent outbursts in favour of Sacheverell and the furore had an impact on
the elections in every open constituency in the country.[136] There
seems little reason to doubt that in the general elections
between 1701 and 1715 there were major shifts in public
opinion in the contested elections, and not just changes in the
deployment of crown patronage or changing attitudes among

the political elite. Professor Speck concluded his examination of constituency politics in these years by claiming that the best explanation for the volatility of the electorate and for the rapid change of electoral fortunes of the two parties was the impact of party propaganda on the attitudes of the ordinary electors.[137]

In the elections after 1715, although party rivalry persisted in parliament and in the constituencies, national issues did not impinge so forcefully or so regularly on the ordinary voter. Occasionally, however, a major national issue did arouse the wrath of the more independent electors, whose reactions then produced a significant shift in the voting pattern in the larger and more open constituencies. By the time polling took place in the 1734 general election, for example, the widespread and deep-seated resentment caused by Walpole's Excise Bill of 1733 had still not dissipated, although the measure had already been withdrawn. The issue had a major impact on the election results in the contested seats. Supporters of the Excise Bill lost seats in about ten counties and in a number of the larger boroughs, including Bristol, Coventry, Canterbury and Newcastle upon Tyne. No supporter of the Bill dared even to contest any of the city of London's four seats. The administration lost most of the largest constituencies in the country and, although it retained its parliamentary majority because of its success in the smaller boroughs, it suffered the clearest electoral rejection of any government in the eighteenth century. The Duke of Dorset had no hesitation in imputing this humiliation to the popular resentment created by the ill-fated Excise Bill.[138] Prior to the general election of 1754 the Pelham administration feared that the intense and widespread resentment caused by the Jewish Naturalisation Act of 1753 might produce damaging electoral consequences. Many constituencies protested against the passing of this measure and there was a great deal of virulent, yet popular, propaganda against it and its supporters. The Duke of Newcastle was warned well in advance of the general election that the furore over the Jew Bill would have an impact on a number of constituencies in the West Riding of Yorkshire, 'I am afraid the ignorant populace may be misled by the men of heat, and men of bad designs, and it may be made the adopted cry at the election, and which can only operate against the present members.'[139] The administration took fright and rushed to repeal the Act at the end of 1753, and yet the resentment against the offending measure was still an issue in every contested election in 1754. It affected the contest in Oxfordshire, Gloucestershire, Bristol, Reading, Exeter, Abingdon, Canterbury, Newton and York. In London Sir William Calvert, who had topped the poll in 1747, was now punished by the independent voters for his support for the act and he finished bottom of the poll.[140]

From the later 1760s onwards many voters in the larger constituencies began to show a deeper and more consistent political awareness of national issues and parliamentary politics. This development owed much to the seriousness and divisiveness of specific issues, the growing political influence of the press, the spread of clubs, societies and party organisations, the increased knowledge of how to organise election campaigns, and the rise of nationwide petitioning campaigns organised by sophisticated extra-parliamentary pressure groups. Many thousands of voters were mobilised into nationwide political campaigns on various major issues from Wilkes through the American crisis to the French Revolution. These issues were significant factors in the election contests in 1774, 1780, 1784 and 1796. In several counties and in many of the larger boroughs radicals and reformers contested seats and even won a number of notable victories. Political radicalism also began to develop among the voters themselves in an enduring and coherent way. Perhaps more significant in electoral terms was the growing number of constituencies where independent voters could play an important role in contested elections. By the later eighteenth century independent electors were active and organised in perhaps 30–40 constituencies (mostly the larger and more important constituencies in the country). Increasingly, the parliamentary elite began to bring party politics into the constituencies. In about ninety boroughs there were signs of party organisation by the late eighteenth century. In a dozen major boroughs, including London, Westminster, Bristol, Leicester, Nottingham and York, party involvement with the voters was very strong. In another 19 boroughs, including Norwich, Coventry, Oxford, Worcester, Maidstone and Newcastle upon Tyne, it was significant. As a result of the efforts of the radicals, the independent voters and party organisations perhaps as many as half the total electorate was conscious of national issues when they went to the polls in the late eighteenth century.[141]

One of the most dramatic examples of the way in which a nationwide shift of opinion could once more occur among the electorate in the more open constituencies took place in the general election of 1784. In that campaign a vast amount of propaganda expressed considerable hostility to Fox's India Bill and the Fox-North coalition of 1783, while just prior to the election well over 200 addresses to the crown (several from large, but unrepresented, towns such as Birmingham and Leeds) announced their firm support for William Pitt and his minority government. With some justice, Bishop Watson could observe:

> The numberless addresses ... against the Coalition Ministry sufficiently showed the voice of the people to be with Mr Pitt. Now I consider the voice of the people to be superior, not only to the House of Commons, but to the whole Legislature: I hope therefore no harm will come to the Constitution from this example. It was not so much the prerogative of the Crown that kept Mr Pitt in his place, and set the House of Commons at defiance, as it was the sense of the nation, which on this occasion was in direct contradiction to the sense of the House of Commons.[142]

In the general election of 1784 the sense of the nation, or at least the votes of the independent electors, sided with Pitt rather than Fox. Charles James Fox did win one of the Westminster seats, but the tide of independent opinion resulted in a clear electoral victory for Pitt and his supporters. William Wilberforce won a sensational victory in Yorkshire, two Pittite candidates recorded the highest number of votes ever recorded in the city of London, whereas leading Foxites surprisingly lost seats in such constituencies as Surrey and Norfolk. The Foxites were reduced to depending on their successes in the smaller boroughs, while the Pittites triumphed in the larger and more open constituencies.[143]

There is considerable evidence to suggest that, at times, party loyalty and national issues did influence a great number of voters, although there is no evidence to suggest that the eighteenth-century electorate clearly divided along socio-economic lines, with an elector's social status determining how he cast his vote.[144] Perhaps the most constant and deep-seated ideological division within the electorate was over religion. From the highly partisan years of the early eighteenth century, through the quieter decades of the mid-century, to the sharply polarised 1790s, the opposition between Anglicans and Dissenters was a marked feature of electoral politics in a number of constituencies. The disputes between Anglican and Dissenters underpinned the rivalry between Tories and Whigs in Anne's reign as it inflamed the hostility between conservatives and radicals in the late eighteenth century. Throughout the century religion was important as a focus of political rivalry in about forty constituencies. The Dissenters were actually the dominant electoral force in Coventry and Nottingham, and they were the major opposition force in a handful of counties and about fifteen boroughs.[145] Occasionally, the Dissenters voted *en bloc*, as at Abingdon in 1734 and 1774, and an attempt was even made in these years to get all the Dissenters in the country to vote for candidates who supported civil and religious liberty.[146] The Anglican majority, of course, never all voted on the same side, but they often voted together in those constituencies where they faced a coherent Dissenting opposition and there is no doubt that the high church parsons voted overwhelmingly for Tory or conservative candidates throughout the century.[147]

Sir Lewis Namier once observed about the issues affecting the voters in the eighteenth century that 'Political issues do not, as a rule, deeply affect the lives or consciousness of ordinary men, and little real thought is given to them by these men.'[148] In the same work, however, he also wrote:

> the knights of the shires, independent of the Government in their constituencies and, as a rule, not soliciting personal favours, and the representatives of the larger boroughs, responded more freely to public opinion than the members of rotten boroughs and close corporations. Still, the difference was marginal, ... even the Members for the worst of the rotten boroughs did not remain impervious to currents of popular feeling.[149]

The burden of most recent research would indicate that both observations were true, but that the second opinion is more accurate and valid for much of the eighteenth century than Namier had recognised.

2 Vested Interests and Pressure Groups

Many recent historians have stressed that there were two political worlds in eighteenth-century Britain. On the one hand, there was a narrow landed elite, composed of the aristocracy and the greater gentry. This remarkably cohesive and integrated group dominated the court, the cabinet, both houses of parliament and the administration of the counties. They regarded the possession of land as the essential qualification for those who desired to serve the king or to sit in parliament. The possession of landed property was also seen as the best means of attaching men to the interests of their country and of providing them with the independence, leisure and judgement needed to govern others. On the other hand, historians have also detected another political world which, if not entirely separate and distinct, at least sought to escape from the patronage of the aristocratic elite and was sometimes in conflict with it. This political world, both bourgeois and plebeian, existed outside the narrow confines of court, cabinet and parliament and flourished in urban areas. In the towns merchant oligarchies, popular radicalism or crowd demonstrations were largely beyond the control of the landed elite.[1]

While there is some justice in this view of eighteenth-century politics, it is possible to offer an alternative interpretation which stresses the links between these two political worlds. These links were forged by the sustained efforts of a whole variety of vested interests, which were not heavily represented in parliament but which were still capable of exerting considerable influence on the political institutions dominated by the landed elite. Sometimes these vested interests were so essential to the smooth operation of the political system that the landed elite readily recognised their importance and acted accordingly. Other vested interests could only influence the decision-making processes of the state by organising themselves into sophisticated pressure groups able to employ a whole range of tactics to ensure that their voices were heard by those in positions of authority. In both cases however these vested interests were able to achieve some success in influencing the decisions taken by the legislature because eighteenth-century parliaments spent much of their time debating legislation introduced by ordinary backbench MPs at the behest of their constituents and the propertied elite who dominated parliament were fully conscious that in a commercial society such as Britain, parliament needed to preserve and promote the welfare of other economic interests than those of the landed classes.

Vested interests and pressure groups soon learned that parliament did not exist simply to raise revenue or to pass legislation required by the executive and hence devised by the government. Parliament met every year in the eighteenth century and in every session it spent much of its time discussing and promoting bills of a private or local nature.[2] Vested interests outside parliament regularly approached backbench MPs to enlist their backing for this kind of legislation. By the 1720s parliament was passing an average of thirty such bills every session. Forty years later the average had increased to about one hundred and it stayed around this number for the rest of the century. A high proportion of these bills resulted from the desire of particular economic interests to enclose land, build turnpike roads, dig canals, improve harbours, clear rivers or pave, light and cleanse the streets. These private and local bills were printed at the expense of their sponsors so that they could be discussed by all interested parties before the bills were introduced into parliament. Both houses of parliament declared at the end of the seventeenth century that all parties affected by a proposed enclosure bill had to give their consent. In 1774 the House of Commons ordered that notices of intended enclosure, drainage and improvement bills should be posted on the church doors in the parishes concerned and should be proclaimed at quarter sessions, while applications for turnpike roads had to be advertised in local newspapers. In 1791 the provisions of bills for paving, lighting, cleansing or improving any town had also to be publicised at quarter sessions and advertised in local newspapers. Often local legislation was also discussed at public town meetings before any bill was submitted to parliament. In addition to this kind of legislation parliament also regularly responded to the large number of petitions promoted by those who sought political influence in order to further their interests and to protect them from foreign rivals or domestic competitors.[3] In its handling of local legislation and in its response to petitions parliament was therefore seen as the representative of a whole variety of interests and not just as an institution serving the interests of the landed elite.[4]

Landed property certainly conferred great status on its owners and the protection of that property was regarded as an essential reason for creating civil government in the first place and as one of the prime duties of the state thereafter.[5] The landed elite undoubtedly dominated government and parliament and so they naturally acted in these two institutions to protect or to promote their own economic interests. The eighteenth century saw the landed elite act, for example, to shift the burden of taxation off their own shoulders and onto those of the middling and lower orders.[6] Meanwhile, parliament passed bounties encouraging the export of corn, high tariffs hindering the importation of foreign corn, and thousands of enclosure acts to benefit the landed interest.[7] None the less, although the majority of MPs were capable of rising up in fury to ward off threats to the landed interest,[8] they did acknowledge that they must represent other important interests in the nation.[9] As early as 1711 an opponent of the Landed Qualification Act, which established that MPs must possess substantial landed property, argued that it was also important to have men in parliament who represented trade and industry.[10] In 1728 *The Craftsman*, a periodical normally associated with the interests of the landed gentry, admitted: 'Trade is of that general use and importance to every country, that whatever relates to it can never be unseasonable, nor too often discussed; especially in this nation, which has so great a dependence on it.'[11] David Hume, in his discussion of political parties, accepted that it was natural and legitimate to have parties representing different interests, though he hoped that efforts to divide the landed and the trading interests of the nation would prove ineffective.[12]

Edmund Burke, however, was probably the first important politician to acknowledge that parliament should represent all the important interests in the nation:

a great official, a great professional, a great military and naval interest, all necessarily comprehending many people of the first weight, ability, wealth and spirit, had been gradually formed in the kingdom. These new interests must be let into the share of representation, else possibly they may be inclined to destroy those institutions of which they are not permitted to partake.[13]

Although conscious of the existence of different interests Burke hoped that in parliament 'all these widespread interests must be considered; must be compared; must be reconciled if possible.'[14] Sir James Stewart claimed in 1755 that 'Every interest in a state must influence the government of it in proportion to its consequence and weight.'[15] Adam Smith was more concerned about the consequences of allowing some interests to influence parliament. He wrote disparagingly of 'the mean rapacity, the monopolising spirit of merchants and manufacturers, who neither are, nor ought to be, the rulers of mankind', but he still acknowledged that the deliberations of the legislature were often directed 'by the clamorous importunity of partial interest.'[16]

By the late eighteenth century radicals often complained about the over-representation of the landed interest in parliament and some of them demanded that the financial, the commercial and the manufacturing interests should be given greater representation. James Burgh promoted the needs of the commercial interests in particular:

> The interest of merchants is so much the interest of the nation, that there can hardly be too many merchants in parliament. ... It is objected, that each merchant will probably vote in parliament for what is most for the advantage of his own particular branch. True. Therefore let a considerable number of merchants always have seats in the house, and then all different interests will be consulted.[17]

In response to such criticisms the conservative defenders of the existing system repeatedly insisted that, while most MPs were landed men, all important interests in the nation were in fact well represented. In opposing the parliamentary reform bill of 1783 Lord North claimed: 'it is the beauty of the constitution of the House of Commons, that like the general fabric of the British legislature, it provides for, and preserves the due balance, between the several great interests of the empire – the landed, the commercial, and the monied.'[18] William Paley and Charles Jenkinson also opposed the need for parliamentary reform because they believed that parliament represented not only the great landowners, but the commercial and manufacturing interests, and the major professional interests, including the army, the navy, the law and the servants of the state.[19] By the end of the eighteenth century James Mackintosh was claiming:

> The best security which human wisdom can devise, seems to be the distribution of political authority among different individuals and bodies, with separate interests and separate characters, corresponding to the variety of classes of which civil society is composed, each interested to guard his own order from oppression by the rest.[20]

An examination of the political activities of the vested interests and pressure groups of eighteenth-century Britain will show that the landed elite did respond to many of the campaigns waged outside parliament by the middling and lower orders of society. Some campaigns were much more successful than others however and an examination of this discrepancy gives us an opportunity to test whether conservative opinion was justified in asserting that all the important interests in the nation were properly represented or whether the radicals were right to claim that those interests representing the middling and lower orders were insufficiently represented in government or parliament.

I ECONOMIC INTERESTS AND PRESSURE GROUPS

Every government and every parliament in the eighteenth century was dominated by the greater landowners.[21] These men resented any challenge to their authority or their privileges by new or rising interests in the state. The prejudices of the country gentlemen, for example, were aroused by fears that a small group of immensely rich financiers were exerting a political influence quite disproportionate to their numbers or their status. In both parliament and the press a war of words was waged by the defenders of the landed interest who feared that the monied men would corrupt the whole political system and undermine the independence of parliament and the liberties of the subject. This conflict was particularly bitter in the earlier eighteenth century,[22] when the financial interest was a relatively new phenomenon, but even in the mid and later eighteenth century there was much resentment against the 'nabobs' of the East India Company who, having enriched themselves in India, bought landed estates and parliamentary seats on their return home.[23] These fears were never fully justified because the financial interest never wielded as much influence as its critics feared. Although many of the directors of the great financial institutions, especially the Bank of England, the East India Company and the South Sea Company, gained seats in parliament, their numbers were never large enough to give them significant direct influence over the legislature. What gave these institutions political power was not their votes, but their ability to raise substantial loans for the Treasury whenever the government required them.[24] Every government in the eighteenth century raised a substantial proportion of its revenue through loans and so the ability to raise huge loans was essential to the survival of any administration. As head of the Treasury every Prime Minister had to maintain good relations with the great financial institutions or face a political crisis. Robert Harley's new Tory administration almost came to grief in 1710–11 because of the hostility of Whig financiers.[25] The Stanhope-Sunderland ministry, the Devonshire-Pitt administration and the Fox-North coalition all ran into major difficulties because they mishandled their relations with the great financial institutions.[26] In contrast, the political success of Godolphin, Walpole, Pelham, Lord North and the Younger Pitt all benefited from establishing good relations between Treasury and the monied corporations.

This was not a relationship between equals however. Whenever a strong administration decided to exert itself it could always bend the monied interest to its will because the major financial corporations could never risk a complete breach with the government. On several occasions the Bank of England and the South Sea Company had to accept political interference in their financial affairs,[27] while the East India Company's activities in India were eventually brought under close political supervision by the British government.[28]

None the less, although they were the servants, not the masters of eighteenth-century governments, the great financial corporations could influence the decisions taken by ministers. The Bank of England was able to protect its interests from being damaged by the South Sea Company's grandiose scheme to take over the whole national debt in 1720 and it emerged from the subsequent crash with its reputation enhanced.[29] In 1737 Walpole defeated parliamentary attempts to reduce the rate of interest on the Bank's loans and in 1750 the Bank successfully campaigned for compensation when the rate of interest was reduced by Henry Pelham.[30] It was government action which secured the South Sea Company's trading privileges with Spanish America and it was partly in response to the company's pressure that Walpole reluctantly went to war with Spain in 1739.[31] The East India Company too learned how to exert political pressure in order to protect its interests. It lobbied successfully to secure its charters in 1698 and 1709 and to have them extended in 1730 and 1744.[32] In the 1720s it embarked on a long campaign to persuade Walpole to work towards destroying a rival East India Company which had been set up in Ostend.[33] In 1762 the East India Company arranged with the government just what demands should be made in the peace negotiations with France now that the company was deeply involved in Indian affairs.[34] Over the next twenty years or so it campaigned vigorously to ensure that government supervision of its activities in India would not be too damaging to its trading interests. In opposing Fox's India Bill of 1783 a special sub-committee was set up to sponsor the dissemination of critical pamphlets and hostile caricatures and to ensure that the Company's case was well publicised in the newspapers across the whole country. This campaign helped to defeat the bill. When William Pitt drew up his India Bill in 1784 in order to regulate the East India Company he made sure that he first reached an acceptable compromise with the Company's directors.[35]

The great financial institutions represented the high bourgeoisie, the richest men among those below the landed elite in the status hierarchy, and so it is not surprising that they could exert political influence in the eighteenth century. They were not however the only economic interest able to influence the political decisions taken by government and parliament. The

landed elite fully recognised that Britain's strength and prosperity rested heavily on its commercial success and that political action often needed to be taken to protect the interests of
those substantial merchants competing for a greater share of
world trade. For their part, these wealthy merchants were not
slow to learn that they too could influence the political decisions of the governing elite by adopting pressure group tactics.

In this struggle for political influence the chartered trading
corporations had an advantage because their original charters
gave them monopoly rights over certain types of trade. Moreover, their trade often had peculiar difficulties, because of the
risk involved and because of the competition from foreign
rivals, and so the government was particularly conscious of
their need for political support. On the other hand, independent merchants outside these companies often resented the
latter's monopoly over a particular trade and their close
relationship with the government. Thus, the major chartered
trading companies had to campaign for government support
not only against foreign rivals, but against those domestic
critics who wanted to open up their trade to independent
merchants.

The Russia Company, although not a very large trading corporation, worked hard to gain considerable influence over Sir
Robert Walpole's administration. It established links with MPs
and with merchants in various ports. It gathered detailed information on the state of its trade and what was needed to promote its commercial activities. The directors of the company
also lobbied MPs, petitioned parliament, and provided witnesses to be examined by both houses of parliament. The government responded by going to great lengths to meet the
needs of the Russia Company and to foster its trade. In nego-
tiating the Anglo-Russian Commercial Treaty of 1734 the
British government met all the Russia Company's objectives
and the treaty proved very advantageous. In 1741 and 1750 the
company was also allowed to breach the Levant Company's
monopoly of trade with Persia by trading with that country
through Russia.[36]

Other chartered companies had to face serious political
challenges to their privileges and they had to make determined political efforts to safeguard them. After 1698 the rights
of the Hudson's Bay Company, which conducted a small, but

reliable and moderately profitable trade, were perilously dependent on the shaky foundations of royal prerogative and were not guaranteed by parliamentary legislation. Although the government did secure the restoration of the company's posts and territories by the Treaty of Utrecht in 1713, there was no firm guarantee of its commercial privileges. Increasingly, the company's failure to conduct an expansive trading policy or to look vigorously for the supposed North West Passage, combined with unfounded rumours that it was reaping vast profits from its existing trade, built up resentment of and opposition to its trading monopoly. In the early 1740s the company's critics embarked on a political campaign to abolish its monopoly privileges. Arthur Dobbs orchestrated a lengthy pamphlet war and also produced the substantial *Account of Hudson's Bay* (1744), which was a powerful piece of special pleading. In 1748 independent merchants from London, Bristol, Liverpool and Glasgow petitioned the crown for their own charter to trade with all territories in Hudson's Bay not occupied by the company. A new propaganda war was initiated and both sides presented parliament with evidence and affidavits. In March 1749 a committee of the House of Commons was appointed to investigate the trade, while outside parliament a well-organised campaign against the Hudson's Bay Company was mounted. Twenty-eight petitions against the company's monopoly were sent in by ports and manufacturing towns. Although the wording of petitions was not identical, it was sufficiently similar to suggest a coordinated campaign. The lead appears to have been given by the Liverpool merchants, who traditionally favoured an open trade, but they established links with merchants in Bristol and in other ports. Alarmed that a distinctly unfavourable impression of its activities was being created, the company produced a pamphlet, *The Case of the Hudson's Bay Company*, and delivered it to every MP. In evidence before parliament, in May 1749, the company's servants also doggedly insisted that cost, terrain and transportation problems ruled out any large-scale movement inland. The campaign against the company's monopoly was defeated, as was a further effort in 1752. In order to safeguard its privileges, however, the company had to break its traditional total secrecy about its activities and it had to make greater efforts to explore and to exploit the huge area under its control.[37]

Other chartered trading corporations were less successful in warding off the assaults on their monopolies launched chiefly by merchants outside London who wanted to open up overseas trade to unrestricted access. The Levant Company's monopoly of British trade to the eastern Mediterranean was subject to much criticism in the earlier eighteenth century. Its ability to resist these assaults was greatly weakened when its own trade to Turkey declined, whereas the trade conducted by French merchants expanded. In 1744 petitions from clothiers and silk-weavers in at least eight towns and three counties blamed the decay of trade with the eastern Mediterranean on the exclusive privileges of the Levant Company. In 1753 there was a flood of petitions from at least thirty-two towns, including Liverpool, Bristol, Norwich, Chester, Leeds, Hull, Lancaster and Gloucester. Parliament agreed to modify the Levant Company's charter and to open up the trade to other British merchants.[38] The Royal African Company, which was even less successful at exploiting its monopoly trading privileges, soon succumbed to the onslaught launched by those merchants in Liverpool and Bristol who were active in the slave trade. In March 1749 petitions from both of these cities complained of monopoly trading companies 'whose interest hath been, and ever will be, found incompatible with that of a free and open trade'.[39] In 1750 the House of Commons received eighteen petitions on the African trade and the Royal African Company was abolished. It was replaced by a new company of merchants trading to Africa. This company was placed under a committee representing the merchants of London, Bristol and Liverpool who traded with Africa. This committee established good relations with the government and kept ministers regularly informed of its needs. As a result the company gained valuable concessions in the peace treaty of 1763. It was also protected by the government when it faced Dutch rivals between 1768 and 1775 and when it was attacked by domestic critics in 1772 and 1777.[40]

Clearly, even chartered trading companies with monopoly privileges could succumb to well-organised assaults. The lesson that commercial success depended upon sophisticated organisation was soon learned by merchants who did not enjoy the benefits of a charter or of trading rights guaranteed by crown or parliament. The commercial group which undoubtedly learned this lesson best were those merchants and planters involved in the West Indian trade. Although eventually one of the most effective economic pressure groups, the West India interest did not find it easy to build up a regular and permanent organisation because it had first to reconcile differences between resident and absentee proprietors of West Indian plantations and between the planters and the London merchants conducting the trade with the West Indies. Joint action and a concerted policy were seen to be advisable, however, in the face of threats to the security of the islands and competition from foreign rivals.[41] An effective West India interest was gradually built up, though it was never as strong inside parliament as some historians have claimed. In 1733 it petitioned parliament and provided it with the propaganda and the witnesses necessary to convince MPs of the need to levy prohibitive duties on all foreign sugar, molasses and rum imported into Britain's North American colonies. In 1739 it lobbied successfully for the Sugar Act, which gave the West Indies permission to ship their products to southern Europe without first landing at a British port. This was achieved despite opposition from other British merchants, who feared it would reduce the West Indian demand for British manufactured goods and also increase the price of sugar within Britain.[42] In 1744, when the government proposed to increase the duty on imported sugar, the West Indian merchants organised a sophisticated campaign of resistance. Their case against the tax was printed as a pamphlet and a copy was sent to every MP. Copies were also sent to all the major seaports throughout the country and the principal arguments were published in the *London Evening Post*. Groups of West India merchants went about London and Westminster lobbying those MPs who were particularly influential or who were known to be friendly to their cause. William Pitt showed an interest in their cause and so the merchants drew up a brief for him to use in his speech against the tax. In return for offering their support for a tax on foreign linen they also received the backing of some Scottish and Irish MPs. The merchants were determined that 'nothing shall be wanted to make the clamour popular, and if possible to get this d[amne]d Bill as much abhorred as the Excise Scheme'.[43] This well orchestrated campaign was in fact entirely successful. The West India interest continued to defend its commercial advantages for the rest of the century, resisting efforts to drive down the price of sugar, securing a monopoly over the sugar supplies to the American colonies and staving off very determined efforts to abolish the slave trade. In 1769 a formal Society of West India Merchants was established. It coordinated activities with the long-established Planters Club and for many years it held meetings once a month to protect the economic interests of its members.[44]

Although no other group of independent merchants could rival the political influence of the West India interest, there were occasions when several different commercial groups combined to bring heavy pressure to bear upon the government. In 1721–2, for example, merchants in London, Bristol, Liverpool, Whitehaven and Lancaster complained bitterly about Scottish merchants smuggling goods into England and undercutting their prices. Their campaign persuaded Walpole to try the experiment of a single Customs Board for the whole of Britain.[45] In 1733 the merchants engaged in the wine and tobacco trades combined with other merchants, traders and shopkeepers to resist Walpole's Excise Bill. The lead was certainly given by merchants and traders in London, where the instructions requesting the city's four MPs to oppose the bill were supported by both the Court of Aldermen and the Common Council. Many of London's livery companies joined in the protests and there were mass demonstrations outside the House of Commons. At least fifty-three other constituencies also petitioned against the bill, including towns represented by pro-government MPs. The campaign was so successful that it forced one of the strongest governments in the eighteenth century to withdraw one of its most important measures.[46]

In 1735, when parliament was contemplating a measure to license and restrict the sale of gin, the Distillers Company appointed a committee to lobby the Treasury, the city authorities and parliament with a proposal to curb excesses in the trade by enlarging the company's powers. The company also distributed pamphlets, broadsheets and petitions against the new law, while its agents swarmed around parliament buttonholing MPs and perhaps even offering bribes. The West India merchants also petitioned against the measure's impact on colonial imports, while retailers in London, Bristol and

Norwich protested and distributed ballads and prints. This
campaign did not prevent the act being passed, but opposition
continued to grow. The implementation of the act depended
heavily on informers and they were deeply unpopular. They
were often physically abused, not only by the poor but by
respectable householders. Government and parliament finally
recognised reality and repealed the Gin Act in 1743, replacing
it with more liberal controls.[47] In the late 1730s Walpole faced
an even greater crisis when a pressure group campaign started
the process which led to his eventual fall. The cause was the
disputes with Spain over illicit British trade in the Caribbean.
In 1739 many independent merchants, in both London and
the other major ports, combined with the South Sea Company
in whipping up public opinion, petitioning parliament and
lobbying MPs in order to ensure that the government would
attempt to protect British ships from Spanish attacks. This
public clamour reached such heights that it drove Britain into
an unnecessary and largely unsuccessful war with Spain that
eventually brought Walpole down.[48]

Many more merchants than manufacturers sat in parliament
and many of the rapidly growing industrial towns were denied
direct representation in the House of Commons, but this did
not mean that the landed elite had no interest in the development of British industries. Many great landowners were in
fact directly involved in exploiting the coal, wood and mineral
resources of their estates and in reducing transportation costs
by improving roads and canals. Some also took a closer interest
in the manufacturing interests in their own areas. The Marquis
of Rockingham regularly spoke up in parliament on behalf of
the woollen industry in Yorkshire, Earl Gower did so for the
Staffordshire potters and the Earl of Dartmouth assisted the
Birmingham metal industries.[49] Manufacturers in various
industries were also capable of acting to protect their own
interests. The woollen manufacturers belonged to the largest
industry in the country and they often combined as an effective political pressure group. Adam Smith declared of their
activities:

> Our woollen manufacturers have been more successful than
> any other class of workmen in persuading the legislature
> that the prosperity of the nation depended upon the success

and extension of their particular business. They have not only obtained a monopoly against the consumers by an absolute prohibition of importing woollen cloths from any foreign country, but they have likewise obtained another monopoly against the sheep farmers and growers of wool by a similar prohibition of the exportation of live sheep and wool.[50]

To protect this second monopoly they mounted intense lobbying campaigns in 1720, 1731, and 1739 in order to prevent the illegal export of wool to foreign manufacturers.[51]

Whenever they perceived their profits, markets and jobs to be under threat, the woollen manufacturers and merchants mounted sustained lobbying campaigns to defend their economic interests. On several occasions the representatives of the woollen interest in England successfully campaigned to restrain and, if possible, destroy competition from foreign woollens, even those from Scotland and Ireland. Those who produced the lighter woollen cloths were particularly concerned about the threat posed by the importation of wrought silk, linen and cotton cloth. They therefore tried, with some success, to constrain competition from linen cloth produced in Ireland and Scotland and to ban the importation of Asian cloths. From the mid-1690s prolonged agitation, including printed propaganda, petitions, the lobbying of MPs, and popular disturbances by distressed workers in the domestic woollen and silk industries persuaded parliament to take action. Imports of wrought silk and finished calicoes were banned from 1701, customs duties were imposed on plain calicoes in 1701, 1704 and 1708, and excise duties were placed on printed calicoes produced in Britain. These political successes did not satisfy the woollen interest which persisted in agitating for a total prohibition on the finishing and sale of all calicoes. The initial campaign in 1704 failed – it was resisted by the East India Company and some West Indian interests – but a major sophisticated and more successful campaign was waged in the winter of 1719–20. Petitions flooded in from all over the country and this lobbying campaign was accompanied by serious disorders in London. By 1721 the East India Company had clearly lost its protracted battle to keep the English market open to Asian textiles. An act of parliament that year agreed to the ban on the sale and use of foreign calicoes requested by the woollen and silk manufacturers and merchants. This act effectively closed the home market to further penetration by Asian textiles. Thereafter domestically produced linen and cotton were the major threats to those who produced lighter woollen cloths.[52]

Even those woollen manufacturers who were based in towns with no direct representation in parliament proved that they could influence the political decisions taken by the landed elite. The woollen manufacturers of Leeds, for example, were able to have their views represented in every House of Commons committee and on every piece of legislation that touched upon the Yorkshire woollen industry throughout the entire eighteenth century. The cloth merchants were liberal with their purses and tireless in their journeys up to London where they lobbied MPs representing various Yorkshire constituencies.[53] On some occasions the wool merchants could even prove more effective than representatives of the landed interest. In 1781–2, for example, the landowners of Lincolnshire drew up a petition to parliament to press for an act of parliament to allow the limited export of combing wool because of the slump in home prices. The West Yorkshire woollen manufacturers recognised this as a threat to the cost of their supplies and they organised a much more effective campaign to resist the proposal. A well-publicised meeting was held in Leeds on 19 December 1781 and the resolutions which were adopted were printed and widely distributed. Public opinion was rallied not only throughout West Yorkshire, but as far as Cumberland, East Anglia and the south-west of England. The woollen manufacturers also sent delegates to London to seek out not only MPs, but government ministers and even Lord North himself. Petitions, handbills and pamphlets were widely disseminated. A joint meeting with the Lincolnshire graziers was dominated by the more numerous woollen merchants and manufacturers who attended. The graziers were outgunned and outmanoeuvred. They failed to rally many MPs to their cause and they soon abandoned their efforts. The woollen manufacturers had clearly demonstrated that they could operate effectively in a political system dominated by landed men.[54]

Other important manufacturing interests, particularly the iron and the other textile industries, were also capable of mounting sophisticated campaigns to safeguard or improve their economic position. For years the British ironmasters combined to dissuade parliament and the Board of Trade from adopting measures to encourage iron manufacturing in the American colonies that might compete with British production.[55] When, however, bar and pig iron from the American colonies were finally admitted into London duty free from 1750, the iron masters in other areas of the country were resentful of the economic advantage which was thus gained. In 1756 petitions seeking a similar concession were sent to parliament from a number of places, including Bristol, Liverpool and Birmingham. Public meetings were held to pass resolutions and to secure support, and pamphlets on the issue were published and distributed. The iron masters rallied other related industries behind their campaign and won over tanners, leather manufacturers and the owners of forges and woodlands. In 1757 this pressure secured the admission of colonial bar iron into any British port duty free.[56]

One of the best organised and most successful extra-parliamentary campaigns on an economic issue was waged in the mid-1760s against the cider excise tax of 1763. Opposition to this exaction in the cider counties of west and south-west England united people from all levels of society against an exaction which they thought would do serious damage to their regional economy. Criticism of the measure had been mounted within both houses of parliament, but this had not prevented the measure being enacted. It was the vociferous and widespread extra-parliamentary campaign that eventually persuaded government and parliament to repeal the measure in 1766. Outside parliament Benjamin Heath, a bookseller and the town clerk of Exeter, did much to unite the opposition in several counties behind a respectable and sophisticated propaganda campaign. Pamphlets were published and widely disseminated, while local newspapers printed polemical essays and reported extensively on the activities of the critics of the excise. Opponents in some 37 constituencies organised letters of thanks to MPs who opposed the measure or sent letters instructing their local MPs to press for the repeal of the tax. Some critics of the excise suggested that the best way of putting pressure on MPs was to form an association 'among all the inferior freeholders by which none, under a very large penalty is to give voice for any one of the present members at the next

general election who does not exert himself towards a repeal
of the cider-law'. Some seventy political meetings were held
across six counties between July 1763 and January 1766, and
some forty petitions were sent in from constituencies in seven
cider counties and from the city of London and the Society of
Merchant Venturers in Bristol. The Court of Common Council
in London unanimously resolved to petition the House of
Commons and to instruct the city's four MPs to vote for repeal.
Leominster in Herefordshire sent in two petitions; one from
the bailiffs and capital burgesses and the other from the mere
'inhabitants'. Many other humble folk demonstrated their
hostility to the cider tax in more ritualistic and direct ways.
They processed through the streets, they hanged or burned
Lord Bute in effigy, and they drank anti-excise toasts. When
the tax was repealed in 1766 there were widespread popular
celebrations, including bell-ringing, the illumination of streets
and houses, public dinners and feasts, and excited crowds processing around many of the towns in the region. A long and
sophisticated campaign had united many interests and sectors
of society over several counties and it had ended in resounding
success.[57]

Campaigns such as this taught manufacturers whose
industries had only recently become vital to the economy how
to manipulate the political system. In 1765 Josiah Wedgwood
and other leading manufacturers in the West Midlands organised a highly effective campaign to secure parliamentary
approval for a proposal to build the Trent and Mersey canal.
Supporters were recruited from the different towns affected
and an informed political discussion of the scheme was generated. Thomas Bentley drafted a pamphlet, *View of the
Advantages of Inland Navigation,* and the scheme was publicised
in the *St James Chronicle* in London and in the provincial press
in a number of important towns including Liverpool, Birmingham, Nottingham, Derby and Chester. This ensured that widespread local backing was secured before Earl Gower was
encouraged to promote a successful bill through parliament.[58]
Matthew Boulton, another leading industrialist, organised two
sophisticated lobbying campaigns in the area in the mid-1770s.
In 1773 he drew up the necessary legislation, wrote to many
MPs and personally canvassed the support of over forty peers
in order to secure parliamentary backing for the setting up of

assay offices in Birmingham and Sheffield. Two years later Boulton went to even greater lengths to rally parliamentary support for an extension of James Watt's patent for an improved steam engine. He approached many local MPs in person and despatched letters and appeals to many more. Over a hundred MPs had been contacted by the time his campaign reached a successful conclusion and the patent was extended for another twenty-five years.[59] Sir Richard Arkwright and his associates also had to combine to promote their innovations in the new cotton industry. When they first tried to mechanise production they encountered tremendous legal barriers which had been erected in the past in order to encourage the purchase of woollens and linens. They also had to combat the opposition of the East India Company which imported foreign cotton goods. In 1774 Arkwright and his Nottingham 'spinners of cotton stuffs' petitioned parliament for relief. Basing their claims on the value of their new methods and the extent of their enterprises, they convinced parliament of the need for legal redress. The House of Commons passed resolutions approving the new industry and declaring that various prohibitions ought to be removed. The necessary legislation soon followed, permitting people to wear goods made entirely of cotton and reducing the tax on textiles mixed with cotton. By 1780 the cotton masters were also allowed to import raw cotton in neutral ships and to breach the East India Company's monopoly.[60]

By the late eighteenth century industrial lobbying and pressure group tactics had become standard practice among the manufacturing interests in the country. Trade associations were founded in the 1770s and commercial committees had been established in such towns as Birmingham, Sheffield, Manchester, Liverpool, Norwich and Glasgow. Samuel Garbett and Josiah Wedgwood, manufacturers who had already learned how to lobby parliament effectively, tried to combine the efforts of several different industrial interests, including the ironmasters of the West Midlands, the potters of Staffordshire and the cotton masters of Manchester. In 1783–4 their efforts were aided by the fears aroused by William Pitt's decision to tax both the raw materials and the finished products of industry. In 1785 a General Chamber of Manufacturers was set up to coordinate policy and, when necessary, to influence parliament on behalf of the manufacturers. Although not as united or as well organised as some of the great financial and commercial interests, this industrial pressure group did achieve some significant political successes. In 1785 the Manchester cotton masters persuaded William Pitt to abandon his cotton tax and to amend his trade concessions to Ireland. The manufacturers held frequent meetings in the Manchester area in order to unite local opinion, they sent out circular letters to other areas of the country interested in the cotton trade, and they ensured that their case was fully reported in the press. Over sixty petitions flooded into the House of Commons, one reputed to have 80 000 signatures appended to it. The cotton masters also sent a committee to London to canvass support in parliament. This activity was so well coordinated that it effectively ruined Pitt's commercial plans for 1785.[61]

Pitt deeply resented this setback at the hands of the cotton masters who, until 1790 when Robert Peel entered the House of Commons, did not even have a single member of their ranks sitting in parliament. Although he acknowledged the wisdom of consulting individual members of the manufacturing interest, Pitt was angry at the success of the General Chamber of Manufacturers and he resisted its attempts to involve itself in the negotiations he was conducting for a new commercial treaty with France. He informed his chief negotiator, William Eden, that 'there are many reasons which make it desirable to give as little employment or encouragement as possible to the Chamber of Commerce taken collectively.'[62] In February 1787, in a speech to parliament, he was critical of 'a few manufacturers collected in a certain Chamber of Commerce', a body which was absurdly wandering 'into the paths of legislation and government' and attempting to take from parliament 'the trouble of legislation'.[63] Despite this reaction, and despite the fact that the Chamber of Manufacturers collapsed, many of the more influential manufacturers did in fact succeed, on an individual basis, in influencing the policy of Pitt. His negotiator, William Eden, both corresponded with and personally interviewed Josiah Wedgwood, and the commercial treaty he signed with France did secure valuable concessions for Britain's iron, pottery and cotton masters. While the industrial economy was not yet sufficiently integrated to make a union of the major industrial interests a feasible proposition, leading manufacturers had proved that they had learned the art of political lobbying and that they could secure valuable concessions from a government and parliament in which they had only limited representation.[64]

The political success of the lobbying campaigns of important commercial and manufacturing interests in the country was used by prominent politicians to deny that there was any need to reform the parliamentary system in order to ensure that the growing towns gained direct representation in parliament. In 1784, for example, Lord North pointed out to the House of Commons that the large, unrepresented towns had already clearly demonstrated that they were able to influence the deliberations of parliament:

> Did any gentleman imagine that a petition from Manchester, or Halifax, or Leeds, or Birmingham, would be less attended to in that House than a petition from Helleston which did send members or from Old Sarum ... petitions from Manchester, from Halifax, from Leeds and from Birmingham always received as much attention as petitions from boroughs that were represented.[65]

There was some justice in this claim. During the preceding decade sixteen unrepresented parishes in outer London and at least fourteen unrepresented towns in the north and midlands had brought legislative proposals before parliament. This persuaded William Combe to claim, 'Though Manchester, Birmingham, and other considerable towns have not actual representation in Parliament, is there a Member of the House of Commons who would be too proud to transact their parliamentary business.'[66] This situation perhaps explains why many important manufacturers in the large unrepresented towns did not support the radical demands for parliamentary reform in the later eighteenth century. None the less, while there are grounds for believing that no important economic interest in the country was neglected by the landed elite who dominated the political system, there are clear indications that some economic interests, even when they did organise lobbies and did adopt pressure group tactics, had much less influence than those which we have already examined.

The economic interests of Ireland, for example, were generally subordinated to those of Britain and, indeed, sometimes they were sacrificed to them. The Irish, of course, had a separate parliament, but, until 1782 at least, this could always be overruled by decisions taken at Westminster. This did not mean, however, that the Irish were entirely powerless or that they never learned how to apply pressure on the political elite in Britain. Intense and sophisticated propaganda campaigns within Ireland, such as that which clearly aroused widespread resentment against Wood's patent to mint halfpenny coins, were capable of forcing the British government to retreat.[67] Within Britain itself the Irish also learned how to mount successful lobbying campaigns. By using Irishmen sitting in the Westminster parliament or Irishmen long resident in Britain or Irish agents sent across especially for the purpose, Ireland did wring a number of important economic concessions out of the British parliament. In 1705 the Westminster parliament allowed Irish linen to be exported directly to British colonies despite the opposition of vested interests within England. In 1731 the Irish were allowed to import some colonial goods directly into Ireland, while in the 1750s the various restrictions on the export of Irish cattle, sheep, butter and cheese to Britain and her colonies were lifted.[68] On the other hand, the Irish lobby was no match for the powerful British commercial and manufacturing interests which were incensed by the efforts of Lord North in 1778 and William Pitt in 1785 to encourage Irish trade. Major propaganda and petitioning campaigns were waged in Britain to wreck these proposals.[69]

The American colonies were also conscious that their economic interests could be sacrificed to those of the mother country. Since only a few Americans ever gained seats in the Westminster parliament and there was no large body of rich Americans living in Britain, the colonists employed colonial agents to protect their interests. A few of these, such as Benjamin Franklin of Pennsylvania and Jared Ingersoll of Connecticut, were very well informed about the colonial situation, but others were either English merchants or sympathetic backbench MPs such as Edmund Burke who had no direct knowledge of the colonies. These agents could sometimes be assisted by colonial leaders sent to London for the purpose, or by religious groups, commercial interests, land companies, etc., which had links with the colonies.[70] In the earlier

eighteenth century the colonial agents often worked effectively behind the scenes with members of the Board of Trade
and Plantations, the Customs Boards and the Privy Council.
Their prime task was to put the views and interests of the
colonies before the British government and, in particular, to
prevent legislation passed by the colonial legislatures being dis-
allowed by the Privy Council. They were also active in blocking
attempts to increase the powers of the colonial governors and
to dissuade the British parliament from passing legislation
regulating internal colonial affairs.[71] The Americans sometimes enlisted the support of British merchants. Together they
pressed parliament to support the new colony of Georgia, to
allow iron exports into Britain and to deal with the problem of
the paper currency in the colonies.[72] The last great political
success of the colonial agents and of sympathetic commercial
interests in Britain was the repeal of the Stamp Act in 1766.
Thereafter, there was growing hostility within Britain to
American claims which were seen as a threat both to Britain's
economy and to the sovereignty of the Westminster parliament. Lord George Germain spoke disparagingly of the
political ambitions of American mercantile interests: 'I would
not have men of a mercantile cast every day collecting themselves together and debating about political matters; I would
have them follow their occupations as merchants, and not consider themselves as ministers of that country.'[73] While this attitude gained support in parliament, some British merchants
did continue to protest against the government's policies
towards the American colonies. There were demands for the
repeal of the Townshend duties and many petitions for conciliation from such towns as London, Bristol, Liverpool,
Norwich, Manchester and Newcastle. These were to no avail
and the protests were largely ignored by king and parliament.[74]
There is no doubt that the failure of British policy in America
owed much to the inability of important economic interests
in the colonies to exert significant influence over the
Westminster parliament.[75]

Sometimes economic interest groups within Britain itself
competed with each other in their efforts to secure parliamentary support for their activities. The Weaver Navigation
bill produced some epic confrontations between the brine and
rock salt producers and other interests which supported them.

Canal transport from the salt mines of Northwich to the
Mersey threatened to undercut brine prices, with disastrous
consequences for Droitwich, Nantwich and Middlewich. The
brinemen were supported by the Newcastle coal trade, which
supplied the salt pans with fuel, while the rock salt producers
were supported by landowners with estates on the proposed
waterway, by merchants and salt refiners in Bristol and
Liverpool, and by fish-curers in the south-west. The proposed
bill was defeated in 1699, 1709 and 1715, before finally passing
in 1721. Later in the century, battles such as these became
quite common. The Coventry–Oxford canal bill of 1769, for
example, involved disputes between a whole series of landowning, commercial and manufacturing interests in the west
midlands.[76] There were also interest groups within Britain
which failed to gain the support of government or parliament,
despite their efforts to mount political campaigns of
considerable sophistication. Some of these groups were not
very powerful in purely economic terms and they found it difficult to influence the government elite especially when their
demands were often opposed by more powerful vested
interests. This was the fate of the Liverpool Canal projectors
who had to withdraw their proposed enabling bill in 1772
when it became clear that Lord Derby and many other local
landowners opposed the scheme.[77] It was certainly the case
with the Chester tanners when they took political action to
defend their economic interests in the early eighteenth century. The Chester tanners were worried about new duties
imposed on tanned and untanned skins, about the export of
oak bark to Ireland where a rival tanning industry was being
developed, and about the petitions of curriers and shoemakers
against the encouragement given to export unfinished tanned
skins. The Chester tanners were therefore struggling against
the government's need for revenue and against the economic
interests of Irish tanners, the exporters of oak bark and British
curriers and shoemakers. The Chester tanners responded as
best they could. They were in regular contact with their most
active MP, Peter Shakerley, who frequently supported their
cause in parliament. They also drafted petitions, sought information about the export of oak bark and made contact with
tanners in other towns such as Bristol and Kendal. In 1717 they
sent representatives around the county of Cheshire and to

North Wales in order to collect subscriptions from other tanners to support a national petition. They also made contact with the London tanners, who themselves were in communication with tanners in such places as Exeter, Worcester, Gloucester and Shrewsbury. Despite these efforts the petitions from the Chester tanners were rejected and their trade continued to decline.[78]

Economic interests as insignificant as that of the Chester tanners were not always unsuccessful in their efforts to influence parliament. In the early 1770s, for example, the various companies of tradesmen in Newcastle upon Tyne decided to challenge the decision of the wealthier merchants on the town corporation to lease part of the common land of the Town Moor for enclosing and cultivation. The Newcastle tradesmen regarded this as an infringement of an important economic privilege belonging to the town's freemen and so they resolved to take the matter to law and they raised a subscription to pay for this. When legal action proved unsatisfactory they decided to appeal to parliament. After many months of pressure and agitation they secured the Town Moor Act of 1774, despite the opposition of Newcastle's two MPs who were both members of the town corporation. This act, which was revised repeatedly in the freemen's favour during its committee stage, limited the leasing of land on the Town Moor, allowed the freemen of Newcastle to determine the terms of the lease and secured the money raised from the lease for the benefit of poor freemen or their widows and orphans.[79]

Lower down the social scale groups of ordinary working men, even when quite well organised, could rarely achieve this kind of success. When they took action they were usually in opposition to better organised groups of employers and the governing elite were more likely to support the latter rather than the former. Parliament certainly passed several pieces of legislation aimed at preventing the development of effective combinations of workers seeking improvements in wages and conditions of employment. There were acts of parliament against individual combinations of workers in 1721, 1726, 1749 and 1767, long before all such combinations were declared illegal in 1800. Nevertheless, parliament was still prepared to listen to the grievances of working men and they occasionally

responded favourably to their protests. The weavers of the
south-west, the stocking-makers of Nottingham, the coal-
heavers of London and the weavers of Colchester all combined
strikes and industrial disorder with the peaceful petitioning of
parliament. Bills to redress their grievances were actually discussed in parliament, but only that for the Colchester weavers
proved effective. For the other groups of workers either the
laws were not passed or, when enacted, they were never
properly enforced.[80] The keelmen of Tyneside also failed to
gain redress when they combined industrial disorder with
political action. In 1768 they sustained a long strike and
created an effective union of all the workers. They raised a
subscription in order to hire an attorney to help them to draw
up a petition to parliament for the redress of their grievances.
When the House of Commons agreed to enquire into their
complaints the keelmen produced a stream of witnesses, who
provided damning evidence of the oppressive methods of the
men's employers. Opinion in parliament was sufficiently sympathetic to produce a bill for the relief of the keelmen's
grievances. Victory was snatched from them only because their
employers lobbied parliament even more successfully. The bill
was first emasculated and then quietly dropped. [81]

It would be a mistake to conclude from these examples, however, that parliament was never sympathetic to the plight of the
labouring poor and was never susceptible to pressure applied
by the lowest ranks in society. There were many occasions
when riots and other forms of protest forced parliament to
take action to assist the weaker elements in society. On many
occasions in the eighteenth century parliament limited the
profits which could be made by the rich food producers and
reduced the price of food to the poor consumer by prohibiting
the export of grain and by reducing the duties paid on
imported foreign grain. The need to maintain order and to
sustain the working population forced these concessions.
Violent protests, combined with more sophisticated lobbying,
including the organising of over 90 petitions from all parts of
the country, also forced parliament to act in 1721 to forbid the
importation of foreign calicoes which was causing considerable
unemployment among English weavers.[82] Although rarely as
organised as their employers, workers were not always politically powerless and were conscious of the fact that the

governing elite could be made to act in their economic interests if sufficient pressure were applied to them. Only rarely was
that pressure applied through sophisticated lobbying tactics
however. Much more common was the riot, crowd protest and
industrial dispute. These deserve detailed treatment and this is
provided in Chapter 4.

II   RELIGIOUS AND MORAL PRESSURE GROUPS

Organised pressure groups were established in eighteenth-
century Britain not only to satisfy material needs and ambitions, but to promote particular religious and moral causes. As
the established church, enjoying many benefits and privileges,
the Church of England was the most powerful religious organisation in the country, but religious minorities were also
capable of making up for their lack of numbers, status and
wealth by developing sophisticated political skills. Furthermore, both religious and secular groups endeavoured to
influence the moral climate of the nation and to shape the
decisions taken on moral issues by the governing elite. This
desire too led to the development of advanced pressure group
tactics.

The Church of England was possibly the most powerful and
certainly the largest and best organised vested interest in the
country. It rarely needed to act as an extra-parliamentary
pressure group, however, because it was a rich state institution
with political influence at every level of society from the royal
court to the smallest parish. When its interests and privileges
were threatened, it was able to mount major propaganda campaigns and to enlist both influential and popular support on
an impressive scale. The cry of 'the Church in Danger' taught
Whig politicians a powerful lesson in the earlier eighteenth
century. The impeachment of Dr Henry Sacheverell in 1710,
the anti-Dissenter riots in 1715–16, and the enormous controversy over the Bishop of Bangor's views on the privileged
status of the Church of England, expressed in 1717–18, all
created enormous difficulties for Whig administrations.[83] The
Whigs also learned that they could only forge and benefit from
an effective alliance between church and state if they defended
the most important privileges of the Church of England.

Although after 1717 they ceased to let Convocation meet to attend to the church's business, successive Whig governments opposed all efforts to repeal the Test and Corporation Acts or to undermine the special status of the established church.

The bishops or clergy of the established church could normally be counted upon to lead any resistance to attacks on the church's privileged position, but occasionally it was the Anglican laity who organised in defence of their church. Fierce opposition to the Jewish Naturalisation Act of 1753, for example, led to virulent propaganda in the press, formal protests from grand juries and municipal corporations, public petitions, and constituency instructions to MPs. This campaign was sufficiently coordinated to humiliate Henry Pelham's administration and to secure the repeal of the offending act, but it was not the work of a structured and organised pressure group.[84] On the other hand, the resentment created by the passing of the Catholic Relief Bill of 1778 did lead to the establishment of a formal and nationwide Protestant Association dedicated to securing its repeal. The relief offered to Catholics by the act was very limited, but the scale of the protest was both massive and alarming. The Protestant Association, which was founded in Edinburgh in December 1778 and had spread to London by November 1779, persuaded very large numbers of people in both countries that the established churches of England and Scotland were in serious danger (despite the fact that the act did not apply to Scotland). It was even argued that the whole Protestant constitution was under threat. There were serious anti-Catholic riots in Edinburgh and Glasgow in February 1779, but this was just a prelude to the massive and alarming Gordon Riots in London in June 1780. Prior to that disaster, Protestant Associations had been set up in many parts of the country and they began to organise massive petitions. Some eighty-five societies in the Glasgow area gathered over 20 000 signatures on their petition. The petition from the Newcastle area secured 7661 signatures, while that organised by the parent Protestant Association in London claimed to have over 120 000 signatures. It was probably the largest single petition presented to parliament in the eighteenth century.[85] Only the mindless and alarming violence of the rioters of June 1780 persuaded parliament to resist this pressure and to refuse to repeal the offending act.

No other religious group could hope to match the numerical support which the Church of England could rally, but they tried to make up for lack of numbers by developing sophisticated organisations in order to bring pressure to bear on parliament. The Quakers were a tiny group with no direct representation in parliament, but they were the first to develop a nationwide pyramid structure of closely linked cells from a base of local 'monthly meetings' up through 'county quarterly meetings' to the 'yearly meetings'. From Charles II's reign onwards this structure gathered information on the problems and grievances of the Quakers and fed this material to a central executive 'Meeting for Sufferings', which was in permanent existence in order to devise the best means of protecting the interests of the movement and, whenever necessary, to secure political concessions. Through this structure the Quakers developed the capacity to engage in regular, constant and peaceful political agitation. A sub-committee regularly attended parliament to keep an eye on business, while the local meetings raised funds if it proved necessary to mount a political campaign. When lobbying campaigns did prove necessary they were conducted at both local and national level, with MPs canvassed in their constituencies and lobbied at parliament, with propaganda widely distributed through newspapers and pamphlets, and with leading politicians approached by prominent Quakers in London. In 1696 the Quakers secured the passage of the Affirmation Act which allowed them to affirm rather than to swear oaths. In 1715 this act was made perpetual, but the Quakers were still not satisfied because they wanted to remove the offending phrase 'in the presence of Almighty God'. Throughout 1721–2 the county quarterly meetings lobbied as many local MPs as possible in order to secure this concession. Circular letters were despatched from the Meeting for Sufferings, petitions were sent to the king and to the House of Commons, and well-disposed MPs were encouraged to attend the parliamentary debates on the issue. This effort paid off and the concession was secured early in 1722. In the early 1730s the Quakers waged a lobbying campaign on the grand scale in an effort to secure a bill which would save them from persecution in case of non-payment of tithes. They approached Sir Robert Walpole directly, they canvassed many backbench MPs, they printed a great deal of propaganda and they prepared a petition to parliament. The Quaker Tithe Bill was finally brought before parliament in 1736. Despite the opposition of the Anglican clergy, who petitioned against it, the bill passed through the House of Commons, but it was defeated in the Lords where the bishops led the outcry against it. On this occasion the Quakers learned that their sophisticated organisation could not counter the superior political weight of the established church, but they themselves still retained a political influence greatly in excess of their numerical strength and social status.[86] The number of cases in which Quakers were subject to vexatious prosecution for the non-payment of tithes declined in the later eighteenth century, but this did not prevent attempts being made to enact legislation, similar to the Quaker Tithe Bill of 1736, in 1750–3, 1772, 1786, 1789 and 1796–7. On most of these occasions the Quaker Meeting for Sufferings endorsed the projected legislation, though it did not organise national lobbying campaigns. In 1786 and 1796 measures actually passed through the House of Commons, but they were defeated in the Lords where the bishops and a majority of peers rallied to defend the privileges of the established church.[87]

The major Dissenting churches – the Presbyterians, Baptists and Independents – were slower to organise for political action than the Quakers, but they soon learned from them. By the beginning of the eighteenth century they had established their separate organisations and were united in their opposition to Tory bills to prevent the practice of occasional conformity and to close the Dissenting Academies. By 1727 the three Boards of London Dissenting Ministers had set up a joint committee to combine together in a more formal and active manner. One of their frequent achievements from 1727 onwards was to encourage parliament to pass annual Indemnity Acts which allowed Dissenters to evade the restrictions imposed by the Test and Corporation Acts and so to hold public office, especially in town corporations. Indemnity Acts were passed each year thereafter, except on seven occasions, until the Test and Corporation Acts were finally repealed in 1828. By the end of 1732 the Dissenters had established the Protestant Dissenting Deputies, a committee of 21 laymen which was to collect information about any grievances and to canvass MPs when some form of redress seemed to be necessary. The greatest grievance of the Dissenters was the restrictions imposed on their political ambitions by the Test and Corporation Acts. In view of their evident political loyalty to Whig principles, they resented the equivocation needed to take advantage of the frequent Indemnity Acts. They wished instead to see the Test and Corporation Acts repealed. Although advised by some of the leading Protestant Dissenting Deputies that such a concession was unlikely to be granted, because of the opposition it would meet from the Church interest, Dissenting groups across the country often pressed the need for determined action. A major campaign was launched in 1735–6. MPs were lobbied in their local areas, prominent politicians were approached directly, funds were raised, and pamphlets and short statements of the Dissenters' case were widely distributed. Despite these impressive efforts the powerful Church interest carried the greater weight in parliament in 1736, and again when another effort was made in 1739.[88]

It was nearly fifty years before the Dissenters mounted another determined campaign to repeal the Test and Corporation Acts. By this time their case for repeal was couched in different terms. They no longer requested a political favour as loyal Whigs and reliable supporters of the constitution, but demanded an essential civil liberty based on the natural rights which God had given to all men.[89] While these views were articulated in depth by leading Dissenting intellectuals, many influential pamphlets pitched their arguments at a more mundane level and great store was put on circular letters, broadsheets, advertisements in the local press and petitions to parliament. Across the country Dissenters called public meetings to demonstrate both their numerical strength and their unity. Local committees corresponded with each other in order to coordinate efforts on a national scale. In London the lobbying campaign was managed by the Aggregate Committee of 21, chaired by Edward Jeffries, which was established by the General Body of Dissenting Ministers and the lay Protestant Dissenters. This committee circulated a publication, *The Case of the Protestant Dissenters*. They also distributed Samuel Heywood's *The Right of Protestant Dissenters to a Compleat Toleration Asserted* (1787) and issued on *Address to the People* after their third defeat in 1790. Contact was made with Dissenters and potential supporters across the country. These efforts enabled

the Dissenters to persuade the House of Commons to debate
motions to repeal the Test and Corporation Acts in 1787, 1789
and 1790. Although there were never more than six Dissenting
MPs at this time, these motions secured the support of 98, 102
and 105 MPs respectively.[90] Some of these MPs were clearly
influenced by the size of the Dissenting interest in their own
constituencies, but others had probably been convinced by the
sophisticated campaign waged by the Dissenters. On the other
hand, potential supporters may also have been alienated by the
activities of those Dissenters, especially in parts of Lancashire,
who had adopted some of the tactics and some of the demands
of the political radicals. This not only worried some of the
more moderate Dissenters, but aroused the intense resentment of staunch Anglicans who responded with a virulent campaign against any concession to the Dissenters. In a country
increasingly polarised by the French Revolution and the
demand for parliamentary reform at home, the campaign
waged by the more radical Dissenters proved counter-
productive and it provoked the kind of Anglican backlash
which had been so potent a political force in the early
eighteenth century.[91]

Although the Church of England and the Dissenting
churches were often in dispute over the privileges of establishment and the extent of religious toleration, men of religious
conviction in all denominations sometimes combined together
to combat what they saw as an increase in irreligion and a
decline in moral standards. Since no single religious authority
could reach the whole population or coerce them effectively,
those interested in moral reform or in waging a moral crusade
had to accept that success might depend on an alliance of the
clergy of different denominations together with laymen of all
religious persuasions. Although some high Churchmen were
hostile to the need for such an alliance, others accepted that a
lay and interdenominational approach was necessary. The
authority of the ecclesiastical courts had been seriously eroded
and so other, voluntary organisations had to be set up to
achieve moral reform by temporal means. Some of these
organisations, such as the Society for Promoting Christian
Knowledge and the Society for the Propagation of the Gospel
were, in effect, extensions of the Church of England, but the
Society for the Reformation of Manners, which operated from

the 1690s to the 1730s, and the Proclamation Society, which was active for a few years from 1787, both looked beyond the Anglican clergy and sought to influence both the secular authorities and the ordinary layman. The Society for the Reformation of Manners, in its campaign against swearing, drunkenness, lewdness, blasphemy and profaning the Sabbath day, won the backing of Queen Mary and Bishop Stillingfleet and the active support of some Anglican clergy, Dissenting ministers, JPs, churchwardens and parish constables.[92] It eventually collapsed because of its lack of real political influence in government or parliament. The Proclamation Society deliberately recruited support for its campaign against vice from among peers, MPs and other prominent laymen. It had some success in infusing new energy and instilling new attitudes into county and urban magistrates and it persuaded parliament to discuss several measures for moral reform in the 1790s, including the regulation of vagrancy and prison. Although dominated by an elite group, the Proclamation Society did win sympathisers from among the middling ranks of society.[93] Very similar in many ways was the Society for Bettering the Condition and Increasing the Comforts of the Poor. It too was dominated by men of substance, but through its Reports and its propaganda it sought both to influence the political elite and to enlist the middling and lower orders in their campaign to improve the lot of the poor.[94]

The later eighteenth century saw many other unofficial efforts to solve or alleviate the most pressing moral and social problems of the day. Individuals, groups of activists and more organised pressure groups were established to improve the administration of the poor law, to reform prisons and to establish Sunday schools. Social reformers of all kinds were conscious of the value of publicity and propaganda, the need to mobilise support across a very broad spectrum of society, and to secure support in high places. This led to the creation of many associations and societies dedicated to advancing a particular project and ready to exploit all the means of influencing opinion. Many of the most remarkable, popular and vociferous campaigns for social and moral reform were demands for peace and the campaign against the slave trade.

During the wars and rebellions of the eighteenth century Anglican clergymen and Dissenting ministers had often produced jeremiads and Fast Day sermons urging the laity to mend their ways and to rally in defence of the nation. These campaigns, usually encouraged by the political elite, had frequently produced hundreds of printed sermons, but they had not created organised political campaigns to influence the policies of government and parliament. Twice in the later eighteenth century, however, campaigns were mounted to enlist popular support behind demands to change government policy. During the crisis with the American colonies in 1774–6 leading liberal spokesmen in London and the provinces urged a policy of conciliation. Several London and provincial newspapers, monthly periodicals and individual pamphlets adopted a pro-American stance and dozens of petitions, signed by over 50 000 people in the British Isles, encouraged king and parliament to seek a peaceful resolution of the crisis.[95] Twenty years later, in the 1790s, liberal opinion across Britain campaigned for an end to the brutal and costly war against France. Once again, London and provincial newspapers, periodicals and individual pamphlets were produced and disseminated across the nation. These put forward a rational, Christian and moral message, and they portrayed the horrors and waste of war and urged the benefits and profits of peace. They helped to rally tens of thousands of people behind an organised peace campaign. In November–December 1795 some 71 petitions to parliament and 20 addresses to the king, reputedly signed by 131 000 people, urged a rapid end to what was widely regarded as a wasteful and unnecessary war. Again, in 1797, petitions in support of peace were organised in 12 counties and many leading towns in the home counties and in the manufacturing regions of the north and midlands. This peace campaign failed to persuade the government to bring the war to a rapid end, but it did succeed in enlisting support from large numbers of the middling and the lower orders in some of the most important towns and counties of England.[96]

Even more significant, though not immediately successful either, was the campaign against the slave trade.[97] By the later eighteenth century many intellectuals had mounted a powerful critique of slavery, and men of deep religious convictions were committed to its abolition. It was the Quakers who first established an effective pressure group to campaign for the abolition of the slave trade, but they were soon joined by

Methodists and Evangelicals and then by supporters from across the religious spectrum. The Quakers set up the first permanent committee in London and the first national network of sympathisers in order to gather evidence about the trade, to distribute propaganda and to organise petitions. In May 1787 the London Abolition Society was established to produce and distribute propaganda on a massive scale and to lobby government ministers and MPs. Correspondents in many parts of the country distributed this propaganda and promoted the cause in their area. Soon local committees were established to gather information on the slave trade and to collect subscriptions to defray the expenses of the agitation. They appeared in many of the most important towns in the country, including Bristol, Manchester, Birmingham, Sheffield, Coventry, Norwich, Hull, York, Leicester, Nottingham, Newcastle and Glasgow.[98]

Although Quakers and Evangelicals remained at the forefront of the campaign for the abolition of the slave trade, the movement was not simply an offshoot of the religious revival of the later eighteenth century. Nor was it simply a cause which appealed to merchants anxious to damage their West Indian rivals or to capitalists who saw it as a means of reinforcing their domination and exploitation of labour. The appeal of the movement went well beyond denominational boundaries and the interests of capitalist employers. Indeed, it had the broadest popular base and the widest support across the whole spectrum of society of any pressure group in the eighteenth century. Although the High Church clergy remained hostile, abolition won the support of many Anglicans. While middle-class support was very significant, it also recruited substantial backing from craftsmen and artisans. Local committees were capable of recruiting members of town corporations, local officials, parish vestries, prominent leaders of the radical opposition, workmen, and significant numbers of women. Newspapers which took different sides on other issues were capable of uniting in support of this cause. Abolition appears to have appealed to a wide variety of people who, for different reasons, aspired to independence and were appalled by such a blatant attack on personal freedom and human dignity.[99]

Enormous efforts were made to mobilise public opinion, especially in the years between 1787 and 1792. The lead was given by the Committee for the Abolition of the Slave Trade, or London Committee. Thomas Clarkson, William Dickson and others travelled extensively to gather information, to enlist support and to encourage the setting up of local committees. Printed propaganda was distributed on a vast scale and public meetings attracted very large attendances. Plans and models of packed slave ships were produced, whips and chains were displayed, West Indian sugar boycotted by 300 000 families in 1791, and Wedgwood produced thousands of cameos of a kneeling slave with the motto 'Am I not a man and a brother'. Most impressive of all was the mobilisation of popular support for petitions to parliament. Some 102 petitions were presented in 1788 from counties and towns across the country. Support was particularly strong in Lancashire, Yorkshire and the Midlands. Some 10 639 people supported the Manchester petition of 1787, 2000 subscribed to the petition from Sheffield and 1800 signed that from York. The petitioning campaign in 1792 dwarfed these efforts and was on an unprecedented scale. Some 519 petitions, the largest number gathered so far on any single issue, rained down upon parliament. This time the Manchester petition had 20 000 subscribers, the radical London Corresponding Society collected 10 000 signatures, the Sheffield petition had 8000 names appended, the Norwich petition some 3700, while that from Edinburgh stretched the whole length of the floor of the House of Commons.[100]

The West Indian slave interest attempted to combat these efforts. It too set up local committees in such towns as Bristol and Liverpool, distributed propaganda on a major scale, secured favourable comments in some newspapers and organised counter-petitions. It made no effort to defend the slave trade on moral grounds, however, but justified its national, imperial and economic benefits. While its propaganda never matched the abolitionist effort in quality or quantity and it never recruited mass support for its case, it did convince conservative opinion in both houses of parliament.[101] This success forced the abolitionists to move from extra-parliamentary agitation to lobbying campaigns designed to influence votes inside parliament. In this effort the lead was taken by William Wilberforce, an MP with close links with William Pitt and other leading politicians. His efforts were undoubtedly assisted by the propaganda and petitions which demonstrated the moral support for abolition, but he distrusted some of the systematic agitation favoured by the radical adherents of the cause. His reaction was symptomatic of his own political conservatism, but events proved that his fears were not entirely unjustified.[102]

It was Wilberforce who first moved for the abolition of the slave trade in the House of Commons in May 1789. He also supervised the production of a selective *Abstract of the Evidence* so that it could be distributed to all MPs elected to the new parliament in 1790. Defeat in 1791 only led to redoubled efforts in 1792, when large numbers of MPs were personally lobbied by leading abolitionists. This, and the massive petitioning effort, persuaded the House of Commons of the wisdom of ending the supply of slaves to foreign colonies and of terminating the British trade by 1796, but the will to implement this vote dissolved and the House of Lords employed delaying tactics by requesting yet more evidence on the slave trade.[103] The abolition cause was undoubtedly weakened by its supposed association with Jacobin ideas and levelling principles. The opponents of abolition deliberately linked the cause with the dangerous demands of domestic political radicals, with the revolutionary violence in France, and with the major slave revolt in San Domingo.[104] At the very moment when abolition had become massively popular, the main basis for its popularity came under political attack and suddenly became a liability. None the less, the abolition issue had been put firmly on the political agenda. Renewed public pressure was needed now only as a complement to, and not as a substitute for, astute parliamentary management. There was now a sufficiently solid base to promote abolition within parliament itself. Abolition proposals were put forward on many occasions in the 1790s and a bill was finally carried in 1807, when fears of revolution principles and domestic radicalism no longer alarmed the parliamentary elite.[105]

III CONCLUSION

The vested interests and pressure groups in eighteenth-century Britain were of many kinds. Some represented very narrow and specific groups, whereas others enlisted very considerable support and appealed across a wide social and geographical range. Some worked very closely with the political elite, while others had to wage their campaigns from outside parliament and even in opposition to the ruling oligarchy. Some achieved political success and clearly influenced the decisions taken by government or parliament. Others never gained much influence within the political elite, but they still demonstrated an ability to organise outside parliament and at a local level. Despite these differences, the various vested interests and pressure groups seeking to protect or to promote their interests against those of the dominant landed and Anglican interests did have some features in common. By and large, they drew their active support from the middling ranks of society, those below the landed elite and above the labouring poor. Most of them operated in an urban environment and they all exploited the opportunities provided by such an environment to establish associations, call public meetings, disseminate propaganda and organise petitions. While an examination of their achievements demonstrates that not all groups could exercise equal influence over the decision-making processes of the state, the *fact* of their existence proves that the political system acknowledged a plurality of interests and was at least willing to let a variety of voices be heard. In allowing some influence to so many different and competing interests, the British political system avoided revolution. On the other hand, by not allowing some groups the influence which they craved, the political system eventually provoked a radical challenge to its existing structure. None the less, the very existence of this challenge and the constitutional nature of much of its activities are further evidence that the political system of eighteenth-century Britain allowed a whole range of interests to express their views and to promote their causes.

3 Politics in the Urban Community

All historians interested in the politics of the people must pay particular attention to urban communities. After all, it was in the towns, especially the larger towns, that popular politics in all its manifestations flourished most vigorously and most persistently. It was in the larger urban constituencies that parliamentary elections were most frequently contested and where the voters and even the non-voters were most often drawn into partisan activities. The activities of both popular radicalism and popular conservatism, whether they involved distributing propaganda, organising petitions, forming associations or holding public meetings, were mainly based in urban communities. The overwhelming majority of riots and crowd demonstrations also occurred in urban settings. All of these aspects of urban politics deserve and are given separate treatment in this study. In this chapter the focus is on the extent to which local government in the urban communities involved the townspeople at large and revolved around political issues which divided men along partisan lines. The first aim here is to show that access to office in the various institutions of local government was not always restricted to a narrow oligarchy and that the few who held office were not in fact able to ignore the interests of their fellow townsmen. The second objective is to demonstrate that many towns were plagued by political disputes not only among the members of the corporation or council, but also between the various different, and often competing, institutions which exercised authority in these urban committees. Following this, I shall argue that the urban oligarchies in many, perhaps most, towns were under challenge at various times, and particularly in the last decades of the eighteenth century. Significant groups of townsmen were clearly dissatisfied with the way the local elite exercised their power. Finally, I shall show that the resentment at this misuse of power provoked many demands for municipal reform and for an end to the exclusive political structures which governed

93

most towns. Before embarking on these four tasks, however, I wish to sketch in briefly why urban communities provided the most fruitful soil for the growth of a thriving political culture.

I   THE POLITICAL CULTURE OF URBAN COMMUNITIES

Eighteenth-century Britain saw not only a doubling of the total population, but a significant growth both in the absolute and the relative number of people living in towns. In 1700 the number of people in England and Wales who were living in communities of over 2500 inhabitants totalled less than one million and they made up less than 20 per cent of the whole population. By 1801 around 2.75 million people, some 30 per cent of the total – and these are conservative estimates – appear to have been living in such communities. For communities with populations of 5000 or over the increase over the century was from 13 to 25 per cent. Greater London, far and away the largest urban centre, grew from about 575 000 to about 950 000 during the century, but it remained throughout the period at about 11 per cent of the total population. It was the provincial towns which grew at a more rapid rate than the overall increase in the size of the population. In 1700 only two other towns, besides London, had over 20 000 inhabitants, a mere four had between 10 000 and 20 000 inhabitants and some 68 had over 2500 citizens. By 1801 these figures had increased to 15, 33 and 188 towns respectively. Several provincial towns, including Bristol, Norwich and Newcastle upon Tyne, remained significant urban centres throughout the century, but other towns experienced quite exceptional growth. The most important of these in England were Manchester, Liverpool, Birmingham, Leeds and Sheffield – in that order – though in Scotland Glasgow also matched their remarkable growth rates.[1]

Rapid urban growth clearly created major town-planning problems and there was soon a pressing need for improvements to buildings, streets, policing, sanitation and water supplies. There were also demands for improved social and recreational facilities, including assembly rooms, theatres, concert halls, bowling greens, walks and town races. Spearheading these demands were the smaller, wealthy elites, but their campaigns also involved the middling orders – the smaller merchants, traders, shopkeepers, master craftsmen and professional men – who made up as much as 30–40 per cent of the population in most provincial towns. These rapidly expanding middling groups in urban society had surplus wealth which allowed them to pursue and compete for status and influence. Towns undoubtedly offered greater opportunities of advancement for the ambitious. Whereas birth and inherited rank were still important assets, wealth could be gained by the ambitious, the able, the determined, the ruthless and the lucky. Wealth could then be translated into possessions and education and also used for personal display and as a means of competing for social distinction. Towns were undoubtedly more open societies than rural areas and in them men could use their recently acquired wealth to buy status and to rival those of superior birth. Greater opportunities to acquire wealth and a more fluid social structure helped therefore to generate a more competitive and aspiring society. This enabled the more prosperous urban bourgeoisie to emulate the landed gentry in the pursuit of culture, status and power. In this competitive world the richest urban citizens were rarely united as an impregnable elite. They were more often divided into rival groups pursuing separate aims and competing with each other for control. Below this elite there were many men of moderate wealth and growing independence who refused to be excluded from all the decision-making processes in their community. Power in the towns was never won without a struggle and it could rarely be retained for long if compromise and balance were not regularly sought.[2]

The ethos of the great commercial and manufacturing towns in particular was robustly utilitarian and independent, while their competitiveness sharpened a sense of the different interests of individuals and of social groups. In such an environment the poorer inhabitants might sometimes be less secure than in rural communities, but even for them towns could provide certain advantages. Urban communities could be knitted together by a variety of social bonds and networks. Close contact could be maintained by quite sizeable groups of people through kinship, work, churches, societies, social activities and residence in a distinctive neighbourhood. Growing rapidly in numbers and living in crowded, often tightly-knit,

communities, the urban poor often gained in social visibility,
confidence and assertiveness. Their sense of the inequalities of
wealth and status was greatly sharpened by the conspicuous
consumption, the social mobility and the sheer competitiveness evident in the larger towns. Expectations were undoubtedly raised and the more able and ambitious among
them became less fatalistic about simply accepting the status
quo. Towns provided them with a greater range of occupations, skills and earnings. Although the urban poor were
often hit by sudden fluctuations in the economy, they did learn
to protect their interests by developing a range of organisations, including journeymen's associations, box clubs,
friendly societies and worker's combinations. Unity among the
poor sometimes allowed them to exploit the divisions in the
ranks of the rich. In desperate situations the poor were also
quite prepared to resort to crowd demonstrations and even to
violent riots. Prudence as well as fear ensured that the dominant elements in urban societies took the threat of disaffection
seriously. Social control in the larger towns was never easy and
the absence of a professional police force made an appeal to
force fraught with danger. Most rich townsmen clearly recognised that compromise, concession and the shrewd deployment of their greater wealth, status and influence were usually
preferable to requests to the central government to send them
an armed force to overawe their fellow citizens.[3]

Economic growth, occupational diversification and an
expanding, competitive population created a variety of social
tensions in urban communities. These tensions were often
exacerbated by religious divisions because towns provided
much greater opportunities for religious diversity and most
churches were vital and important communities in their own
right. They invariably met a range of social needs and they
usually provided highly cohesive and structured patterns of
community and organisation. Churches provided an alternative society, capable of looking after their own members, and
their ministers were often able and articulate men who could
give their congregations a clear lead on matters of importance.
With a large membership, able direction and a ready platform,
churches could provide an organisation capable of enlisting
the support of significant numbers of townspeople. In many
towns there were rival churches, with large and lively

Dissenting congregations which competed for influence and support with the established Anglican church. Many urban communities were sharply divided over religious issues and the resulting disputes were often a decisive factor in local politics. In several towns, including Nottingham, Coventry and Cambridge, the Dissenting community was so influential that it could play a prominent role in local government, despite the restrictions apparently imposed by the Test and Corporation Acts. In many other towns, including Exeter, Norwich, Newcastle upon Tyne and Taunton, there were significant Dissenting minorities whose interests could not be ignored, while in Birmingham, Manchester and Southampton conflicts between Anglicans and Dissenters degenerated into violence. Even in Liverpool and Leicester, where determined efforts were made to exclude all Dissenters from the corporation, the Anglican elite were occasionally embarrassed by the efforts of their religious opponents.[4]

Urban communities were not only the centres of economic growth, social mobility and religious tensions; they were also the main force and the chief locus for the introduction of new ideas and different ways of doing things. Literacy rates were nearly always higher in urban than in rural communities and, among the urban middling orders in particular, they were very high. Provincial newspapers, periodicals and circulating libraries, which did not even exist in 1700, expanded remarkably during the eighteenth century. No longer was London the only urban centre provided with a mass of printed material containing political news and views. By the late eighteenth century nearly every important provincial town not only received the London press, but had its own newspaper, and sometimes two or three. In most towns inns and coffee houses stocked a wide range of newspapers for their customers and it is clear that even humble tradesmen and apprentices read the public prints. Most towns in the eighteenth century also witnessed the creation of a wide variety of clubs, societies and voluntary associations. London had several hundred clubs of every conceivable type. Over sixty different clubs were set up in Norwich between 1715 and 1750 and over fifty different societies were established in Newcastle upon Tyne between 1754 and 1785.[5] Voluntary societies provided fellowship, entertainment and instruction for men in the middling orders and artisan trades.

Many consciously engaged in the discovery and transmission of new ideas and deliberately encouraged debate and discussion. Their members displayed a commitment to intellectual innovation and social improvement and a growing willingness to participate in public life. Among the most active clubs in London and the provinces were the Free and Easy Johns, the Independents, the Lumber Troop, the Bucks, the Albions and the Antigallicans. Most of these lodges and societies were designed to provide mutual assistance for their members in order to help them become socially, economically and politically independent. An elaborate system of mutual obligations was created so that members could assist each other and make themselves free of political dependence. Subscriptions were raised in order to provide insurance against sickness, old age and unemployment, but also to support schools, hospitals, libraries and other amenities. In this way members were freed not only from certain cares and worries, but also from political dependence upon the growing elite. These associations refused the patronage of the elite and demonstrated their independence by organising all their own activities and entertainments. In these societies all members were equal, they made their own rules and they elected all their own officials. Collective power freed them from the constraints of the client economy and from the political control of the elite. In the mid- and later-eighteenth century a rash of Robin Hood Debating Societies, Conversation Clubs, Literary and Philosophical Clubs and other associations with a social and educational purpose were set up in most of the larger towns. By the 1760s and 1770s these clubs were often debating political questions and were discussing issues of public concern. Urban radicalism was to find in them a ready-made foundation for the creation of overtly political societies.[6]

Urban communities were also the location for a whole range of civic ceremonies and public rituals which could strengthen the bonds of society and provide a focus for demonstrations of local pride and political loyalties. Large numbers of townspeople could be involved in ceremonies to mark civic occasions such as the election of the mayor, to celebrate national achievements such as military or naval victories, or to honour visiting dignitaries. Every year and in every town there was a full political calendar when public notice was taken of such events as the monarch's birthday, accession day and coronation day, and of such major political incidents in the past as the execution of Charles I (30 January), the restoration of Charles II (29 May), the landing of William III at Torbay (4 November) and the Gunpowder Plot (5 November). In wartime too, many towns celebrated major British victories. On celebratory days such as these there might be public meetings and speeches, civic processions and church services, and, on days of great excitement, there might well be bonfires, fireworks, bell-ringing, gun salutes, music, songs and drinking. The local press might also mark the occasion with a special issue or a flood of handbills, while a whole range of manufacturers might rush out medals, badges, plates, jugs, teapots and other commemorative artefacts.[7]

II POLITICAL AUTHORITY IN URBAN COMMUNITIES

The notion that most towns were governed by narrow, inefficient and corrupt oligarchies was first established by the commissioners examining the state of local authorities before the passing of the Municipal Corporations Act of 1835 and it was reinforced later by the prodigious historical research done by Sidney and Beatrice Webb.[8] While modern historians have confirmed some of the strictures of the commissioners and many of the observations of the Webbs, they have not concluded that oligarchy, corruption and inefficiency were the hallmarks of all local authorities in eighteenth-century Britain.

It is clear that in over two-thirds of the 180 or so incorporated boroughs in England and Wales, and in all the royal burghs of Scotland, the town councils or corporations were composed of the wealthiest inhabitants, who served for life and who filled any vacancy by co-opting new members. In the small boroughs, such as Grimsby or Nairn,[9] a single family could dominate the town for several decades, but in the larger towns the self-perpetuating oligarchies usually included the majority of the wealthiest men in the community and there was therefore some justification for their political influence. In the third or so of English boroughs where the freemen or burgesses had some legitimate political influence over the corporation there was still no truly democratic franchise or popular mandate. In those towns, such as Liverpool, where the mayor and other officials were still elected annually by the freemen, the choice none the less was usually restricted (mainly to members of the town council itself). In other towns the position was a little better. In some, the members of the corporation or common council were elected for life by all the freemen in the town, but the freemen were only a part, and invariably a declining proportion, of the adult males. About twenty boroughs did possess a constitution which allowed the whole body of freemen to constitute the Common Hall, which had a role in governing the town, but only in the handful of towns where all the householders or all those paying scot and lot were freemen was there anything approaching a democratic form of municipal government.[10]

Some of the greatest boroughs in the kingdom, including Bristol, Liverpool, Coventry, Leeds and Exeter, were 'close' corporations governed by self-perpetuating oligarchies.[11] Some of the most rapidly growing towns, such as Manchester, Birmingham and Sheffield, were not even incorporated boroughs, but were governed by manorial courts, parish vestries and the neighbouring county justices.[12] Even Westminster, which had one of the widest parliamentary franchises in the kingdom, had no corporation, but was governed by twelve burgesses chosen for life by the High Steward.[13] In other important towns, however, the freemen or burgesses had rather more influence over how they were governed. In Leicester, for example, the freemen elected the 48 members of the Common Council, but it was the councilmen who chose the 24 aldermen and it was their chamber which dominated the corporation.[14] A similar system prevailed in Maidstone.[15] In Newcastle upon Tyne all the members of the twelve incorporated companies of merchants and tradesmen started off the electoral process to choose the corporation, but there were seven further stages in an incredibly convoluted system and so the wealthiest men invariably ended up being elected.[16] In Nottingham some 3000 freemen had the right to elect the eighteen Senior Councillors, but their choice was restricted to those who had already served as chamberlain or sheriff and it was the mayor who appointed to these particular offices. On the other hand, the freemen could elect six Junior Councillors from among their own ranks, though these councillors had much less influence within the corporation.[17] Norwich at the beginning of the eighteenth century had a very open system. Several thousand freemen elected 60 members of the Common Council every year, chose the 24 aldermen who served for life, and elected the mayor each year from the two candidates put forward by the aldermen. This system produced a very vigorous urban polity.[18]

The most open and vibrant municipal government in the whole country was in the city of London itself. There the citizens formed the largest, most politically sophisticated and most articulate urban community in the whole country. The elaborate infrastructure of 26 wards and 242 precincts and the existence of many large livery companies ensured that many citizens gained experience of limited self-government and had some opportunity to participate in civic affairs. Perhaps two-thirds of the adult male householders in the city possessed the municipal franchise at the beginning of the eighteenth century. In all, about 15 000 resident freemen elected 234 (later 236) members to the Common Council each year and also chose the 26 members of the Court of Aldermen who served for life. Most of the common councilmen were small merchants, shopkeepers and master craftsmen, but, since they needed to possess a substantial property qualification, the aldermen were usually rich merchants and financiers. In addition to these elections, some 8000 liverymen, about one-third of all male householders, also met in Common Hall to elect the city's four MPs, to choose the chamberlain and the sheriffs, and to put forward two candidates for lord mayor. Even the 'mere' inhabitants of London, who were not freemen, but who did pay rates, could elect the petty officers in their own ward and precincts and could even hold these offices themselves.[19]

Obviously, no other urban community was as large or as open as the city of London, but even in the more restricted corporations the ruling oligarchy was rarely entirely divorced from the interests of the freemen or the other moderately prosperous inhabitants of the borough. Most town corporations were composed for the most part of the kind of merchants and small businessmen who made up a third or more of the inhabitants. Few corporations thought they could entirely ignore their fellow townsmen, particularly on matters of public concern. Members of town corporations had to live with their fellow citizens and prudence often dictated that they should seek consensus rather than confrontation. Public meetings, open to all inhabitants, were an occasional, but an accepted and effective, means of obtaining the general approval of the town on any controversial issue or whenever there was any proposal for improving the amenities of the town or changing how it was governed. Town governments usually required a broad measure of agreement, at least from among the middling orders of society, if they were to function effectively and harmoniously.[20]

Furthermore, although there were no urban democracies, town corporations were not the only institutions with political influence. Indeed, a corporation's power was often severely circumscribed by the existence of other administrative bodies, old and new, which met the needs of the town's inhabitants and which allowed other citizens to exercise political influence over the local community. In many towns parish vestries and manorial courts still retained a wide range of powers, while new statutory authorities were established in nearly all large towns before the end of the century in order to solve the growing problems of these rapidly expanding communities and to meet the burgeoning needs of the more prosperous inhabitants.[21]

In all urban communities the parish vestry was the basic unit of local government. Like the town corporations these vestries were either 'open' or 'close' (or 'select'). In open vestries all rate-paying householders could attend the meetings, which were usually held either every quarter or once a year. In Taunton it was claimed that the poorest citizen could 'hold up his head against the insolence of wealth and rank'.[22] These came near to being communal democracies. In contrast, the select vestries were attended by a restricted number of specified individuals who filled any vacancy by co-option. All vestries were served by a variety of minor officials, including a clerk, sexton, beadle and constable, but their principal task was to elect the churchwardens, the overseers of the poor, the collectors of the poor rate and the surveyors of the highway. This meant that many important duties and functions were administered by the vestries rather than by the town corporations. Because these tasks were often onerous, time-consuming and unpaid, it was usually the local tradesmen, shopkeepers and professional men who were called upon to take them up. With urban parishes facing growing problems with the poor and the state of the highways the trend in the eighteenth century was to replace the open with select vestries in order to attract the services of the wealthier inhabitants.[23] All nine vestries in Westminster were select and they virtually governed the city from the 1720s.[24] Over the century the number of select vestries grew in London and the metropolitan area as a whole and in other towns such as Bristol and Brighton.[25] On the other hand, only about a quarter of the 200 metropolitan vestries became select. Some vestries, such as those in Whitechapel, Bethnal Green and St Pancras remained very open and several hundred householders attended their meetings.[26] In Lincoln the vestry was particularly important because only it, and not the corporation, could levy the rates needed to pay for improvements in the town.[27] The qual- ification for voting in the open vestry of Newark was simply the occupation of property worth one pound per annum. In 1791, when the town was bitterly divided between the reforming 'Blues' and the conservative 'Reds', each side put up a separate slate of three candidates for the three posts of churchwarden. Over a thousand votes were cast and the 'Blues' celebrated their victory in the church itself.[28] In Liverpool, despite its size, there was only one parish and the vestry remained open to all inhabitants paying the poor rate. By devolving all detailed administration to a standing committee, which reported annually to the whole vestry assembled, Liverpool retained some of the advantages of a relatively democratic parish government whilst avoiding the inconvenience of government by a large public meeting.[29]

Manorial courts also existed in many towns and, in those communities where there was no corporation, they still elected several dozen local officials and could make by-laws about the upkeep of streets and buildings. In Manchester, which was without a corporation, the Court Leet could appoint over a hundred local officers and it could exercise considerable juris- diction over the state of the roads, bridges and buildings and over the conduct of trade. Large numbers of the adult male inhabitants could attend this court.[30] Birmingham and Sheffield were also without a town corporation and they too had a manorial court exercising considerable powers.[31]

In addition to these older institutions, the eighteenth century also saw the creation of hundreds of new statutory authorities to deal with the needs and desires of the larger urban communities. These new authorities covered a larger area and a greater proportion of the total population than the town corporations and they affected the lives of the people to a much greater extent. Arising out of local demands they were established by separate acts of parliament which defined their function, locality, organisation and composition. These authorities covered a very wide range of activities and they included bodies to maintain harbours, docks, bridges, canals, markets and burial grounds.[32] Some 96 local acts of this kind applied to Manchester alone in the eighteenth century.[33] Much the most important of these new statutory authorities, however, were the new incorporated guardians of the poor, the turnpike trusts and the Improvement Commissions which were set up to deal with the lighting, paving, cleansing and watching of the streets. As early as 1698 Exeter had established a new Corporation of the Poor, which not only included the mayor and eight aldermen, but also an additional 40 guardians who were elected by those householders who paid the poor rate.[34] Similar schemes were adopted in many other towns and so responsibility for the poor was taken away from the town corporation and given to a new body which often included guardians who were elected by the rate-paying householders.[35] Many towns, including Newcastle upon Tyne, Norwich, Manchester and Birmingham, also established hospitals or infirmaries for the poor and they too were governed according to more democratic principles in that all those who subscribed to the upkeep of these charitable foundations were given a single vote in deciding how they were to be managed and conducted. This often resulted in several hundred subscribers taking an interest in these institutions and in the wider interests of their town.[36] Several hundred separate turnpike trusts were also established in the eighteenth century, but Improvement Commissions were the most important of the new authorities, however, because they affected more people directly, they dealt with novel public services, and they levied new taxes on every householder. The first Improvement Commission was set up for St James's Square, Westminster in 1725 and the first established alongside an existing town corporation was in Salisbury in 1737.[37] Commissions of this kind spread very rapidly in the later eighteenth century and over a hundred had been set up by 1800.[38] The local acts setting up these commissions usually named between 30 and 80 specific inhabitants to be responsible for the improvements, but one act named as many as 302 commissioners.[39] In about one-third of these acts it was laid down that some of the commissioners had to be elected on quite a wide franchise. In Boston, Manchester, Nottingham and Worcester, for example, relatively small property-owners were able to join the improvement commissions.[40] Elsewhere, the commissions might involve all the local rate-payers or, occasionally, even all the adult male inhabitants. This was the case in Plymouth in 1782 and Cambridge in 1788 when quite humble parishioners, including a few women, elected the commissioners.[41] The improvement commissioners themselves usually needed a property qualification, however, and so men in the middle ranks of society were invariably elected by the more humble rate-payers.[42] None the less, through these commissions many more men of modest property were able to participate in the shaping of their environment and the management of their community as the eighteenth century progressed.

The local acts establishing these new statutory authorities were usually promoted initially by private individuals acting informally, but these men very rarely proceeded without seeking to enlist quite widespread support. At an early stage they usually approached the parish vestry and the town corporation. They then often called a public meeting to discuss the terms of a draft bill and their proposals were usually published in the local press to allow for further public discussion of their merits. Prudence and good sense clearly dictated that expensive schemes should gain widespread backing within the local community. Indeed, parliament increasingly took care to ensure that proposals of this kind were fully discussed within the local community before they reached the House of Commons. As early as 1699 it was established that all parties to enclosure bills had to give their consent to the proposed measure. Throughout the eighteenth century parliament paid close attention when it was suggested that the local community had not been consulted in advance before a local bill was introduced. The Wareham Road Bill of 1776, for example, had to be revised because of protests from three towns affected by the measure that no public meetings had been held to discuss it. The defenders of the Birmingham Street Bill of 1769, on the other hand, were able to assure the House of Commons that they had 'repeatedly taken every method to obtain the sense of the Town, which law and custom have established in cases of a like nature'.[43]

In 1773–4 the House of Commons ordered that notices of intended enclosure, drainage and improvement bills had to be posted on the church doors in the parishes concerned and should be proclaimed in quarter sessions. Bills for turnpike roads also had to be advertised in the local press. In 1791 the provisions of local bills concerned with paving, lighting or watching streets were made more stringent. Notice had to be given at the September quarter sessions, details had to be fixed to the sessions house door and they had to be advertised in the local newspaper at least three times during the August or September preceding the session of parliament in which the bill was to be introduced. Compliance with these standing orders had to be proved in both houses of parliament.[44] Clearly, no small group of wealthy townsmen could expect to get any kind of improvement bill through parliament without consulting their fellow citizens and obtaining a wide measure of approval. The regularity with which such proposals were opposed and the frequency with which they were actually abandoned are clear proof of this.

III   POLITICAL DISPUTES WITHIN AND BETWEEN THE URBAN AUTHORITIES

When we examine all the different institutions which might exercise some authority over urban communities, it becomes clear that local influence was generally *not* restricted to a handful of the wealthiest citizens. Of course, the men of greatest wealth and status exercised the most influence, but they could rarely achieve the stability and harmony they clearly desired if they did not consult the interests of their fellow citizens. As we shall see in the next section the way town officials exercised their power and the attempts they made to defend their privileges could create considerable tension and formidable opposition. But what we ought to note here is that even the minority who did enjoy the privileges of office could not always agree among themselves on how best to govern their local communities. The ruling elites in urban communities were not, in fact, cosy oligarchies who smugly protected their own selfish interests and quietly decided the fate of their fellow townspeople behind closed doors. On the contrary, members of the same institution were often divided into hostile camps and the different, sometimes overlapping, authorities in the urban communities were sometimes engaged in major demarcation disputes. The existence of severe conflict within the ruling oligarchies could easily spill over and involve the rest of the urban population. When this happened the ruling elite often lost credibility among substantial sections of the community and the result was vociferous demands for reform and for a wider distribution of political power.

The corporation of London was riven by intense political disputes in the late seventeenth and early eighteenth centuries. Chicanery and intimidation were widespread in the elections for both common councilmen and aldermen and the disputes between these two bodies threatened at times to paralyse the government of the nation's capital. Partisan feelings were frequently aroused over national political and religious issues, as the trial of Dr Sacheverell clearly demonstrated, while within the city itself the Common Council championed the interests of the ordinary freemen whereas the Court of Aldermen sought ways of restricting popular participation in the city's affairs. In 1725 Walpole's administration tried to ensure greater political stability in the capital by passing the City Elections Act. This measure restricted the municipal franchise to those freemen who were £10 householders and who paid church and poor rates (thus disfranchising over 3000 poor freemen) and it also gave the aldermen the right to veto measures passed by the Common Council, but it only served to create widespread and deep-seated hostility in London to the ruling oligarchy both in parliament and in the city. The Common Council did not quietly submit, but, thereafter, frequently put itself at the head of political campaigns critical of Walpole in particular and the ruling elite in general. The offending act was eventually repealed in 1746, but this only increased the political dominance of the Common Council and ensured that it would take the lead in nearly all subsequent political disputes in which aristocratic exclusiveness was challenged and popular participation was encouraged.[45]

Other town corporations were also riven by internal disputes which affected more than just the narrow oligarchy directly engaged in the quarrel. In Norwich, elections of the mayor and members of the corporation were often very lively affairs. Party and religious disputes also frequently divided the members of the Assembly or Corporation. In 1728 the aldermen withdrew from the Assembly because they were being regularly outvoted by the common councilmen. Since the Assembly could not act without their participation there was deadlock for more than a year and considerable conflict in the municipal elections of 1729. The next year the aldermen persuaded their Whig friends in parliament to pass an act laying down that in future no official municipal action could be taken without the consent of the majority of both the aldermen and the common councilmen, who were henceforth to meet separately and to reach independent decisions. Although it was designed to given the wealthier aldermen a veto over the decisions of the common council, this act failed to prevent subsequent disputes between the two bodies and the whole system worked badly. In nearly every subsequent dispute the common council tried to enlist the support of the freemen of Norwich.[46]

In many other towns there were similar conflicts within the corporation. In Liverpool in 1726–7, and again in 1734–6, disputes within the town council led to the mayor refusing to call any meetings with his colleagues and seeking to govern with the approval of the wider body of freemen. On both occasions, once the council did get a chance to meet, it immediately condemned these proceedings and rescinded the decisions taken without its approval.[47] This did not stop another protracted dispute in the 1750s when Alderman Joseph Clegg challenged the council's authority and appealed for support from the town's freemen. Expelled from the council, he condemned his colleagues in print, took the issue to court and was reinstated.[48] Other town corporations experienced even worse internal disputes. In Scarborough disputes reached such a height that in 1736 the factions on the close corporation proceeded to appoint two entirely different corporations. For three years each of these two corporations claimed to be the legitimate government in the borough, but neither could, in fact, do very much at all. It took seven years of litigation in the courts before the dispute was finally resolved.[49] In Colchester the situation was even more serious. There a dispute about the legality of the municipal elections of 1742 led to court action which resulted in the corporation falling into complete abeyance until a new charter was granted in 1764.[50] Disputes in Scarborough and Colchester went to extreme lengths, but internal friction of this kind was not at all unusual. Devizes had two rival mayors in 1707–8, as did Grampound in the 1740s, while Bewdley had two rival corporations from 1708–10.[51] The corporation of Cambridge was sharply divided in 1769, in 1774–5 and, from 1785, its members were locked in a very protracted legal wrangle over the methods of electing the mayor and the common council.[52] Many other corporations, including Banbury, Bridgwater, Dartmouth, Exeter, Harwich, Leicester, Maidstone, Nottingham, Southampton and Tiverton were involved in internecine disputes at some stage in the eighteenth century. The disputes in Totnes lasted for more than a quarter of a century and they frequently obstructed council business.[53]

Parish vestries were also sometimes the scenes of bitter conflict. At Clapham, Surrey, in 1701 and 1704 and at Walton upon Thames in 1760 the vestrymen vigorously defended their right to choose both of their churchwardens and resisted the claims of the local rector to select one of them.[54] Much more serious was the question of who was qualified to attend vestry meetings. In St Marylebone, for example, which had been rapidly transformed from a small village into a prosperous urban parish, there was a four-year struggle by the aristocratic newcomers to establish a select vestry which would wrest control from the tradesmen who had previously administered this open vestry. In February 1764, and again in October 1767, the majority in the parish protested against attempts to secure a local act making St Marylebone a select vestry. The petition to parliament on the first occasion helped to defeat the bill, but the second campaign was unsuccessful and a select vestry was set up in February 1768.[55] In other parishes too there was popular opposition to proposals to create select vestries. There was a twenty-year conflict in St Pancras before a select vestry was established.[56] St Saviour in Southwark actually bucked the trend towards oligarchy and successfully moved from being a select to an open vestry in 1730.[57] Even when a select vestry was established, it did not mean that disputes would cease. The select vestry of St Martin-in-the-Fields, for example, was so divided over proposals to improve the parish that plans put forward in 1739, 1757–8, 1785 and 1789 were all dropped because of internal opposition within the vestry.[58]

Disputes did not occur just within the different institutions of local government, but also between them, particularly when their spheres of authority overlapped. In Liverpool there was only one parish and so the vestry covered precisely the same geographical area as the town corporation. Since the corporation was closed, whereas the vestry was open and included all the householders assessed for poor rates, the two bodies were open to different pressures. Moreover, since the vestry administered the poor law and could levy rates, whereas the corporation appointed the rector and could interfere in the management of the church, disputes between the two bodies could scarcely be avoided.[59] In Taunton there were disputes in the 1720s between the manorial court and the town council because both claimed the right to control various local charitable funds. The opponents of the council, led by a humble carpenter, were unable to change the composition of the corporation and so they concentrated their attention on getting themselves elected to the manorial court.[60]

As new statutory authorities were created conflicts of interest with established local institutions multiplied. In both Bristol and Exeter new Corporations of the Poor were erected in the 1690s. In both cases the mayor and aldermen were members *ex officio*, but the majority of guardians were elected by the ratepaying householders. These new bodies often met with hostility from the corporations over their tax-raising powers and because they claimed to be more representative of local opinion.[61] Throughout the eighteenth century proposals for local acts of parliament to improve the amenities of many towns produced resistance from sections of the local community. In some towns it was the inhabitants who resisted the creation of new authorities which could levy taxes, but, in other places, it was the established institutions which resisted encroachments on their own powers. A proposal to improve the streets of Bristol, for example, was abandoned in 1738 when it met determined local opposition. It took another ten years before such a measure was passed, but, when a scheme to establish a force of salaried watchmen was put forward by the corporation in 1754–5, there was renewed opposition. A body of citizens protested at having to pay for the services of men who would be under the control of the town corporation.[62] In Southampton in 1769–70 there was a prolonged conflict of jurisdiction between the town corporation and the proposed improvement commission. A more acute controversy was aroused in Plymouth where the corporation protested to parliament in 1772 that the Paving Act of 1770 imposed unjust taxation on the town and infringed the rights granted by charter to the mayor and corporation.[63] Improvement schemes were opposed without success in Coventry in 1762, but various schemes were defeated in Leicester in 1749–50, in Nottingham in 1786 and 1792, in Bristol in 1787, in Sheffield in 1791, in Bath in 1792, and in Liverpool in 1799; all on the grounds of cost.[64] In Birmingham the opposition voiced at public meetings was so persistent that it held up a scheme to light the streets from 1765 until 1769 and it delayed a subsequent proposal for improved policing from 1789 until as late as 1801.[65]

In other towns it was the corporation which resisted changes that might diminish its authority. In Chester the citizens favoured a scheme to revive the declining trade of the town by deepening the river Dee which had silted up. The proposal grew so popular that it became the slogan of one of the candidates for mayor in 1732, and when it was dropped it provoked serious 'tumults and disorders' in April 1732.[66] In Southampton the corporation feared a diminution of its authority when some inhabitants petitioned parliament in 1791 to be allowed to create a new Poor Law Union whose guardians would be elected by the rate-paying householders. The corporation counter-petitioned and a prolonged propaganda war broke out. Feelings reached such a pitch of intensity that, when the printed matter produced by both sides was republished in 1793, the collection was entitled *The Civil Wars in Southampton*. The corporation's campaign resulted in the proposed bill being defeated in 1792, but the other side responded by obstructing the corporation's own proposals to extend the town's quays, docks and pier.[67]

IV CONFLICTS OVER THE EXERCISE OF POWER

As we have seen, disputes within and between the institutions of local government might originate among the members of these authorities, but the conflicts soon spread beyond their restricted numbers to incorporate a significant proportion of the townspeople at large. What provoked greater comment and incited wider opposition within urban communities, however, were those instances when it was popularly believed that those in positions of authority were deliberately encroaching on the privileges of their fellow citizens or were guilty of lining their own pockets at the public's expense.

In most towns the rights of a freeman or burgess could be secured by inheritance, marriage, apprenticeship, purchase, or as a gift from the corporation. Freedom could confer various privileges. These usually included the right to practise a trade or to buy and sell goods, exemption from various dues and tolls, and access to the benefits of town properties and charities. It might also confer on the freeman the municipal, or even the parliamentary, franchise. Not surprisingly, these rights and privileges were jealously guarded and infringements of them were liable to arouse political opposition. The freedom of a town was usually granted by the town corporation and considerable resentment could be provoked if the honour were denied to those who believed they had a legitimate claim to it or if it were too readily granted for partisan electoral purposes. In many towns, including London, Bath, Bristol, Coventry, Exeter, Leicester, Lincoln, Liverpool, Newcastle upon Tyne, Norwich, Southampton and York, the proportion of adult males who qualified as freemen declined steadily throughout the eighteenth century. When men of substance were denied the privilege they often protested. Disputes of this nature were frequent in such towns as Bath, Liverpool and Southampton.[68] In Plymouth three men won a court action against the council in 1728 when they were denied their freedom, while in Northampton some 44 freemen recovered their rights in 1740 when they challenged the corporation's authority to disfranchise them.[69] On the other hand, some corporations provoked opposition when they created huge batches of freemen, many of them non-residents, simply in order to increase the number of those qualified to vote in an approaching general election. In Liverpool, for example, the corporation created between 300 and 750 freemen at a time prior to the general elections of 1734, 1761, 1790 and 1796.[70] In Northampton nearly 400 new freemen were created prior to the election of 1734; in Leicester over 800 freemen were created in 1754; in Newcastle upon Tyne over 600 were created in 1774; while in Bristol hundreds of freemen were created before most elections in the eighteenth century including an astonishing 2080 in the month prior to the general election of 1774.[71] When it was rumoured, in October 1732, that the corporation of Chester planned to create some 300 honorary freemen overnight, a crowd, incensed at this suggestion, drove out the aldermen and demolished the city hall.[72] In Coventry the freemen tried to prevent such creations by taking legal action in 1769 and by securing an act of parliament in 1781 which restricted the parliamentary franchise to those who had served a seven-year apprenticeship within the city.[73] In many towns there were also protracted disputes over the corporation's attempts to force those who were not freemen to pay a variety of dues and tolls on their commercial activities. In towns such as Liverpool, Manchester, Nottingham, Southampton and York the opposition became so widespread and persistent that the corporations had to abandon their efforts to collect the customary dues from those who were not freemen.

In several towns the inhabitants became incensed at the way members of the vestry or corporation used the income derived from the dues, charities and properties under their control. They protested that the parish's or the town's revenue was being misapplied on extravagant entertainments or was being used to line the pockets of the local ruling oligarchy. Sometimes these complaints led to court action or to public protest meetings. In 1710 and again in 1721 there were repeated accusations against the select vestry of St Botolph, Bishopsgate, that its members were raising too much revenue and were applying it for their own benefit.[74] In the 1750s Joseph Clegg published a series of pamphlets which charged the treasurer of Liverpool with not keeping proper accounts and warned the freemen that the town clerk was 'seeking means to establish the exercise of arbitrary power upon the ruins of your liberties'.[75] In Newcastle upon Tyne in 1774, in Exeter in 1782, in Birmingham and Bath in 1789, in Cambridge for a decade after 1788, in Southampton throughout most of the 1790s, and in Manchester in the mid-1790s, there were public accusations that local officials were improperly using local funds and were not keeping proper accounts. In Cambridge, Manchester and Southampton the aggrieved inhabitants went to court, but, despite prolonged litigation, they failed to make local officials more accountable.[76]

The most intense resentment against the actions of local corporations was provoked by their mismanagement of the towns' common lands which were traditionally meant to be used for the benefit of the whole body of freemen. The corporations of Bath, Cambridge and Southampton were all accused of this offence, but the most serious disputes occurred in Leicester, Newcastle upon Tyne and Nottingham. In Leicester there were repeated protests at the way the corporation regularly favoured the interests of the great farmers in the area and endeavoured to disregard the pasture rights belonging to the freemen. Attempts by the corporation to enclose some of the common land were frustrated by effective opposition in 1708, 1711 and 1730. The most bitter and protracted controversy occurred in 1752–4 when 550 acres of the land were leased at a low rent to three members of the town corporation. Indignant protest meetings were held in November and December 1753 and angry crowds threw down the fences and damaged the buildings erected on the land which had been recently enclosed. The corporation insisted that it had a legal right to draw up such leases, but it was careful to avoid such outbursts in the future. An attempt to destroy the rights of the freemen of Leicester by an enclosure act in 1777–8 was defeated and it was not until 1804 that agreement was finally reached on enclosing the town's common land.[77] In Newcastle upon Tyne the opposition to the corporation's plan in 1771 to lease part of the common land making up the Town Moor was very well coordinated by the local radicals. The freemen's rights were widely publicised in the local press, a public subscription was raised and Serjeant Glynn, the Wilkite lawyer from London, was hired to take the matter to the assize court. In order to instigate legal proceedings a crowd quite deliberately damaged the fences and gate used to enclose part of the Town Moor. In August 1773 the verdict handed down at the Northumberland assizes vindicated the claims of the free-

men and instructed the corporation of Newcastle to join the
freemen in securing an act of parliament to confirm this
decision of the court. This victory was celebrated throughout
the town with the ringing of bells, the firing of cannon and the
setting off of fireworks. The freemen also illuminated their
houses and paraded through the streets in triumph. In 1774
the Newcastle Town Moor Act limited the leasing of land on
the Town Moor to one hundred acres and a term of seven
years. The decision whether to lease was to be taken by the
freemen themselves and the money raised was to be used for
impoverished freemen or their widows and orphans.[78] In
Nottingham a similar proposal, in 1787, to enclose and lease
the common land of the town also produced an unprecedented
outburst of popular hostility and 'an uncommon Union of the
Lower Orders'. A high proportion of freemen turned out to
vote against Samuel Heywood, the candidate for senior
councilman, who had advocated the scheme. Insisting that
they would not barter away their rights for gold, the freemen
defeated Heywood. Thereafter, candidates for any office in
Nottingham fell over themselves to swear their opposition to
enclosure and their determination to preserve the rights of the
freemen inviolate. In 1791 and 1795 the freemen again protested, and even took court action, to protect their remaining
rights of pasture on common or waste land in the town.[79]

V DEMANDS FOR THE WIDER DISTRIBUTION OF POWER

Clearly, the performance of local authorities in urban
communities often came under intense scrutiny and became
the subject of fierce public debate. Too ostentatious a monopoly of privilege and too flagrant an abuse of power provoked
hostility and attracted widespread condemnation. There was a
great deal of open discussion and printed comment on the
activities of the urban oligarchies in most of the larger towns
and there was a growing sense that public bodies were legitimate targets for public scrutiny and criticism. Most significant
of all was the increasing recognition that the only way to make
urban governments accountable to the public was to allow a
higher proportion of townsmen a legitimate political role in

their local communities. Dissatisfaction at the way existing
authorities exercised their power, and anger at the frequent
failure of attempts to remedy abuses, forced some townspeople
to reflect on how these authorities gained their power in the
first place. By the end of the eighteenth century there were
demands in some towns for an end to the existing oligarchies
and for the creation of institutions which had more popular
support.

Accusations that the ruling oligarchies who dominated most
town corporations were exceeding their authority and were
ignoring the interests of the wider body of freemen began
quite early in the eighteenth century. Popular challenges to
oligarchy had been mounted in London from as early as the
1690s and by the last years of Anne's reign the Common
Council had gained the right to regulate aldermanic elections.[80] From 1725 to 1746 the popular element in the
Common Council vigorously opposed the aldermanic veto and
eventually saw it rescinded.[81] In Liverpool, when John Hughes
was mayor in 1727, he increased the number of freemen, put
himself at the head of an anti-corporation party and
endeavoured to govern with the support of the freemen. For
the next two years, and again from 1733 to 1736, the government of Liverpool was in some confusion as the authority
of the town council was challenged by the more numerous and
more popular Assembly of Freemen. It was not until 1736 that
the council regained the upper hand and expelled its critics
from the corporation. Throughout the 1750s Alderman Joseph
Clegg waged another campaign to increase the influence of
the freemen of Liverpool at the expense of that wielded by the
corporation. He insisted that the free burgesses 'now look
upon themselves under a necessity of endeavouring by the
most prudent measures they can be advised to, to give a check
to the progress of an illegal and unwarrantable exercise of
power over them, which, if not prevented, must evidently
entail vassalage upon them and their posterity'.[82] This charge
encouraged some of the freemen to draw up a remonstrance
supporting their rights against those of the town council, but
they were unable to vindicate their claims.[83] Around the same
time, in Bristol, there were disputes over who should be
commissioners on the turnpike trust in 1749, while in 1754–5
there were protests against the authority of members of the

corporation, who 'are quite independent of their fellow citizens, either as to their being chosen into office, or as to their continuance in power after being chosen'.[84] The dispute centred on whether control over the new Night Watch should be exercised by the corporation alone or by trustees chosen by the citizens of Bristol as a whole. In a debate on the bill setting up the new Night Watch, on 15 January 1755, several MPs accused the corporation of being 'a sort of oligarchy' that was not responsive to the interests of the city's inhabitants. Sir John Phillips argued that too much power in such an important city should not be placed in so few hands and he insisted that good government required the citizens to have effective power over their corporation.[85]

Scottish towns, more so than English towns, were notorious for being governed by narrow oligarchies in the eighteenth century and yet, here too, there were a number of fierce conflicts provoked when the local elite tried to dominate elections to the town council and endeavoured to undermine the traditional rights of incorporated merchants and craftsmen. There were protests in Cupar in 1722 and considerable litigation after the council elections in Irvine in 1754 had produced two rival sets of magistrates and councillors. In Dumfries in 1758–9 protests against the town council took several forms; the town's craftsmen resorted to both legal action and crowd demonstrations in their efforts to protect their old liberties, while merchants and professional men advocated a reform of the municipal electoral system.[86] In Edinburgh too there was a long history of opposition to the domination of the burgh council by an external aristocratic patron and a narrow oligarchy of wealthy merchants. On several occasions, most notably in 1746, 1763 and 1777, the incorporations of lesser merchants and master craftsmen, encouraged by wealthier men who had been excluded from influence within the town, campaigned unsuccessfully to have the council's constitution altered and more power given to ordinary freemen.[87]

One of the most protracted and successful campaigns waged by freemen burgesses in defence of their municipal privileges occurred in Maidstone. In 1747 the members of the town council sought a new charter which would create a close corporation and exclude the freemen from any real influence over the town's affairs. This effort failed and the new charter actually

confirmed the right of the freemen to participate in the selec-
tion of all the borough's officers. In 1764 the corporation again
tried to exclude the freemen from the municipal franchise by
altering the town's by-laws. This time the freemen took the corporation to the Court of King's Bench and once more successfully vindicated their rights. Two years later the corporation
passed another by-law restricting the municipal franchise to the
members of the council and to the town's forty most senior freemen. Again the freemen successfully defended their rights by
court action. In 1767 the corporation tried yet again, this time
marginally increasing the municipal electorate by giving the
franchise to the sixty most senior freemen. The freemen refused
to be intimidated and once more they won a favourable decision
in the law courts. Lord Chief Justice Mansfield dismissed the
corporation's case on this occasion with the withering comment:
'They would overturn the constitution itself, if it were in their
power.'[88] Thereafter, Maidstone was sharply divided between
well-defined corporation and anti-corporation parties which
engaged in very vigorous and intensely partisan municipal election campaigns. When vacancies needed to be filled on the corporation there were generally twice as many candidates as
vacancies because each party put up a different slate of candidates. In 1786, for example, there were eighteen candidates
contesting nine seats and all freemen, whether resident or non-
resident, were able to cast nine votes each. Two-thirds of the
freemen voted consistently either for the nine corporation or
the nine anti-corporation candidates. In 1788 there were six candidates for the three vacancies and 648 freemen voted, each one
casting three votes. Some 91 per cent of the freemen refused to
spilt their vote, but cast all three for either the three corporation
or the three anti-corporation candidates. The three corporation
candidates defeated their opponents by a mere 31, 18 and two
votes in what was obviously a very close contest. The Maidstone
community was clearly divided between two parties, one of them
supporting oligarchy and the other favouring a more open political society. These local parties were moreover aligned to the
parties in parliament and they took different sides on most of
the great issues of the day.[89]

Few towns were divided quite so sharply as Maidstone or
possessed such well-defined local parties, because few towns
allowed the freemen such a clearly demarcated role in munici-

pal politics. Nevertheless, by the last quarter of the eighteenth century, a number of towns witnessed determined efforts to make the ruling elite more accountable. Protracted campaigns were waged to give the freemen or the inhabitants in general a greater role in civic affairs. In Newcastle upon Tyne, for example, a radical party emerged in the early 1770s and one of its demands was for municipal reform. One critic of the corporation observed: 'What has been said of the riches of kingdoms, are equally applicable to corporations where the revenues are great, uncontrollable, and centred in few hands, then the community soon sorts itself out into two classes – the slaves and the tyrants.'[90] In 1775 the freemen not only stridently asserted their right to speak at will in the Guildhall, but claimed that they had coeval power with the corporation. The corporation took the matter to court in order to confirm its privileges.[91] In Nottingham protests from the freemen forced the elitist aldermen and senior councillors to accept that the six junior councillors, who were more representative of the ordinary freemen, were part of the corporation. Once fully admitted to the town corporation, in 1776, these junior councilmen acted as the leaders of a popular campaign to reduce the authority of the ruling oligarchy. They became a tolerated, almost official, opposition, but they were too few in number to dictate corporation policy.[92]

Many other towns witnessed campaigns to make the local authorities more accountable and more representative of the inhabitants at large. In 1782 a Constitutional Society for the Redress of Grievances was established in Exeter. It condemned the Chamber for abusing its authority, failing to keep proper accounts and infringing the rights of the Corporation of the Poor. The disputes eventually produced a letter to the press, signed by 'many citizens', urging that the members of the Chamber should be elected by all the householders in Exeter.[93] In Cambridge a by-law was actually passed in August 1789 granting the whole body of freemen the right to elect both the common councilmen and the aldermen, but within a few weeks the concession was rescinded by the elitist majority on the corporation.[94] In 1790 the freemen of Scarborough attempted to participate in the choice of the town's bailiffs, coroner and chamberlain, but their efforts failed when the corporation successfully challenged them in the law courts.[95] In

Bath the freemen protested on several occasions about their exclusion from municipal government;[96] in Bristol the corporation was denounced in 1792 as 'a local tyranny ... an immovable, uncontrollable, unaccountable power';[97] while in Southampton the bitter disputes between the corporation party and its popular critics in the early 1790s was described as a local civil war. The supporters of oligarchy in Southampton claimed that the distinctions between 'gentlemen' and 'tradesmen' were necessary and were indeed the cement which held society together.[98] The demands of the popular party were rejected because they would 'destroy the peace and subvert the good government of the town, render the magistracy contemptible and its authority of no effect towards restraining the dangerous spirit of liberalism which is daily increasing in the kingdom.'[99]

Some of the most significant challenges to urban oligarchy occurred in those towns which were experiencing the most rapid economic changes and the fastest demographic expansion in the later eighteenth century. In Birmingham there was growing political discontent among the smaller property owners. They feared that a few prominent individuals, some of whom did not even reside in the town, were seeking to push through changes which would increase their own powers while putting the financial burden on the middling ranks of townsmen. Resentment over the unsatisfactory distribution of power generated opposition which frustrated practical measures needed to deal with genuine problems. In order to combat this opposition some efforts were made to concede greater influence to the ordinary rate-payers. In 1783 the members of the Board of Guardians who dealt with the poor in Birmingham were elected by ballot by the rate-paying householders. In 1790 a proposal for a Police Bill, which would require an additional rate, conceded that the commissioners of the new force should be elected by ballot for three years by the rate-paying householders. This attempt to sweeten the pill failed to conciliate the bill's critics. It was not until the last day of 1799 that a public meeting in Birmingham finally approved the suggestion of petitioning for a local Police Bill. The measure was finally passed in 1801.[100] In Manchester the Court Leet handed over much of its responsibilities for law and order to newly created police commissioners in 1792. Every inhabitant who owned or rented property to the value of £30 per annum was allowed to participate in the police commission's affairs. Within two years a public meeting in the town elected a committee to investigate accusations of corruption against the civic officials, especially one of the deputy constables.[101] When its investigations were resisted, Thomas Battye, who published *A Disclosure of Parochial Abuses*, declared:

> I am at a loss to discover from whence they derive an authority to put a negative on the public will. What! have the inhabitants of this town no *right* or *power* to enquire into its abuses, and into the conduct of its servants? Are they quietly to witness the *enormities* and *abuses* that disgrace its civil regulations, without a liberty to investigate and remove them![102]

In 1797 the reformers temporarily gained the upper hand and voted to stop a deputy constable's salary, but he took the issue to court and won. The reform movement then collapsed, although the government of Manchester did improve thereafter.[103]

In Liverpool there was an even more impressive campaign to open up the town's government to a much wider body of citizens. After some years of criticism of the corporation's handling of municipal affairs, an anti-corporation party gained considerable public support. This popular party was able to elect its candidate to parliament in 1790, defeating the corporation's candidate in the process. In October 1790 a petition signed by 1098 freemen, including many prominent merchants in the town, requested the mayor to summon a 'Common Hall' or assembly of all the freemen in order to fill the existing vacancies on the council and to review its past conduct. The petitioners expressed their 'disapprobation not only of the mode of election of the Councilmen, but of the persons who are frequently chosen into that body. ... We think we are warranted in saying that the Council, in choosing their own body, do not consult the wishes or the interests of the burgesses.'[104] Well-attended meetings of the freemen, summoned in 1791, insisted that the right of co-option by the council should be annulled. The freemen then proceeded to elect five men from their own ranks to fill the existing vacancies on the council. The corporation refused to accept the new members who were foisted upon it, declaring the actions of the freemen to be illegal. The assembly of freemen then appointed a committee to examine the corporation's books and to audit its accounts and elected another committee to look into the existing by-laws and to draft new ones if necessary. New by-laws were in fact drafted and an annual meeting of the freemen in Common Hall was instituted. The Liverpool corporation resisted all of these developments and determined to vindicate its privileges in the law courts. In the protracted litigation which ensued the freemen were not able to validate their claim to elect the members of the council, but they did win the right to have the corporation's accounts audited. Unfortunately for them, the corporation kept up the legal struggle until the funds of the popular party ran out and the reform campaign collapsed.[105]

The best coordinated and most sustained campaign to achieve municipal reform in the later eighteenth century was waged in Scotland, where narrow urban oligarchies were firmly entrenched in every town. Accusations that burgh councils were corrupt and unaccountable had been made at various times in the eighteenth century, but it was in 1784 that a national campaign for municipal reform was first mounted. In March a Convention in Edinburgh was attended by representatives of 33 out of the 66 royal burghs in Scotland. These representatives appointed a committee to consider two bills, one dealing with the parliamentary franchise, but the other dealing with abuses in municipal government. After further evidence of abuses had been gathered a second convention was summoned in October 1785. The 49 representatives who attended decided to institute annual meetings in future and meetings of this kind were held every August from 1786 to 1791. In 1787 the annual meeting issued a Memorial accusing existing burgh councils of alienating public property, illegally contracting debts and raising taxes, and misapplying the money so raised. These abuses were the inevitable outcome, it was asserted, of the unsatisfactory municipal constitutions operating in the royal burghs:

> The Magistrates and town-councillors in the Royal Burghs of Scotland are the governors of the police of the towns and the administration of the common property; yet these men

are totally unconnected with the burgesses whose common affairs they administer. They are self-elected into office; derive no power from the citizens; are not subject to their control in matters of public police; and are not in any respect accountable to them for the application of public money.[106]

When, however, a test case over the burgh of Dumbarton was brought before the Convention of Royal Burghs in 1786, the legal decision was that neither the Convention nor the Court of Exchequer had any jurisdiction over the actions of burgh councils. Scotland's leading politicians, including Henry Dundas, were unwilling to take up the cause in parliament in order to secure burgh reform by legislative means. Although Richard Sheridan very tentatively introduced the issue into the House of Commons five times between 1787 and 1792, and although some 46 petitions were sent to parliament from royal burghs in 1788, a motion for municipal reform in Scotland was not put to the vote in parliament until 1792 and then it was easily defeated in a thinly attended House of Commons. Few English MPs were prepared to support municipal reform in Scotland in case it set a precedent for action in England.[107]

VI CONCLUSION

An investigation of urban politics in eighteenth-century Britain undoubtedly reveals that political tension, even partisan disputes, were quite common. It also shows that, while most towns were governed by a fairly narrow oligarchy composed of the wealthiest inhabitants, these men could never totally ignore the interests of the substantial middling orders within these communities or even those of the urban poor. Those who held office preferred consensus and compromise to confrontation and conflict. While there was a discernible trend towards a more entrenched urban oligarchy in the early Hanoverian period, as there was in national politics too, at no stage could the ruling elite in any urban community be absolutely convinced that it could master all potential opposition. In the late eighteenth century the rapid growth of many towns and the desire for a whole range of urban improvements widened the scope for disagreements and disputes. The potential for the abuse of power and for a conflict of interests between different local authorities both increased. With many men of wealth and·status excluded from any official role in municipal government it is hardly surprising that demands for greater accountability and eventually for greater representation began to be voiced. Just as a national movement for parliamentary reform began to emerge from the late 1760s onwards, so popular challenges to municipal oligarchies began to appear in many of the same towns where radical groups had gained a foothold. Demands for parliamentary reform and for municipal reform peaked in the same years. Both movements also declined at the same time in the late 1790s as the fear of revolution created a conservative backlash which stiffened the resolve of those who defended oligarchy and demoralised those who advocated change. The benefits gained from the existing political order, at national and local level, seemed worth defending when the alternative seemed to be complete anarchy and the breakdown of all social order. None the less, the fact that municipal reform was long delayed should not blind us to the fact that for most of the eighteenth century urban oligarchies generally sought to allay the fears, even if they did not seek the consent, of their fellow townsmen when they took those decisions which affected the community as a whole.

4 The Politics of the Crowd

Although many of the middling orders and even some of the lower orders were drawn into parliamentary elections and pressure group politics the most common and the most effective form of plebeian politics was the crowd demonstration and the riot. Crowd activity, both peaceful and violent, was a major form of group expression by the common people of eighteenth-century Britain. It brought together in public places significant groups of ordinary people whose numbers and proximity allowed them to influence each other's behaviour and whose collective strength was sufficient to impress or even alarm their social superiors. The common people engaged in a wide range of collective behaviour, much of it stressing social order and integration, on festive, ceremonial and celebratory occasions and in recreational, patriotic and popular assemblies. Peaceful crowds might gather to celebrate coronations, military and naval victories, and local festivals or they might provide audiences at political rallies or be spectators at an execution or a sporting occasion. In periods of tension, however, crowds could gather together in a more aggressive and hostile mood in order to engage in social protests and political demonstrations.[1] Riots were, in fact, endemic, widespread and frequent throughout the eighteenth century.

Until relatively recently most historians largely ignored the violent protests of the common people because they saw them as the frequent, spasmodic actions of a mindless or criminal rabble, reacting in a spontaneous, almost mechanical, fashion to material distress, social deprivation or sheer licentiousness of spirit. Riots were viewed as the inevitable product of a society lacking an effective police force or sophisticated organisations capable of representing the interests of ordinary people. Since the 1960s, however, the work of George Rudé and Edward Thompson[2] (and of a host of other scholars influenced by their pioneering efforts) has rescued the crowd and the popular disturbance from neglect, incomprehension and condescension. Riots are now seen as rational and legitimate protests against a variety of grievances and as an expression of the social attitudes and the political will of the common people. The study of these popular disturbances enables the historian to understand the world as it was experienced and perceived by the lower orders, who have rarely left written evidence of their belief and attitudes.[3] Much recent historical research has informed us of the number and range of popular protests, the context in which riots occurred, the motives and objectives of those involved, the conduct of riots and the types of person who rioted, the response of the authorities and the consequences of such widespread disorder.

I   THE INCIDENCE AND NATURE OF POPULAR DISTURBANCES

Britain experienced a very large number of popular disturbances throughout the eighteenth century. They occurred mainly in towns, both large and small, and across the length and breadth of the country. Some protests involved only a few dozen people shouting insults and hurling little more than abuse. A few were almost urban insurrections causing very considerable damage to property. They were sparked off by a wide variety of specific grievances, both public and private, though most of them fall into a few general categories.

Historians are continually discovering evidence of previously unknown riots, but it is unlikely that we will ever know with any degree of precision how many occurred during the eighteenth century. We can be certain that Rudé and Thompson underestimated the total, but the absence of much evidence from rioters themselves and the lack of complete court and newspaper records mean that we will never know about all the outbreaks of popular protest.[4] The total certainly runs into several thousands, with the incidence increasing as the century progressed. One historian has found evidence of 167 riots (some on a very small scale) resulting in prosecutions in Middlesex alone in the year 1720,[5] another has identified 383 labour disputes (many involving a measure of violence) between 1717 and 1800,[6] while a third has identified over a thousand popular disturbances between 1790 and 1810.[7] All historians agree that the most common form of popular protest was the food riot. These were widespread in 1709–10, 1727–9, 1739–40, 1756–7, 1766–8, 1772–3, 1782–3, 1792–3, 1795–6 and 1800–1.[8] George Rudé estimated that two out of three popular disturbances were food riots.[9] Since he first made his calculations, other historians have found evidence of many more food riots. Roger Wells, for example, has traced over 200 food riots between 1795 and 1801.[10] None the less, the growing evidence about other types of violent disturbances suggests that Rudé has over-estimated the proportion of food riots. Of the 617 popular disturbances examined by John Bohstedt only 39 per cent (48 per cent of the riots outside London) were food riots.[11] It seems likely that Rudé underestimated both the number of violent labour disputes and the number of popular disturbance that occurred in London.

Given its size, wealth and political importance, it is not surprising that London experienced more riots than any other part of the country. Rioting in general was very much an urban phenomenon. Popular disturbances of all kinds occurred in such long-established regional centres as Nottingham, Norwich, Bristol, Exeter and Newcastle upon Tyne; in the smaller woollen towns of the south-west; in the rapidly growing industrial towns such as Manchester, Birmingham and Sheffield; and in Edinburgh and Glasgow. Even the numerous food riots mainly occurred not in small villages, but in smaller industrial towns, market towns, ports and other centres of communication.

Popular disturbances varied considerably in their size and nature. Sometimes, even quite large and noisy crowds demonstrated peacefully or tried to intimidate by psychological pressure, weight of numbers or shouts of ridicule and abuse. Even quite threatening demonstrations were not always described as a riot by contemporaries. On arriving to face a tense situation in Sheffield, in September 1800, Earl Fitzwilliam calmly noted:

> we found large numbers collected in the principal streets. However no act of outrage was committed (save hissing, hooting and indeed pelting the Sheffield Volunteers, who were going singly to parade; three of these have been much hurt). Though in such numbers, these people were not rioting.[12]

There was in fact no precise definition of how many people had to be involved in a protest for it to be classed as a riot. The common law required a mere three people, whereas the Riot Act of 1715 required a crowd of twelve or more before the participants could be found guilty of rioting.[13] John Bohstedt considered only violent protests of fifty or more to constitute a genuine riot.[14] By imposing this limit he clearly underestimated the number of popular disturbances that occurred between 1790 and 1810, since many riots involved smaller crowds than this. It does appear that most disturbances that were reported by local authorities involved between fifty and two hundred participants, but some riots were much larger than this. It was reckoned that some 2000 tinners took part in a food riot in Falmouth in November 1727,[15] while some 3000 people were involved in a food riot in Stockton on 10 June 1740.[16] Some industrial disputes were on a similar scale: hundreds of London weavers were involved in the calico riots in London in 1719–20,[17] while some 3000 seamen rioted in Liverpool in August 1775.[18] An astonishing 5000 were involved in a militia riot in the small town of Hexham on 9 March 1761.[19] By far the largest and most alarming riots of the eighteenth century, however, were sparked off by religious bigotry. The Priestley riots in Birmingham, which started on 14 July 1791, involved hundreds of rioters, lasted four days, and resulted in very considerable damage to the chapels and houses of local Dissenters.[20] The Sacheverell riot in London, on 1–2 March 1710, saw about 5000 rioters systematically destroying some of the largest Dissenting meeting houses in the capital as well as attacking the Bank of England and the houses of leading Whig politicians.[21] By far the worst rioting of the eighteenth century were the Gordon riots of 2–9 June 1780 when crowd demonstrations of 60 000 people got entirely out-of-hand and ended in an orgy of violence. Over £100 000 worth of damage was done to property, over 450 casualties were inflicted by troops attempting to restore order and a similar number of arrests were made.[22] Smaller riots however could also stretch the resources of law and order if several dozen occurred at the same time over a wide area of the country. This was certainly the case in 1715–16, 1740, 1756–7, 1766–8, in the early 1790s, in 1795–6 and in 1800.

Crowd demonstrations and riots could be sparked off by a wide range of private and public grievances. Among the former were disturbances caused by arguments in taverns, brothels and gaming houses, and disputes over property. Some of the riots caused by public grievances had very specific causes and are difficult to classify. There was a riot in Lincoln in 1726, for example, in opposition to a proposal to remove the spires on the cathedral because they were judged unsafe.[23] In April 1751 there was a violent attack on a suspected witch in Tring, Hertfordshire, while in 1765 rioters demolished a workhouse at Bulcamp, Suffolk.[24] The great majority of riots caused by public grievances, however, can be placed into three main categories: riots provoked by economic motives, by actions taken by the government, and by political and religious tensions. Violent protests caused by economic grievances were particularly common. They included the numerous food riots which were widespread after nearly all the disastrous harvests of the eighteenth century; industrial disputes, involving textile workers, miners and transport workers in particular; some violent protests against tolls charged on roads and bridges; a relatively small number of disturbances over enclosures in both rural and urban areas; and some violent clashes involving poachers, smugglers and wreckers. Disturbances caused by opposition to government actions included demonstrations against unpopular taxes (such as the Malt tax, the Gin tax and the Cider tax); violent resistance to recruiting practices employed by the army, navy and militia; and violence sparked off when the forces of order overreacted to what was essentially a peaceful demonstration or high-spirited celebration. Riots caused by political partisanship or religious prejudice included, among the former, over-enthusiastic celebrations of sensitive public events (such as the King's birthday or the Pretender's birthday), election riots, anti-Union protests in Scotland in 1706, anti-Hanoverian demonstrations in 1715–16, pro-Wilkes riots in 1768 and loyalist demonstrations in the early 1790s; and, among the latter, the numerous violent demonstrations against Catholics, Dissenters and Methodists.

II THE CONTEXT OF POPULAR DISTURBANCES

Eighteenth-century riots were both frequent and widespread, but they were more common in some areas than others, occurred at certain times more than others and involved some groups in the population more than others. To understand why riots were particularly common in some places and among certain groups in society we need to appreciate the socio-economic changes which created tension and resentment, to be acquainted with the popular culture which made direct action appear a legitimate response to grievance, to comprehend the political attitudes which encouraged the resort to crowd action, and to consider the nature of those communities where group activity was most likely to take a violent form. We need, in other words, to understand the many factors which promoted riots and the various conditions which sanctioned them.

Population growth, agricultural improvement and an increase in the size of the manufacturing and service sectors of the economy all created circumstances in which the poorer sections of society were in danger of being exploited by their social superiors. This applied particularly to the food market and conditions of employment. To cope with the increased demand for food, especially in London and other major urban centres, a highly sophisticated trade in foodstuffs developed. The chain between the primary producers of food and the individual consumer became longer and more complex as the number and range of middlemen proliferated. The old laws against monopolistic offences were increasingly regarded as a hindrance to the development of a national market in grain. They were therefore only imposed in times of crisis and they were formally repealed in 1772. The Assize of Bread, which had long established the size and quality of a loaf of bread, was also increasingly abandoned and was finally abolished in 1815.[25] To encourage the free market in food the authorities were therefore prepared to abandon the regulations which had previously protected the small consumer. In times of dearth this was likely to breed resentment among the poor who had to spend between half and two-thirds of their income on bread. Many workers, particularly those engaged in manufacturing, mining and transport work, faced not only high food prices in years of bad harvest but employment conditions which left them feeling increasingly defenceless.[26] They lived in an ever-evolving capitalist market economy and experienced exploitation at work as well as in the market place. A growing number of workers no longer lived with their employers and were hired by the day. Moreover, as it became more expensive to establish a business, many skilled workers could no longer hope to become independent masters, but had to remain paid journeymen for life. In many trades, especially in the textile and clothing industries, employers increasingly hired semi-skilled workers or larger numbers of apprentices at cheaper rates, weakening the employment opportunities and reducing the wages of fully-trained craftsmen. In certain areas, such as the clothing towns of East Anglia and the south-west, industries were in decline as manufacturing moved to the north. In addition, workers such as miners, keelmen and seamen faced increasing competition for employment as the population expanded rapidly in the later eighteenth century. Not surprisingly, uncertain wages, irregular employment and the lack of economic independence among certain groups of workers helped to breed insubordination and indiscipline.[27]

Popular disorder could be sanctioned in many ways in eighteenth-century Britain. Among many of the lower orders street protests were regarded as legitimate behaviour because plebeian culture had long licensed various forms of popular action and public disorder. The English legal system relied heavily upon private citizens, often acting in groups, for the arrest of suspected criminals and occasionally for their punishment. Any subject could be required to assist any officer of the peace who raised a hue and cry in the pursuit and arrest of suspected felons and breakers of the peace. Anyone could also legally arrest suspected criminals and could help to punish convicted criminals who were sentenced to stand in the pillory or to be whipped through the streets at the cart's tail. Ordinary citizens might also decide to punish, without the sanction of the courts, those whose misdeeds were not illegal, but which violated popular norms of behaviour. Popular definitions of illegal behaviour might not coincide with those of the courts, but crowds did sometimes explicitly imitate legal forms in order to give their actions the appearance of legitimacy. Popular belief in the legitimacy of disorder also derived from the ritualised inversionary disorder often expressed in traditional holiday celebrations, when grievances could be expressed and tensions released in the form of processions, plays, violent sports, the burning of effigies, mock executions, etc. Another spontaneous type of traditional disturbance was the riding (or skimmington or charivari) when violators of sexual or marital norms were publicly shamed by the clamorous ridiculing of their behaviour.[28]

Public disorder might also be encouraged, or at least sanctioned, by the governing elite during a wide variety of public ceremonies and celebrations, including election and military victories, royal birthdays, coronation days, Restoration day and Guy Fawkes day. On such occasions as these, contending political parties or factions might seek to prove that public opinion was on their side or was hostile to the views of their opponents. During times of political crisis the people were encouraged to demonstrate that those who favoured constitutional change had no popular support for their demands. Those in power in 1715, 1745 and in the early 1790s deliberately encouraged popular loyalist violence in an effort to intimidate those who were regarded by the governing elite as enemies of the state. In almost all of the religious riots of the eighteenth century there is ample evidence to show that at least some of the political elite and even more of the Anglican clergy were ready to incite or at least condone violent hostility to religious minorities. Popular hostility to Catholics, Protestant Dissenters, Methodists and Jews was given a certain legitimacy because religious prejudice of this kind was shared, and was sometimes propagated, by the local squire and parson. In the Sacheverell, Gordon, Priestley and anti-Methodist riots, the rioters were motivated by genuine, if misguided, religious convictions that were also held by their social superiors.[29]

Those who engaged in violent disturbances also possessed a strong and deeply-entrenched notion of their political rights which they were ready to defend when they feared that they were in danger. Throughout the eighteenth century some of the political elite had proclaimed a patriotic and libertarian ideology which stressed the ancient rights of Englishmen. In the later eighteenth century many middle class reformers propagated the more radical notion of the rights of man. These ideas were not restricted solely to those with an education or a sophisticated view of politics. They clearly percolated down to the lower orders so that many humble citizens were conscious that they were freemen and not slaves.[30] There were many popular appeals to Magna Carta, the

Bill of Rights and the rule of law. There was widespread criticism of royal absolutism and arbitrary power, as exercised in Britain before 1688 and in much of Europe throughout the eighteenth century. The popular prejudice against Catholics and against foreigners (including the Irish) was due, in part, to the conviction that they did not enjoy the liberty or the modest prosperity of the free-born Briton. Plebeian Britons prided themselves on being free of oppression, on enjoying a considerable measure of independence from government authority, and on being equal before the law. They also cherished a free press, the right to petition king and parliament, and the right of free assembly. In the campaign against the Gin Act in 1736 a circular letter declared:

> If we are Englishmen let us show that we have English spirits and not tamely submit to the yoak just ready to be fastened about our necks. ... Let them [the Whig ministers] see that *wooden shoes* are not so easy to be worn as they imagine.[31]

When an angry crowd attacked a workhouse at Nacton in Suffolk, on 5 August 1765, they claimed 'that they came in defence of their liberty and were resolved that the poor sho^d be maintained in their sev^{ll} parishes as usual.' When the magistrates demanded that they disperse, they replied, 'The ground was as free for them as for the magistrate.'[32] In their repeated protests against taxes on items of popular consumption and in their violent resistance to attempts to recruit them into the army, navy and militia, ordinary British subjects demonstrated that they would not submit to oppressive actions even if they were legally sanctioned by duly constituted authority. In organising violent strikes, in demonstrating for Wilkes and Liberty, and even in joining the loyalist protests of the 1790s, many ordinary people were expressing their belief in the rights of British subjects. They clearly possessed a concept of justice, a little knowledge of the law and a perception of what constituted the proper behaviour of those in positions of authority. They believed that those who ruled them should be accountable both in law and to the law.[33] They were convinced that all men had some right to participate, if not in government, at least in the securing of justice. If necessary, therefore, they were prepared to take direct action to redress their grievances.

While notions of the rights and liberties of the subject were widespread, not all parts of Britain were equally prone to riot as a means of redressing their grievances. Some types of community were much more likely to engage in popular disturbances than others. Urban communities, for a start, were much more likely to riot than small, isolated rural villages dominated by squire, parson and substantial farmers. Moreover, urban communities of certain types were more likely to riot than others. Although it experienced very few food riots, the most common type of popular disturbance, London witnessed more disturbances than any other urban centre. It was widely regarded as a centre of unruliness and insubordination. There were various reasons for this: London was rich and populous, its street were crowded, some parts were dominated by large working-class communities, it had many institutions and organisations capable of organising group activities, and it had a very active press, a well-developed popular culture and established traditions of collective action.[34] Many regional capitals, such as Norwich, Bristol, Exeter, Nottingham and Newcastle upon Tyne, shared many of the same characteristics as London. They were fairly open parliamentary boroughs, they possessed well-established municipal corporations, and they had a tradition of partisan conflict in politics and religion. The common people in these towns were used to acting collectively, publicly and forcefully. Groups had established networks and relationships through work, leisure activities, neighbourhood, worship and membership of combinations and box clubs. Familiarity and understanding helped to nurture a plebeian tradition of resorting to direct action when under threat. Even in smaller towns, where long-established working-class communities had created dense and stable social networks and a tradition of plebeian autonomy – in the textile towns of Devon, for example – natural leaders readily appeared to articulate the demands of the local community through disciplined direct action.[35]

By way of contrast, less disciplined riots were also likely to appear in centres which conspicuously lacked these particular features. In rapidly growing towns, such as Manchester, Birmingham and Sheffield, rioting became endemic precisely because the old community links had been swamped and the local government structure proved inadequate. With large parts of these urban areas lacking magistrates or a propertied elite, the rapidly expanding lower orders had to create their own sense of community solidarity. Bargaining by riot was one way of achieving this.[36] In these and other types of industrial community the workers possessed the ability and the determination to resist changes to their living standards. Large concentrations of independent and self-assertive workers, who shared a common experience and who were not easily disciplined by a distant elite or a multiplicity of small employers, created their own organisations capable of promoting group loyalty and effective direct action. Relatively isolated and distinctive groups, such as weavers, miners, seamen, keelmen and coalheavers, learned to be disciplined, resolute and cohesive.[37] In certain rural areas too, in forest, fenland and wasteland (such as Cannock Chase, Kingswood Forest and the Forest of Dean), there were no resident gentry, clergy or substantial farmers, most of the inhabitants were quite poor, and parochial and manorial institutions were almost non-existent. Here, too, the exercise of authority by the propertied elite was tenuous, uncertain and ineffective while the local communities were proud of their independence and their own customs and practices. When under threat, they too proved to be virtually ungovernable.[38]

III MOTIVES AND OBJECTIVES

Although many, perhaps most, popular disturbances were influenced by economic factors and by threats to the livelihood of the poor, it is now widely accepted that riots were not simply spontaneous and automatic responses to threats to the material interests of the lower orders of society. Edward Thompson, in particular, has warned us to reject the 'crass economic reductionism' of those who seek to explain popular disturbances in 'spasmodic' and 'mechanical' terms.[39] Instead, he has taught us to look for the deeper motives and aims behind popular disturbances so that we can more fully understand what notion of right the crowd was endeavouring to defend and what legitimate objective they were seeking to attain. In Thompson's view:

It is possible to detect in almost every eighteenth-century crowd action some legitimizing notion. By the notion of legitimation I mean that the men and women in the crowd were informed by the belief that they were defending traditional rights or customs; and, in general, that they were supported by the wider consensus of the community.[40]

Thompson's thesis was applied to eighteenth-century food riots in particular. Since he first articulated it, some criticisms have been levelled against it,[41] but it has stood up remarkably well and it has had a profound impact on the research of all those seeking to understand the motives and objectives of the crowds involved in other kinds of popular disturbances.[42]

In seeking to trace the motives and objectives of the crowds involved in food riots Edward Thompson and others have accepted that bad harvests, dearth and high prices were the necessary but not the sufficient causes of these frequent and widespread popular disturbances. They have acknowledged that food riots obviously occurred in those years when the short supply of grain pushed up the price of bread to a level which, while it very rarely threatened outright starvation, had a disastrous impact on the living standards of the poor. A sudden and dramatic rise in price often provoked more resistance than a slow, steady climb to a higher price level because it was harder to adjust to a rapid change in circumstances. On the other hand, riots did not inevitably occur in all places or at all times when food prices reached alarming levels. It is therefore necessary to find other explanations for food riots than simply the price of grain. Edward Thompson found this explanation in his notion of 'the moral economy'. He maintained that the poor had a well-developed notion of how the supply and quality of food should be regulated for the benefit of the small consumer. The poor approved of the traditional paternalistic legislation which had long defended the consumer against what were stigmatised as illegitimate and oppressive practices in the marketing and processing of food (practices such as the forestalling, engrossing, or regrating of the grain supply or the adulteration or short measure of the bread itself). When, as we have seen, the authorities began, from the late seventeenth century onwards, to abandon the regulation of the market in order to facilitate the development of a national free market in grain that would keep London and other large urban centres supplied with food, the activities of a growing number of grain merchants and millers came to dominate the market at the expense of the small consumer. The power they had thus gained could sometimes be abused. It was when a natural dearth caused by a bad harvest was exacerbated by the sharp practices of particular farmers, grain merchants, millers or bakers that the small consumers were most likely to rise up in protest. The poor understood perfectly well that a bad harvest would result in higher prices, but they reacted vigorously and even violently when they believed the depth of the crisis was artificial because it was created by the unrestrained desire of producers and suppliers to make a quick profit. They believed that the whole community should share the burden of a bad harvest. While prices might legitimately go up, this should be done to compensate for the loss to suppliers produced by a reduced yield and not because those who controlled the supply could greatly increase their profits because of the desperation of those who utterly depended upon bread for their very existence. The poor were therefore quick to blame malpractice and exploitation when grain clearly existed but failed to reach the market or when prices seemed artificially inflated. In these circumstances they expected those in authority to protect the interests of the poor by enforcing the traditional regulation of the food supply and by restricting the profits made by the suppliers. When peaceful demands failed to produce a ready supply of food at affordable prices, the poor regarded violent direct action as a legitimate response to their grievances. In Thompson's words, 'An outrage to these moral assumptions, quite as much as actual deprivation, was the usual occasion for direct action.'[43] Food riots therefore were the symptom of a conflict between a traditional set of values relating to the marketing of food and the aggressive commercial exploitation of the farmers and middlemen involved in the food trade. They were an attempt to preserve an older moral economy of provision, based on the needs of the consumer, in opposition to the extortionate mechanisms of an unregulated market economy.

This 'moral economy' thesis has attracted much support, but it has also been subjected to some criticism and refinement.[44] It has been emphasised that, although food riots were quite common, they were still the exception rather than the rule in

times of dearth and so the notion of a moral economy could
not have been very popular or deeply entrenched. It has also
been pointed out that most rioters participated in, and did not
consistently oppose, a capitalist market system and that most
food riots occurred in the later eighteenth century, long after
the old regulations of the market had been abandoned and
the national market in grain had appeared. Rioters therefore
were not resisting the development of a market economy so
much as demanding practical measures of relief in a sudden
crisis. Other historians have not gone so far in rejecting the
'moral economy' thesis, but they have argued that food rioters
were not always as rational and as respectable as Edward
Thompson claimed. They have also stressed that it is necessary
to look at why food riots were more likely to occur in some
places than others. To answer this question they have looked
more closely at the social framework of the local communities
and at the types of person most likely to resort to direct action.
Some communities were clearly more likely to act together to
defend their interests. Food riots were not the protests of the
common people as a whole, but were primarily the response of
workers in the industrial districts of middle-sized towns,
especially those towns that were ports or communications
centres from or through which grain might be transported out
of the area in which it was grown. The sight of food leaving an
area where it had been produced, and where it was already in
short supply, was often enough to provoke a riot.

While it is advisable not to invoke too rigid a notion of the
moral economy nor to assert that all food rioters based their
claims to legitimacy on ancient paternalistic practices, Edward
Thompson has certainly performed a valuable service in alert-
ing historians to the fact that the protests of the crowd were
based on rational beliefs and understandable attitudes and
were not simply a mindless response to economic distress.
While the moral economy ideology may not have been an
established feature of plebeian culture in general, food riots
were undoubtedly protests against what were widely perceived
as exploitation and sharp practices and they certainly indicated that the lower orders sought to legitimate their protests
by reference to their traditional rights and their concept of
justice. Protesting communities demonstrated their solidarity,
discipline and sense of justice when they sought to compel

suppliers to bring grain to market, when they endeavoured to prevent food leaving the area where it was produced, and when they tried to establish a just price. When local magistrates and parsons shared this belief that the poor consumers were being oppressed and exploited in order that rich producers and suppliers could make a profit, we can be confident that some notion of a moral economy was widely held.[45]

When other kinds of popular disturbances are examined, we find that those who engaged in them consistently claimed to be defending traditional rights and customary values. They sought to legitimise their conduct and they tried to act with the support and sympathy of the wider community. Enclosures (in both rural and urban areas) were sometimes violently resisted because they destroyed some customary rights and they changed established farming practices.[46] In forest areas too great landowners destroyed customary rights of grazing and restricted general access to timber, clay, peat, turf, chaff, etc.[47] In both rural and forest areas there was also considerable resentment against the introduction of the numerous game laws, from the later seventeenth century onwards, which restricted the right of hunting to the landed elite and allowed hunting to damage the land of tenants and smallholders. In the opinion of the latter, wild animals should be for the benefit of anyone with the skill to hunt them successfully.[48] Many small men of property also resented the introduction of tolls on traffic using improved roads and bridges built by private investors. On routes which they had long used free of charge they now found themselves liable to pay fees to more prosperous men who had formed trusts to improve communications for their own benefit.[49] While violent protests against such innovations as these were not legitimised by appeals to a moral economy ideology, they were reactions against sudden alterations to established practices and they were in opposition to changes which could be regarded as unjust and oppressive. Riots against new taxes, such as the Malt tax riots of 1725, the Gin riots of 1736 and the Cider tax riots of 1763, were also expressions of popular resentment against taxes on the small luxuries of the poor passed by authoritarian and uncaring governments.[50] The various anti-recruitment riots of the eighteenth century can also be seen as a defence of individual liberty against oppressive and unjust practices approved of by authoritarian regimes. Recruitment fell unequally upon the poor who could least afford to give up their normal employment and leave their families without an adequate bread-winner.[51]

In most labour disputes those involved were also seeking to defend established interests and to preserve traditional rights. Although a few industrial disputes were about pushing up wage levels and improving conditions of work,[52] most were about preserving customary rates of pay, maintaining traditional working practices, preserving regular hours of work and steady employment, or defending craft skills. Direct action was usually taken in order to prevent employers driving down wages, paying by truck rather than by cash, using unskilled or semi-skilled men, or introducing new machinery or working practices which would reduce employment, skills or rates of pay. Labour disturbances were also provoked by employers using cheap immigrant labour (mainly from Ireland) or by merchants importing cheap foreign goods. Industrial action was not simply a mechanistic response to economic distress, but was a conscious and purposeful statement of outraged common values. Only when employers refused to play according to customary rules, and when magistrates failed to act as arbitrators and conciliators, did industrial workers believe that they had a right to unite in defence of their own interests. While they did not oppose capitalism *per se*, did not regard their employers as class enemies and did not want to engage in a permanent conflict of interests, they did wish to see a labour market circumscribed by custom and law so that workers were protected from oppressive and avaricious employers.[53]

Not all popular disturbances were motivated by factors which were essentially socio-economic. Many ordinary citizens took to the streets in defence of their religious beliefs and their political prejudices. It is quite clear that, while the common people might not have understood the theological, ceremonial and organisational distinctions between the different religions practised in Britain, they did seek to preserve the privileged position of the established church (in both England and Scotland) and they were deeply prejudiced against other religious groups. Anti-Catholicism had a long history in Britain and Catholicism was popularly associated with idolatry, persecution, absolutist regimes, foreign enemies, domestic unrest and poverty. Foreign Catholics living in Britain and Irish Catholic immigrants were frequently the targets of abuse in times of crisis.[54] The passing of the Catholic Relief Act in 1778, for example, led to the creation of a major pressure group, the Protestant Association, dedicated to its repeal. When it failed to change the opinion of parliament, some protesters embarked on the worst riots of the century.[55] Although he acknowledged that the rioters attacked Roman Catholic priests, schools, chapels and houses during the Gordon riots and that there is no evidence that loot and plunder were the primary motives of the rioters, George Rudé has argued that the 'No Popery' slogan covered a desire to settle accounts with the rich. This, he maintains, explains the attacks on the Bank of England, the Inns of Court, the prisons and the toll-houses on Blackfriars Bridge, and also the fact that there was no general attack on the Roman Catholic community.[56] Subsequent research into the Gordon riots, however, has shown that anti-Catholicism *was* the major cause of the rioting and that most of the victims were either Catholics or supporters of the Relief Act. This hostility did lead to attacks on poorer Catholics and to demonstrations against them in several provincial towns. Only in the last stages of the Gordon riots did the rioters attack targets not associated with the 'No Popery' slogan.[57]

Popular hostility to other religious minorities was also based on deep-seated prejudice. The popular outcry against the Jewish Naturalisation Act of 1753 was undoubtedly fuelled by religious and racial hatred.[58] Violent attacks on Protestant Dissenters in 1710, 1715–16 and in the early 1790s were motivated by religious prejudice, although there were also political overtones in these riots.[59] The prime targets were not the rich or political enemies, but Dissenting meeting houses and the homes of prominent Dissenters or their closest political allies. The Dissenters were accused in each case of being enemies of the established order in church and state and on each occasion there is evidence of the Anglican clergy encouraging the populace to express their opposition to religious dissent. The violent attacks on the early Methodists were also motivated to a significant extent by hostility to a movement which challenged established order and authority, and which introduced unwelcome changes into the local community. Methodist preachers were resented as highly articulate men who appealed to the poor and whose conversion of women and young people sometimes disrupted family life. They aroused suspicion as itinerant agents whose origins were unknown, whose persons were obscure and who acted without any formal authorisation. Outside the control of squire and parson, they intruded into the community and unleashed unwanted religious and social innovations. They threatened to undermine attachments to the local parish church and they criticised drinking and various forms of popular entertainment. Hostility was created by their ability to attract large crowds and to induce conversion hysteria. Class meetings and the suspiciously named 'love feasts' were sometimes seen as a cover for clandestine or even obscene practices. Since they were a threat to the authority, the status and the livelihood of the parish clergy, it is hardly surprising that violent opposition to itinerant Methodist preachers was incited or at least condoned by the local parson, but it is also clear that many in the local community shared this resentment against intruders who created tensions and divisions within the parish.[60]

In the political riots of the eighteenth century there are also indications that disorder was organised or condoned by men of property, but once again it appears that the plebeian rioters were not simply the tools of their social superiors. Regardless of elite leadership, political riots depended on plebeian participants showing considerable initiative and independence. Political riots were often easy to instigate precisely because the local community had been schooled in more spontaneous street protests when expressing other types of grievances.[61] Plebeian rioters might be influenced by their social superiors, but this does not mean they were motivated by exactly the same political grievances. Indeed, even when they cooperated with the elite, it is clear that they were expressing their own political prejudices and convictions. Participants in the anti-Union disturbances in Scotland in 1706 and in the loyalist disturbances of the early 1790s were not simply following the lead of the political elite. They were undoubtedly defending established practices and entrenched customs, which they held dear, against innovations which they feared would have a detrimental effect on their lives.[62]

IV RIOTS AND RIOTERS

To the governing classes of eighteenth-century Britain the terms 'mob' and 'riot' conjured up visions of death, destruction and mindless looting. The later stages of the Gordon riots certainly justified these fears that crowd demonstrations could easily descend into social anarchy. In a few other riots too there was very considerable damage to private property. What is notable and to some extent remarkable about the vast majority of eighteenth-century riots, however, is the very considerable restraint and discipline shown by those who participated in them. While some petty pilfering and some minor acts of violence certainly did occur in many popular disturbances, most riots were surprisingly disciplined and highly ritualised forms of protest in defence of a coherent set of beliefs and values. Whether entirely spontaneous or the result of some preparation the vast majority of popular disturbances were distinguished by their restraint rather than their violence. In choosing their targets, in conducting their protests and in organising themselves, the rioters showed that they understood how best to engage in the process of 'collective bargaining by riot'.

Although many magistrates complained of violence and tumult during riots and sought military assistance to quell the disorder in their communities, most riots did not involve indiscriminate violence. Rioters usually showed care and discrimination in selecting their targets. They almost invariably attacked only those who could be held responsible for their grievances and, while rioting might prove contagious, it rarely spread to areas untouched by these original grievances. In food riots the participants went directly to individual farmers or merchants who were refusing to bring grain to market, they stopped the ships or carts which were transporting grain out of their area, they attacked mills where adulterated flour was being used, or they protested outside bakers' shops where loaves of inadequate weight or quality were being sold. In enclosure riots fences were torn down, in turnpike riots toll booths were smashed, while in militia riots the lists of men to be balloted were destroyed. In industrial disturbances the rioters attacked the machinery, equipment, goods or property of those employers directly involved in the dispute or they tried to intimidate strike breakers. In religious riots they mainly damaged buildings where the unpopular minorities held their services, though some Methodist preachers who held services in the open air were physically manhandled.

Popular protests usually started with attempts at peaceful negotiation, with requests to the local magistrates to enforce traditional regulations and customary practices, or with demands that the government should rescind unpopular policies. When these efforts failed, protesters might resort to handbills, posters and anonymous threatening letters or to shouts of abuse and spoken threats. Violence was usually the last resort and, when it did occur, it was usually disciplined and directed. In most riots there were no serious injuries to the person targeted by the rioters and there was relatively little damage to his property. Where there was violence, most direct action took the form of attacks on the property rather than the persons of those regarded as the enemies of the protesters. Grain ships might be dismasted, granaries ransacked, mines and machinery damaged, toll booths destroyed, and Catholic chapels or Dissenting meeting houses demolished. There was very little gratuitous looting or entirely mindless violence. In some food riots the crowd simply forced the suppliers to sell grain at a just price and the proceeds from the sale were handed over. Occasionally, the crowd even punished some of its own members caught pilfering.[63] It has to be acknowledged that in some riots the damage done to property was considerable and the victims sustained severe losses. In most riots however the aim was simply to humiliate or intimidate the victim and not to do severe injury to his person or his property. Only a handful of deaths were inflicted by rioters in the whole eighteenth century and nearly all of these were accidental. Captain Porteous was certainly lynched by an Edinburgh mob in 1736, but his death was the exception, not the rule.[64] When fatalities did occur, the vast majority were caused by the forces of order employed in suppressing riots. Some riots were also followed by the execution of a few participants. Violence by rioters was rare and was mainly provoked by the heavy-handed response of the authorities. This was the case with the Guildhall riot at Newcastle in 1740, the Hexham militia riot of 1761, the seamen's strike at Liverpool in 1775, the Gordon riots of 1780, the Bristol Bridge riot of 1793 and the Tranent militia riot of 1797.[65] None the less, while the discipline and restraint of most crowds were remarkable, some historians have perhaps underplayed the fear and alarm that could be caused by dozens or even hundreds of angry people armed with clubs and staves, and occasionally with swords and pistols. Their human targets were put in fear of their lives even if very few were ever killed. More than a few victims were beaten up and humiliated, and many more suffered material loss when their property was damaged.

Most protesting crowds were not uncontrolled mobs, but were a disciplined and cohesive force, because of their underlying belief, their organisation and their leaders. United by a strong sense of grievance, convinced that their protests were legitimate and sustained by the consensus of their community, and, on some occasions, buttressed by the tacit support of the local authorities, many crowds spoke with a single voice. They often mustered to the beat of drums or the sound of a horn and they marched behind colours, carried emblems such as a loaf on a pole, and shouted slogans such as 'Bread and Fair Prices', 'No Popery', and 'Wilkes and Liberty'. Occasionally, rioters might wear masks, don women's clothes or adopt some other form of disguise. They might act as a single body or divide into several smaller groups in order to accomplish separate tasks or to start protests at new locations. Sometimes a sense of direction was provided by leaders from outside their ranks and in whose name they rioted or demonstrated. 'Heroes' such as John Wilkes and Lord George Gordon reached the crowd by the written or spoken word and helped to give them unity and direction. They were always in danger of losing control of the crowd however or of seeing their ideas used for other purposes, since the rioters might demand more than these outside leaders desired.[66] Most crowds, however, threw up their own natural leaders or 'captains' – 'Irish Tom', 'Barley Will' and 'Tom the Barber', for example.[67] These were invariably local men who exercised a temporary influence over the crowd. Most crowds were drawn from the area where the riot occurred, but they were usually composed of different elements. There were generally a few leaders who instigated the protest and directed operations; a band of activists who readily joined the protest, took orders and were equipped for their purpose; a larger body of sympathisers who were drawn into the protest and who shouted encouragement; and then the mere onlookers and passers-by who wanted to see the action, but who took no active part in proceedings. Although riots might attract very large crowds indeed, the real activists were usually a militant minority, but they were drawn from the same social groups as those who did no more than provide encouragement and sympathy.[68]

It is impossible to identify every member of any riot since evidence on the composition of crowds comes mainly from legal records that can be unreliable and incomplete. What can be clearly shown, however, is that most participants were not criminals, vagrants and misfits. George Rudé's pioneering research seemed to prove that rioters were a fairly typical cross-section of the working population. According to him perhaps two-thirds of rioters were wage-earners (apprentices and journeymen in skilled trades, domestic servants and common labourers), nearly a third were small employers, master craftsmen, tradesmen and shopkeepers, while a sprinkling were professional men. Few of them had criminal records before they were arrested for rioting; nearly all were in some kind of employment, and many were married and in their late twenties rather than delinquent youths. In the capital they were the respectable poor drawn not from the worst slum areas, but from areas such as the City, Strand, Southwark, Shoreditch and Spitalfields. In the provinces the most active rioters were drawn from such groups as the Cornish tinners, the miners and keelmen of the north-east and the weavers and other textile workers from the south-west.[69]

Rudé's research has been extended and refined by other scholars. It is now clear that riots were not in fact the work of a representative cross-section of the common people of Britain, but were largely the protests of distinctive minorities within the working population.[70] Agricultural labourers, the largest group of working people in the country, played very little part in riots. They rarely participated in food riots (except in East Anglia where a high proportion were wage labourers) because they might lodge with their employer, be paid in kind or have access (licit or illicit) to food. They were also less riot-prone than some other groups of workers because they were more isolated, they were less well-informed, their cottages were often tied to their work, they had little independence from their employers and they lived in small communities dominated by men of substance.[71] Most rioters lived very different lives and were drawn from a minority of the working population. Those chiefly involved in popular disturbances were those who worked in manufacturing, mining and transport and who lived in urban communities (even if these were relatively small towns).[72] In the metropolis it was the Spitalfields silk weavers, the coalheavers and other dock workers on the Thames, and craftsmen such as tailors, shoemakers and building workers. Groups that were active in riots elsewhere included the Cornish tinners; the textile workers of West Yorkshire, South Lancashire, East Anglia, the east midlands, the south-west, and Clydeside; the miners, ironworkers, seamen and keelmen of the north-east; the coal and lead miners of Wales; and the nailers and metalworkers of the west midlands. Thus, both skilled and unskilled workers participated in riots. In some riots other groups were quite prominent. Women were quite active in food riots because they bought more food than men, they were more sensitive to change in price and quality, and they may have believed that they were more likely to avoid severe punishment. Women were also active in other riots about economic issues (toll-booth riots, for example) and in disputes concerning sexual morality.[73] Religious and political riots might also draw in middling and professional men and even a few clergymen and gentlemen.

V   THE RESPONSE OF THE AUTHORITIES

Although the governing elite might insist that respect for rank, property and authority was a moral duty, they had to come to terms with the fact that there was widespread popular discontent and social disorder throughout the eighteenth century. The poor generally accepted the social hierarchy and were often deferential, but, under stress, they were prepared to ridicule their superiors and treat authority with contempt. Their deference and subordination could not be taken for granted. Often irreverent and unruly, they could become almost ungovernable in a crisis.[74] Violent popular disturbances proved that the common people could create major problems for the governing elite and they tested, sometimes to the limit, the resources of force and persuasion available to the authorities.[75] There was no effective civilian police force and so major riots in London or other large cities or a rash of smaller riots across several counties compelled the governing elite either to think in terms of conciliation or to resort to suppression by military force. The latter was rarely possible and was always unpopular even with the propertied elite. Remedial action, on the other hand, required a recognition of the grievances of the people, a willingness to redress these complaints, and policies designed to ameliorate the distress of the poor.

The governing authorities, both at Westminster and in the localities, were anxious to maintain law and order, to defend property and to prevent social anarchy. Riots led to a direct confrontation between rulers and ruled and so forced the former to devise ways of restoring stability as quickly as possible. An obvious response was to use the law, the forces of order and the legal process to suppress riots, to punish the participants and to warn potential transgressors of the consequences of their actions. This was more easily proposed than accomplished however. To preserve the rule of law an immense effort was made to project the image of a ruling class which was itself subject to the law. The ruling elite therefore became to some extent the prisoners of their own rhetoric and their own ideology. They certainly found it impossible to rule in a truly arbitrary fashion and they recognised that armed force could be used only as a last resort.[76] There was no doubt that rioting was a crime, but that did not make suppression easy, especially when it was on a large scale or a considerable part of the local community was involved. At common law participation in a riot was considered a misdemeanour punishable by imprisonment, whipping or a fine. After the passing of the Riot Act in 1715 rioters were guilty of a felony punishable by death if they had not dispersed, but remained in a crowd of twelve or more persons, one hour after a magistrate had read the Riot Act.[77] Reading the Riot Act before large angry crowds however sometimes required more courage than magistrates possessed.[78] Some conspicuously failed to do their duty. The magistrates of Glasgow after the Malt tax riots of 1725 and those of Edinburgh after the Porteous riot of 1736 were criticised by the government because of their failure to confront the rioters in the manner prescribed by the Riot Act.[79]

In trying to suppress a riot magistrates might find it difficult to command the required force. Justices of the Peace were authorised to command the assistance of any private citizen to suppress a riot or they could summon the *posse commitatus* (consisting of all able-bodied loyal subjects of the crown in the county), but, when rioters articulated the grievances of the local community, it was very difficult to recruit such assistance.[80] In 1740, for example, the sheriff of County Durham did successfully call out the posse. Although it managed to arrest seven food rioters (out of several hundred) in Stockton, the posse soon melted away and two of the prisoners escaped before they reached Durham.[81] The regular civilian forces of order (the constables and the nightwatchmen), that were available in urban areas where most riots occurred, were not trained or suited to deal with riots on any significant scale. In cases of major disturbance therefore the magistrates could only call upon the assistance of troops, either the militia (only available from 1756) or the regular army. The militia was not well trained for riot duty and resented being used on such occasions, especially against food rioters. (In the 1790s some of the recently instituted Volunteers resigned rather than suppress food riots.[82]) The regular army played the major role in restoring order, especially in the case of the larger riots.[83] The decision to call out the troops lay with the local magistrates, who often hesitated to take this step. In a few cases (in election, Church and King, and some food riots, for example) this was because they had some sympathy with the cause of the rioters. In some other cases it was because the magistrates expected the riot to subside long before any troops could reach the scene.[84] More often it was because they did not want to bear the responsibility for subsequent casualties; an attitude that was reinforced when two magistrates were put on trial for murder in 1757 and 1768 for using excessive force in restoring order. Although acquitted, their ordeal discouraged others from using troops.[85] So did the fear of losing popularity or being socially ostracised in their community if casualties were caused in suppressing a riot. The magistrates of Bristol certainly earned public opprobrium when troops caused heavy casualties in the city during the Bristol Bridge riot of 1793.[86] When troops were summoned, magistrates found that billeting them could cause endless bickering and the local community was anxious to see the back of the licentious soldiers.[87]

For its part, the central government was always anxious not to use regular troops unnecessarily. The use of the army for internal policing was always likely to cause public controversy because it was regarded as a threat to liberty and no British government in the eighteenth century ever wished to give the impression that it ruled by force of arms. Since there were not enough troops, in any case, to deal with widespread rioting, the government tried to ensure that troops were not despatched simply because a local magistrate had lost his nerve. When regular troops were despatched, their officers were repeatedly advised to follow the instructions of the civil magistrates and to act with extreme discretion. It was generally accepted that it was legal to use regular troops against rioters, but only if the civil magistrates had called for their assistance and commanded them to act.[88] Soldiers were certainly reluctant to act without the authority of a civil magistrate. During the Porteous riot of 1736, when a large number of rioters seized control of Edinburgh for several hours, troops in the castle refused to intervene because no city magistrate was brave enough to risk the wrath of the mob by reading the Riot Act or commanding the troops to restore order.[89] This caution was reinforced when, on several occasions, officers and men were charged with wilful murder because they appeared to use excessive force in suppressing a riot. After the Malt tax riots in Glasgow in 1725 Captain Bushell was found guilty of using excessive force and only avoided punishment by receiving a royal pardon.[90] After the St George's Field 'Massacre' of 10 May 1768 the troops accused of murder were acquitted, but the decision aroused much public controversy.[91]

Sometimes, however, militia (rather than regular) troops were ill-disciplined or poorly commanded and they did use excessive force. In the Hexham militia riot of 1761, the Bristol Bridge riot of 1793 and the Tranent militia riot of 1797, the militia on duty lost control of the situation and caused heavy casualties. Regular troops were better trained and disciplined and they were very effective in quelling some serious riots. In the Sacheverell riot of 1710 the regular troops handled a dangerous situation extremely well and restored order with minimum casualties. In the notorious Gordon riots of 1780 however the situation got rapidly out of control and regular troops had to be ordered to restore order at all costs. Such was the scale of the problem that even disciplined troops could not suppress the rioting without killing or wounding 458 people. On this occasion the government had to act because the London magistrates had proved too timid. The ministers were more prepared to contemplate heavy casualties in order to end the anarchy in the nation's capital. Thereafter, the government insisted that troops could act on their own initiative to suppress a riot and did not need to be commanded by a civil magistrate.[92] This more determined attitude caused some public controversy, but in the 1790s riots were more readily suppressed and the Volunteers were raised, in part, as an additional policing force to maintain domestic order.

In seeking to suppress riots the forces of order were generally outnumbered and so it was impossible to arrest all the participants. Even reading the Riot Act might only encourage the rioters to disperse; it did not facilitate their arrest.[93] Moreover, magistrates were sometimes reluctant to arrest rioters because to do so could provoke even greater violence or lead to attempts to rescue those placed under arrest. In some election, religious and political riots magistrates so sympathised with the rioters that they did not contemplate making arrests.[94] When arrests were made in any kind of popular disturbance only a small proportion of those involved could be apprehended. The authorities then faced the dilemma of what to do with them. In many instances the authorities were lenient because they were anxious to restore good relations within their community and they were conscious of the bitterness and tensions that criminal prosecutions could produce. If many in the community were still angry and resentful, then potential prosecutors, witnesses and juries, and even the magistrates themselves, might be subjected to threats, intimidation, social ostracism or acts of revenge.[95] The law could work effectively only when the local community supported it and rioters could be prosecuted only if their victims were prepared to come forward. This could prove expensive and troublesome.[96] When the Kingswood colliers rioted against turnpikes in 1738 the mayor of Bristol found that even offers of rewards for information failed to produce any evidence.[97] After the Stockton food riot of 1740 most of those who were arrested were released without ever being brought to trial.[98] It was never easy or prudent to bring all arrested rioters to trial. Hundreds of weavers were involved in the calico riots in London in 1719–20, but only 35 were prosecuted.[99] The available evidence suggests that the authorities never prosecuted all those who were arrested for participating in a riot and many of those who were prosecuted were never convicted. Of the 220 Londoners indicted for riot in 1720–1 only 20 per cent were actually convicted because so many prosecutors abandoned their cases or because sympathetic juries brought in verdicts of not guilty. Most of those convicted of riot were prosecuted for a misdemeanour under the common law and not for a felony under the Riot Act. These rioters were generally fined a small sum or were imprisoned for a short period.[100] Even after the serious rioting in Newcastle upon Tyne in June 1740 the magistrates inflicted only light sentences. They recognised that they had to tread a careful line between enforcing respect for the law and restoring some measure of social harmony. The fact that most pits in the area went on strike while the verdicts were awaited helped to persuade the magistrates to be lenient.[101] The violent riot by seamen in Liverpool in 1775 resulted in some fifty arrests, but only eight men were eventually prosecuted and all were discharged on agreeing to serve in the Royal Navy.[102] During the serious and widespread food riots of 1795 some 64 people were arrested, but only 30 ever appeared in court, only eight of these were sent for trial and only five of these were sentenced (to between two weeks and three months in prison).[103] Only when the authorities were thoroughly alarmed, and were convinced that they must demonstrate the need for a restoration of law and order, did they seek to impose exemplary punishments. Even in these cases they usually sought to execute a few ringleaders as a warning that some types of disorder would not be tolerated. About 5000 people were involved in the Hexham militia riot of March 1761, but only two men were sentenced to death for treason and only one of these was actually executed.[104] The food riots of 1766 were so widespread and so alarming that a Special Commission was set up by the government to tour the worst affected areas to bring hundreds of rioters to trial in order to produce summary and salutary warnings to the populace of what could befall those who created such disturbances. Yet only 96 prisoners were finally arraigned. Forty-three of these were eventually discharged and only three were finally executed.[105] The Gordon riots of 1780 caused more alarm than any other disturbance of the century. The authorities were determined to inflict exemplary punishments on this occasion and, to that end, they created Special Commissions in Southwark and Surrey and they offered rewards for information that would help to bring in convictions. Over 450 arrests were made, but only 160 rioters were brought to trial. Of these 62 were sentenced to death, though only 25 were eventually executed.[106] The authorities had again recognised the need to temper justice with mercy.

The authorities clearly recognised that the use of force and the resort to executions were not effective solutions to popular grievances and were a poor means of restoring social harmony. In general, they preferred conciliation, arbitration and mildness to the prolonged odium caused by a policy of repression. In the case of some religious and political riots they were even prepared to condone attacks on unpopular minorities. In many other instances, especially in the case of food riots, they were prepared to tolerate disturbances which did not get seriously out-of-hand. In most riots with a clear economic motive, when the poor could point to a legitimate grievance, the authorities were prepared to investigate the causes of the disorder and to take remedial action. When industrial disputes were widespread, the government sent agents to inquire into the causes of these disturbances and peaceful and negotiated solutions were sought. In the winter of 1726–7, for example, when many weavers rioted in the south-west, a secretary of state sent two commissioners to investigate whether the protesters had a legitimate grievance. One agent itemised the many grievances of the weavers and concluded that these miserable workmen were oppressed by the clothiers. Two weavers had already been arrested for rioting and he urged that they should be released. Commenting on the clothiers, he noted: 'here are some angry & revengfull people who think that all authority consists in punishment, it is my humble opinion a little show of prudence in ye governing of this Country wou'd keep it in perfect tranquility without ye assistance of troops.' In his opinion it was the clothiers who deserved to be punished.[107] The Privy Council reprimanded the clothiers and suggested articles of agreement which were subsequently embodied in an act of parliament, though, unfortunately, they were never fully implemented.[108] In other industrial disputes, involving the coalheavers and silkweavers of London and the keelmen and seamen of the north-east, for example, the authorities also tried, without complete success, to persuade employers not to oppress their workmen.

Both the central government and local magistrates showed particular sympathy for the poor involved in food riots and they sought a variety of remedies. One solution, urged by local magistrates and implemented by the government, was to regulate the grain trade more effectively. After many bad harvests (in 1709–10, 1740–1, 1756–7, 1766–74, 1789–90, 1792, 1795–7 and 1800, for example) the government prohibited the export of grain. Less frequently, it withheld the bounties on grain exports (in 1697–1700, 1764–5 and 1782–3) or it suspended the duties on grain imports (in 1757–8, 1764–8, 1772–4 and 1795–7).[109] Local magistrates (in Newcastle upon Tyne and in Flintshire, in 1740, for example) also placed embargoes on grain leaving their particular region.[110] To ensure that available supplies would get to the poor the government urged the rich to curtail their own bread consumption and they prohibited the use of wheat in distilling, starching and hair powder.[111] On several occasions the authorities condemned the forestallers, engrossers and regraters who failed to bring grain to the local market. In June 1740, for example, the Lords Justices, urging the implementation of the laws governing the trade in grain, complained that 'divers ill disposed persons for their private lucre do presume to buy up and ingross great quantitys of corn and grain in order to export and sell the same beyond the seas contrary to the said laws & to the great oppression of the poor.'[112] Local magistrates also often sought to implement the old laws regulating the market in grain (as those in Gloucestershire did in 1765).[113] Long after these laws were repealed in 1772 the authorities still instigated prosecutions of forestallers and other offenders. As late as 1800 one Staffordshire magistrate admitted:

> As a Conservator of the Peace I shall always stand forward to protect it, but I can never attempt it, at the hazard of my life,

for enriching one part of the community and supporting them in the most glaring acts of oppression at the expense of the comforts, Happiness and even the existence of the other.[114]

When the government and local magistrates responded in this way they bestowed a degree of official sanction on the rioters and this helped to convince the poor that their actions were legitimate.[115] To some extent it also benefited the governing elite by diverting the wrath of the rioters against the middlemen in the grain trade and away from those in positions of authority.[116] Those in authority however did make determined efforts themselves to get grain to market at a price the poor could afford.[117] Local magistrates put pressure on farmers and merchants to bring their grain to market. The government itself tried to import grain from as far afield as Egypt, Sicily, Canada and the Baltic so that London would be supplied with food in the hard years of the 1790s.[118] Individual landlords often urged their tenants to release grain onto the market at an affordable price.[119] When such measures failed, the propertied elite turned to outright charity. Food subsidies and increases in poor relief were sanctioned and soup kitchens were established. The expenditure on poor relief increased sharply after the food riots of 1795, for example, and this response did much to reduce the level of disorder.[120]

VI THE IMPACT OF POPULAR DISTURBANCES

What most worried the authorities about riots was the belief that they were manifestations of a deeper political conspiracy designed to subvert the constitution and the fear that they would defeat the resources of law and order and make the poor ungovernable. In other words, they feared that popular disturbances might be the prelude to political revolution or social anarchy. As one commentator noted: 'As for our Common People many of them must be confess'd to be very rough and savage in their dispositions, being of levelling principles and refractory to Government, insolent and tumultuous.'[121] Government ministers frequently asked their agents or local magistrates to investigate popular disturbances in order to see whether they were the harbinger of more serious attempts to destroy the existing constitution or subvert the established social order. The Riot Act of 1715 itself was passed at a time when the Whig ministers feared that widespread rioting was linked to a Jacobite conspiracy against the constitution.[122] In September 1735 Lord Chancellor Hardwicke warned the Duke of Newcastle of the dangerous consequences of allowing the common people, who were at that time protesting about turnpikes, to get the better of the laws and the legislature.[123] During the widespread food rioting of 1740 one commentator warned Newcastle that the people 'have got the old cry of levelling and I'm affraid that unless timely prevented it will come to it.'[124] After serious industrial disputes in Manchester in 1759 an assize judge commented: 'If inferiors are to prescribe to their Superiors, if the foot aspire to be the head, if every man is aiming to follow the evil of his ways without restraint or controul, to what end are laws enacted?'[125] In the 1790s the government enquired into the many industrial disputes of the period to see whether they might be part of a radical conspiracy against the constitution. One shipowner informed the Home Secretary in November 1792 that Tyneside was 'covered with thousands of pitmen, keelmen, waggonmen, and other labouring men, hardy fellows strongly impressed with the new doctrine of equality, and at present composed of such combustible matter that the least spark will set it ablaze.'[126]

Whatever the fears of some contemporary witnesses, the research of modern historians has shown that riots very rarely served overtly radical aims. Although some rioters did shout their support for the Pretender, for John Wilkes or for Tom Paine, most rioters did not seek to change either the constitution or the distribution of power. The vast majority of riots were 'extra-institutional' rather than 'anti-institutional'.[127] Those who participated in them believed that they had been provoked into action to redress specific grievances because those in authority had failed to come to their aid. It was never their intention to replace that authority, but to compel it to act as the rioters desired. They did not rebel against authority *per se*, but rather protested because those in authority had failed to act responsibly. Riots were a means of holding authority to account and of putting pressure on those in power to implement specific remedies. While rioters temporarily subverted the established order, they usually claimed to be performing for themselves the tasks which the magistrates ought to have fulfilled. Rioters, moreover, knew that street protests were not the way to achieve wider political objectives and there is little evidence to suggest that they saw such disturbances as the means of achieving radical political reform or a new social order. Nor is it possible to see much evidence of serious class hatred or a desire for social levelling in most of the popular disturbances of the eighteenth century. While there were many criticisms of the rich and threats of levelling, these were largely rhetoric. Only in the widespread riots of the 1790s was there a genuine undercurrent of subversion and, even then, militant loyalism probably attracted greater popular support. Most rioters practised the art of the possible and tried to achieve what was practical and within their reach. They sought concrete and local remedies to specific grievances not a fundamental overhaul of the whole political and social order. While violently protesting about particular grievances, most rioters affirmed their loyalty to the powers that be and claimed to be acting legally or at least justly.[128]

The common people generally accepted the existing political and social order, out of necessity and out of self-preservation. They were fully conscious of the fact that they lacked the resources to replace their rulers or to redistribute property by their own direct actions. Their aims were more limited and more conservative. Much of the time they sought to defend established customs and traditional practices. This did not mean that they were powerless, however, or that they had always to be passive, acquiescent or deferential under the hegemony of the landed elite. Popular disturbances were not simply a confirmation of the political and social order. Most riots were not approved of by the authorities. They were a clear challenge to the authority of the governing elite and their outcome was always uncertain. The immediate gains of crowd activity were not very great, but there were some successes. Food riots, as we have seen, often goaded the authorities into action and they sought a variety of remedies. Many industrial disputes forced minor concessions from employers, while government and parliament responded with legislation to disputes involving silkweavers, coalheavers and keelmen. After popular protests the Excise Bill was dropped, the Gin Act was abandoned and the Jewish Naturalisation Act was repealed. In other riots Captain Porteous was lynched, Wilkes was supported, and religious and radical minorities were oppressed. Success was always greater where the cause was also supported by some of the elite or by the middling orders. It is a mistake, however, simply to add up the victories and defeats of the crowd in specific riots. What popular disturbances regularly and repeatedly demonstrated was that the common people of eighteenth-century Britain would become ungovernable unless the governing elite acknowledged their genuine grievances, recognised their right to protest about them, and sought more often to ameliorate their condition than to suppress their protests. Arbitration and conciliation rather than punishment and repression were seen to be the best remedies for popular grievances. The ruling elite could not govern by force alone and they had to recognise that they could be held to account even by those who had no voice in parliament and no vote in elections. The widespread and endemic rioting of the eighteenth century offered clear and repeated proof that Britons were freemen and not slaves.

Part Two
The Politicisation of the People

5 The Debate on British Liberties and Natural Rights

Part One endeavoured to show that, although the governing elite undoubtedly dominated politics at court and in parliament, the people at large still managed to exert political influence because of their participation in parliamentary elections, pressure groups, urban politics and popular demonstrations. The British people were able to exploit their role in these activities in order to influence or at least to constrain the political decisions taken by the ruling class. Throughout the eighteenth century these activities provided the people with both a range of political opportunities and a political education that enabled them to limit the power of their political superiors. In addition, as we shall see in Part Two, both the ideological debate initially waged within the governing elite and the political actions taken by government and parliament eventually politicised a much wider public. In defending themselves against the power of the crown and in criticising the misuse of royal patronage, the propertied elite defended various rights and liberties of the subject. These actions initiated a prolonged and sometimes intense ideological debate on the rights and liberties of the subject; a debate which soon involved those outside the narrow circle of the ruling oligarchy and eventually led to demands for a wider range of liberties for a larger proportion of the population. The political disputes within the governing elite and, especially their manifest political failings, also eventually provoked criticisms from the people 'out-of-doors' and encouraged the more active of these critics to demand that those in positions of power should be accountable to a wider public. By the later eighteenth century there were campaigns in support of a much more representative and responsible system of government. Thus, an ideological campaign was waged in support of greater rights and liberties and extra-parliamentary pressure groups were established to give

voice to the political and constitutional demands of the middling and even of the lower orders. At the same time, these
ideological and political developments also provoked a conservative reaction against such a radical campaign to change
the existing political and social order. Here too, conservative
arguments and loyalist organisations were first promoted by
the propertied elite, but they soon influenced and involved a
much wider public. The people at large therefore were
brought into politics by the governing elite and they were
provoked into both challenging and defending the existing
political system as a result of examples provided by and lessons
learned from their political superiors.

I   RIGHTS AND LIBERTIES

In seeking to understand the political role that ordinary
British citizens played in the eighteenth century we need to
know what rights and liberties contemporaries believed that
British subjects could and should possess. Throughout the
eighteenth century we can find many favourable comments on
the advantages which British subjects enjoyed as free men
living in a free society. Although a narrow propertied elite
clearly played the dominant role in government and parliament, those who admired the existing constitution confidently asserted that the British people possessed as much
liberty as was consistent with the preservation of order. On the
other hand, there were many other commentators who criticised the actual working of the constitution and they often did
so on the grounds that it was failing to safeguard the liberties
of the subject. There was, in fact, a profound and prolonged
debate throughout the eighteenth century between those who
were confident about the existence of 'English liberties' and
those who believed that the people did indeed have an historic
claim and a natural right to liberty, but were being denied
their just deserts by a corrupt administration. These differences rested, in part, upon conflicting assessments of what
government and parliament were in fact doing to and for the
subject and, in part, on different perceptions of what legitimate rights and liberties the people as a whole ought to
possess. Defenders of the *status quo* believed that government

and parliament were doing as much as possible to preserve the liberties of the subject, whereas critics feared that the ruling elite posed a permanent threat to the rights of the people. These opposed views were underpinned by different notions of what rights and liberties British subjects ought and could reasonably hope to possess. No commentator, no matter how conservative, was prepared to assert that the people were without any rights or liberties or that these liberties were subject to the whim of an arbitrary tyrant. On the other hand, there was a great deal of discussion and many heated disputes over the precise nature and the exact extent of the liberties which British subjects could legitimately demand as their historic or natural rights.

An examination of this debate on the rights and liberties of the subject shows that those who were engaged in it often held different, even conflicting, notions of what constituted freedom. It was certainly accepted by all that every subject had the right to enjoy some negative freedoms or civil liberties. There was general agreement, for example, that there has to be an area of human activity within which each individual is left free to do what he wants without interference from others. There was a natural limit on the power of any government or any individual to interfere with the activities of other men. It was also agreed that this sphere of free action could not be unlimited, because this would mean that no civil government could possess any legitimate or effective authority over its subjects. In such an anarchic situation the liberties of the weak would be at the mercy of the freedom of the strong. The freedom of the individual therefore had to be limited by law, but, many argued, the sphere of civil liberties ought to be as extensive as possible without undermining law and order. The advocates of extensive personal freedom claimed that one of the most important motives in creating civil government was the desire to convert the natural right to personal freedom into secure civil liberties.

Whereas all commentators admitted that a measure of civil liberty was the legitimate right of every individual, there was obviously some dispute over how extensive these civil liberties could be. There was much greater disagreement over how these civil liberties could be protected from those in positions of authority who might be tempted to increase their own power.

Those who feared an oppressive state claimed that, in any emergency, subjects could legitimately act to defend their civil liberties because they had a natural right to resist arbitrary tyranny, by force if necessary. They based this right on the notion that the people as a whole were the sovereign authority in the state since they had agreed in the first place to the creation of civil government as a means of defending their freedom.

The suggestion that the people were the supreme authority in the state ran up against the counter-argument that sovereignty was in fact located in the combined legislature of King, Lords and Commons and that undue emphasis on the right of resistance would undermine the stability of any political regime. The force of this argument encouraged those anxious to safeguard the extensive civil liberties of the subject to demand that the people had a right to be their own masters or, at least, they ought to have an active role in deciding who should govern them. While men of a conservative disposition were content to see the right to shape the decisions of the state confined to a narrow propertied elite, men of more radical opinions began to demand that most, perhaps even all, men had a legitimate right to choose who should govern them and to hold these governors to account. The logical conclusion of this claim was the demand for a democratic republic, though few radicals went this far. An even smaller number of radicals believed that a democratic republic would remain an inadequate defence of civil liberty so long as men remained so unequal in wealth and status. They feared that some men would be too poor to protect their civil liberties in the law courts and too dependent upon others to make an independent choice of their political representatives. To ensure therefore that all men could effectively protect their civil liberties and freely exercise their political rights, it was essential to achieve a measure of economic equality.[1]

In seeking to justify different concepts of liberty, political commentators used a range of arguments and they appealed to quite different intellectual traditions. One line of argument put great stress on the appeal to history, experience and prescription. It was asserted that England possessed an ancient constitution which had long guaranteed the historic rights of Englishmen. Some radicals claimed that these historic rights had been very extensive in the distant past, had been undermined at the Norman Conquest, and were in the process of being slowly recovered by sustained pressure for reform.[2] A very different defence of liberty rested on the claim that God had endowed all men with inalienable natural rights. These natural rights to 'life, liberty and property' had to be converted into civil liberties and could only be protected if all men were able to exercise a positive role in the decision-making processes of the state. A number of those who appealed either to historic English liberties or to natural rights also employed utilitarian arguments. They maintained that civil government was established for the benefit of the governed, not to exalt the authority of those in positions of power, and, hence, governments should be judged according to how well they served the interests and preserved the liberties of the people as a whole. By the end of the eighteenth century this test of utility had not yet produced a fully articulated utilitarian defence of liberty, on the basis that civil government ought to seek 'the greatest good of the greatest number', but it was not long before Jeremy Bentham and James Mill sought to replace the appeal to history and natural rights with their own felicific calculus.[3]

II THE DEBATE ON NATURAL RIGHTS AND CIVIL LIBERTIES

In nearly all civil societies the power of rulers is limited, legally or morally, by laws, customs or some higher authority. This was quite definitely the case in eighteenth-century Britain, but there was still considerable debate over the exact nature and the precise extent of those civil liberties which all subjects possessed. It is clear that both conservative and liberal commentators accepted that all subjects possessed civil liberties, usually defined as 'life, liberty and property', which were justified as either natural rights or the historic liberties of Englishmen. Even at their most limited these civil liberties defended the right of subjects to live under the rule of law and to have an equal opportunity of justice. Arbitrary authority was restrained by positive law, ancient custom or natural law to the extent that no subject could be imprisoned without trial; all men were subject to the same laws administered by the same law courts; no torture could be used to secure a confession; and no accused person could be convicted of a serious offence except after a trial by jury. As Lord North claimed in the House of Commons in 1784:

> He was free, because he lived in a country governed by equal laws. Where the highest and lowest were governed by the same laws, where there was no distinction of persons, there freedom might be said to exist as purely and as perfectly as in the nature of things it could exist.[4]

Equal justice for all however was not seen as the full extent of every subject's claim to civil liberty. There was also almost universal agreement that all subjects had an inalienable right to their property. In his *Second Treatise* (1690) John Locke had gone to great lengths to prove that private property and its unequal distribution had originated in the state of nature, before the appearance of civil government, and he had also stressed that civil government was usually established because of the pressing need to defend this natural right to property. Locke was so convinced that civil government was created to protect private property that he insisted that no government could legitimately seize or even tax any man's property unless the subject gave his consent to it.[5] A whole host of eighteenth-century commentators endorsed Locke's views on this particular issue.[6] William Blackstone, who rejected some of Locke's more radical political opinions, supported Locke's efforts to defend private property:

> So great moreover is the regard of the law for private property, that it will not authorise the least violation of it; no, not even for the general good of the whole community ... the legislature alone can, and indeed frequently does, interpose, and compel the individual to acquiesce. But how does it interpose and compel? Not by absolutely stripping the subject of his property in an arbitrary manner; but by giving him a full indemnification and equivalent for the injury he sustained.[7]

Even most of the radicals of the later eighteenth century were prepared to defend both private property and its unequal distribution. Some quite explicitly denied that they desired to invade the rights of property. The radicals of Manchester, for example, protested:

The *inequality* derived from labour and successful enterprise, the result of superior industry and good fortune, is an *inequality essential to the very existence of Society*, and it naturally follows, that the property so acquired, should pass *from a father to his children*. To render property insecure would destroy all motives to exertion, and tear up public happiness by the roots.[8]

The right to freedom of conscience was another important civil liberty which was widely conceded by political commentators in the eighteenth century. The intellectual defence of religious toleration had made great strides in the seventeenth century and had been supplied with a profound philosophical justification in John Locke's *Letters concerning Toleration* (1689–92). Locke maintained that every man has a natural right to hold and profess whatever opinions he chooses, provided these are not a threat to the stability or morality of society. In his opinion, each individual is responsible for his own salvation and no one could have good grounds for entrusting his salvation to the necessarily incompetent discretion of another person. Each man is responsible for his own beliefs and has to answer for them to God. The state therefore has no right to concern itself with the condition of any man's soul and no church has the right to impose its own religious views by seeking to deprive any man of his civil liberties. While Locke was not prepared to tolerate Roman Catholics or atheists, on the grounds that their opinions were a threat to society, he did provide a wider interpretation of freedom of conscience than any of his contemporaries. He combined the moral argument that any human attempt to interfere with religious belief or worship was blasphemously presumptuous with the utilitarian argument that toleration should be granted whenever it could be expected to promote civil order and social harmony.

The Toleration Act of 1689 conceded freedom of worship only to Protestant Dissenters. Various penal laws against Roman Catholics and the Test and Corporation Acts, which sought to deny Protestant Dissenters access to office under the crown or in local corporations, remained in force throughout the eighteenth century, but the case for freedom of worship, if not for full religious equality, won increasing support and ultimately prevailed. Even conservative Anglican clergymen, such as Archdeacon William Paley, came to accept that an established church was only justified on utilitarian grounds because it was best suited to preserving and communicating religious knowledge. He fully accepted that Dissenters should be allowed freedom of worship.[9] Edmund Burke was prepared to go even further, he defended the liberty of conscience of any religious group, including Jews and Muslims. Only when religious beliefs threatened to undermine the state could action be taken to restrict the political influence of such beliefs, but not to prevent any man holding them.[10]

Many Protestant Dissenters were not satisfied with religious toleration on such terms. They fought a prolonged campaign for an extension of their religious and civil liberties, and for the repeal of the Test and Corporation Acts in particular. At first, their case was based on references to their political loyalty or to scriptural authority in support of their religious practices. By the later eighteenth century, however, they had changed tack and were insisting that their demands were consistent with the natural and inalienable rights of all men.[11] David Williams advised his fellow Dissenters in 1777:

> Your very existence depends on your changing the reason of your dissent, which used to be an opinion of superior orthodoxy and superior purity of faith and worship, for another which is the only rational and justifiable reason of dissent – the inalienable and universal right of private judgment, and the necessity of an unrestrained enquiry and freedom of debate and discussion on all subjects of know-ledge, morality, and religion. This may be called *Intellectual Liberty*. This should be the general reason of dissent ...[12]

Joshua Toulmin protested that a mere relaxation of religious persecution would not do and he demanded: 'Give us back our full natural rights!'[13]

The demand for religious toleration generally advanced hand-in-hand with the campaign for a free press and for free-dom of expression in civil matters. The free expression of political views, provided they were not libellous, seditious or subversive, was advocated on the grounds of expediency and was regarded as a means to advance truth and justice. In eighteenth-century Britain there was no pre-publication censorship and, while stamp duties and other commercial restrictions might hinder the distribution of critical opinions, a wide variety of political, religious and philosophical views were propagated. The principle of a free press was rarely challenged and indeed the existence of such a press was widely recognised as one of the most valuable civil liberties possessed by the British people.[14] Even the conservative William Blackstone defended a free press:

> The liberty of the press is indeed essential to the nature of a free state. ... Every free man has an undoubted right to lay what sentiment he pleases before the public; to forbid this, is to destroy the freedom of the press; but if he publishes what is improper, mischievous or illegal, he must take the consequence of his own temerity. ... Thus the will of individuals is still left free; the abuse only of that free will is the object of legal punishment.[15]

The more liberal Charles James Fox was prepared to go much further. He asserted in 1789:

> Men ought to be judged by their actions and not by their thoughts. The one can be fixed and ascertained, the other can only be a matter of guess and speculation. I am so far of this opinion that if any man publishes his political sentiments and says in writing that he dislikes the constitution of this country, and gives it as his judgment that principles in direct contradiction to the Constitution and Government are the principles that ought to be asserted and maintained, I hold that he should not, on this account be disabled from filling any office, civil or military; but if he carries his detestable opinions into practice, the law will then find a remedy and punish him for his conduct.[16]

Although radicals in the later eighteenth century advocated extensive political liberties, they were careful to deny that they were encouraging anarchy or licentiousness. They believed that all men were subject to a superior moral or natural law and that all men had a duty to pursue what was 'right', should exercise responsibility and must regulate their freedom. While all men had an absolute liberty to think, to discuss and to worship, they did not have an absolute right of action. They were not free simply to please themselves, but must acknowledge a higher moral law and must also accept the restraints of the law of the land. On the other hand, no conservative commentator was prepared to argue that British subjects had no claim to natural rights and civil liberties. William Blackstone, though he might not have interpreted them quite so liberally, acknowledged that British subjects possessed the same natural rights that Locke had defended: 'the rights of personal security, the right of personal liberty, and the right of private property'.[17] Edmund Burke, even in his most conservative phase when he was denouncing the whole natural rights school of radicals, fully recognised that all subjects had a right to certain vital civil liberties:

> Men have a right to live by that rule [of law]; they have a right to justice; ... They have a right to the fruits of their industry; and to the means of making their industry fruitful. They have a right to the acquisitions of their parents; to the nourishment and improvement of their offspring; to instruction in life, and to consolation in death. Whatever each man can separately do, without trespassing on others, he has a right to do for himself.[18]

III THE DEBATE ON RESISTANCE AND POPULAR SOVEREIGNTY

Whether they were defending a minimum of civil liberties or seeking greatly to extend them, all eighteenth-century commentators proclaimed the crucial importance of the rule of law which established the boundary between the legitimate authority of the government and the liberty of the subject. It was recognised that the rule of law could be secured and preserved only so long as any claim to tyrannical or arbitrary authority could be defeated. In the last resort therefore it was generally acknowledged that subjects possessed the natural right to use force to resist tyranny. Those with complete confidence in Britain's mixed and balanced constitution believed that this right of resistance would never need to be exercised because the combined and sovereign legislature of King, Lords and Commons could be trusted to safeguard the liberties of the subject. Those who were less confident of the virtues of the existing constitution or who were more alert to the danger that power corrupts, believed that the people as a whole must be allowed to resist any serious abuse of power. Moreover, in an emergency, they must be free to assert their superiority even over the legislature itself. Thus, the right of resistance ultimately rested on the belief that the final source of sovereign authority in the state was the people themselves.

The radicals, from the late seventeenth century to the late eighteenth century, proclaimed the natural right to resist any government which seriously abused its trust and acted in an arbitrary and tyrannical manner. Some argued that the right of resistance should be exercised only by men of property and that ordinary subjects should not act unless given a lead by their superiors.[19] Locke and most late eighteenth-century radicals were prepared to concede the right of resistance to all men, but even they were careful to suggest that its use was not justified out of sheer caprice, but only in order to resist manifest tyranny.[20] This position was endorsed by most commentators in the eighteenth century, even those of a conservative disposition such as David Hume, Adam Smith, William Blackstone and Edmund Burke.[21] Those of a more liberal persuasion went further and vigorously campaigned against the growth of a large standing army under the government's control. They advocated instead a citizen militia which would be capable of defending the country from invasion and its subjects from arbitrary authority.[22] A large professional army was seen as a potential instrument of tyranny and also, because of the money, appointments and contracts needed to service it, as a means of increasing crown patronage. This patronage could be used to influence both parliament and voters. It was widely feared therefore that a nation which relied for its defence on a hired army had taken a major step towards sacrificing its liberties. On the other hand, a citizen militia promoted civic virtue and civic responsibility and it allowed the people to act for themselves in defence of their property and their liberties. A citizen who was not also a soldier had alienated a vital part of his freedom and had sacrificed his independence. A free society could only be preserved so long as the sword remained in the hands of the people. Whereas many proponents of a citizen militia in the earlier eighteenth century expected this force to be commanded by men of substantial property, the radicals of the later eighteenth century stressed that the right to bear arms was the mark of full citizenship and it was a badge which should be worn by all adult males. According to William Jones all men not only possessed the right to bear arms, but should be practised in the use of them.[23]

Those radicals who explicitly defended the right of resistance often did so because they believed that civil government was a trust established by the consent of the people and for their benefit. In their view, the sovereign authority in the state was only legitimate so long as it fulfilled its trust. When it failed to do so, then sovereign authority reverted to the people who had created civil government in the first place. According to this view, the sovereign legislature of King-in-Parliament could retain its legitimate authority in eighteenth-century Britain only so long as it preserved the natural rights and civil liberties of the subject. Whenever it clearly ceased to do so, then its constitutional authority was dissolved and power reverted to the sovereign people. According to Richard Price:

> Nothing, therefore can be more absurd than the doctrine which some have taught, with respect to the omnipotence of parliaments. They possess no power beyond the limits of the trust for the execution of which they were formed. If they contradict this trust, they betray their constituents, and dissolve themselves. All delegated power must be subordinated and limited. – If omnipotence can, with any sense, be ascribed to a legislature, it must be lodged where all legislative authority originates; that is, in the PEOPLE. For their sakes government is instituted; and their's is the only real omnipotence.[24]

The danger in relying on this claim, as in relying on the right of resistance, to safeguard the liberties of the subject, was that it could be asserted only in an emergency when it might already be too late to preserve freedom. Those who were conscious of the potential threat posed by a supreme, absolute and uncontrolled legislature were forced therefore to think of ways in which its authority could be continuously and effectively restricted. Some critics of parliamentary sovereignty insisted that the legislature had no legitimate power to command what was contrary to the inalienable rights of man, the law of nature or such fundamental laws of the constitution as the Bill of Rights, the Triennial Act and the Act of Union with Scotland. A few critics suggested the possibility of a divided sovereignty and advocated either a complete separation of legislative, executive and judicial powers or a judicial review of legislative or executive actions in order to test whether they were constitutional or not.[25] By the late eighteenth century a number of radicals had come to the conclusion that Britain needed a constitution which would clearly secure the civil liberties of the subject and would lay down detailed restrictions on the exercise of power by the legislature and the executive. Whereas in Locke's *Second Treatise* the sovereignty of the people lay dormant between the time civil government was first created and whenever it was subsequently dissolved, for Thomas Paine and most other radicals of the 1790s the sovereign will of the people was actively and continuously expressed in the making of the constitution, in its operation and in any amendments made to it. According to these radicals the sovereignty of the people remained active throughout the existence of civil government because it was the will of the people that first created civil society, as a compact between equals, and it was this society of equals which subsequently created civil government. So the first and most important contract was not that between subjects and rulers, but that between free and equal individuals who voluntarily agreed to associate with each other. The civil government which they then established remained subordinate to the democratic arrangements which first constituted civil society. In the words of Thomas Paine:

> It has been thought a considerable advance towards establishing the principles of freedom, to say, that government is a compact between those who govern and those who are governed: but this cannot be true, because it is putting the effect before the cause; for as man must have existed before governments existed, there necessarily was a time when governments did not exist, and consequently there could originally exist no governors to form such a compact with. The fact therefore must be, that the *individuals* themselves, each in his own personal and sovereign right, *entered into a compact with each other* to

> produce a government: and this is the only mode in which governments have a right to arise, and the only principle on which they have a right to exist.[26]

To achieve a continuous popular supervision over the actions of those in power, Paine and many other radicals were ready to confer extensive positive rights on the people at large. It is to his debate on precisely what positive political rights might be conferred, and on whom, that we should now turn our attention.

IV   THE DEBATE ON POSITIVE POLITICAL RIGHTS

Many of those who were particularly concerned to defend the liberties of the subject recognised that it was hazardous to allow the abuse of power to proceed to the point where the remedy for manifest grievances required a resort to armed resistance and the dissolution of civil government. Radicals might agree with the assertion that the people had a 'right to chuse our own governors; to cashier them for misconduct; and to frame a government for ourselves',[27] but they often feared that this could be a recipe for perpetual revolution. It clearly made greater sense to devise ways and means of ensuring that those in positions of authority were always responsive to the wishes and interests of the people as a whole. It was generally agreed that the best means of achieving this happy state of affairs was to give the legislature the right to limit the power of the executive and to make the legislature responsible to the people.

Many commentators believed that this state of affairs had been achieved by the beginning of the eighteenth century. They could point to the various restrictions imposed on the royal prerogative since the Glorious Revolution, they could glory in the fact that parliament sat every year after 1688, and they could claim that parliament virtually represented every important interest in the nation.[28] Throughout the eighteenth century, however, there were many critics who maintained that parliament was not successfully curbing the power of the crown and it was not properly representing the nation as a whole. For much of the century spokesmen for a sophisticated Country ideology condemned the growth of crown patronage and expressed the fear that it was being exploited in order to undermine the independence of parliament and to subvert the liberties of the subject. It was widely believed that once a majority of MPs had been seduced by court favours and enough voters seduced by crown patronage, then arbitrary power would be as firmly established as if parliament and voters no longer existed. During the debate on Walpole's Excise Bill in 1733, for example, William Pulteney protested:

> It is certain, that the liberties of this country depend upon the freedom of our elections for members of parliament; our parliament, especially the representatives of the people in parliament assembled, are designed for, and generally have been a check upon those, who are employed in the executive part of our government; if the executive have such an influence over most of the elections in the kingdom, as to get any person chosen they please to recommend, they will then always have a majority of their own creatures in every House of Commons, and from such representatives what can people expect? Can it be expected, that such a House of Commons will ever be any check upon those in power, or that they will find fault with the conduct of the most rapacious, the most tyrannical ministers that may hereafter be employed by the crown.[29]

To counter the danger which crown patronage posed to the subjects' right to have a parliament truly representative of the nation, Country (and Tory) spokesmen advocated a three-pronged response. In the first place, they urged MPs and voters to cultivate civic virtue and their responsibilities as patriotic citizens. Liberty, it was maintained, could be preserved only if public-spirited men were eternally vigilant and were continually aware of the need to oppose the abuse of power and to defend the liberties of the subject. The second response was a vociferous campaign for economical reforms which would reduce the scale and the effectiveness of crown patronage. Attacks were launched on the size and expense of the executive, on the national debt and on the armed forces, and efforts were made to exclude recipients of crown patronage from the House of Commons. A minority of Country spokesmen advocated a third approach designed to ensure that the political voice of the electorate was more effective. Demands were made for free, fair and frequent elections. This led to proposals to eliminate electoral corruption, to transfer seats from the small rotten boroughs to the larger counties and growing towns, and to secure more frequent general elections. If reforms such as these were passed, then the crown would no longer control so much patronage. It would be unable to influence the conduct of MPs and, consequently, these representatives would become more responsive to the interests of those who elected them to parliament. The voters would gain greater control over their representatives and might even be able to instruct them how to vote on crucial issues affecting the vital interests and cherished liberties of the people.[30]

Campaigns such as these were designed to ensure that the electorate could influence the composition and the decisions of the House of Commons, but they were based on the premise that only a minority of subjects – those who possessed the necessary property qualifications to become voters – deserved to be classed as full citizens. Those without such a stake in the community – chiefly the labouring poor – could be justifiably excluded from the franchise and denied a positive voice in the decision-making processes of the state. Indeed, many spokesmen for Country policies frequently voiced their contempt for the lower orders. They often described them as an ignorant and disorderly mob, incapable of resisting bribery and corruption or of exercising independent political judgment. Even if successful, their campaign to defend the positive political rights of the people would have benefited only those who were already qualified to vote.

There were, however, other voices raised in defence of the positive political rights of those without a vote and in support of a radical extension of the electorate. Several scholars have recently suggested that John Locke himself wished to extend positive political rights to all men, although he did not make any explicit statements about the franchise he favoured in England. In stressing the natural equality of all men and in demonstrating that every man has property in his life, liberty, person, actions, and possessions (however limited), Locke was implicitly acknowledging the right of all men to possess the vote.[31] Other scholars have maintained that Locke was consistently *inclusive* in his definitions of who qualified for full membership of the political nation. By claiming that all men had a natural right to life, liberty and property, and by interpreting property to include every man's own labour and his own person, Locke was implying that all men had a legitimate claim to active political rights. It has also been suggested that Locke was prepared to include all men, even domestic servants and dependent wage labourers, as full participants in political society and he would have excluded only children, slaves and lunatics.[32]

Other radical Whig theorists of the late seventeenth century, including Algernon Sidney, James Tyrrell, John Toland and John Trenchard, were more forthcoming than Locke on precisely which men were qualified to be full and active members of political society. They, however, restricted positive political rights to the property-owning minority. When they used the term 'the people' or 'free men', they invariably meant those men who owned sufficient property to be economically independent of other men. They were quite content to restrict the franchise to the freeholders in the counties and to merchants, shopkeepers and master craftsmen in the towns.[33] One radical Whig went so far in 1701 as to claim:

It is owned, that all governments are made by man, and ought to be made by those men who are owners of the territory over which the government extends. It must likewise be confessed, that the FREEHOLDERS of England are owners of the English territory, and therefore have a natural right to erect what government they please.[34]

Demands for a massive extension of the electorate were not voiced until the later eighteenth century, but, long before this, it is possible to detect a growing recognition that all men deserved to possess positive political rights. Without explicitly campaigning for an extended franchise, a number of critics of the existing constitution were prepared to claim that all men had an equal right to freedom and a right to scrutinise the actions of those in power.[35] One critic of Sir Robert Walpole claimed that every man had 'an equal right to nominate the makers and executors of the laws, which are the guardians of person and property'.[36] By the early 1740s several opposition spokesmen were maintaining that even the 'meaner sort', and not just the electorate, had the right to instruct MPs on their conduct in the House of Commons. This was because the actions of the legislature affected every man and so all men had the right to concern themselves with the decisions taken by parliament. Even poor men paid taxes and contributed to the support of the state and hence such men had a right to take an interest in how they were governed.[37] It is, in fact, possible to detect the emergence of the concept of 'no taxation without representation' in Britain, before it was articulated so much better by the American colonists and the British radicals of the later eighteenth century. Certainly, by the early 1760s, James Burgh wanted to see the franchise extended to all those who paid taxes to a specified amount and, by 1766, another radical came close to justifying universal manhood suffrage on the basis that every man was taxed and hence every man was entitled to the vote.[38]

By the late eighteenth century a whole host of political writers and organisations were demanding a radical extension of the franchise. Almost all radicals agreed that God had created all men equal in the sense that they all possessed 'the same senses, feelings and affections to inform and influence; the same passions to activate; the same reason to guide; the same moral principles to restrain; and the same free will to determine all alike.'[39] A high proportion of radical propagandists were either Dissenters or liberal Anglicans, who were engaged in a prolonged campaign for religious toleration and who based their demands on the natural right of all men to enjoy liberty of conscience. While the campaign for religious liberty often took precedence, spokesmen such as Joseph Priestley and Richard Price insisted that religious freedom could only be secured and defended if men also possessed the positive political right to choose and judge those who are in positions of authority. It was essential that all men should be free both to judge and to legislate for themselves in matters of religion and politics.[40]

While they all claimed that the franchise should be extended, radical reformers justified their demands in different ways. Some, most notably John Cartwright, Obadiah Hulme and Catharine Macaulay, insisted that in the distant Anglo-Saxon past it had been the historic right of all Englishmen to elect their parliamentary representatives. They claimed that according to the principles of England's ancient constitution all men had enjoyed positive political rights, but that these had been lost at the Norman Conquest. English history from 1066 was the story of a continuous struggle to regain these lost rights. The Glorious Revolution had witnessed a partial victory only and much more needed to be done to restore the full and positive political rights of Englishmen.[41] Other radicals, especially Richard Price and Thomas Paine, appealed to the doctrine of natural rights as the basis of their demands for active political rights in civil society. It seems quite clear, as Isaac Kramnick has argued, that John Locke's ideas on natural rights and the original contract made a dramatic and decisive comeback among the radicals of the late eighteenth century.[42] Locke's political ideas were interpreted in a more straightforward fashion and they were now used explicitly to defend a radical extension of the franchise. It was confidently asserted that the state of nature was an actual historical experience in which primitive man had enjoyed equal liberty. In this golden age most men had been naturally benevolent and their reason had been uncorrupted. Only the corrupt designs of a few powerful men had rendered the creation of civil government a pressing necessity. The original contract which established civil government had guaranteed to preserve the universal, natural and inalienable rights of all men, including the positive right to a voice in the legislative process. Unfortunately, the original democratic institutions of civil society had been corrupted and undermined by a selfish minority. In order to recover their positive freedom, men must return to the original principles of civil society and reclaim the legitimate political equality which they had once enjoyed.[43] Thomas Paine, in particular, was conscious of the fact that appeals to the historic rights of Englishmen were a poor basis on which to demand an extension of the franchise. He recognised that the historical evidence supported the conservative claim that there had always been a propertied franchise, so he preferred to reject an appeal to history. He preferred to go back to original natural rights in order to justify what ought to be done and he also insisted that each age had the right to establish whatever political system would most satisfy its needs.[44]

Paradoxically, many radicals, whether they appealed to natural rights or the ancient constitution in order to portray a golden age in the distant past, also believed in the possibility of unlimited future progress.[45] Joseph Priestley, for example, believed that it was the intention of Divine Providence to bring everything to perfection by degrees. He believed that enlightenment, truth and liberty would all progress, enabling man to master his environment and create a new world in which all men were equal. The French Revolution encouraged him to have a millennial vision that a new world was at hand.[46] Richard Price also believed that the full potential of man's God-given reason could be achieved only if men were granted the fullest possible political freedom. Progress therefore depended upon an equal political right to self-determination. The outbreak of the French Revolution also convinced Price that a new age of liberty was at hand and that oppression was being rapidly extinguished.[47]

A few radicals rejected both the appeal to historic English liberties and to universal natural rights. They appealed instead to the test of utility. William Godwin's belief that a democratic republic was the best system of government rested on the assumption that it was the form of government most likely to achieve the greatest general good.[48] Jeremy Bentham was even more scathing in his denunciation of natural rights and even more committed to the utilitarian ethic of the greatest happiness of the greatest number. He claimed that every man prefers his own interest to that of other people and that he was likely to be the best judge of his own interest. If every individual is the best judge of his own interest then all individuals together must be considered the best judges of the public interest. The only way to ensure that a government served the proper end of government – that is, to promote the greatest happiness of the greatest number of subjects – was to allow every man to judge that government and to give all men the right to choose their representatives in the supreme legislature. In Bentham's opinion, therefore, political liberty was to be promoted because its consequences were beneficial. By the early 1790s he was coming to the conclusion that the demand for universal manhood suffrage could be justified on utilitarian grounds, but he had not yet articulated his views in the public prints.[49]

Appeals to natural rights, to the ancient constitution and to utilitarian values all encouraged and justified the radical campaign for an extension of positive political rights. Not all those who advocated such political reforms were convinced, however, that this must necessarily mean conceding the vote to *all* adult males. Obadiah Hulme and James Burgh both advised extending the franchise only to those who paid rates and other specific taxes.[50] Both Richard Price and Catharine Macaulay were prepared to exclude paupers and domestic servants from the franchise because they were not sufficiently independent and lacked that firm stake in society which they would actively defend.[51] Joseph Priestley argued that the right to vote should be annexed to educational qualifications of some kind. He proposed a literacy test which must be passed before any man could claim the right to vote.[52] In Christopher Wyvill's view, those in favour of parliamentary reform should enlist the support

> not of that class at the lower end of society, many of whom wish for universal suffrage only to abuse it, but of those middle classes, who have some education, who have some property and some character to preserve, and who probably would prefer some limitation of the right of suffrage, as more friendly to peace, to order, and even to rational liberty.[53]

William Belsham also was not convinced that all men should have an equal and inherent right to share in the power of government. While he accepted the equality of men in a state of nature, he claimed that the distribution of positive political rights in civil society was chiefly a question of utility. It must be carefully calculated whether it would bring to society the greatest number of advantages and the greatest sum of human happiness:

> The grand axiom of equitable government is this – that as all men are ultimately equal, all civil or political equality must rest upon the basis of public utility. If then any class of men be disqualified, in a moral view, by extreme ignorance, gross venality, abject dependence, or any other cause, from exercising the privilege of voting in the elections of those who are to guide the great concerns of the community, they have no more right to complain of the injustice or hardship of not being permitted to nominate the rulers of the state than of the injustice of not being allowed to rule the state in person.[54]

There were, however, other radicals who were prepared to argue that all men, irrespective of their social status and economic position, ought to have the vote. In John Cartwright's view the franchise should be attached to the person and not to the property of a man. Poverty was no justification for stripping a man of his natural right to elect his governors. Indeed, labour itself was a species of property, as Locke had recognised long ago and, hence, all men possessed a property qualification to vote. Cartwright, therefore, suggested that all men over the age of eighteen should have the vote because they all paid taxes of some kind:

> The first and most natural idea which will occur to any unprejudiced man, is, that every individual of them, whether possessed of what is vulgarly called property, or not, ought to have a vote in sending to parliament those men who are to act as his representatives; and who, in an especial manner, are to be the guardians of public freedom; in which, the poor, surely, as well as the rich have an interest. ... All are by nature free; all are by nature equal: freedom implies choice; equality excludes degrees in freedom. All the Commons, therefore, have an equal right to vote in the election of those who are to be the guardians of their lives and liberties.[55]

Cartwright justified his claims by reference to England's ancient constitution, whereas other radicals reached the same conclusion on the basis of an appeal to natural rights. They argued that men voluntarily agreed to the creation of civil society and civil government in order the better to safeguard their natural rights. In deciding to convert their natural rights into civil liberties, they deliberately preserved their right to influence the choice and decisions of those who were to govern them. Even after agreeing to submit to the authority of civil government all men retained their right to mould and supervise the government placed over them. They continued to possess the right to elect those who could pass laws on their behalf. If any man was denied the right to choose his governors, he was little more than a slave: 'He is compelled to obey laws, made without his consent, given either personally, or by his representative: he, therefore, wears the distinguishing, humiliating badge of a bondman.'[56] In Thomas Paine's opinion all men must possess the franchise if they are to protect their natural right to preserve their life, liberty and property:

> The right of voting for representatives, is the primary right by which other rights are protected. To take away this right, is to reduce man to a state of slavery, for slavery consists in

being subject to the will of another, and he that has not a vote in the election of representatives is in this case.[57]

Universal manhood suffrage was supported by many other radical propagandists, including John Jebb, David Williams, Daniel Isaac Eaton and Mary Wollstonecraft, and it was one of the principal demands for reform put forward by the Westminster Association, the Society for Constitutional Information and the London Corresponding Society and other radical clubs of the 1790s. None the less, there are good grounds for accepting Isaac Kramnick's conclusion that the vast majority of reformers in the late eighteenth century wanted the educated middle classes to govern and expected the poor to follow their lead.[58] There is certainly plenty of evidence to suggest that only a minority of them could be classed as full and unequivocal democrats. Joseph Priestley believed that the progressive middling orders of society were the proper representatives of the people and the natural rulers of the country. He assumed, without questioning the premise, that the interests of the middling and lower orders were the same. He praised the industrious classes and tended to believe that poverty was the natural result of idleness and failure.[59] Richard Price supported the notion of popular sovereignty, but he did not expect authority to be exercised solely by that part of the legislature elected by the people.[60] James Burgh expected MPs to be men of ability, education and character drawn from the prosperous landed, commercial and professional classes.[61] James Mackintosh expected the multitude to 'value the superiority of enlightened men' and to 'retain a sufficient consciousness of ignorance to preclude rebellion against their dictates'.[62] Even John Cartwright, a supporter of universal manhood suffrage, expected the voters to elect men of birth and station to the House of Commons and he referred to MPs as an 'elective aristocracy'.[63] John Thelwall, normally ranked among the most determined radicals of the 1790s, also had reservations about instituting a genuinely democratic system of government. Restore to men their natural rights, he claimed, and they would learn to exercise them properly. Yet Thelwall never expected the poor ever to become sufficiently qualified to govern or to hold important political office. He insisted that government of any sort was only necessary because very few men were qualified to rule themselves or to choose good representatives. While, therefore, he supported a government of the people, Thelwall never envisaged a government by the people. He expected the lower orders to follow the lead of enlightened men from the middle and upper ranks of society.[64] Indeed, at times, he feared that democracy might actually obstruct progress. Like Godwin he argued that the voice of the majority was not necessarily the voice of truth and he insisted that the majority had no right to suppress the opinions of the minority.[65]

The democratic leanings of nearly all the reformers and radicals stopped short of advocating the positive political rights of women. Adult females were regarded as mere appendages of men and as existing on the same level as children or domestic servants. They were entirely dependent on their male superiors and hence were incapable of exercising the rights of an independent citizen. John Cartwright argued that women had no right to representation in parliament:

> women being by nature unable to qualify for and to perform various labours of magistracy and office in civil government, and of serving as the military defenders of their country, which are equally duties appertaining to dominion, and necessary to the preservation of political liberty, their right to the latter falls to the ground.[66]

John Longley claimed that nature fitted only men for public activity, whereas women were best fitted for domestic occupations.[67] Even Mary Wollstonecraft, who was devoted to improving the social status and economic condition of women, admitted that, so long as women remained in a position of subordination and dependence, they would remain unfit to play a full, active and equal role in public life. Women, in her view, certainly had the potential for full rationality and equal moral responsibility, but, until their social and economic inferiority was redressed, they could not expect to possess the same active political rights as men. She therefore refrained from campaigning for votes for women, though she did hint that she might do so at a future date 'for I really think that women ought to have representatives instead of being arbitrarily governed without having any direct share allowed them in the deliberations of government.'[68] Thomas Spence went further. At first he made a distinction between fully active citizens (men) and proprietary citizens with rights to an equal share in the revenues of society (women and children). Later he conceded that women should be given the vote, but not an active role in public life because of the delicacy of their sex.[69] A few other radicals were also prepared to give the vote to women, including George Phillips and Thomas Cooper, while an anonymous contributor to *The Cabinet*, published in Norwich, argued unequivocally for adult female suffrage and even for the right of women to sit in parliament and to hold important public offices. Yet even this radical recognised that most men would laugh his arguments out of court.[70]

Most radicals were also content to limit their political demands to a reform of the process by which the people elected their representatives to the House of Commons. They had no wish to abolish monarchy, aristocracy or the hereditary right to rule. James Burgh, Richard Price and John Cartwright, for example, all explicitly denied that they wished to undermine monarchical government or planned to abolish aristocratic privileges.[71] By the 1790s, however, a few radical theorists were prepared to launch a forthright attack on aristocratic privileges and hereditary government. Titles, honours and special privileges could not be tolerated in a society which desired to treat all men as political equals. Neither the monarchy nor the House of Lords could be defended on any rational principle and so they must be cast aside by the march of progress. John Oswald bitterly attacked all hereditary distinctions and concluded that:

> in a State really free, a privileged caste of men cannot possibly exist; for it could never enter into the minds of free people to establish so absurd a barrier between man and man. In a free state, there can be but one class of men, which is that of citizen; as there is but one will, which is that of the people.[72]

Other radicals endorsed this view, but it was Thomas Paine who revealed himself as the most determined advocate of a democratic republic. In his view, there could be no justice in a political system which tried to create hereditary legislators out of a tiny minority of the population. A free people would never willingly set up a monarchy or approve of an hereditary aristocracy. These institutions could have been established only by force or fraud, at the expense of the political rights of the rest of mankind. The present British constitution was therefore corrupt, expensive and unjust and it ought to be abolished.[73]

Paine was determined that every man should enjoy the same positive political rights. The possession of wealth or titles was no proof of moral worth and poverty was not evidence of the lack of it. Every man had his person, his liberty and the fruits of his labour to preserve and so every man deserved the same political right to influence the making of the laws under which he lived.[74] William Godwin reached a similar conclusion by a different route. Although he stressed a man's duties rather than his rights and although he did not support organised campaigns for political reform, he insisted nevertheless that there could be no equity or justice in a society which conferred special privileges or hereditary honours on particular categories of men or which denied other men their right to influence directly the decisions of all their legislators and all those in positions of authority:

> The most insignificant individual ought to hold himself free to animadvert upon the decisions of the most august assembly; and other men are bound in justice to listen to him, in proportion to the soundness of his reasons, and the strength of his remarks, and not for any necessary advantage he may derive from rank or exterior importance.[75]

By the late eighteenth century advanced radical views on the positive political rights of man had progressed to the stage where inherited political power was condemned and all men were deemed to possess an equal right to express their political opinions and to vote for their representatives in parliament. Such advanced radicals were often convinced that the summit of political liberty would be reached when all men were given the same *opportunity* of exercising a positive political influence on the decision-making processes of the state. Few of them wished to go beyond a demand for political equality. Indeed, they explicitly denied that their campaign, even for universal manhood suffrage, was the prelude to demands for social and economic reforms. They denied that they had any levelling ambitions. The radicals of Sheffield protested:

We demand equality of rights, in which is included equality of representation; ... We are not speaking of that visionary equality of property, the practical assertion of which would desolate the world, and replunge it into the darkest and wildest barbarism; but that equality we claim is, to make the slave a man, the man a citizen, and the citizen an integral part of the state; to make him a joint sovereign, and not a subject.[76]

The radicals of Liverpool distributed a handbill, entitled *EQUALITY*, which insisted:

The rule is not 'let all mankind be perpetually equal'. God and nature have forbidden it. But 'let all mankind start fair in the Race of life.' The *inequality* derived from successful enterprise is the result of superior industry and good fortune an *inequality* essential to the very existence of society.[77]

Many radicals, however, had long argued that political equality was impossible until all men had sufficient reason and judgement to exercise their positive rights properly. Rational argument and accurate information were seen to be essential to political progress. This led all radicals to stress the importance of educating the people, at least in the sense of fully informing the people about political matters and encouraging the free and rational discussion of political questions. William Godwin was perhaps the radical most convinced of the connection between the spread of reason and knowledge and the advance of democracy, but he refused to encourage the formation of debating societies and he opposed the creation of a state education system because he feared both types of organisation might seek to impose views rather than open minds.[78] Most other radicals sought to educate the people in political matters by using the press and a whole range of clubs and societies. A few went further than this and pressed for the provision of more education for the poor. Like Godwin, Joseph Priestley feared a state system of education, but he did encourage parents to educate their children and he did approve of Sunday schools.[79] Thomas Cooper, however, was prepared to advocate a national system of liberal education so that the ordinary people would learn how best to improve their conditions. A lack of education had kept the people in ignorance and had prevented them from enquiring into abuses and discussing remedies for their grievances. Until a system of public education was created the middling and lower orders should set up their own clubs and societies for the express purpose of encouraging political discussion and disseminating ideas and information. By these means the people might become more fully informed of their political rights and of the political privileges to which all men were entitled.[80] George Dyer not only wanted the government to provide a system of education, but suggested that rich and poor should attend the same schools because this experience would help to equalise all and exalt all.[81]

A handful of radicals went further still and argued that political equality was impossible in a society where gross economic inequality was allowed to persist. They maintained that mass poverty was in fact the direct consequence of the existing political system in which corruption enriched the few and oppressed the many. In a society which allowed great disparities of wealth, clearly unconnected with differences in ability or merit, the rich could sustain their privileged position only by arbitrary and oppressive actions. They could deny the poor the full exercise both of their civil liberties and their positive political rights by using their own wealth to corrupt and manipulate all the executive, judicial and legislative institutions of the state. Thomas Paine was confident that political reforms would permanently alter this unsatisfactory state of affairs. He believed that extensive political reforms would so change the nature of government that economic oppression would be significantly reduced. He was convinced that a democratic government would save considerable sums of money by eliminating the enormous costs of a corrupt court, a parasitic aristocracy, a bloated bureaucracy and an unnecessarily large army and navy. These savings would allow the government to reduce the level of taxes paid by the poor, while taxes on the rich could be used to provide a whole variety of grants and social welfare payments to improve the conditions of the labouring classes.[82]

John Oswald, William Ogilvie and a few other radicals suggested ways in which a democratic government could use waste and common land to help to improve the condition of the poor,[83] but only Thomas Spence maintained that this was to approach the question of the relationship between democracy and economic reforms from the wrong angle. In his view, even the most extensive political reforms would not lead to any significant improvement in the condition of the poor because, so long as gross inequalities of wealth persisted, the rich would always possess the means of oppressing the poor. Convinced that extensive political rights alone could never prevent the rich from oppressing the poor, he argued that the way to full democracy did not lie along the road to parliamentary reform, but along the route to economic equality. For Spence the real source of power was land and until this was placed under the firm control of all citizens there could be no real political equality. The achievement of democracy depended upon first securing the common ownership of land and the more equal distribution of wealth. Spence's famous Land Plan, which was promoted in nearly all his numerous publications, urged the elimination of private ownership of land and other natural resources. He wanted these to be placed under the control of parochial corporations involving all those who lived in the parish. The land and natural resources of the parish would be rented out to the highest bidders. Part of the money so raised would be used for the limited expenses of government and justice, and for public works. The rest would be shared out equally among every man, woman and child in the parish. Under this system excessive wealth and power could no longer be accumulated and dire poverty would be eliminated. Spence favoured extensive civil rights, defended popular sovereignty and the right of resistance, and wanted all citizens to have an equal voice in the decision-making processes of the community, but his vision of a democratic republic was predicated on first creating a social system in which there would be no private property in land and no oppression of the poor by the rich.[84] Although his scheme was impractical, and even eccentric, it took the debate on political rights into new territory which was to be explored more fully in the nineteenth century.

6 Radical Ideas and Popular Politics before Wilkes

Historians interested in the study of popular politics and in the development of political radicalism have, not surprisingly, paid relatively little attention to the period between the Glorious Revolution and the accession of George III. Extra-parliamentary movements dedicated to the radical reform of the constitution did not exist in the early eighteenth century and did not develop until the era of the American and French revolutions. Historians interested in the politics of the first half of the eighteenth century have largely been preoccupied with the rage of party, the rise of oligarchy and the growth of political stability. Much recent work on this period has stressed the conservative nature of the Revolution Settlement, has traced the dominance in parliament and in the constituencies of parties led by the propertied elite, and has revealed the means by which a narrow oligarchy, proclaiming a rather conservative Whiggism, came to monopolise executive power and to exercise very considerable influence over parliament.

This preoccupation with party rivalry and with the growth of oligarchy in the eighteenth century is entirely understandable. These were clearly the most important and the most significant political developments between the Glorious Revolution and the early 1760s. None the less, in recent years, a few historians have been prepared to challenge this heavy concentration on high politics and this concern with the political activities of the ruling oligarchy. These scholars have insisted on the need to appreciate the efforts of those who resisted the growth of oligarchy and of those who laid the foundations for the rapid flowering of radical activity in the later 1760s.[1] Their research has shown that in the earlier eighteenth century the roots of a radical ideology were nourished, a political platform critical of the ruling oligarchy was built up, and the means of enlisting popular support for radical change were beginning to be developed and exploited. A large-scale and sustained radical moment failed to appear, but the essential elements of such a political

movement – ideology, platform, organisation and popular support – can certainly be detected in the early eighteenth century.
Their potential was not fully developed at this time, however,
and the different elements were never properly integrated until
later in the century. A radical ideology stressing universal and
inalienable natural rights had appeared in the late seventeenth
century, but it was many more decades before support for these
natural rights was translated into demands for positive political
rights. The opposition platform in early Hanoverian Britain did
learn to challenge the ruling oligarchy on many fronts, but it
failed to rid itself of its attachment to a propertied franchise and
it was too cautious to commit itself to a demand for universal
manhood suffrage. The harnessing of the middling orders
behind this opposition platform was occasionally achieved in
the earlier eighteenth century, but the attachment of the middling orders to a radical platform required the full developments of a bourgeois culture which was just beginning to
emerge at this time. Moreover, these various sources of radicalism remained disparate elements before the later eighteenth
century. The doctrine of universal and inalienable natural rights
appealed to only a small coterie of radical Whig intellectuals,
who were mainly active in the 1690s. This doctrine was too radical for the Tory and Country elements which played such a
large part in developing a sophisticated critique of the corrupt
tactics and authoritarian tendencies of the ruling oligarchy in
early Hanoverian Britain. For its part, this opposition campaign
only occasionally rallied mass support from the people 'out-of-
doors'. During the earlier eighteenth century the middling
orders and, to a lesser degree, the lower orders were becoming
increasingly disenchanted with the policies and political tactics
of the patrician elite and they were also beginning to develop
their own forms of political organisation, but they did not adopt
the doctrine of natural rights before the late eighteenth century
and they had not yet fully absorbed the political programme of
the parliamentary opposition.

I THE ROOTS OF A RADICAL IDEOLOGY

The Tories, who still made up a majority of the political nation
after the Glorious Revolution, remained attached to a

sophisticated ideology of order until well into the eighteenth century. Although most Tories reluctantly accepted William III in the place of James II, they did not readily abandon their support for the doctrines of divine right, indefeasible hereditary succession, non-resistance and passive obedience. Ranged against such notions however was a significant body of Whigs whose commitment to limited monarchy, the rights of parliament and the rule of law made even the most conservative of them appear to be dangerous radicals in the eyes of the Tories. A minority of these Whigs did develop an even more radical ideology, while John Locke, the most intellectually sophisticated of them all, advanced ideas which were inherently revolutionary. The natural rights ideology of late eighteenth-century radicalism could undoubtedly trace its origins to the Whigs of a century earlier and to the radical Whigs and to John Locke in particular.

The ideology of the mainstream Whigs of the late seventeenth century was certainly more liberal than that of their Tory opponents. All genuine Whigs rejected absolute and arbitrary monarchy and they insisted that the authority of the monarch must be limited by the power of parliament, especially in matters of legislation and revenue raising. In their view ultimate sovereignty lay not with the monarch alone, but was located in a combined legislature of King, Lords and Commons. The Whigs also claimed that all subjects should possess certain civil liberties, chiefly the rights to life, liberty and property, which no government could infringe without due process of law. In the last resort subjects could forcibly resist an arbitrary tyrant who sought to subvert the constitution and who endeavoured to destroy the essential liberties of the subject. In making such claims the Whigs mainly appealed to England's ancient constitution and to the traditional rights of Englishmen. They did not claim to be demanding new rights or to be seeking a radical overhaul of the constitution. Indeed, most Whigs regarded as dangerous and absurd the notion that the labouring poor should have any voice in the decision-making processes of the state. The poor might be allowed to enjoy the benefits of the rule of law under a limited monarchy, but they must be denied the positive right to choose their governors or to supervise the conduct of those in positions of authority. The full and positive rights of citizenship therefore were restricted to men of property. They alone were regarded as possessing the education, the leisure and the economic independence needed to cultivate those civic virtues which were required by those men who deserved to be entrusted with executive or legislative authority.[2]

While the majority of Whigs developed a liberal ideology which was essentially aristocratic rather than democratic, a small coterie of advanced Whig intellectuals did propagate a much more radical ideology which was designed to confer, or at least could be construed as conferring, more extensive political rights on the mass of the adult male population. These radical Whigs assumed that all men were naturally equal in the eyes of God, that God had conferred upon them extensive and inalienable natural rights, and that the only legitimate forms of government were established by consent and must be based on the ultimate sovereignty of the people. Men only agreed to accept the authority of civil government in return for the protection of their natural and inalienable rights to life, liberty and property. Whenever a government sought to infringe these rights, by punishing criminals or raising taxes for example, then it must secure the consent of the community for such measures. This consent could be most readily obtained when the legislature incorporated some kind of representative assembly. Should the civil government betray the trust placed in it, through sustained action of a tyrannical or arbitrary nature, then the people were absolved of their duty to obey and were free to resist the government in order to defend their inalienable natural rights. They could force the government to return to the terms of the original contract or they could set up a new civil government following the dissolution of the old.

Clearly, the radical Whigs claimed rights whose implications, in the context of the times, were revolutionary. They insisted that all men possessed natural rights, that civil government must be based on some form of contract, that subjects must consent to decisions which affected their natural rights, and that, since ultimate sovereignty lay with the people, they could forcibly resist an illegitimate exercise of power by those whom the community had entrusted with authority. Perhaps most revolutionary of all was the notion that civil government was an artificial construct, made by man and sustained or undermined by human action. Civil government was not created by divine authority and religious sanctions did not dictate the nature of a subject's submission or the extent of his duties. Put in these terms, it might be concluded that the radical Whigs favoured a democratic form of government. It is not clear, however, how far this was indeed the case since the radical Whigs of the late seventeenth century did not always spell out the full implications of their ideology and modern commentators remain divided on how best to interpret their writings. These Whigs certainly put forward political notions with considerable revolutionary potential even though this potential was not fully exploited until the late eighteenth century.

The radical Whigs wished to see men's natural rights converted into civil liberties. They hoped that this would have the effect of securing for every man his life (unless he committed some serious offence which justified execution), his liberty to think, speak, act and move as he wished (provided that, in doing so, he did not infringe the same rights of his fellow men) and the possession of his labour, property and estates (unless these were required, in the form of military service or taxes for example, in order to safeguard civil society itself). Many of the radical Whigs were also particularly anxious to extend freedom of conscience. Indeed, many of them were bitterly anti-clerical and they desired to strip the Established Church of all its political, economic and social power.[3] It has even been claimed that their radicalism was religious rather than political in both its intellectual origins and its overriding aims.[4] It can certainly be doubted whether the radical Whigs were genuine democrats who were determined to extend positive political rights, as distinct from negative civil liberties, to all men. When they used the term 'free men', most radical Whigs appear to have meant those men who owned sufficient property to be economically independent and they were quite ready to accept a propertied franchise which restricted the vote to a minority of the adult male population.[5]

Clearly, the radical Whigs of the late seventeenth century had propagated some advanced notions of the liberty of the subject, but only John Locke developed a highly theoretical and coherent political ideology with considerable revolutionary potential. Whereas most radical Whigs were content to locate sovereignty

in the combined legislature of King, Lords and Commons, John
Locke granted sovereignty to the legislature only so long as it
did not abuse the trust placed in it by the people upon the original creation of civil government. In Locke's view ultimate sovereignty lay with the whole community which had created civil
government and which could reclaim its original authority if its
natural rights were threatened. While most radical Whigs were
concerned simply to defend the actual decision to renounce
allegiance to James II, Locke was proclaiming the right of revolution whenever there was a calculated design to subvert the
constitution and to reduce the people to a state of servitude. In
these circumstances the community was released from all obligations to the civil government and was completely free to choose
whatever form of government best suited its needs.[6] Other
radical Whigs wished to restrict the right of resistance to men of
property,[7] but Locke was prepared to grant all men the right to
resist a government which betrayed its trust; though even he was
careful to suggest that it was a right which could be justified only
in an emergency when it became necessary to oppose manifest
acts of tyranny. It is not clear whether Locke wished to extend
positive political rights to all men because he did not make any
explicit statements about the franchise he favoured in England.
Some modern commentators have insisted that Locke maintained that only men of property consented to the original contract which created civil government and that he therefore
believed that only this minority of the community at large could
participate actively in the decision-making processes of the
state.[8] Recently, however, several scholars have stressed the
implicit radicalism of Locke's views on the question of who had
the right to elect the nation's representatives to the legislature.
James Tully has claimed that, in demonstrating that every man
has property in his life, liberty, person, actions and possessions
(however limited), Locke was implicitly extending the right to
vote to every adult male. Although he does not explicitly state
the criterion in the *Two Treatises*, Locke does assume that the
natural equality of *all* men should be the basis of discussions on
political representation.[9] Other commentators have also argued,
that whereas most of Locke's political associates were explicitly
exclusive in their definitions of who qualified for full membership of the political nation, he himself was consistently *inclusive*.
By claiming that all men had a natural right to life, liberty and

property, and by interpreting property to mean that every man had a property in his own labour and his own person, Locke was implying that all men had a claim to active political rights.[10] Locke therefore included all men, even servants and dependent wage labourers, as full participants in political society.[11]

Unfortunately, Locke did not make his radical views on the franchise explicit and so his views were not fully understood by his contemporaries. None the less, his views were certainly seen as too radical to be endorsed by the majority of the Whig party.[12] Though once regarded as *the* philosopher of the Whig party and as the principal defender of the Glorious Revolution, Locke has recently been located on the radical fringes of the Whig party and is now perceived as a rather neglected political philosopher in his own day. Few contemporaries quoted his political works with approval and even fewer might have done so had they interpreted his work in the radical manner of some recent commentators. None the less, it is going too far to suggest that Locke had no admirers in his own day or in the decades immediately following his death. The *Two Treatises* had appeared in three separate editions by 1700 and many of Locke's ideas were popularised in that highly influential pamphlet, *Political Aphorisms* (1690), which reappeared in 1709 as *Vox Populi, Vox Dei* and again in 1710 as *The Judgement of Whole Kingdoms and Nations*.[13] The contract theory was certainly debated in the late seventeenth and early eighteenth centuries.[14] What is much more significant, of course, is the way in which the radical potential in Locke's political ideology was appreciated and extended nearly a century later by such radicals as James Burgh, Richard Price, Joseph Priestley and Thomas Paine.[15] Locke's sophisticated ideas were interpreted in a straightforward literal fashion by late eighteenth-century radicals and his theoretical concepts were adopted as the ideological foundations for practical political reforms. The radicals of the later eighteenth century believed that they were merely reiterating Locke's views when they claimed that the doctrine of natural rights, the contract theory and the concept of popular sovereignty (which were all to be found in Locke's writings) were the ideological foundations of a democratic system of government and of such positive political rights as universal manhood suffrage, equal electoral districts and annual parliaments.

II   THE DEVELOPMENT OF A RADICAL PLATFORM

Although John Locke worked out an extended theoretical defence of natural rights in the late seventeenth century, he did not explicitly advocate radical political reforms such as universal manhood suffrage and no group of radical Whigs built up a political platform based on the demand for a fully democratic political system. None the less there were mainstream Whigs, radical Whigs and even Tories who supported an array of practical reforms which aimed to reduce the power of the executive and to promote the liberties of the subject. To sustain these efforts appeals were made to the evidence of history, to England's ancient constitution and to the traditional rights of Englishmen rather than to the natural rights of man. Within this more conservative intellectual framework, however, various propagandists did succeed in putting forward practical proposals for limiting the authority of the government, making the legislature more independent of the executive and more responsive to the people, and extending the rights of the subject.

Although the Revolution Settlement of 1689 was not a triumph for the radicals and was in many ways a compromise between the Whigs and the Tories, it is probably a mistake to regard it in too conservative a light. James II did lose his throne and the royal prerogative was criticised even if it was not significantly curtailed. The Declaration of Rights and the Bill of Rights did lay claim to some traditional liberties which the crown had not fully conceded in the past. These included criticisms of the crown's suspending and dispensing powers, the rejection of a standing army without the consent of parliament, the right to freedom of speech in parliament and the demand for frequent parliaments. It is true that increasingly thereafter the main body of Whigs readily accommodated themselves to a political system which was highly aristocratic and far from democratic. The more the leading Whigs came to enjoy the benefits of office, the more willing were they to endorse a relatively conservative political settlement which left real power in the hands of a narrow, propertied oligarchy. None the less, the establishment Whigs never entirely abandoned their former principles and they remained attached to a number of liberal policies. Even as the ruling oligarchy the

mainstream Whigs retained practical limits on the authority of
the monarch, supported regular sessions of parliament, paid
more than lip-service to the notion of government by consent,
and allowed most subjects considerable liberty of conscience
and freedom of expression. The establishment Whigs created
and ruthlessly exploited a vast system of patronage, but, by
accepting limits on the power of the executive and by acknowledging that they were governing free men, they had established a political context in which others could voice demands
for more radical political changes.

The radical Whigs had hoped to secure more constitutional
innovations in 1689. During the discussions on the nature of
the Revolution Settlement they put forward a number of
entirely new claims, including attacks on the monarch's
prerogative to summon and dissolve parliament at will, a proposal to give judges security of tenure during good behaviour
and a demand for full religious toleration for all Protestants.
There were also several schemes for limiting the power of the
executive and for increasing the authority of parliament. The
radical Whigs failed to carry through a fundamental revision of
the constitution in the wake of the political crisis of 1688, but
this does not mean that they ceased to exist or to propagate
their demands. Throughout the 1690s two radical Whig
groups, the 'Calves Head' republicans and the more aristocratic coterie who met at the Grecian Tavern, provided the
Whig cause with intellectual depth and political respectability.
These men waged a major campaign against a standing army
in 1697–9 and even helped to impose further limitations on
the crown in the Act of Settlement of 1701.[16] It is also possible
to detect radical Whig groups campaigning for political
reforms in 1705–6 and again in the early 1720s. None the less,
any serious investigation into the development of a radical
political platform before 1760 must examine not only the propaganda of those small coteries of radical Whigs who occasionally rose to political prominence, but must also explore the
programme of the Country and Tory opposition that campaigned throughout the early Hanoverian period for reduc-
tions in the power of the executive and the increased
independence of parliament.

Only occasionally during the period from 1688 to 1760 did a
Country *party* manifest itself and, even when such a party did

exist, it drew the bulk of its support from men who, on most issues, were Tories. Although a Country *party* rarely existed, a Country attitude and a Country interest, even perhaps a coherent Country ideology and platform, did have a continuous existence throughout the late seventeenth and earlier eighteenth centuries. Country policies were sometimes propagated by those radical Whigs who were disenchanted by the conservative nature of the Revolution Settlement and they were sometimes supported by malcontent Whigs who hoped such policies might be a means of pushing themselves into office, but they were mainly advanced by the bulk of the Tory party once it had been forced into the position of a permanent opposition by the Hanoverian succession and the triumph of the Whig oligarchy. For many years *The Craftsman* was at the centre of a formidable array of literary and journalistic talent that mounted a scathing attack on the corrupt political methods of Robert Walpole and his ministry. It is ironic that it was attacks such as these, largely mounted by the Tories, that built up the most effective indictment of executive authority and led the way to demands for constitutional change that were to be adopted by the radicals of the later eighteenth century. Thus, the Country ideology, with significant Tory backing, did much to show how royal patronage threatened to corrupt both parliament and people and first advocated many of the policies designed to curtail this patronage and to purify the constitution.[17]

The Country interest believed that Britain could enjoy the best system of government in the world if only the balanced constitution of King, Lords and Commons was safeguarded from the alarming threat posed to it by the growing patronage at the disposal of the executive. Whereas the royal prerogative had been successfully curtailed since 1689, a new, more insidious, danger had appeared in the form of crown patronage which could be used to corrupt both parliament and people. This patronage system had been created since 1689 by the financial revolution, by the deployment of large armies and navies, and by the growing bureaucracy needed to manage the national debt, to supply the armed forces and to raise the revenue needed for both. Crown patronage enabled the executive to build up a Court and Treasury party in parliament and to persuade peers and MPs to sell their political integrity and their political independence in return for places, promotion and profit. Fearing that the Court was approaching the position where it might count upon a subservient majority in parliament – a fear that was greatly exaggerated – the Country spokesmen attacked the sources of political corruption and propagated the ethic of civic virtue. Widespread and persistent criticisms were launched on the fraudulent practices of monied men involved in the whole system of public credit. Numerous bills were introduced to prevent many categories of placemen and pensioners from sitting in parliament and to disfranchise revenue officers. Frequent demands were made for a citizen militia to replace the large standing or professional army which was seen as a direct and indirect threat to the liberties of the subject. Armed force had been used against parliament in the past, but the Country opposition was more alarmed at the indirect consequences of a large standing army. The raising of the loans for war, the appointment of army officers and the awarding of contracts to supply the troops all threatened to combine to give the Court undue political influence over important sections of the political nation. Moreover, a nation which hired mercenaries to defend its liberties was corrupting its own public spirit. A nation which lost the willingness to defend itself had already surrendered its right to remain free.[18]

Efforts to curb crown patronage failed and so Country spokesmen were driven to consider other means of establishing the independence of parliament from Court influence. They were not prepared to endorse the genuinely radical notion of popular sovereignty, but they did propose a variety of measures designed to increase the electorate's influence over its representatives. Frequent appeals were made to the electors urging them to reject candidates who were courtiers, placemen, monied men or stockjobbers and to vote instead for men of large landed estates who could be trusted to preserve their own integrity and the liberties of the subject.[19] To reduce the costs of parliamentary elections (and hence the scope for corruption) and to make MPs more responsive to their constituents, Country propagandists campaigned for shorter parliaments and more frequent general elections. Some spokesmen went out of their way to remind the electorate that voters only delegated their authority to their MPs, but did not surrender it absolutely. Since MPs held their power in trust for the people, they were not free to sacrifice the liberties of the people in order to please the Court. In order to remind the MPs of their duties, voters were regularly urged to mount 'instruction' campaigns which were designed to pressurise their representatives into supporting Country measures.[20]

In addition to demands for more frequent elections and for the right of voters to instruct their MPs, radical Whig and Country propagandists occasionally suggested the need for changes in the system of parliamentary representation. These proposals sought to ensure the return of more independent and more honest country gentlemen rather than to increase the authority of the electorate. Shortly after the Glorious Revolution several radical Whigs complained about the over-representation of the poorer counties such as Cornwall and the decayed boroughs such as Old Sarum. They favoured a significant redistribution of seats from such constituencies to the rich counties and to the growing towns of the north and midlands.[21] Forty and fifty years later several Country propagandists condemned rotten boroughs and urged a redistribution of seats according to the contributions which counties and boroughs made to the land tax.[22] One opposition journal asked why rotten boroughs should return two MPs, when each member for Yorkshire represented 10 000 freeholders and when such towns as Birmingham and Leeds had no representation at all; and why Cornwall should return over forty MPs when Middlesex, London and Westminster together, with twenty times the population and one hundred times the wealth, elected a mere eight representatives.[23] Another journal advocated a radical redistribution of seats according to population and wealth. It suggested that the decaying boroughs of the south-west should be grouped together to form larger constituencies, while such towns as Birmingham, Manchester and Halifax should secure direct representation in parliament for the first time.[24]

Some radical Whigs and Country propagandists were prepared to consider other means of reforming the system of representation. John Wildman advocated the secret ballot as early as 1689[25] and this particular means of eliminating electoral corruption was revived by opposition spokesmen in the 1730s and 1740s.[26] There were also suggestions for changes in the franchise. Several radical Whigs advocated not an extension of the franchise to the propertyless masses, however, but urged instead a restriction of the franchise to the substantial £40 (instead of the existing 40 shilling) freeholders who were much less likely to succumb to bribes offered by parliamentary candidates.[27] This reform, and the others mentioned above, would have weakened the ruling oligarchy's ability to influence election results by the distribution of patronage and would have strengthened the Country interest by increasing the number of independent country gentlemen who would be returned as MPs for the rich counties and the large towns. These reforms, however, would not have greatly increased the political voice of the ordinary people because insufficient attention was paid to the question of improving the representation of the middling and lower orders by a radical extension of the franchise. Neither the radical Whigs nor the leading Country propagandists can be classed as genuine democrats interested in the equal representation of the people.

Demands for a radical extension of the franchise did not appear as an important element in the opposition platform until the late 1770s, but, long before this, it is possible to detect a growing recognition in radical circles that all men deserved to enjoy active political rights. As we have seen, although he did not make his position plain, John Locke did imply that all men should enjoy positive political rights in civil society. Without explicitly campaigning for an extended franchise, a number of radical Whigs did claim that all men had an equal right to freedom and had the right to scrutinise the actions of the government under which they lived.[28] As early as 1701 one radical Whig suggested that the number of voters in certain boroughs should be increased, though not to the extent of enfranchising those without property.[29] In 1732 one critic of Robert Walpole claimed that every man had 'an equal right to nominate the makers and executors of the laws, which are the guardians of person and property'.[30] By the early 1740s several Country spokesmen were arguing that even the 'meaner sort' and not simply the electorate had the right to instruct MPs. This was because the actions of the government concerned every man and so every man had the right to concern himself with the decisions taken by parliament. Even poor men paid taxes and contributed to the support of the government and hence such men had the right to take an interest in government.[31] Here were the beginnings of the concept of 'no taxation without representation' and it was being articulated in England long before it was raised by the American colonists. By the early 1760s James Burgh wanted to see the franchise extended to all those who paid taxes to a specified amount and another radical came close to justifying universal manhood suffrage on the basis that every man was taxed and hence every man was entitled to representation.[32]

Clearly, while critics of the ruling oligarchy in early Hanoverian Britain concentrated their attentions on the need to preserve civil liberties, discussions about extending the political rights of subjects were also being articulated and these were laying the basis for the radical demands of the later eighteenth century. Even more surprising was the occasional reference to the economic rights of the poor that pointed to radical demands much further into the future. A few commentators recognised that oppression not only took political forms, but could also involve the abuse of the economic power which the rich could exert over the poor. There was some discussion of the need to redistribute property more equally among the whole population if political liberty was to be effectively safeguarded.[33] There was the occasional condemnation of oppressive employers who refused to pay their labourers wages necessary to the upkeep of themselves and their families and who used the law against those who would not submit to such arbitrary conduct. It was suggested that efforts to reduce the wages of the poor would be destructive of both individual liberty and the prosperity of the nation at large. Food and clothes belonged of right to all industrious men and therefore the price of labour should correspond to the price of such necessities and care should be taken not to load unjust taxes upon the poor.[34]

III POPULAR POLITICS: ORGANISATIONS AND METHODS

It was not until the later eighteenth century that there appeared an extra-parliamentary political movement which proclaimed its attachment to a radical ideology and stood on a radical platform. Even then this movement found little support inside parliament and it could only occasionally enlist mass support out-of-doors. The political groupings who criticised the ruling oligarchy and

who sought some reform of the constitution in the late
seventeenth and early eighteenth centuries however were both
smaller and less permanent than the radical movement of the late
eighteenth century. At various times small coteries of radical
Whigs campaigned for effective restrictions on the royal prerogative, while, more persistently, a Country opposition, drawing
the bulk of its support from the Tories, challenged the political
abuses and the corrupt tactics of the ruling oligarchy. Although
both radical Whigs and Country/Tory opposition failed to rally
mass support for a genuinely radical political programme, they
did learn to exploit the power of the press in order to propagate
their views. They also sought to rally the electorate behind their
demands by encouraging petitioning and instruction campaigns
and they learned to influence public opinion through their contacts with constituency clubs, pressure groups and even popular
demonstrations. Although the parliamentary opposition usually
succeeded in controlling and restraining the political demands
put forward by the middling and lower orders, they did, inadvert-
ently, help to create an extra-parliamentary force which would
later break free of control from above. Furthermore, social and
economic developments-throughout the nation were creating
potential support for constitutional reform that the radical Whigs
and Country propagandists never fully harnessed to their own
causes. It was left to the radicals of the later eighteenth century to learn how to enlist mass popular support behind their
programme of reform.

The arguments of radical Whigs and Country spokesmen
were disseminated by a burgeoning political press which
became increasingly critical of the ruling oligarchy and deeply
conscious of the liberties of the subject. Although rival groups
within the political elite sponsored publishers, printers and
journalists for their own ends in their struggle for power, they
also helped the press to play an important role in encouraging
popular involvement in national affairs. A substantial proportion of the public prints was devoted to political issues and
this intense debate helped to bring politics out of the
restricted arena of court and parliament. All forms of newspapers commented on politics and most adopted an ident-
ifiable political stance, especially during periods of intense
excitement. The press undoubtedly played a crucial role in
informing the people of the conduct of their rulers and in

acting as the principal medium for the articulation and distribution of popular protests against the government. The press often acted as the political instructor and as the political agent of those who wished to resist the growth of oligarchy. Its influence was undoubtedly greatest among the middling orders of London, but it also grew to be a significant force acting upon the merchants, shopkeepers, tradesmen and professional men of the large provincial towns.

Despite efforts by various ministries to control the press by Stamp Acts or by prosecutions for seditious libel, the authorities were unable to stem this tide of political propaganda. A burgeoning free press became a marked feature of the political life of the nation in the earlier eighteenth century. By the middle of the century there were several daily and tri-weekly newspapers in London and 40–50 newspapers in the provinces. The best and the most influential newspapers and periodicals in London, including the *Daily Post*, the *London Evening Post*, *The Craftsman*, and *The Monitor*, were vehicles for Country propaganda. No ministerial periodical could rival the influence of *The Craftsman*. No newspaper subsidised by the government was as popular as the *London Evening Post* which, from its launch in late 1727, was usually critical of the ministry. This influential newspaper played a major role in rallying public opinion against Walpole in 1733 and again from 1739 to 1742. During both crises it gave its readers the clear impression that the nation at large was united against Walpole.[35] The cheapest newspapers in London, especially the illegal unstamped prints, also invariably came down against the Whig governments of the early Hanoverian period. They tried to cash in on the anti-ministerial and anti-Hanoverian sentiments that existed at the lower social levels.[36] Despite Walpole's efforts to subsidise a pro-ministry press, his government generally lost the propaganda battle.[37] The fact that such a successful minister as Walpole, with strong backing at court and with a clear majority in parliament, believed it was necessary to spend large sums of money subsidising the publication and dissemination of political propaganda is a clear indication that he too recognised the need to win the hearts and minds of those outside parliament who read the public prints.

The choicest political items from the capital's press were often reprinted in the provincial press which grew in numbers and circulation, and increased its interest in politics, during the long ascendancy of Sir Robert Walpole. The provinces were therefore fed with a diet of political news about national affairs rather than with information about local matters. Many of the best provincial newspapers, including the *York Courant*, the *Newcastle Courant*, the *Exeter Journal*, the *Chester Courant*, the *Lancashire Journal*, the *Norwich Gazette*, *Farley's Bristol Newspaper*, the *Worcester Journal*, and *Jopson's Coventry Mercury*, were determined opponents of the ministry. Indeed, it seems clear that the majority of the provincial press was critical of the executive and sympathetic to the defence of liberty.[38] The *York Courant* was perhaps the most outspoken provincial critic of Walpole. From 1729 onwards it reprinted each week the leading political essay from *The Craftsman* and from 1739 it bitterly attacked Walpole's policies, rejoiced at his fall and then campaigned for his prosecution. In 1740, when the virulent press campaign against Walpole was in full swing, the Bishop of Chester complained to the Duke of Newcastle of

> the unwearied industry of some to poison the common people with ill thoughts of the Administration, with fair pretences of great respect to the King. This poison is, by my observation, chiefly conveyed by a course of newspapers dispers'd all over these and neighbouring parts. We have a printing press here at Chester, another at Manchester, another at Leeds, and other places, all under the direction of seditious and disloyal men, scattering their papers all over the countys at low prices. ... The authors pick their news out of the London prints, and take care to publish everything that is against the government, but give by half, or with some sneer, whatever is favourable to it.[39]

It seems clear that the majority of the provincial press and perhaps a majority of provincial readers of the press were hostile to the policies and methods of Walpole. In any local press war the newspaper espousing Country views was usually the victor. This was the case in Bristol, Chester, Newcastle upon Tyne, Nottingham, York and other towns. Only in Exeter, Northampton and Norwich did the pro-government newspaper prevail, but even these newspapers were sparing in their praise of Walpole. The provincial press generally, following the lead given by Country propaganda printed in London, published all the major arguments against oligarchy and corruption and disseminated the various radical proposals for constitutional and electoral reform. The major campaigns against Walpole in 1733 and 1739–42 were promoted across the country by the provincial press and the press gave a voice to popular opinion out-of-doors.

The demands of radical Whig and Country/Tory propagandists were also promoted by political organisations in the constituencies and by the sophisticated campaigns to rally the electorate behind them. Despite the growth of oligarchy and the spread of electoral patronage, a significant number of large and open constituencies continued to exist and in these the voters were never under the complete control of the propertied elite. As we have seen (in Chapter 1) elections were often bitterly contested in such large boroughs as London, Westminster, Southwark, Bristol, Norwich and Coventry, and in such populous counties as Yorkshire, Middlesex, Surrey, Kent, Norfolk and Essex. In the large boroughs, in particular, the electorate began to reject the leadership of the propertied elite and endeavoured to control its own representatives. As early as 1695 the Tories had set up a political society at the Castle tavern in the City of London. Known as the Centenary Club this society of professional men and retail traders later played an active part in encouraging popular resistance to Walpole's oligarchical policies in the City. In 1714–15 the City Whigs formed the Hanover Society, the most sophisticated political club of its day, in order to combat Jacobitism. Among its proposals was a scheme to extend the franchise to those men of property who were not freemen. In the 1720s and 1730s a political society meeting at the Half Moon tavern in the City coordinated the opposition of the London liverymen to the policies of Walpole. By the late 1730s a Society of Independent Electors had emerged in Westminster to combat oligarchy, while a second, more plebeian, group met at the Crown and Anchor tavern. Even outside the metropolitan area electors were beginning to establish their own independent political organisations. By the late 1730s there were two electoral clubs in Bristol, the Steadfast Society and the Union Society. The former was supported by many smaller, satellite clubs in the poorer parts of Bristol. Soon there were local clubs of independent electors in other towns, including the Bull Club in Cirencester, the Charter Club in Colchester, the Bean

Club in Birmingham and the Independent Electors Society in Coventry. These clubs monitored the parliamentary conduct of MPs and orchestrated popular resistance to aristocratic control in the larger constituencies. Hard-fought contests in such constituencies frequently involved the unenfranchised as well as those qualified to vote. There were violent demonstrations of popular opinion in numerous urban constituencies.[40]

The casting of votes in elections however was neither the most frequent nor the most important way in which the electors or organised opinion 'out-of-doors' could influence the behaviour and the decisions of the ruling oligarchy. When it was effectively organised popular opinion could persuade or pressurise parliament into taking decisions which would be to the advantage of those who united to propose them. Both the ministry and parliament could be influenced by petitions, by organised extra-parliamentary pressure groups and by nation-wide instruction campaigns. All subjects enjoyed the right to petition crown or parliament, not simply those men qualified to vote. Although electors were more likely to petition than those who were not enfranchised, borough petitions in particular were frequently signed by non-voters.

Indeed, some petitions came from urban areas which were not represented in parliament. In 1731, for example, several Lancashire MPs were pressurised into supporting a petition from Manchester, which was not a parliamentary constituency, requesting a popularly elected Board of Guardians for the town's workhouse.[41] As we have seen (in Chapter 2) it was always open to extra-parliamentary groups to approach individual MPs to present petitions on their behalf or to sponsor private bills. Remarkably well organised pressure groups, both economic and religious, were able to influence the policies of the government and the decisions taken by parliament. The West India interest[42] and nonconformist groups[43] were among the first to develop sophisticated organisations of this kind.

During periods of national political crisis extra-par-liamentary opinion went beyond the humble petition and the sophisticated lobbying campaign. Nationwide campaigns were mounted in an effort to dictate the conduct of MPs. In these coordinated and concerted movements petitions for the redress of grievances were combined with 'instructions' from constituents to their MPs, requesting them to vote in a particular way and to bring forward certain resolutions in parliament. In 1733 there was a vigorous national protest against Walpole's Excise Bill, while between 1739 and 1742 there was concerted extra-parliamentary pressure of this kind against Walpole's political conduct in general and his handling of the crisis with Spain in particular. Walpole himself claimed that these campaigns were instigated and orchestrated by the disaffected leaders of the parliamentary opposition.[44] Some historians have endorsed this claim, but this view ignores the substantial evidence which suggests that these campaigns were generated by genuine popular hostility to Walpole's policies.[45] The parliamentary opposition undoubtedly used the press to alert public opinion to the dangerous implications and alarming consequences of the government's conduct, but both the press war and the instruction campaigns had a natural appeal at constituency level.

In 1733 some petitions were formulated by opposition MPs and by meetings of the county gentry, but even these had an impact beyond their particular constituencies. Many of the 54 petitions (and this is a conservative estimate) had instigators who did not belong to the landed elite.[46] The lead in this almost unparalleled display of public anger was given in fact by London where the campaign was not organised by the city's parliamentary representatives. In the Common Council it was the Lord Mayor, John Barber, who promoted the resolution which instructed the city's MPs to vote against the Excise Bill. This initiative was taken up by the Court of Aldermen and supported by a broad coalition of tobacco and wine importers, Dutch and Hamburg merchants, linen drapers and brewers, and a substantial section of the middling liverymen. The general populace also rallied against the Excise Bill, parading wooden shoes through the streets, manhandling Walpole himself at the door of the House of Commons and burning him in effigy. London's lead was soon followed in Westminster, Southwark, Bristol, Liverpool, Nottingham, Newcastle and Exeter.[47] Instructions even came from constituencies such as Bath, Carlisle, Coventry, Harwich, Wigan and York that were represented by supporters of the government, not by opposition MPs. Eight towns, including Daventry and Towcester, also petitioned against the Excise Bill even though they were not parliamentary constituencies. There can be no doubt that much of this opposition came from the urban commercial classes; a sectional interest certainly, but a substantial one and one which appears on this occasion to have represented a very considerable body of extra-parliamentary opinion. The financial exactions of the Excise Bill and the army of investigative excise officers needed to enforce it aroused real hostility among the British people as a whole. Walpole's retreat on the issue did not immediately defuse the climate of excitement and bitterness. In the general election of 1734, when the Excise was the only significant issue, the government suffered over twenty defeats in the more open constituencies and in several counties the highest polls of the whole eighteenth century were recorded. Although Walpole was saved by the results in the rotten boroughs, the general election certainly registered a popular defeat for his administration.[48]

Between 1738 and 1742 Walpole was faced by an even more popular and broad-based anti-ministerial coalition. This extra-parliamentary opposition originated in hostility to the government's conduct of commercial negotiations with Spain, but it was soon extended into a general and sustained attack on the policies and the methods of Walpole's administration. Once again the lead was taken by London merchants, this time those who traded in Spanish American waters. On 3 March 1738 Micajah Perry, a London alderman and tobacco merchant, seconded by Sir John Barnard, presented a petition to the Commons from the London American and West India merchants condemning the Spanish attacks on British commerce and demanding a tougher response from Walpole's administration. Within weeks there was similar petitioning from Bristol, Liverpool and Glasgow and a well-orchestrated press campaign which drove the government onto the defensive. The convention which Walpole negotiated with Spain in 1739 confirmed the worst fears about his conciliatory policy and inaugurated a new wave of protests. Over the next few months the court Whigs lost control of the City of London, even of the Court of Aldermen. The independent opposition in London seized control of the city's political institutions, promoted a petition against the Spanish convention and delivered 'instructions' to the city's MPs on no fewer than five occasions by 1742. These instructions condemned Walpole's whole political system and adopted a programme of constitutional reform that included attacks on placemen in parliament, a large standing army in peace time, septennial parliaments and the veto possessed by the city's Court of Aldermen. There were demands for a vigorous inquiry into Walpole's mismanagement of public affairs and for the implementation of reforms which would eliminate political corruption.[49]

In this campaign London gave a lead to popular opinion throughout the country. The livery's instructions of October 1739, which called for the introduction of a Place Bill, were copied by 12 other boroughs and five counties. The resolutions of Common Council in June 1740 rallied at least 36 other constituencies, while the city's instructions of 1741–2 encouraged even more constituencies to follow this lead.[50] In Bristol the petty merchants, drapers and tobacconists of the Steadfast Society asked Edward Southwell, a candidate in the election of 1741, to pledge himself in support of a Place Bill, a reduction in the size of the army and the repeal of the Septennial Act.[51] In November 1742 the merchants and tradesmen of Exeter dispatched instructions to their two MPs requesting them to support constitutional reform and to refuse to grant supplies until concessions were forthcoming.[52] In Scotland, where the tiny electorate was usually dominated by aristocratic influence, instructions were sent from Edinburgh, Aberdeen, Stirling, Kincardine, Dumfriesshire, Ayrshire, Aberdeenshire, Lanarkshire and Ross.[53] In Edinburgh the instructions were drawn up by the merchant companies and such tradesmen's corporations as the surgeons, goldsmiths, skinners and weavers.[54] This wave of protests undoubtedly represented genuine popular hostility to Walpole's administration and it certainly had a significant impact on government and parliament. A contributor to *Common Sense* claimed that the electorate was the sovereign authority in the kingdom: 'If the electors of England should declare to you (the Parliament), you shall not make laws for us, we will do it ourselves: will any man say they may not do it?'[55] While rejecting such radical conclusions even the ministers themselves recognised the need to bow before this storm of popular resentment. The Duke of Newcastle acknowledged: 'If we go on despising what people think and say, we shall not have it long in our power to direct what measures shall be taken.'[56] Walpole himself confessed: 'If the City of London

showed their inclinations against him in this public manner
there was no standing against it, and he should think himself
bound to yield.'[57] He did yield to the clamour for war in 1739,
but his inability to prosecute this conflict successfully only
incited the public to greater fury. In the general election of
1741 most of the open constituencies and a majority of the
electorate voted against Walpole's candidates even though his
majority in seats was not entirely eroded. Walpole was
eventually hounded from office early in 1742, as much because
of public hostility out-of-doors as because of the greater
effectiveness of the opposition within parliament.

On other occasions extra-parliamentary campaigns were
able to force apparently strong administrations to change their
policies or their stance. In 1753, for example, the Pelham
administration passed the Jewish Naturalisation Act through
parliament with little difficulty and they clearly did not expect
much criticism out-of-doors. They were shocked at the extent
of opposition that this measure created. Over sixty individual
pamphlets were printed on the subject, numerous essays
appeared in newspapers and periodicals, a petition against it
was drawn up by the City of London, twelve formal protests
were made by county grand juries and municipal corporations,
and seventeen constituencies instructed their MPs to demand
the repeal of the act.[58] Public clamour and extra-parliamentary
pressure was on such a scale that the Pelham administration
feared the possible consequences in the general election due
to be fought in 1754. To forestall any electoral losses the
ministers decided to repeal the act in late 1753, only a few
months after passing it. The *London Evening Post* claimed that
this repeal 'shews the respect of the Legislature for the Public
Voice.'[59] The Earl of Hardwicke, the Lord Chancellor, admitted the truth of this observation when he confessed to the
House of Lords:

however much the people may be misled, yet in a free
country I do not think an unpopular measure ought to be
obstinately persisted in. We should treat the people as a
skilful and humane physician would treat his patient: if they
nauseate the salutary draught we have prescribed, we should
think of some other remedy, or we should delay admin-

istering the prescription till time or a change of circumstances has removed the nausea.[60]

Three years later, in late 1756, the administration led by the Duke of Newcastle was brought down, despite its parliamentary majority and the backing of the king, when public opinion was aroused by the loss of Minorca, and other military disasters. From July 1756 onwards the press played a major role in condemning the faults and weaknesses of ministers and in demanding an enquiry into the loss of Minorca.[61] A flood of pamphlets appeared and the *London Evening Post*, the *Gazetteer* and the *Monitor*, in particular, fully exploited the issue. On 31 July 1756 the *Monitor* urged the people to 'exert that liberty, which is our birthright' and encouraged grand juries and town corporations to petition parliament and to address the king for an inquiry into the iniquities of the ministers. Some protesters also demanded a reformed militia, limitations on the number of placemen and pensioners allowed to sit in the House of Commons, and even annual parliaments. The crisis was clearly reviving old Country demands. It also provoked more than just printed propaganda. Admiral Byng and the ministers were burned in effigy, Byng's property was attacked and the Duke of Newcastle was mobbed. Addresses to the king and instructions to MPs began flooding in over several months 'all of them breathing a true patriotic and loyal spirit'. Despite the efforts of the ministry's friends in the city, the Common Council resoundingly passed an address expressing its disgust at the mismanagement that had produced such alarming military defeats and instructed the city's MPs to demand political and constitutional changes. In all these protests blame was laid squarely on the lethargy of ministers and admiral alike. The clamour eventually resulted in the execution of Byng and it played a major role in forcing the king and his favourite ministers to accept William Pitt as a leading member of the government, since, in the present crisis, he alone had the confidence of the people at large.

Extra-parliamentary pressure groups and nationwide instruction campaigns clearly show that the Country platform could occasionally influence public opinion and could enlist considerable popular support for its political demands. The radical movement of the later eighteenth century built upon these foundations, but it also benefited from the growth of an independent political culture, hostile to the ruling oligarchy and its aristocratic politics, that had taken root among the middling orders in society earlier in the eighteenth century and from the longstanding tradition of riots, demonstrations and direct action among the lower orders.

The urban bourgeoisie, in particular, had their own social and economic reasons for resisting the authority and criticising the policies of the governing elite. The late seventeenth and earlier eighteenth centuries saw a considerable growth in the size of London and many provincial towns and the consequent expansion in the number of merchants, traders, master craftsmen and professional men who came to dominate these urban centres. With money to spare the middling orders improved the facilities of their towns and pursued culture, status and power. The larger provincial towns followed London in becoming more open societies in which the bourgeoisie could advance their economic interests, achieve social distinction and seek political influence. The growing towns encouraged greater mobility and generated a more competitive, aspiring society that was in the process of breaking away from aristocratic domination.[62] Resentful of the ways in which the governing elite could damage their economic interests, the urban bourgeoisie sought ways of challenging the pretensions of their social superiors. Through the expanding press they imbibed political propaganda which was frequently hostile to the ruling oligarchy. By developing a whole range of masonic and pseudo-masonic lodges, of tradesmen's societies and social clubs, the middling orders learned to combine in mutual support and to organise themselves independently of the patrician elite. These associations allowed their members to organise their own activities without deferring to aristocratic leadership and ultimately to use these institutions as vehicles for coordinating campaigns to challenge the political influence of their social superiors. In these societies all members were equal and the members made their own rules and elected their own officials. Even more political were the reading and debating societies which sprang up in most towns in the mid-eighteenth century. The authorities became very suspicious of the fact that in these societies the middling orders freely discussed politics and religion. These societies spread rapidly and their political views had clearly been radicalised by the time they rallied to Wilkes and his cause in the 1760s.

Despite the growth of oligarchy in the early Hanoverian period the middling orders were not totally excluded from the local political disputes which broke out in their towns. By virtue of its capital status, its commercial supremacy, its sheer size, its special privileges, and its comparatively democratic system of government, the city of London was virtually an independent political community. It certainly dominated the arena of popular politics. The city corporation, divided into a Court of Aldermen and a Common Council, had complete jurisdiction over its own territories and had considerable economic power and patronage at its disposal. Walpole could usually count upon the support of the rich financiers and merchants who dominated the Court of Aldermen, but he increasingly alienated the independent merchants and the middling sort who dominated the election of the Common Council and of the city's four MPs.[63] In the early 1720s most of the independent merchants and liverymen of London were critical of Walpole's close links with the monied interest and his support for the Quarantine Act and the Westminster Bridge Bill, but it was the City Elections Act of 1725 that turned them strongly against the court. This measure sought to remodel the constitution of the city and to circumscribe its more democratic tendencies. The freeman franchise was defined more narrowly (disqualifying nearly 3500 voters), the control of elections was tightened up, the growth of the lesser livery companies was restricted, and the Court of Aldermen was given a veto over all legislative acts and resolutions of the Common Council. The act can be regarded as a sensible attempt to deal with long-standing abuses,[64] but its critics interpreted it as an assault on London's political independence and as a means of strengthening oligarchy. Walpole certainly hoped to inhibit the Common Council from adopting an independent role as a critic of the government and he aimed at increasing aldermanic control over local ward politics. The measure fired partisan disputes in which popular opinion cast Walpole as the villain. It was opposition to the City Elections Act that first encouraged the emergence of a broadly-based anti-ministerial coalition in London. This opposition fought Walpole on two fronts. It endeavoured to oust the court interest in the city corporation, especially in the Court of Aldermen and, as we have seen, it gave a lead to the nationwide petitioning campaigns of 1733 and 1738 to 1742. By 1741 Walpole's opponents in London had severely reduced the court interest on the Common Council, gained a clear majority on the Court of Aldermen, and secured a complete victory in the election of the city's four MPs. For the first time since 1688 the court had lost political control over the nation's capital city. The popular champions of independent opinion in London had vindicated a more open concept of politics and had made a seed-bed for the radical libertarianism of the later eighteenth century.

The example of London spread to the other large boroughs. Westminster was more under the influence of the ruling oligarchy than London because of the presence of the court, parliament, Whitehall and the houses of fashionable society within its boundaries; but it also had the largest urban electorate in the country. While the wealthy western parishes were generally pro-court in their political sympathies, the poorer eastern parishes were more resistant to aristocratic influence and more hostile to Walpole's administration. By the later 1730s the lesser tradesmen of these areas were becoming politically active and were beginning to wrest control from their social superiors. In 1741 this opposition formed a Society of Independent Electors and swept the polls against the court in a violent election.[65] Popular resistance to oligarchy was not confined to the metropolitan area. In many of the larger boroughs there were conflicts between the corporation party which represented the interests of the richer inhabitants and an independent opposition hostile to the political dominance of this local oligarchy. This was the case in Coventry, Exeter, Bristol, Colchester, Tiverton, Leicester, Liverpool, Norwich, Nottingham and Worcester. These local contests often involved a religious division, with the Anglicans usually forming the corporation party and the Dissenters active among the opposition. In Coventry and Nottingham however the Dissenters were the entrenched interest. In many of these towns local issues overlapped with national politics. In both Liverpool and Tiverton the town corporations tried to restrict the number of electors who could vote in parliamentary elections, while the opposition campaigned for wider franchises.[66] In Norwich in 1722 and in Chester in 1732 local and national political tensions fused and provoked considerable bitterness. The election of a sheriff in Norwich was the occasion for a demonstration of several hundred citizens shouting their opposition to the court and their support for the Jacobite Bishop of Rochester. This riot encouraged the local Whigs to suggest remodelling the city's charter in order to increase the power of the local oligarchy on the Court of Aldermen.[67] In Chester there were a number of violent riots during the election of the town's mayor, though the real issue in dispute was whether the town should support a bill in parliament seeking approval to deepen the river Dee.[68]

Direct involvement in elections, pressure groups, petitioning campaigns and borough politics was largely confined to the middling orders. Only occasionally did political activity of this kind involve the poorer sections of society. Nevertheless, as many historians have recently demonstrated, the lower orders did engage in direct action which could influence the political decisions of the ruling oligarchy.[69] In crowd demonstrations the poor revealed a strong sense of corporate identity and a capacity for effective collective action. In the early eighteenth century however the populace failed to develop a coherent critique of society and never adopted a programme for the restructuring of the whole political system. Crowds did wear Jacobite colours at the Coventry election of 1722 and during the Cheshire contest in 1734,[70] while rioters celebrated the Pretender's birthday at Bridgwater in 1721[71] and protested on the anniversary of George I's accession at Harwich in 1724;[72] but these isolated and unconnected incidents were neither proof of serious disaffection among the masses nor the prelude to armed insurrection. Positive support for Jacobitism at grass-roots level collapsed after the widespread rioting of 1715–16,[73] though there is considerable evidence of plebeian hostility to the ruling Whig oligarchy continuing throughout the years of Walpole's ascendancy. Popular antipathy to the Whigs did not lead to violent measures to overthrow the Hanoverian regime, but it did express resentment against Walpole's intimate association with Dissenters and monied men and against the corrupt tactics and anti-libertarian tendencies of his administration. Jacobite symbolism was very much a gesture of popular defiance to the ruling oligarchy. The lower orders preferred to appeal to the English libertarian tradition and to adapt the ideology of the Country opposition to their own conditions, but the limited nature of their political consciousness and the superior power of their social superiors prevented them from developing a radical programme aimed at transforming their own position in society.[74] Although the common people believed that they were free men, not slaves, they were usually on the defensive. They engaged in direct collective action in order to protect their traditional rights and to preserve their established customs. The poor did not expect to decide who should rule them, but they did seek to circumscribe how the ruling oligarchy should exercise its authority. Far from rising in armed resistance to overthrow established authority, most rioters were concerned to enlist the support of that authority in defence of their customary rights.

Faced with the problem of considerable popular unrest Whig administrations frequently resorted to a policy of coercion and ignored the genuine economic grievances which had often sparked off these violent protests. The government feared that riots might be the prelude to revolution or the first step to anarchy. Walpole's own correspondence shows that he was always predisposed to see the hand of Jacobite conspirators behind any manifestation of public disorder.[75] After a riot against turnpikes in 1735 Lord Chancellor Hardwicke argued that it was essential for the government 'to inculcate into men's minds the dangerous consequences, that must follow from suffering the people to get the better of the laws, &, as it were, to override the acts of the legislature'.[76] Ministers frequently encouraged JPs to make use of the unpopular Riot Act, which had been passed in 1715 following widespread rioting, and sent troops to their assistance. In response to a virtual epidemic of poaching across several counties Walpole's government passed the notorious Black Act of 1723 which created no fewer than 50 capital offences connected with poaching.[77] In similar fashion the administration responded in 1735 to a rash of riots against the new turnpike roads by making it a capital offence to destroy the toll gates.[78] The Porteous riot in Edinburgh in 1736 provoked Walpole into an attempt (largely unsuccessful) to punish the city and its magistrates,[79] while the appearance of effective workers' combinations among London tailors in 1720 and among Wiltshire weavers in 1726 propelled the government into passing legislation to ban both of these nascent trade unions.[80]

There were times however when the government clearly recognised the limits of its authority and endeavoured to placate those it could not subdue. In these instances the government's natural response was to retreat from a dangerous confrontation and to make the minimum concessions needed to restore law and order. In 1720, for example, when the popularity of foreign calicoes was creating unemployment among English weavers in London and elsewhere, an act was passed to forbid the wearing of printed, stained and dyed calicoes imported from abroad. Serious and persistent rioting and the presentation of over ninety petitions to parliament persuaded the government to offer concessions on this occasion.[81] Serious rioting among the weavers of the south-western counties in 1726 stirred Walpole's ministry into an even more impressive display of conciliatory tactics. Two commissioners were sent down by Townshend to investigate the causes of the riots. When they reported that the weavers had genuine grievances and that their employers were largely responsible for the crisis the government summoned representatives of both sides to London. There the Privy Council urged them to draw up articles of agreement about wages and the measures of cloth to be regarded as the unit of payment. This agreement was then embodied in an act of parliament in 1727.[82] While insufficient efforts were subsequently made to render this measure effective, its enactment did indicate that the government would occasionally protect the interests of the poor in order to avoid serious disturbances. The dropping of the Excise Bill in 1733 and the embargo on grain exports following widespread food riots in 1740 were further demonstrations that the lower orders were not without influence on government policy.

IV   CONCLUSION

This chapter has attempted to show that radicalism cannot be regarded as a sudden or surprising development of the late eighteenth century. The precursors of a radical movement can be traced back to the late seventeenth and early eighteenth centuries, but these were not of one kind and their full potential was not realised at the time. Later eighteenth-century radicalism owed much to the radical Whig ideology and the ideas of Locke that were propagated in the late seventeenth century, but it also owed a great deal to the campaigning of the Tory and Country opposition, especially under the first two Georges, and to a number of social and economic developments over an even longer period of time. Moreover, before radicalism could fully develop, the doctrine of natural rights had to be extended to a desire for full political rights, the opposition platform had to include a demand for a major extension of the franchise, and there had to be a further growth of a distinctive bourgeois culture. In addition, these elements had to be integrated into a coherent whole. These developments and this integration could only be accomplished during a deep and sustained political crisis and through the talents of a charismatic leader who was capable of fully exploiting the ideology, platform and organisations that had been developing since the Glorious Revolution. The early years of George III's reign produced the first of these and John Wilkes pointed the way towards the second.

7 Radicals and Reformers in the Later Eighteenth Century

While it is clear that even in the later eighteenth century Britain was still governed by an aristocratic, propertied elite, another political world existed in which large numbers of people, mainly but not exclusively drawn from the middling ranks of society were able to influence the decisions taken by the ruling elite and were often able to act independently of them. A century of political, social and economic changes moreover had combined to create a growing body of opinion critical of the power and the policies of the aristocratic elite. The rule of law limited the authority of the ruling elite and the civil liberties of the subject ensured that many Britons believed that they were free men living in a free state, and they acted accordingly. A century of commercial expansion and modest population growth had, by 1760, created towns in which moderately prosperous men had learned to exercise increasing control over their own lives. The population grew very rapidly in the later eighteenth century and much of this increase was concentrated in the larger urban centres. Urban growth produced an expanding middle class whose advancing wealth and improved education inspired demands for greater social status and increased political influence. Many of the middling orders resented their dependence upon the landed elite whose policies could have a profound effect on their economic welfare. Political weakness had economic consequences as the burden of taxation was steadily shifted from the shoulders of the great landowners onto those who produced, sold, used or purchased many items of popular consumption. Furthermore, government policies could result in wars which dislocated trade or in legislative restrictions on the activities of traders and manufacturers. These grievances were felt quite low down the social scale, among small shopkeepers, tradesmen and artisans. Even the labouring poor could express

221

violent resentment of the ruling elite when they suffered from rising prices and declining wages due to the selfishness of their employers or to the particular policies of the ruling elite. Economic crisis and social dislocation, caused by bad harvests or costly wars, recruited many craftsmen and artisans, and not a few labourers, into the campaigns for political reform.

As we have already noted, the growth of towns and the expansion of the press transformed the political culture of these urban centres. This burgeoning political culture enabled the middling orders in particular to establish their own independent organisations, to inform themselves about public affairs and to develop advanced notions of their political rights and liberties. Clubs and societies enabled the middling orders to combine in mutual support and to organise themselves independently of the patrician elite. The members of these associations learned to organise their own activities without resorting to aristocratic leadership. They gradually became critical of the governing elite and ultimately transformed their clubs and societies into vehicles for coordinating campaigns to challenge the political influence of their social superiors. At first designed for social and entertainment purposes these clubs and societies increasingly became educational and political. They formed a nationwide communications network which could later be exploited by political radicals. These societies could never have become more political if their members had not absorbed a wealth of political information and a libertarian political ideology propagated by a rapidly expanding press. By the late eighteenth century London alone was served by 13 daily and 10 tri-weekly newspapers, while in the provinces there were over fifty weekly newspapers. Total annual sales of newspapers were as high as 12.5 million by 1775 and some 17 million by 1793. In addition there was a wealth of political information and propaganda published in the numerous monthly periodicals and in the large number of individual pamphlets produced during any political crisis. Most of the more successful publications were anti-ministerial in their politics. This flourishing and expanding press played a major role in encouraging a wide public to be critical of the governing elite and interested in suggestions for reforming the political system.

Throughout the later eighteenth century critics of the governing elite waged a propaganda campaign in the press against the abuse of executive power and the corrupt means used by ministers to subvert the independence of parliament or to undermine the liberties of the subject. Regular attacks were made on crown patronage and persistent demands were made for economical reforms which would reduce the crown's influence over parliament. These were a prelude to more radical proposals for a redistribution of parliamentary seats, for more frequent general elections and for an extension of the franchise. These demands for parliamentary reform were made by extra-parliamentary movements of a kind not seen earlier in the eighteenth century. These movements developed quite separately from the opposition in parliament and they enlisted greater and more consistent support out-of-doors than the instruction campaigns of the earlier eighteenth century had done. Most supporters of radical reform in the later eighteenth century operated in an entirely constitutional fashion, though the later 1790s did see the creation of a small revolutionary underground movement ready to achieve its aims by conspiracy and insurrection.

In order to understand the nature of the radical and reform movements of the later eighteenth century we need to examine the issues which gave rise to their campaigns, the political aims and ideological assumptions of these movements, their organisation and composition, and their methods and activities. In conclusion, this chapter will look briefly at the nature and extent of the revolutionary underground that appeared at the very end of the eighteenth century.[1]

I ORIGINS AND ISSUES

By 1760 the preconditions for the development of extra-parliamentary radicalism already existed and over the coming decades the tensions produced by economic change and foreign wars, and by the social dislocation which both of these brought in their train, did much to focus attention on the failings of the governing elite. None the less, it was popular reaction to serious *political* crises that did most to stimulate the quite sudden growth of a radical movement 'out-of-doors'. It was the actions of the new king, the dramatic irruption of John Wilkes onto the political stage, the prolonged and ultimately disastrous dispute with the American colonies, and the profound ideological issues raised by the French Revolution that generated the pressure which turned potential critics of the ruling oligarchy into political radicals ready to demand constitutional reform and willing to join extra-parliamentary pressure groups dedicated to political change. Moreover, these four political crises had a cumulative effect in that, as one followed the other, they deepened the sense of unease about the existing constitution and widened the circle of those who supported the cause of reform.[2]

While no historian now believes that George III waged a determined campaign to increase his own prerogative powers at the expense of the rights of parliament or the liberties of the subject, a considerable body of opinion in the 1760s did believe that the king was threatening to disturb the delicate balance of the constitution and was leading a conspiracy against liberty. Public alarm was deliberately created by disgruntled politicians, who resented their sudden loss of power, by an unscrupulous John Wilkes, and by American colonists who were seeking to justify resistance to British interference in their internal affairs. The consequence of all these efforts was a widespread conviction that a constitutional crisis had been created by the political ambitions of George III. The king was accused of exploiting crown patronage as a means of increasing his personal power, whereas George I and George II had used it to create ministerial stability and to secure a measure of consensus within parliament. Opinion within parliament and out-of-doors propagated a conspiracy theory about the unconstitutional aims of George III and led to demands for economical reform as a means of reducing the patronage at the disposal of the crown. Such fears were given wide currency in the press and this critique won over considerable extra-parliamentary support to the cause of economical reform.

John Wilkes was even more successful in convincing a significant number of people out-of-doors that he was a political victim of men who were seeking to undermine the independence of parliament and subvert the liberties of the subject. With unrivalled skill he raised his personal disputes with the government into issues involving fundamental constitutional principles. When, in 1763, following his notorious attack on the king in number 45 of *The North Briton*, the ministry issued general warrants in order to secure incriminating evidence against him, Wilkes exploited the situation to condemn the authorities for abusing their power. He gave his personal plight a more general application by claiming that English liberties were at stake. When, in 1768–9, a majority of MPs was persuaded to embark on a policy of repeatedly expelling him from the House of Commons, although he consistently won the backing of a majority of the electors of Middlesex, Wilkes could claim that the dispute raised the whole question of the freedom of voters to choose their own representatives. If the decision in the Middlesex election case was not reversed, then, he argued, the rights of the electorate would be reduced to a hollow sham.[3] The issue clearly transcended the question of whether John Wilkes should or should not represent Middlesex. It posed the question of whether the membership of the House of Commons was to be manipulated by a narrow aristocratic elite or was to represent the interests of the electorate as a whole.

Even more fundamental questions were raised by the American crisis which developed over a period of twenty years or more. The ill-judged policies of successive British administrations aroused widespread and intense resentment in the American colonies. They eventually provoked an armed resistance which led to a prolonged war that Britain was unable to win. Within Britain the whole dispute generated intense discussion about the very nature of the British constitution.[4] Many British critics of government policies supported the American challenge to the doctrine of parliamentary sovereignty and they endorsed the American stand on the principle of 'no taxation without representation'. These critics began to argue that parliament was not the ultimate sovereign authority in the state, but should be accountable to the people at large. To make the people and not parliament the sovereign authority in the state, crown patronage would need to be reduced and the whole system of representation overhauled. Alarmed by military defeat and inspired initially by Christopher Wyvill, the Association movement launched a nationwide campaign to reform a political system which had failed the nation and had plunged the country into a disastrous war.

The ending of the American war in 1783, the rapid recovery of the economy and the restoration of political stability at home led to a sudden collapse in support for the radicals and for the cause of parliamentary reform. By the early 1790s however radicalism had not only revived, but had made major advances on the position which it had occupied a decade before. A number of factors contributed to this dramatic transformation – including the ratification of the Federal Constitution in the USA, the vigorous campaigns against the Test and the Corporation Acts and for the abolition of the slave trade, and the celebrations of the centenary of the Glorious Revolution – but much the most important was the outbreak of violent revolution in France. The dramatic and astonishing events in France, for a decade and more after 1789, had an electrifying effect on British politics. The revolution in France was sudden and surprising and it produced a political earthquake that sent seismic shockwaves across Europe. The impact on Britain was profound and was widely diffused throughout the whole society. Within a few short months the strongest monarch in Europe was humbled by his subjects, the entrenched privileges of the aristocracy were condemned, the church was placed under secular control, the universal and inalienable rights of man were proclaimed, and a representative assembly was charged with drawing up a new written constitution. British reformers of all shades of opinion were galvanised into action. The French Revolution stimulated veteran reformers such as Wyvill, Cartwright, Price and Horne Tooke to renew their demands for reform. It also awoke the sleeping Society for Constitutional Information and encouraged liberal Whig MPs to renew their efforts at economical reform and to contemplate moderate parliamentary reform. The greatest impact of the French Revolution however was on the new and more radical societies which sprang up in London and the provinces in the early 1790s. The French Revolution aroused many thousands of men to political action and it provided them with new ideas on how best to redress their grievances, but it was the economic distress of the 1790s which enabled the new radical societies to recruit mass support. Bad harvests, trade depression and the financial burdens of a long and unsuccessful war after 1793 created widespread distress which was a major recruiting agent for the radical cause, especially in the years 1792–6.[5]

II IDEOLOGICAL ASSUMPTIONS AND POLITICAL AIMS

The political crises of the later eighteenth century did not produce a single, integrated radical ideology nor an agreed programme of reform. Instead, those seeking reform drew upon several different political discourses and a wide array of moral principles and political ideals in order to provide themselves with a set of values capable of underpinning the practical programme which they favoured. In order to reform the existing constitution some reformers turned to long-established demands for economical reform as a means of reducing the influence of crown patronage over parliament, while others advocated parliamentary reform so that parliament would be made more accountable to the electorate. There was considerable disagreement over how radical the reform of parliament should be, with some reformers suggesting a householder franchise and others campaigning for universal male suffrage. A minority of radicals actually wanted to go beyond political reform and proposed schemes to improve the social and economic conditions of the poor.

In seeking to appeal to a wide range of opinion some leading reformers adopted the traditional Country ideology, with its criticism of executive power and ministerial corruption, in order to demand a return to the original principles of the balanced constitution and to secure an independent House of Commons free of crown patronage and aristocratic influence. Other reformers were influenced by a radical Protestant discourse which stressed personal and individual virtues rather than public or civic virtue. Praising such personal qualities as industry, sobriety, frugality and enterprise, they encouraged self-improvement and they desired equal opportunities and careers open to talent.[6] Many reformers were also influenced by the optimism of the Enlightenment. They believed that there was no limit to the rational faculties of man and that men could achieve unlimited progress in future. Some of the enlightened Rational Dissenters were also influenced by religious millenarianism. For them the political, moral and scientific progress of the age was a preparation for Christ's Second Coming and the French Revolution presaged the approach of the millennium.[7] Other radicals were influenced by secular ideologies. John Cartwright, for example, still adhered to the notion of England's ancient constitution. He appealed to the historic rights of Englishmen because he believed that universal manhood suffrage and the sovereignty of the people had existed before the Norman Conquest and he insisted that these ancient rights should now be recovered.

The most radical reformers however went beyond demands for a meritocracy or a return to historic rights. Instead, they adopted and developed the ideas of John Locke and appealed to equal, universal and inalienable natural rights. Recognising that the weight of historical evidence supported the conservative claim that there had always been a propertied franchise, radical theorists such as Richard Price and Thomas Paine preferred to claim those rights which all men *ought* to have because of their natural equality and common humanity. They insisted that all men were created equal and that they possessed inalienable natural rights which no government could legitimately infringe. These God-given natural rights included the rights to life, liberty, property and the pursuit of happiness. To ensure that these natural rights were maintained in civil society the authority of those in power must be limited and must be subject to the sovereignty of the people. More explicit on practical matters than Locke, they claimed that a man's natural rights could not be safeguarded unless he possessed the right to vote for those who sat in the nation's legislature. Although modern scholars can detect the differences between the various ideological assumptions used by the radicals of the later eighteenth century, these reformers were quite capable of appealing to Country principles, to the historic rights of Englishmen and to the natural rights of man at the same time. They often managed to proclaim the glories of the ancient constitution, while simultaneously advocating future progress on the basis of abstract rational principles.[8]

The radicals and reformers were not only influenced by different ideological assumptions; the reform movements of the later eighteenth century also supported a variety of different programmes. Different reformers tended to see the political crises of the period in a different light and they produced different solutions to these problems. Many Wilkites and most adherents of Wyvill's Association movement were convinced that the real dangers to the existing political system were posed by crown patronage and aristocratic influence. To defeat this insidious threat the people were urged to adopt the traditional Country or patriot ethic of civic virtue. They were encouraged to prize their liberties and voters were urged to reject courtiers, placemen and monied men as their representatives and to elect honest, independent country gentlemen in their stead. Support was also given to proposals to exclude placemen from parliament, eliminate bribery and corruption in elections, secure more frequent general elections and redistribute some parliamentary seats from small rotten boroughs to the largest counties and the more populous urban centres. Christopher Wyvill wanted to abolish at least fifty rotten boroughs and to transfer the hundred seats to the counties and large towns. He showed little interest in securing direct representation for such growing manufacturing towns as Birmingham, Manchester and Sheffield, however, and he was content to restrict the franchise to men who possessed sufficient property to be independent of crown and aristocracy.[9]

Some Wilkite radicals were ready to contemplate a more drastic redistribution of seats and John Wilkes himself appeared to favour an extension of the franchise. He certainly raised the issue in a speech which he delivered in the House of Commons in 1776.[10] The metropolitan radicals did praise the virtues of the industrious middle classes. They insisted that independence could derive from all kinds of property, not simply from the possession of landed estates, but they stressed that independence could also be a matter of conviction and attitude. They were convinced that the middling ranks of urban society had the capacity to judge the merits of those who governed them and that they ought to have the right to choose more of the nation's representatives. In their opinion, industry, frugality and talent had gained the middling orders sufficient wealth, status and expertise to engage actively in public affairs. A small group of Rational Dissenters, including John Cartwright, James Burgh, Richard Price and John Jebb urged a much more substantial redistribution of seats and a major extension of the franchise. In 1780 John Jebb and other members of the sub-committee of the Westminster Association endorsed what later became known as the six points of parliamentary reform: universal manhood suffrage, equal constituencies, annual elections, the secret ballot, the abolition of property qualifications for parliamentary candidates and the payment of MPs. Very few reformers at this stage supported such a radical programme. Even those that did, did not generally advocate votes for women and did not seek to abolish monarchy or aristocracy.[11]

In the 1790s many more radicals endorsed the six points of parliamentary reform. There was widespread agreement among the British Jacobins that the right to vote should be attached to the person and not to the property of man. To deny any man the franchise was to cast a slur on his moral character and to assert that he was less than a man. The possession of wealth was no proof of moral worth or civic virtue and nor was property any evidence of the lack of these qualities. This emphasis on the equal political rights of all men led some radicals to go further than any of the earlier reformers and to condemn all hereditary honours, titles and privileges. Thomas Paine advocated the creation of a democratic republic, but few other radicals went so far. Indeed, it is not absolutely clear that they desired a fully democratic system. Most of the leading radicals were men of modest property and few of them could entirely escape the assumption that men of property should govern and should give a political lead to the labouring masses. Furthermore, in the struggle for the rights of man, most radicals were concerned quite literally with the liberty of adult males rather than with the freedom of all mankind. They regarded the position of women as analogous to that of children; they were dependent creatures incapable of exercising independent judgement. A handful of radicals did contemplate giving the franchise to women, but the radical campaign was overwhelmingly preoccupied with securing the vote for adult males.[12]

Most radicals in the 1790s were convinced that the social and economic grievances of the poor could be removed only by radical political reform. In their opinion it was the unequal distribution of political power, rather than the unequal distribution of wealth, that was the chief cause of the economic grievances of the poor. It was the need to support an extravagant monarchy and aristocracy, to corrupt parliament and to finance foreign wars that combined to place a crippling tax burden on the middling and lower orders. Parliamentary reform would result in lower taxes and much cheaper government, and it might also lead to the abolition of tithes, the repeal of the game laws and the reform of the laws which put so many small debtors in prison. Thomas Paine also hoped that a democratic government would bring in such welfare reforms as maternity benefits, child allowances and old age pensions and would also levy a special property tax on the rich in order to pay for these welfare reforms and to give all poor men a lump sum when they came of age. Even Paine, however, feared social revolution and opposed the forcible confiscation of property. Most radicals of the 1790s explicitly denied that they were social and economic levellers anxious to redistribute the wealth of the nation. Only Thomas Spence put forward a detailed Land Plan which would place all the land and natural resources of each parish under the control of parochial corporations composed of every man, woman and child in the parish. The land and resources would be rented out to the highest bidder and the income would be used on public amenities and on equal quarterly payments to every inhabitant in the parish.[13]

III COMPOSITION AND ORGANISATION

In the early Hanoverian period the critics of the ruling oligarchy had no effective national leaders outside parliament, they only occasionally enlisted widespread support for their aims, and they lacked the sophisticated organisations needed to rally mass support across the nation as a whole. In the later eighteenth century these weaknesses were addressed even if they were not always overcome. National leaders did sometimes reach out beyond their local base, some reform movements enlisted significant support for several years of political campaigning, and some political clubs and societies achieved a national standing.

John Wilkes was the first radical to achieve a national reputation by his extra-parliamentary activities. Although he was a rake and a politician whose sincerity and integrity are open to question, he played an indispensable role in exciting popular interest in major constitutional issues. Employing his pen, his wit and his theatrical talents to brilliant effect, he was able to exploit his charismatic personality and his outrageous behaviour in order to reach and captivate a wide public. By deliberately creating incidents and issues capable of arousing intense excitement he was able for several years to sustain unrelenting pressure on the governing elite. His own personal objectives were raised to the level of grand constitutional principles and abstract concepts of liberty and justice were made tangible to ordinary people. Wilkes made himself the personification of liberty and played the role of a political martyr suffering at the hands of an unprincipled and corrupt oligarchy. Never remote, aloof or patronising, he deliberately flattered his public by praising the political sense and even the political sophistication of ordinary freeholders and tradesmen.[14]

No other radical leader could command the loyalty of reformers across the country to the same extent as Wilkes, but a few proved to be almost as indispensable. In the late 1770s and early 1780s Christopher Wyvill played a vital role in holding together the scattered elements of the Association movement. In many ways the antithesis of Wilkes, Wyvill was sober, honest, direct and industrious. A man of courage, broad humanity and scrupulous integrity, he had a clear vision of what was needed and he displayed a remarkable tenacity and persistence in pursuit of his goals. Both the inspiration and the driving force of the Association movement, he showed a respect for the opinion of others and he remained an excellent judge of what was feasible.[15] No radical leader in the 1790s dominated the reform movement in the way Wilkes and Wyvill had done. Thomas Hardy, the founder and secretary of the London Corresponding Society, was not as charismatic as Wilkes and was not quite as well connected nationwide as Wyvill, but he had an excellent reputation for industry and integrity and he was an inspiration to many provincial radicals. He proved that men of quite humble origins could play a significant role in extra-parliamentary politics.[16]

Perhaps even more crucial to the radical movement were the leading theorists and propagandists who developed radical ideas and programmes for reform. Writers such as John Cartwright, James Burgh, Richard Price, Joseph Priestley and Thomas Paine provided the radicals with inspiration and with convincing moral, historical and rational justifications for their practical proposals. Much of the routine work of the radical societies was performed by a relatively small number of activists: men such as John Horne Tooke, John Sawbridge, Richard Oliver, Thomas Brand Hollis, John Glynn, Brass Crosby and Maurice Margarot in London and provincial activists such as George Grieve, Richard Gardiner, Crisp Molyneux, Thomas Walker, and Joseph Gales in such towns as Newcastle upon Tyne, Norwich, King's

Lynn, Manchester and Sheffield. The ideas and the activities of the radicals were propagated by a whole coterie of publishers and distributors in London, as well as by many newspaper proprietors in the provinces.[17]

Initially, support for political reform came from a wide spectrum of society, though it was mainly drawn from the middling orders. A handful of the propertied elite (the Duke of Richmond and Lord Stanhope for example) took an interest in parliamentary reform and John Wilkes was occasionally able to involve some of the urban poor in his activities. Both Wilkes and Wyvill secured some support from rural freeholders, but most of their support came from the urban areas. They recruited sympathisers from among the moderately prosperous merchants, wholesalers, small manufacturers, shopkeepers, retailers, traders, master craftsmen and professional men, as well as from more humble tradesmen and artisans.[18] Some urban groups were particularly prominent in the reform movement precisely because their fortunes were closely tied up with the success or failure of radicalism. These groups included middle-income lawyers involved in the campaign for the reform of legal abuses, those involved in the print and book trades which provided information about radical opinions and activities, those who kept or supplied the inns, taverns and public houses frequented by the various radical groups, and those tradesmen who manufactured the pottery, ceramic and other commemorative artefacts bought by radical sympathisers.[19] A few eminent Rational Dissenters played a distinguished role in the development of radical ideas and a number of prominent Dissenting ministers preached sermons in support of both the American and the French revolutions[20] but there is little evidence to suggest that the majority of ordinary Dissenters were deeply involved in the reform movement.[21] In the first phase of radicalism the movement flourished in London, in the urbanised areas of the southeast and in the small clothing towns of the south-west and the rather larger clothing towns of the West Riding of Yorkshire, in the manufacturing areas of the west midlands and in a number of important ports or commercial centres such as Bristol, Norwich, Portsmouth and Newcastle upon Tyne. It had not yet gained a strong foothold in such rapidly expanding manufacturing as Birmingham, Manchester and Sheffield and it had made no real headway in Scotland.

In the second phase of radicalism, in the 1790s, the movement not only revived in London and in the older provincial
towns such as Norwich, Nottingham, Derby, Leicester,
Newcastle upon Tyne, but expanded into many of the rapidly
growing industrial towns (such as Manchester, Birmingham,
Sheffield and Leeds), into the central belt of Scotland, and
into a host of small towns that had previously shown little interest in reform. This expansion has convinced some historians
that the radicalism of the 1790s was a genuinely mass movement and one that reached a significant number of the
labouring poor. The evidence does not fully justify such claims
however. The London Corresponding Society (LCS) claimed a
total membership of around 5000 (not a huge number in a
metropolis with a population of nearly a million people) and
this number has been accepted by many historians. The latest
estimate on active as distinct from total membership suggests
that the number of regular members attending meetings
fluctuated between a few hundred and two thousand. Only in
the autumn of 1795 did the weekly attendance rise to around
3000, with a peak attendance of 3576 members. By 1797 the
active membership had shrunk to around 600 and this was
reduced to about 400 in 1798.[22] Artisans and tradesmen played
a significant, but not a dominant, role in the LCS. Many of the
more prominent members were booksellers, printers,
publishers, authors and men in the legal and medical
professions.[23] There is no evidence that the LCS ever had
much appeal, except in periods of acute economic distress, for
unskilled labourers or the very poor. Despite the accusations of
its enemies and the claims of some historians, the LCS was
never a mass society nor a genuinely proletarian one.

In some ways the Sheffield Society for Constitutional
Information was more impressive. Its total membership was over
1500 by March 1792 and was about 2500 by June 1792 (in a town
with less than one-tenth the population of London), though the
active membership was probably around 600. Most of the more
active members appear to have been small masters and skilled
journeymen employed in the small workshops of the Sheffield
steel industry.[24] Although there were a great many other provincial radical societies none could rival the size or success of the
Sheffield SCI. The membership of most of them rarely grew to
more than a few hundred and some were short-lived organ-

isations of a few dozen activists. Membership was largely made up of small merchants, professional men, shopkeepers and tradesmen. Radicalism in the 1790s actually declined in some large towns (including Liverpool, Bristol and Portsmouth). It failed to penetrate into the rural areas and it failed to enlist the active support of large numbers of the urban labouring poor. On the other hand, in the later 1790s when radicalism had largely been driven underground, economic distress, political repression and the strains produced by military defeat in the war against France, created widespread passive disaffection among the labouring population of Britain if not active support for political reform.[25]

Throughout the later eighteenth century the main radical organisation was the local club or society that generally met weekly in a tavern or public house to discuss recent events, debate current issues and plan future activities. Their most active members printed public addresses, distributed propaganda, organised petitions, raised subscriptions, staged celebrations and street demonstrations, and coordinated activities with other societies. In periods of political excitement they rented larger rooms where political meetings, public debates, lectures and celebration dinners could be held. In London and some of the more open parliamentary boroughs they canvassed voters during elections and even helped to elect a small number of radical MPs.

John Wilkes was the first to benefit politically from the existence of dozens of clubs, lodges and associations which had been set up in London and other large towns for a variety of purposes long before the 1760s. The majority of these voluntary associations, including the Albions, the Bucks, the Leeches, the Lumber Troop, the Free and Easy Johns and the Robin Hood debating societies, had been established originally for commercial, educational, convivial and civic purposes, but most of them soon rallied to the radical cause in the 1760s. The club of Honest Whigs, which brought together many of the leading Rational Dissenters in London, also soon changed its focus from debates on general religious or philosophical questions to discussions on more explicitly political subjects. The issues raised by Wilkes soon spawned new, overtly political, clubs such as the Anti-Caledonian Club, the Retribution Club, the Liberty Beefsteak Club and, most important of all, the Society of the Supporters of the Bill of Rights (SSBR) and the Constitutional Societies.[26]

The SSBR, which was explicitly Wilkite, was only the tip of a broad base of clubs in the metropolis. Set up on 20 February 1769 by a band of London radicals it sought to provide the organisation needed to mount a nationwide petitioning campaign in support of Wilkes. By collecting funds and distributing propaganda it was able to give a lead to protesters not only in London, Westminster and Middlesex, but also in Yorkshire and parts of the West Country. Money and presents, often in units of 45, were sent to Wilkes from bands of sympathisers in many parts of the country and even in the American colonies. Much to the chagrin of Wilkes, however, the leaders of the SSBR were not devoted only to advancing his personal political career or to reversing the decision in the Middlesex election case. They were also concerned to achieve shorter parliaments and a redistribution of seats and they believed such objectives could be gained only if they embarked on a long-term programme of political education. Such aims soon clashed with the more limited and immediate goals of Wilkes. The resulting dispute rapidly revealed that many of these metropolitan radicals distrusted Wilkes and were suspicious of his delight in promoting crowd demonstrations. John Horne Tooke was soon accusing Wilkes of making patriotism a trade and a fraudulent trade at that. By 1771 the breach between them was a matter of public and acrimonious debate and Horne Tooke and others resigned to set up a rival Constitutional Society in London. The SSBR thereafter lost momentum, but, within a short time, there were provincial Constitutional Societies in such towns as Birmingham, Norwich and Newcastle upon Tyne. Wherever they were established they worked hard to return candidates to parliament who had explicitly pledged themselves to support political reform.[27]

After Wilkes was returned to parliament in 1774 the SSBR foundered and the Constitutional Societies languished. It was another five years before the heavy costs of an unsuccessful conflict with the American colonies encouraged Christopher Wyvill to set up the Yorkshire Association dedicated to economical reform. Wyvill was soon in regular correspondence with sympathisers in Yorkshire and with more radical reformers in many parts of the country. He fully recognised the necessity for association and he organised a conference in London in order to unite reformers in a coordinated campaign for a common programme. At least sixteen counties and several boroughs established associations modelled on that set up in Yorkshire and, in March 1780, some 30–40 delegates from these associations attended Wyvill's conference in London. Some of these associations proved to be short-lived and the whole movement was torn by internal disputes and suffered from frequent defections. There was much dispute about whether to support moderate economical reform or radical parliamentary reform. None the less, Wyvill performed heroics to keep the Association movement united and in being. He was able to mount a significant nationwide petitioning campaign in 1780, but further efforts in 1781, 1782 and 1785 met with more limited success. Racked by continuous quarrels the associations were divided over what reform programme to adopt.[28]

Less of a national movement, but undoubtedly a major contributor to the education of many political reformers, was the Society for Constitutional Information (SCI). Set up in April 1780 by a number of prominent Rational Dissenters, the SCI sought to increase support for political reform by the systematic production and distribution of printed propaganda. Always small in size its membership included several peers and about fifteen MPs, but its more active members were recruited from the professional middle classes. They undertook the printing of a vast range of political propaganda, most of which endorsed the radical programme of parliamentary reform favoured by the committee of the Westminster Association. Many of its publications were distributed free of charge and it achieved a great deal in educating reformers across the country. None the less, it was too radical to secure widespread support and it declined like the other reform movements after the failure of Pitt's reform bill in 1785. After the outbreak of the French Revolution however the SCI renewed its efforts to distribute radical propaganda across the country and it helped to educate a new generation of reformers.[29]

Easily the most important of the new radical societies of the 1790s, and the one which established a new structure for a radical organisation, was the London Corresponding Society, founded on 25 January 1792 by Thomas Hardy, a humble shoe-maker, and a mere eight colleagues. Soon Hardy and his allies had established branches or divisions of the LCS across the metropolitan area. Each one was expected to recruit a minimum of thirty members and a maximum of forty-six. Once the latter total was reached the last sixteen enrolled were supposed to set up a new division. In fact, many divisions exceeded the suggested maximum: division two, the most active of them all, had nearly 700 members by late 1795. By May 1792 there were nine divisions of the LCS, each sending a delegate to the general committee that met each Thursday evening. Each division elected its secretary and its delegate every three months. The general committee elected a smaller executive committee consisting of a secretary, president and six ordinary members. This executive committee, consisting of a secretary, president and six ordinary members, coordinated the activities and policies of the LCS. Its members met two or three times each week and so the leading activists in the LCS were busy with political meetings for four or five evenings in the week. As the LCS spread over a wider area, which imposed travel problems on its members, it was decided to divide London into four geographical districts and to insert a district committee between the divisions and the general committee. Members of the district committee were also elected by the divisions. Thus, by 1795, the LCS possessed a sophisticated organisational structure designed to overcome the legal, financial and geographical restrictions on its political activities.[30]

London also possessed dozens of less organised political groups and three or four very active debating societies in the 1790s,[31] and there were dozens of radical clubs, formal and informal, in the larger provincial towns. The most important of these were in Sheffield, Manchester and Norwich. The members of the Sheffield SCI met weekly in their local branches or divisions and each group elected a delegate to a general executive committee which distributed political literature, organised petitions, communicated with the LCS and the SCI in London, and advised radical groups in such neighbouring towns as Leeds, Derby, Nottingham and Stockport.[32] Most provincial radical societies of the 1790s however had insufficient members to establish branches or divisions, though in some towns several different political societies flourished at the same time. Manchester, for example, had a Patriotic Society, a Reformation Society and a Constitutional Society, while Norwich had a Revolution Society, a Patriotic Society and a Constitutional Society.[33]

IV   METHODS AND ACTIVITIES

As we have seen elsewhere middle-class reformers sought to gain influence in local municipal corporations and to elect sympathetic MPs to parliament. They achieved some limited success. They also fought legal cases, sometimes with considerable success, over such issues as general warrants, parliament's efforts to restrict press reports of its debates, and the abuse of authority by officials seeking to control crowd demonstrations.[34] In the Printer's Case of 1771, for example, the corporate privileges of the House of Commons to restrict press reports of its debates was opposed by the jurisdictional autonomy of the City of London in order to protect those printers who published parliamentary debates. In a brilliant campaign, executed with characteristic audacity, Wilkes won a major victory.[35]

Much more important than these achievements however were the radicals' successes in educating themselves and a wide public on political questions and in securing popular support for their reform programme. This was done by a variety of methods and activities. The most important of these were the political education provided by debating clubs and the public prints, the organisation of petitioning campaigns, the calling of conventions, the exploitation of crowd demonstrations and the addressing of mass meetings.

The radical activists who joined the various debating societies and political clubs spent much of their time listening to someone reading political literature or taking part in political discussions. Debates were held in an orderly manner according to strict rules of conduct. There was to be no drunkenness, rowdiness or interruption of speeches. All speakers were to address the chairman, no one was to speak for too long and no one was to speak twice until everyone who wanted to speak had spoken once.[36] The aim was clearly to promote the political education of the members while instilling in them both discipline and self-respect. The radical activists must be taught to think for themselves as a prelude to leading and influencing others.

The radicals were also particularly active in exploiting the opportunities provided by an expanding press. The *London Evening Post*, the *Middlesex Journal*, the *Newcastle Chronicle*, the *Leeds Mercury*, the *Birmingham and Stafford Chronicle* and many other newspapers publicised the activities and the objectives of the radicals and condemned government policies during the age of the American Revolution.[37] Individual pamphlets, highly critical of the existing political system, poured from the presses. Well over a thousand separate pamphlets on the American crisis were published in London in the twenty-year period beginning in 1763.[38] Edmund Burke's *Thoughts on the Cause of the Present Discontents* (1770), with its critique of George III and the Earl of Bute, sold about 3250 copies, a respectable total, but its central thesis reached a much larger public because it appeared in review or extract in five London newspapers, several provincial newspapers and six magazines.[39] Richard Price's more radical *Observations on the Nature of Civil Liberty* sold a very impressive 60 000 copies in some 14 editions.[40] Wilkes himself exploited the press to an astonishing extent. He used newspapers, pamphlets, periodicals, handbills, posters, ballads, verse, caricatures and even joke books to publicise his political activities. In the first Middlesex election of 1768 he distributed over 40 000 handbills and he was the inspiration behind *English Liberty Established*, the most famous single-sheet publication of the age.[41] The SCI, concentrating as it did on distributing political propaganda, sent out at least 88 000 copies of some 33 different publications between 1780 and 1783 alone.[42]

In the 1790s the radicals were even more determined to educate the people about their political rights and most optimistically believed that a massive propaganda campaign might be sufficient to achieve their political goals. To propagate its views the LCS sold broadsheets and pamphlets, distributed large numbers of its own printed addresses, and tried to establish its own political magazine. It managed to publish an eight-page weekly, *The Politician*, four times between December 1794 and January 1795, and a forty-eight page monthly, the *Moral and Political Magazine*, twelve times between

June 1796 and May 1797. Both of these publications were collections of letters on political subjects, extracts from political speeches or lectures by radicals such as John Thelwall and John Horne Tooke, brief essays and selected passages from political classics. Unfortunately, the monthly magazine was a heavy financial drain on the resources of the LCS because the society could only manage to sell half of its regular production of between 3000 and 4000 copies.[43] In Manchester too the radicals produced their own weekly newspaper, the *Manchester Herald*, though this flourished for only a year from March 1792 to March 1793 before government prosecution closed it down.[44] In Sheffield Joseph Gales produced the weekly *Sheffield Register* which circulated throughout the whole region and for a time he also produced a fortnightly periodical, *The Patriot*. From April 1792 to June 1794 *The Patriot* reported on radical developments in Britain and France, published editorials and letters, and quoted from all kinds of political literature.[45] An excellent weekly periodical, *The Cabinet*, which published similar material, was produced in Norwich between 1794 and 1795.[46] Elsewhere, the cause of reform was promoted by such provincial newspapers as the *Leicester Herald*, the *Derby Mercury*, the *Newark Herald*, the *Cambridge Intelligencer* and the *Newcastle Chronicle*.

A few radical theorists and publicists made heroic efforts in the 1790s to reach a mass audience with their political views. Some, such as John Thelwall and Henry Redhead Yorke, went on lecture tours, but most relied upon printed literature. Daniel Isaac Eaton produced *Politics for the People*, a cheap weekly periodical selling at twopence per issue that appeared between September 1793 and January 1795; Thomas Spence's *Pig's Meat*, which was the cheapest of all radical periodicals at one penny per issue, appeared between 1793 and 1795; while Thelwall's *The Tribune* was published weekly from March 1794 to April 1795.[47] Anxious to reach a mass audience these men ransacked reform literature of the past two centuries in order to instruct the people in their political rights and they disseminated this information in a cheap and easily digested form. Many other radicals produced an impressive array of individual pamphlets, but none could match the success of Paine's *Rights of Man* (1791–2). Published in many cheap editions it certainly reached many tens of thousands of readers; some historians have suggested a circulation of perhaps 200 000 copies and a total readership of more than twice as many.[48] This enormous success owed much to the appeal of Paine's radical views, especially his proposals for relieving the distress of the labouring poor, but it was also due to Paine's ability to communicate with ordinary men. Paine was very conscious of his readers and of the effect he wished to have on them. His style was bold and clear, his case was well-ordered and carefully marshalled, and he had a rare gift for combining lucid, rational argument with the capacity to touch the heart and stir the imagination. Paine's work was not as philosophically profound as William Godwin's *Enquiry Concerning Political Justice* (1793), which had a very considerable impact on radical intellectuals, but in his ability to reach a mass readership Paine stood head and shoulders above all other radical theorists.[49]

As well as educating a wide public the radicals devised a variety of means to recruit popular support for their aims and to demonstrate that unity was strength. The most consistent way of achieving this was through the public petition to king or parliament. In 1769 the SSBR organised the first nationwide petitioning campaign clearly initiated and fully orchestrated by extra-parliamentary groups rather than being inspired by opposition elements within parliament. The SSBR urged clubs, societies and individuals across the country to petition parliament over the Middlesex election case. About 18 counties petitioned and, in a further eight, radical groups discussed doing so. A dozen boroughs also sent in petitions and several others indicated some degree of support for Wilkes. Nearly 60 000 people altogether signed these petitions.[50]

During the long dispute with the American colonies petitioning was a major response of those who took issue with government policies. As early as 1765 some twenty-five petitions were sent to parliament in protest against the Stamp Act, while at the height of the American crisis in 1774–6 a positive flood of petitions reached king or parliament. More than a dozen counties and nearly sixty towns in England alone sent petitions; in many places rural petitions urging either conciliation or coercion were drafted. In 1775 over 40 000 signatures were attached to the petitions drafted in England, over 10 000 of them in Lancashire alone, while several thousand additional signatures were gathered in Scotland and Ireland. Although few of the petitioners were poor men, most were drawn from shopkeepers, artisans and others in the middling orders. Clearly, large numbers of people were both well informed and deeply concerned about the actions of the British government in the American colonies.[51]

Wyvill and the Association mounted petitioning campaigns more consistently than any other radical organisation. Their greatest effort was made in 1780 when about 60 000 signatures were secured in 26 counties (over 8000 signatures in Yorkshire alone) and in a handful of boroughs. Another petitioning campaign in 1782–3 had less support from the counties (only 12 petitioned), but it aroused greater interest in the boroughs (23 of which sent in petitions). Apart from London, Westminster, York and Gloucester, however, few of these boroughs were of great significance. Several large towns, including Bristol, Liverpool, Nottingham, Newcastle, Manchester and Birmingham, did not petition on this occasion, though they had organised other petitions in recent years. The total number of people who signed the petitions in 1782–3 was only about 20 000, half of them from Yorkshire alone. In 1785 when the Prime Minister himself proposed a modest reform bill, Wyvill could encourage only two counties and 12 boroughs to petition.[52]

The radicals of the 1790s were rarely able to match the petitioning campaigns of the Wilkites and the Association movement. There was no nationwide campaign for parliamentary reform in 1793, when Charles Grey introduced a motion for reform; only a rash of separate petitions which failed to demonstrate overwhelming support for the radical cause. Thirty-six petitions were sent to the House of Commons, but 24 of these were from Scotland and not one was from an English county. The Sheffield petition attracted some 8000 signatures, but that from London could secure only 6000 signatures and the petition from Norwich was signed by no more than 3700 people.[53] Clearly, there was some considerable support for parliamentary reform, but nothing approaching mass support or an irresistible tide in favour of change. The radicals were more successful in 1795 when, allied with the Foxite opposition in parliament and moderate opinion out-of-doors, they organised a nationwide protest against the government's repressive legislation. On this issue some 95 petitions, with over 130 000 signatures, were presented to parliament. In defence of the traditional liberties of free speech and free assembly the radicals could rally an impressive degree of support, even though they were not able to prevent the government's repressive legislation reaching the statute books.[54]

Although there was never a fully integrated radical movement at any stage in the later eighteenth century efforts were made to coordinate the efforts of the various clubs, societies and associations across the nation. The SSBR and later the Constitutional Society in London gave a lead to the provincial clubs and societies. Wyvill's Yorkshire Association, while not the most radical of the local county and borough associations, was usually in the vanguard of the petitioning campaigns and Wyvill himself organised meetings of delegates in London to coordinate strategy and to discuss policy. It was not until the early 1790s however that the radicals took up the idea of calling a national convention, a proposal first suggested by James Burgh in 1774 and more recently advocated by Thomas Paine and Joseph Gerrald.[55] These theorists had suggested that a national convention could emulate the American and French efforts to draw up a written constitution and to challenge the established political institutions of the state. Few radical activists were prepared to take such a revolutionary step, but they did favour a convention which would unite the various radical societies behind an agreed reform programme that could be presented to parliament and the people. The first practical steps towards a national convention were taken by the Scottish reformers in December 1792 when some 260 delegates representing eighty radical societies in Scotland met in Edinburgh. They agreed on resolutions in support of moderate parliamentary reform, though the two leading delegates, Thomas Muir and William Skirving, held more advanced views. Muir read what some regarded as a seditious address from the United Irishmen in Dublin and the convention's adjournment was marked by French revolutionary procedures including the Jacobin oath to 'live free or die'. When the convention reassembled in Edinburgh on 30 April 1793 it was again divided between moderates and radicals, though the latter secured a resolution in favour of inviting English delegates to a larger convention in the autumn. Before that could meet, Thomas Muir was found guilty of sedition and was sentenced to 14 years transportation to Botany Bay.[56]

The apparently vindictive trial of Muir provoked widespread indignation and failed to divert some of the English radical societies from sending delegates to Edinburgh. The LCS sent Maurice Margarot and Joseph Gerrald, while the London and Sheffield SCI and the Norwich radicals also sent delegates. Although only a few English delegates attended the national convention in Edinburgh, their reputation and experience enabled them to play a decisive role in the assembly's deliberations. They devised its regulations, presided over its meetings and initiated its policies. Their commitment to radical parliamentary reform, their adoption of French revolutionary procedures and their uncompromising defiance of established authority impressed the Scottish radicals but alarmed those in power. Though the convention never advocated violence during its meetings in November–December 1793, several of its leading members were arrested. Skirving, Margarot and Gerrald were convicted of sedition and transported to Botany Bay. The idea of a national convention was a significant innovation, but the radicals had seriously miscalculated the extent of popular support for its activities and they had dangerously underestimated the fears which it would arouse among those in authority.[57]

The meetings of clubs, societies and conventions, the signing of petitions and the reading of radical propaganda appear to have attracted the interest of reformers largely drawn from the middling ranks of society. Efforts were made however to enlist the support of the more humble and less literate sectors of society, an endeavour which met with mixed results. John Wilkes was remarkably successful in his attempts to attract popular support by making radical politics enjoyable, entertaining and exciting. He made extra-parliamentary politics a communal activity by recognising the impact of ritual, spectacle and ceremony. Public celebrations, feasts, processions and crowd demonstrations were all seen as vehicles for attaching popular support to the radical cause. Such activities coordinated behaviour, established unity and created a sense of community among the participants. The authority of the established elite was explicitly challenged in such rituals as burning opponents in effigy, while support for Wilkes was demonstrated in a whole series of celebrations commemorating the various achievements of his career. Bonfires, gun salutes, fireworks, music and heavy drinking were features of many of these celebrations. Wilkes himself did much to persuade craftsmen to commercialise radical politics by producing a whole range of artefacts with a political connotation. Pottery of all kinds, including porcelain figures, plates, teapots, shaving mugs and snuff boxes, all appeared with Wilkite decorations. So did medals, buttons, rings, brooches, badges and candles.[58] The number '45' appeared on a vast range of products because it was easy to execute, it was recognised by the illiterate, and it could be attached to or drawn on almost any object. It could be used to denote a unit of time, space or mass. It was even chalked on walls and doors, and embroidered on clothes. This simple device became a sign or symbol for Wilkes, liberty and the whole radical cause. In many parts of the country Wilkite festivities were marked by inspired use of the number '45'.[59] Wilkes's release from prison on 18 April 1770 was celebrated in communities across England. In Gateshead, for example, a tobacco-pipe maker produced 45 pipes 45 inches long for local journeymen who prepared a feast of 45 lbs of mutton, 45 large potatoes, 45 biscuits and 45 quarts of ale.[60]

Much of the crowd behaviour in Wilkite demonstrations was rich in anti-authority ritual, but most of these demonstrations remained orderly. Workers involved in violent industrial disputes at the time occasionally used Wilkite slogans, but they were motivated more by economic grievances than by political demands. There was undoubtedly some violence and intimidation by Wilkite crowds, but violence was not usually seen as a means of applying pressure to the ruling elite. There was certainly nothing revolutionary about these disturbances. Indeed, it is not certain what positive political aims were shared by these crowds. In general, it is doubtful whether they were committed to an extensive programme of parliamentary reform. The crowds were protesting about the abuse of power by those in positions of authority and they wanted to proclaim their independence from the patrician elite, but they were less articulate than those who supported the petitioning campaigns. Wilkes himself and nearly all the radicals of his day had a horror of mob violence and, apart from Wilkes, they rather disdained the labouring poor.[61]

The radicals of the 1790s, despite their more popular support, also failed to exploit the popular tradition of riots and crowd demonstrations as a means of putting pressure on the governing elite and they had not yet appreciated the political potential of organised labour. Although workers' combinations or trade unions had begun to appear in a number of industries and had already demonstrated their strength in a number of violent protests and effective strikes, most radicals had not yet grasped that labour's industrial strength might become a powerful weapon of political change. Most radical theorists were still limited by their bourgeois conceptions of society and still concentrated on the freedom of the individual. There are some indications that a few radical theorists (including Paine, Spence, Thelwall and Godwin) were conscious of the important role which labour played in the production of wealth, and they did argue for a fairer distribution of that wealth, but they did not recognise that the workers might be the means of their own salvation if they put their numerical strength and economic value to good use. None of the radicals advocated economic action, through the industrial strike for example, as a means of wringing substantial political concessions from the propertied classes.[62] Few radicals sprang from the ranks of the poor or fully identified with the labouring masses. In the realm of practical affairs there was some overlap between those who were members of radical societies and those who were involved in trade union activity, but this did not encourage the notion that trade unions should be harnessed to the cause of parliamentary reform. There were also isolated examples of political slogans being used during industrial disputes and food riots as on Tyneside in 1792–3, in Sheffield in 1795 and during food riots in the north-west in 1800, but these riots and strikes were not primarily concerned with political issues and very few of those involved were radicals with an overtly political agenda.[63]

From 1795 onwards, when the radicals were faced with increasing government repression, there were signs that the political activists were beginning to appreciate the value of crowd demonstrations, but there was no coordinated strategy of using widespread rioting as a means of changing the political policies of the governing elite. For many years the radicals had organised large public meetings (on 24 June 1775, for example, 2500 London liverymen had attended a meeting in Common Hall to urge the government to adopt a conciliatory stance towards the American colonies[64]), but it was not until 1795 that the LCS began to organise monster open-air meetings to demonstrate mass support for the cause of reform. On 26 October 1795, a vast crowd, reputed to be 100 000 strong, assembled in the fields near Copenhagen House to hear speeches in favour of political reform and peace with France delivered by John Thelwall, John Gale Jones and John Binns. This meeting provoked government repression in the form of the Seditious Meetings Act and the Treasonable Practices Act, but before these measures were passed the radicals had held similar meetings. On 12 November 1795 a larger crowd, perhaps the greatest gathering yet assembled for a political cause, again met near Copenhagen House to hear John Thelwall, John Ashley and Richard Hodgson condemn the government's policies. A similar protest meeting was held in Marylebone Fields on 7 December. These crowds demonstrated mass opposition to the government's repressive policies and there were also protests against the high price of food and the enormous costs of the war.[65] It is unlikely that all those present supported a radical reform of parliament, but these meetings were a significant innovation in radical strategy. They did not indicate however that the radicals planned to move from peaceful crowd demonstrations to violent riots or mass insurrection as the authorities feared. When the governing classes refused to be persuaded by reason or intimidated by numbers, and resorted to repression and persecution, most radicals lost heart or at least moderated their public conduct. Only a minority turned as a last resort to conspiracy and violence.

V   THE REVOLUTIONARY UNDERGROUND

The radical societies of the early 1790s always explicitly renounced any desire to achieve their aims by force and none of their leaders was actually convicted of promoting violent revolution. Despite their rhetoric and their admiration for the

French Revolution most radicals were parliamentary reformers. Had they achieved their main aims – especially universal
manhood suffrage and annual parliaments – then very drastic
changes might have followed, but they claimed to be acting
constitutionally and few contemplated revolution on the
French model even in the dark days of the later 1790s. Nearly
all the radical theorists were equally cautious about suggesting
the need for revolution. Thomas Spence and John Baxter were
more equivocal when they wrote about the right to self-defence
or the right to resist oppression, though even they envisaged a
popular recourse to arms only after the governing elite had
resorted to outright force to preserve their privileged position.
Thomas Paine, eventually, and James Oswald, in his *Review of
the Constitution of Great Britain* (1793), are among the exceptions who came to believe that only violent revolution could
secure the rights of man in Britain.[66] The governing authorities of the day however did believe that there was considerable
evidence to suggest that there were many men of violence plot-
ting revolution in Britain. Later historians have found it difficult to decide whether the evidence available on the
conspiracies of the 1790s shows that they were practical
projects or merely the fantasies of deluded men, the work of a
few fanatics or proof of a profound popular disenchantment
with the prevailing political and social order. Some historians
have tended to play down the significance of the threat of revolution in Britain in the 1790s,[67] whereas others have gone to
considerable lengths to demonstrate how much support the
revolutionaries possessed.[68] Yet others have accepted that a revolutionary movement existed, but are less convinced of its
effectiveness or its degree of popular support.[69] It is unlikely
that historians will ever reach full agreement on the issue.

The militant elements among the United Irishmen certainly
plotted violent rebellion in Ireland and they sought to export
their revolutionary activity to Britain.[70] They made contact
with Irishmen who had settled in Lancashire, central Scotland
and the poorer areas of London, but they were not the only
conspirators in Britain. The government's repressive policies
and the severe economic distress caused by bad harvests, high
taxation and trade dislocation drove some of the more militant
British radicals to contemplate revolution. By 1797 societies of
United Scotsmen, United Englishmen and United Britons – in

central Scotland, north-west England and London – were in contact with the United Irishmen, were collecting arms and were practising military drill. They swore secret oaths of loyalty and dedicated themselves to radical parliamentary reform by force if necessary. They claimed the support of many thousands, though, in fact, these conspirators may only have numbered a few hundred. Most were poor men – weavers, spinners, tailors, shoemakers and labourers.

Their existence however cannot be doubted, nor can their willingness to contemplate violent revolution. Their leaders were drawn from local radical societies – George Mealmaker in Dundee, William Cheetham and James Dixon in Lancashire, and John and Benjamin Binns, John Bone, Thomas Evans and Alexander Galloway from the LCS in London. These men made contact with agents of the United Irishmen and with French revolutionaries. They failed to establish a unified command structure however or to adopt an agreed policy of action. Although they collected arms and plotted insurrection, it is very unlikely that they could ever have achieved much without a French invasion. Apart from conspiring with the French and encouraging some soldiers and sailors to mutiny they had no effective strategy. In the event the government penetrated the various conspiracies throughout the nation and in 1798 made arrests in all areas where insurrection was being plotted. The conspiracy in Britain (if not in Ireland) was crushed long before the movement had enlisted mass support. Subsequent arrests ensured that the revolutionary underground could never develop a coordinated strategy or plan insurrection on a large scale. Isolated groups continued to hold the occasional secret or nocturnal gathering, but violent revolution was never the preferred option of significant numbers of British radicals.[71]

The poor, who did face very harsh economic circumstances in the 1790s, were never fully radicalised. A fusion of popular hardship and political radicalism might have produced an explosive mixture capable of shaking the foundations of the state but such a fusion never occurred. The radical leadership did not succeed in enlisting the poor in huge numbers and the elite attacked the material causes and limited the political consequences of poverty by expanding poor relief and private charity and by encouraging a moral revolution.[72] In many ways therefore the most alarmingly subversive development of the 1790s was not the activities of radical activists or the popular protests of the labouring poor, but the growing disaffection in the Royal Navy, the country's first and most vital line of defence against the French threat. The initial causes, and no doubt the major precipitants of the mutinies at Spithead and the Nore, in April–May 1797, were the bitter grievances of the sailors with regard to their pay and appalling conditions of service, but there may also have been a degree of political motivation. William Pitt, the prime minister, appears to have been convinced that radical instigators had incited the seamen to revolt, though his agents failed to establish any definite link between the mutineers and political radicals. Certainly no mutineer was ever charged with treasonable political activity and most historians have blamed the mutinies on the bad conditions of service in the fleet. A few scholars however have been impressed by the way the seamen's organisation, language and use of oaths reflected the structure and practices of the United Irishmen and the LCS. There is some evidence of cells of United Irishmen being established in the fleet before the mutinies, some mutineers spoke of the need for political changes, and delegates of the LCS visited the naval dockyards and distributed radical handbills. While this evidence is rather sketchy and is not entirely reliable, it does seem likely that the United Irishmen and the LCS made some contact with the mutineers and some seamen were politically conscious. None the less, the weight of evidence and the actual behaviour of the vast majority of the seamen suggest that the dispute was primarily over pay and conditions, and that when these grievances were redressed support for the mutiny quickly collapsed.[73]

VI CONCLUSION

The radicals of the later eighteenth century failed to achieve their major objective, the reform of parliament. There were many reasons for this failure. Probably at no stage were the radical activists a majority of the politically conscious classes and only intermittently could they count upon widespread support. The radicals were divided among themselves over ideology, aims and methods. They faced powerful and resilient institutions which were defended by the ruling elite and were supported by a sophisticated conservative ideology. Circumstances over which they had no control also conspired against them. The ending of the war with the American colonies removed a major issue that had focused attention on the failings of existing institutions, while violence in France and the outbreak of war in the early 1790s alarmed a wide cross-section of society and created a patriotic desire to defend the established order. The radicals also failed however because the more popular support they gained, the more the ruling elite refused to debate the issue with them, but sought instead simply to silence them. Although the term applied to government repression in the 1790s – Pitt's Reign of Terror – is an exaggeration, government persecution and loyalist intimidation did much to destroy the radical threat in the 1790s. The government employed agents, spies and *agents provocateurs* to penetrate and subvert the radical movement. Nearly every leading radical theorist and activist was harassed, arrested, prosecuted, imprisoned, transported or driven into exile. Civil liberties were infringed, radical meetings were restricted and radical societies were banned. Place-holders and place-hunters were hired to produce a veritable flood of conservative propaganda that smeared the radicals by exaggerating their demands and accusing them of levelling aspirations. Worse still, the government encouraged, or at least turned a blind eye to, the intimidatory tactics employed by the militant loyalists who sprang up in opposition to the British Jacobins of the early 1790s.[74]

Because the radicals of the later eighteenth century failed to achieve a reform of parliament it is easy to conclude that they had little influence on British politics. It is a mistake however to make such a crude assessment of their political significance. Even if we look only at the radicals' influence on the existing political institutions, it is possible to point to a number of successes. Crown patronage, for example, was steadily curtailed from the early 1780s onwards and there was a significant revival of partisan politics in the larger, more open constituencies. Parliamentary reform was not achieved, but some committed reformers were elected to parliament and the reform bill of 1785 did secure the support of 174 MPs. The condemnation of general warrants and the relaxation of the restrictions on press reports on parliamentary debates were also significant achievements.

The really important successes of the radicals however were achieved at the local level where they experimented in how to rally support among the middling orders of society. The radicals began to challenge local elites in many of the large towns and they exploited the press more effectively than ever before. Clubs and pressure groups had existed before 1760, but they had not been directed so explicitly towards overtly political objectives. Petitioning and instruction campaigns had also been waged earlier in the eighteenth century, bur rarely had they been so widespread, so well supported and so independent of the parliamentary elite. Crowd demonstrations were also an endemic feature of eighteenth-century Britain, but before the age of Wilkes they had rarely been enlisted in the cause of extra-parliamentary forces challenging the political power of the patrician elite. Never before had politics seemed so exciting, instructive and relevant to so many people outside the ruling classes as they did in the later eighteenth century.

The extent to which extra-parliamentary politics was transformed by the radicals and reformers of the later eighteenth century can be seen most clearly by examining their impact on other groups who sought to influence the decisions of the governing elite. The Protestant Association, for example, had a charismatic leader, established societies across the country, distributed a great deal of propaganda, organised public meetings and crowd demonstrations, and presented a massive petition to parliament. The activities of a whole range of economic and moral pressure groups in the later eighteenth century demonstrated how much they had learned from the radicals. The ironmasters of the west midlands, the potters of Staffordshire, the cottonmasters of Manchester, the Dissenters seeking the repeal of the Test and Corporation Acts and, most of all, those who campaigned to abolish the slave trade, all adopted most of the methods developed and exploited by the radicals in their efforts to influence parliament. Perhaps even more significant was the extent to which those extra-parliamentary groups dedicated to the defence of the existing political system adopted similar tactics to those who were seeking to challenge it. The loyalists who wished to protect the constitution from the attacks of colonial rebels, French revolutionaries or domestic radicals used the press, supported petitions, established local political associations and organised crowd demonstrations at least as effectively as their radical opponents. Extra-parliamentary politics was not restricted to the dissatisfied elements seeking constitutional reform, but embraced even larger numbers in defence of existing policies and practices. This would not have occurred if the radicals had not set the political agenda and raised the political temperature. The radicals succeeded in making politics out-of-doors a vital part of the whole political culture of later eighteenth-century Britain.

8 Popular Conservatism and Militant Loyalism

Nearly all historians interested in the politics of the people in eighteenth-century Britain have concentrated much of their attention on the development of radical ideas and the rise of popular societies dedicated to parliamentary reform. In seeking to explain why radicalism failed, these historians have rarely acknowledged that the reform movement was simply not attractive to large numbers of the middling and lower orders. They have seen failure in terms of aristocratic hegemony and the willingness of the governing elite to use naked force or judicial persecution to frustrate any challenge to their authority. These explanations have failed to carry complete conviction, however, and so, more recently, alternative explanations have been sought. While not denying the power of the ruling elite or their control of the institutions of church and state, Professor Ian Christie has asserted that it was the pluralistic character of British society and the responsiveness of its political institutions that gave it the unique capacity to absorb both the pressures created by major socio-economic changes and the internal conflict generated by opposing interest groups.[1] Professor Christie and other historians have also acknowledged the existence of a sophisticated conservative ideology, which defended the authority and privileges of the governing elite and praised the virtues of the existing constitution.[2] What he and they have failed to do, however, is to examine what kind of conservative political message was disseminated to the people at large and what response these efforts evoked.[3] When explorations in this direction are made, it becomes clear that the middling and lower orders were not only taught a conservative political message; large numbers of them also absorbed it and acted upon it. An examination of popular political attitudes reveals how deep and widespread were popular patriotism and loyalism, and popular support for established institutions and traditional values. Although popular conservatism and militant loyalism was never as autonomous as popular radicalism, in that much of its ideology was written and propagated at the behest of those in positions of authority and many of its actions were incited or legitimated by men of standing, it did occasionally develop political organisations and a whole range of techniques which were similar to, but even more effective than, those of their radical opponents. Moreover, although often requiring a lead to be given by those in authority, popular conservatism and militant loyalism were never simply the creation of the governing elite. Conservative propagandists were clearly reinforcing and tapping prejudices which already existed and which could, on occasion, escape from the control of those in authority or even manifest themselves in spontaneous and independent action. When cherished institutions and traditional values were seriously threatened by domestic radicals and foreign revolutionaries, the majority of the middling and lower orders willingly joined their social superiors in organising a powerful and successful response.

I   THE POPULAR DIMENSION IN CONSERVATIVE IDEOLOGY

Although the governing elite were sharply divided on many constitutional and political questions during the eighteenth century, they came close to unanimity in their hostility to radical change and their fear of popular sovereignty. When faced with demands for a radical redistribution of political power to the middling and lower orders, they rallied to the defence of the existing political and social order with appeals to religion, natural law, utility and history. They insisted on the value of tried and trusted institutions, they urged the need to restrain man's passionate and selfish nature, and they stressed that expedience and experience were much more important than abstract notions of liberty in assessing the value of any particular system of government or social arrangement. In their view, it was dangerously conceited for even the wisest of men to presume to elevate his reason above the judgement of centuries. An acceptance of God's will, submission to duly constituted authority and a reverence for the past were to be preferred above the speculative theories and abstract general principles propagated by those who desired radical change.

In responding to the radical challenge to the existing political and social order conservative thinkers developed a sophisticated ideology of great resilience, power and appeal. Much of
it was too philosophical or intellectually profound to be easily
disseminated to, or understood by, the middling and lower
orders, but those in authority did seek popular support for
their ideological stance. They did so by simplifying and popu-
larising conservative views which not only sustained their
privileged position, but also appealed to the deeply-held
prejudices of large numbers of ordinary citizens. The elite
recognised that there was widespread popular support for the
monarchy, the established church, the constitution, the existing social order and all things British. As well as encouraging
and fostering such views, they also incited popular hostility
against those who favoured radical change.[4]

Although in the earlier eighteenth century there were
serious disputes about which monarch had the more legitimate claim to the throne, there was no hostility to monarchy
as such and there was considerable support for the surviving
prerogative powers of the crown. Conservative opinion had
never quite accommodated itself to the Revolution of 1688 or
the accession of Dutch William. The demise of both William
III and James II at the beginning of the eighteenth century
released the Tories, who were a natural majority in the political
nation,[5] from the restraints imposed upon their loyalty to the
crown. They could not conceal their pleasure at the death of
William III and the proclamation of Queen Anne was met
'with the greatest appearance of Joy among all parts of people,
that ever I yet saw on the like occasion.'[6] Jonathan Swift was
soon to write of the rejuvenated Tories:

> As they prefer a well-regulated monarchy before all other
> forms of government; so they think it next to impossible to
> alter that institution here, without involving our whole
> island in blood and desolation. They believe, that the pre-
> rogative of a sovereign ought, at least, to be held as sacred
> and inviolable as the rights of his people, if only for this
> reason, because without a due share of power, he will not be
> able to protect them.[7]

Anne's reign saw a great revival of the cult of Charles I as the
'royal martyr', and many high-flying clergymen, most notably

Dr Henry Sacheverell, delivered highly-charged sermons on the subject of loyalty to the crown. In 1710, which witnessed a flood of loyal addresses to the crown from all over the country, Tories competed with each other in their submission to the Queen's authority.[8] The address from Gloucester declared: 'We are now, and always shall be, ready to sacrifice our lives and fortunes, in defence of Your Majesty's most sacred person, prerogative and government.'[9] The address from Warwick included the promise: 'We will continue to choose such Representatives, as shall have the profoundest veneration for your Majesty, [and] shall assert and maintain your hereditary title.'[10] The expressions of loyalty in these addresses were sometimes so excessive that even the Queen herself demurred at their tone. When she received the address from the City of London she 'immediately took exception to the expression that "her right was divine", ... [and] having thought often of it, she could by no means like it, and thought it so unfit to be given to anybody that she wished it might be left out.'[11]

During the reigns of the first two Hanoverian monarchs conservative opinion in Britain was divided on whether they or the Jacobite Pretender had the stronger claim to the throne, but *both* camps saw loyalty to the crown as an institution as the prime duty of subjects and as essential to the preservation of the constitution. Although to this day historians still remain divided on how popular the Jacobite cause really was, there can be no doubt that the scale of the propaganda, conspiracies and rebellions in favour of a Stuart restoration showed that loyalty to the Pretender had considerable popular appeal for some years after the Hanoverian succession. During every period of Jacobite unrest there was a minor rash of prosecutions across the country of indiscreet Stuart loyalists guilty of uttering seditious words.[12] Indeed, at times, the Whigs confessed their fear that the Pretender was more popular than the Hanoverian occupying the throne. In 1742 Thomas Winnington, a former Tory but now an ally of Sir Robert Walpole, admitted:

> there is a sort of enthusiastical spirit of disaffection that still prevails among the vulgar: and, I am afraid, there is by far too great a number of men of all ranks and conditions, who now seem to be true friends to the Protestant succession,

that would declare themselves otherwise, if they could do so without running any great or unequal risk.[13]

Neither George I nor George II was widely popular with the people at large. They were too foreign, too attached to Hanover, too aloof, and too much associated with partisan Whigs to be personally attractive to their ordinary subjects. Moreover, little effort was made to produce pro-Hanoverian propaganda during their reign, except when their claim to the throne was under threat, as it was during the 1745 rebellion.[14] None the less, conservative supporters of George I and George II were not content simply to claim that their right to the throne rested on the choice of parliament, still less on the choice of the people. They made great play of the notion that the succession to the crown remained hereditary. While deviations in the strict line of succession had been necessary, primarily as a means of safeguarding the Protestant religion, these had been minor and they had been sanctioned by divine providence. The remarkable success of the Glorious Revolution and the defeat of the Jacobite rebellions were seen as clear proof that God approved of the changes in the line of succession that had been necessary. Although the Hanoverian monarchs owed their crowns to an act of parliament, many conservatives preferred to stress that they occupied the throne as God's vicegerents and that they fully deserved to be honoured and revered by their subjects. In their view the sovereign was ordained by God and he remained the fount of authority, from whence all power descends to lower magistrates.[15] Thus, a Tory address to George I could still congratulate him upon his accession in 'high church' sentiments:

> Wee have been always educated in those principles of loyalty and obedience which are taught by the Church of England and enforced by the laws, which ... strictly enjoyn us to support the right of your Ma[jes]tie and royal house to the imperial crown of this realme.[16]

Even the opponents of George II's ministers were keen to display their admiration for his heir apparent, Prince Frederick, and they themselves hoped to exploit the aura which most men ascribed to kingship. In his *Idea of a Patriot King*, Bolingbroke declared:

I esteem monarchy above every other form of government and hereditary monarchy above elective ... the character and government of a Patriot King can be established on no other [principles], if their office and their right are not always held divine, and their persons always sacred.[17]

By the time of the Jacobite rebellion of 1745 the tide of loyalty in England at least was clearly flowing in the direction of George II. Although nearly a hundred individuals in and around London were arraigned for expressing pro-Jacobite or at least anti-Hanoverian sympathies, Jacobitism had become a minority movement. Relatively few Britons, even fewer Englishmen, actively supported the rebellion. Popular loyalty to George II was widely expressed in drawing up addresses, creating armed associations and raising subscriptions on a large scale. The merchant community expressed unanimous enthusiasm for the king, large crowds burned the Pretender in effigy and there was a veritable flood of anti-Jacobite and anti-Catholic propaganda. In the popular mind the Jacobite cause had come to symbolise the return of absolutism and the denial of national identity and hence it was no longer capable of rallying mass support.[18]

By the time George III ascended the throne in 1760 the Jacobite cause had ceased to be a viable alternative and the new monarch could tap a strong groundswell of loyalty to a genuinely British king. He benefited from a fusion of the old divine right doctrine of hereditary succession with the notion of the divine right of providence.[19] Both old-fashioned Tories and conservative Whigs could rally behind his right to the throne and they could willingly encourage popular loyalty to the monarch. Although the king's attitudes towards the Wilkes affair and the American problem lost him much liberal support in the early decades of his reign, these crises did, in fact, make him more popular in conservative circles. By the end of the American war he had even become a symbol of stability. Thereafter, he was increasingly identified with the nation's achievements and with the preservation of the vital balance between liberty and order. When he recovered from his first serious bout of illness in 1789 his popularity with the people at large was demonstrated by a veritable flood of addresses expressing the nation's sense of relief.[20] This attitude was greatly reinforced in the 1790s when the French Revolution and the French War were seen as alarming threats to the British constitution, the prevailing social order and even Britain's independence as a nation. George III increasingly became the symbol of Britain's interests and the centre of loyalty to existing institutions. The monarch's appeal was heightened by extensive reportage in the press, by an increasing number of popular celebrations in which loyalty to the monarch was a prominent feature, and by a widespread recognition that loyalty to George III was a patriotic duty required of all true Britons who wished to see the preservation of the country from the alarming threat posed by the French.[21] Some high church conservative clergymen, such as George Horne and Bishop Horsley, were so devoted to the monarch and so ready to exalt monarchy that they resurrected older notions of divine right and claimed that the king's authority was in fact superior to that of parliament. Several dozen pamphlets put forward this exaggerated view of monarchy in the 1790s.[22] In his ultra-conservative pamphlet, *Thoughts on English Government* (1795), John Reeves stressed that the government of the country was essentially monarchical and that Lords and Commons were subordinate and subsidiary to royal authority. Even the Younger Pitt's conservative administration felt obliged to condemn such views as 'unconstitutional', but they were clearly indicative of the tide of loyalty flowing in favour of George III in particular and monarchy in general as the eighteenth century drew to a close.[23]

Rivalling the monarchy both as a source of power and as an institution with widespread popular support was the Church of England. Despite the survival of Dissent and, by the later eighteenth century, the growth in the number of people who ceased to attend any church, the Church of England retained the overwhelming support of the English people in all ranks of society. The political power and widespread influence of the Church rested on firm foundations. Its bishops sat in the House of Lords and its communicants dominated the many offices in central and local government. The Church still possessed considerable wealth, property and patronage, and it played a major role in education, charity and the dissemination of news and views. Its parish structure remained the basic unit of local government and administration. Its ceremonies and rituals marked the major rites of passage of nearly all English citizens and, for many, it offered a focus to their daily lives and a consolation in death.

The Church of England also played a central role in conservative political ideology.[24] Throughout the eighteenth century conservatives agreed that government in general was ordained by God and that the workings of civil society were at the mercy of divine providence. It was a view propagated not only by the Tories, but by the majority of Whigs. Most political commentators never abandoned the conviction that it was God alone who sanctioned and supported all authority. Long after the collapse of the old Tory party the House of Lords was being informed by a Whig Bishop of Oxford:

> That civil government cannot subsist without regard to the will of God, or, in other words, without the sanctions of religions, is manifest from the universal experience and practice of mankind ... human laws can never inforce an obedience adequate to their purpose, unless it be grafted upon a prior principle of obedience to the laws of God ... The will of God being the first principle and foundation of civil government; from the same principle the obligation of obedience to legal authority, and reverence to governors, as the ministers of God, immediately arises.[25]

It was believed that God ordained government in order to subdue the passions of men. To preserve society and to enable men to pursue their duty to God there had to be a firmly established authority in the state. This was only possible where power was deliberately limited to the few and obedience was willingly rendered by the many. Both the right to govern and the duty to obey were sanctioned by the will of God. In order to combat the threat posed by those who would rebel against God and nature it was essential to provide civil government with the support and sanction of religion. Neither public morality nor political duties could ever be separated from the Christian religion. The established Church of England, in particular, provided one of the strongest bonds of society and was an indispensable ally of the state. Assertive Anglicanism kept both the Dissenters and the Roman Catholics on the defensive for much of the eighteenth century. Even when the Dissenters did launch major campaigns for the repeal of the Test and

Corporation Acts they not only failed in their objectives, but provoked an Anglican reaction both in parliament and in the nation at large. The Church of England prided itself on preaching obedience to the powers that be and on inculcating the doctrines of non-resistance and passive obedience. It also campaigned against vice and immorality and encouraged citizens to cultivate such moral virtues as humility, sobriety, frugality and industry.[26] Religion, not political reform, was offered as their guide and solace. Those men therefore who undermined organised religion or challenged the special privileges of the Church of England were regarded as the enemies of political order and public morality. By the 1790s conservative opinion was bitterly hostile to the French Revolution precisely because it sought to undermine Christianity and organised religion. The French were accused of forsaking truth and virtue and of substituting the unrestrained will of man for the providential dispensations of God. The ideological crusade against them involved a struggle for religion against atheism.

The legislature could never command such popular and intense loyalty as the person of the monarch or the Church of England, but there can be no doubt that, as both Whigs and Tories came to appreciate the political benefits of annual sessions of parliament, the notion that ultimate sovereignty lay not in the monarch alone but in the combined legislature of King, Lords and Commons proved increasingly attractive.[27] The constitutional settlement eventually reached after the Glorious Revolution was widely credited with saving the country from Catholicism and royal absolutism and with inaugurating a period of unparalleled political liberty, social stability and economic advance. Throughout the eighteenth century most people in Britain were confident that they enjoyed greater freedom than any other country. The preservation of justice, the rule of law, freedom from state oppression and a careful balance between liberty and order were all attributed to the existence of parliament and to the sovereignty of the legislature. The delicate balance between King, Lords and Commons was seen as essential to the preservation of civil liberty and the securing of stability, and as the best means of averting both arbitrary power and political anarchy. An increasing tide of conservative propaganda therefore urged the British people to cherish a constitution which had clearly gained the admiration of the civilised world. This marvellous and intricate system of checks and balances provided firm leadership, important limitations on the power of the state and a legislature which represented property and all the important social and economic interests in the nation. Radical appeals to popular sovereignty were condemned for threatening to unleash the will of the impoverished and uneducated masses and so undermine all liberty, property and order in the state. Since all British subjects already enjoyed the substantial benefits bestowed by the best constitution which human wisdom and long experience could contrive, it was highly dangerous to criticise it and absolute folly to risk changing it merely so that it could accord better with the speculative designs of impractical theorists.

In defending an essentially aristocratic constitution, in which only a minority of men could expect to wield direct power in the legislature, conservative propaganda rejected the concept of natural rights and the notion of natural equality and hence opposed the radical claim that all men should possess the same positive political rights. Although it was accepted that all men shared a common humanity, it was stressed that men were so unequal in their physical abilities and mental capacities that it was both natural and inevitable that they would acquire varying amounts of property and exercise unequal degrees of power in the state. The more prosperous and commercial a society became the more property and power would be unequally distributed. There was a wide measure of agreement that the protection of property therefore was one of the most important duties of civil government and hence men of substantial property could be most trusted to exercise political influence over the affairs of state. The possession of substantial wealth gave the propertied elite a major stake in society and made it more likely that they would have the solid judgement, ample intelligence and ability to command others and to defend the state. Both the majority of those who defended the ruling elite in the eighteenth century and those who employed a Country ideology to oppose them were agreed that only those who possessed a real and substantial stake in the country were the natural leaders. Their property gave them both the independence and the sense of responsibility that were needed to govern the rest of society. Country spokesmen were fearful of the political influence of financiers, stockjobbers and other monied men, whose wealth was fluid, insecure, based on speculation and capable of corrupting the political, social and moral order. Not all conservative spokesmen for the government shared such fears, but both sides engaged in this debate on the political influence to be conferred on landed or monied wealth agreed that those with little or no property of any kind should be excluded from the decision-making process of the state. Propaganda from both sides stressed that inequality was natural and divinely ordained. Those in the middling and lower ranks of society were urged to be content with the station in life to which they had been assigned by providence. Great care was taken to inform them that God had deliberately ordained that there would be rich and poor, each enjoying the benefits and burdens of its particular rank in society and each dependent on the other. The rich certainly enjoyed the fruits of wealth, but they also shouldered greater cares and responsibilities. The poor possessed few luxuries, but they could enjoy the benefits of continuous labour and the pleasures of a simple, frugal existence. The rich depended upon the labour of the poor, but the rich in turn provided the latter with employment, charity and good government. All sections of society therefore would suffer if the natural distinctions between men were eliminated. Most men in the middling and lower ranks of society would have much to lose if property rights were not defended and the rule of law collapsed. Rash attempts to redistribute property would first make all men poor and would then lead to determined attempts to restore inequality, by force if necessary.[28]

Obviously, conservative arguments of this kind were a case of special pleading designed to preserve an hierarchical society and to maintain the special privileges of the propertied elite. None the less, many in the middling and lower orders of society accepted these arguments and fully endorsed the notion that the minority in society who clearly enjoyed wealth and status should also dominate the political system and exercise much greater power than their mere numbers would indicate. Most men were born into a position of dependence upon their social superiors and never questioned the oft-repeated propaganda that this was the natural and divinely ordained state of affairs. Indeed, the popular attachment to established institutions and traditional values – to the monarchy, the Church of England, parliament and the hierarchical social order – was so great that it produced a deep prejudice in favour of all things regarded as uniquely 'English' (or at least 'British') and an almost unthinking hostility to anything deemed 'foreign'. Pride, self-satisfaction and complacency about British institutions and values fed xenophobia and a patriotism which was rapidly advancing towards fervent nationalism.

A pride in things 'English' (or later 'British') influenced attitudes towards the monarchy, the established Church, the constitution and all foreigners. William III and the first two Georges were unpopular because they were clearly foreigners who protected the interests of their homeland and who liked to be surrounded by their fellow countrymen. The Jacobite Pretender, James Edward, enjoyed the benefits of an English birth, but suffered the severe disadvantages of belonging to a foreign church and being dependent upon foreign powers. On the other hand, both Queen Anne and George III were popular precisely because they could boast of their English birth and their attachment to British interests. Popular support for the Church of England was also gained because it was seen as being peculiarly 'English', whereas English Roman Catholics and the various Dissenting churches were regarded as 'foreign'. Religious divisions within Britain were far less important than the virulent Protestantism that did so much to unite the vast majority of Britons and to distinguish them in their own minds from their foreign enemies. A continuous outpouring of propaganda – in sermons, newspapers, pamphlets and works of history and in the most popular works of the age (such as Foxe's *Book of Martyrs*, Bunyan's *Pilgrim's Progress* and the tens of thousands of almanacs produced every year) convinced the majority of Britons that they had a mission to defend Protestantism and to oppose Catholicism. Protestant Britons came to believe that they were a chosen people, that God was watching over them, that His providence had made them peculiarly free and prosperous, and that their rights and privileges were gravely threatened by Roman Catholic enemies, and by the French in particular.[29]

British liberties and Britain's much-cherished constitution were regarded as superior to any other in the world and as under threat from absolutist regimes in Europe. Indeed, Britain's colonial possessions, her overseas trade and her very security were seen as being endangered by foreign enemies. Fear bred a virulent xenophobia which incited bitter hostility even towards foreigners visiting Britain, those seeking to become naturalised British citizens, and those such as the Dutch, who were often in alliance with Britain. Although these foreigners were regarded as inferior, they were perceived as a threat to the established church or to the political and economic interests of the country. The French, on the other hand, were feared precisely because they were a formidable military threat, a dangerous colonial and commercial rival, and the cultural arbiters of Europe. Tensions created by French support for a Jacobite rebellion, a long series of bloody and expensive wars, and a sense of cultural inferiority produced a fierce reaction which led not just to xenophobia, but to efforts to focus loyalty and national self-identification on purely British institutions and values. A great deal of patriotic propaganda highlighted the contrasts between the perceived characteristics of the British and those of the French and the myth of British superiority and national identity was born.[30]

Conservative propaganda tried to defend established institutions and traditional values by asserting that it was a religious duty to submit to the powers that be and that it was immoral to promote reform or encourage rebellion. Throughout the eighteenth century most of the clergy of the Church of England and many of the conservative laity preached the doctrines of non-resistance and passive obedience. At first complete submission and obedience to the monarch alone was demanded, but later subordination to the sovereign legislature was required. Government in general, rather than just monarchy in particular, was seen to be divinely ordained and hence obedience was a religious duty. Indeed, it was one of the prime duties of religion to preach subordination:

> the generality of men must not by any means be left wholly to the workings of their own minds, to the use of their natural faculties, and to the bare convictions of their own reason; but they must be particularly taught and instructed

in their duty, must have their motives of it frequently and strongly pressed and inculcated upon them with great authority and must have many extraordinary assistance afforded them; to keep them effectually in the practice of the great and plainest duties of religion.[31]

Political power could be legitimately wielded only by those whose authority was sanctioned by God and positive law. Subjects could not lawfully oppose the commands of their superiors and could not legitimately decide for themselves who should rule. It was unnatural and dangerous to claim that all men had the right to exercise political power or influence. Men were not, in fact, born free but were born subject to existing authorities and established laws.[32] If order was to prevail, and anarchy and licentiousness were to be averted, then positive political power must be restricted to the qualified few and submission must be demanded of the many. The tyranny of the mob was far worse than the absolute authority of a single ruler.[33]

Views such as these led to harsh attacks on domestic radicals, who favoured popular sovereignty or urged resistance to those in authority, and to bitter condemnation of revolutionaries abroad who threatened to undermine the whole constitution. In the early eighteenth century the Tories frequently accused the Whigs of inculcating schismatic and republican principles and of fomenting rebellion against the powers that be. The loyalist address of 1710 from Lincoln, for example, asserted:

We beg leave to declare our utter abhorrence of such persons who despise all reveal'd religion, and the power thereof; who disavow obedience and non-resistance, the essential ligaments of a well-established monarchy, and who seem to deny what the Scriptures dictate unto us, that all power is of God, and that they that do resist shall receive unto themselves condemnation.[34]

Once the Whigs themselves were firmly established in power there was no shortage of conservative voices raised to condemn those who provoked unnecessary convulsions in the state by 'working upon and corrupting the minds of the people.'[35] When Wilkite radicals began to press for parliamentary reform they were accused of stirring up a ferment among 'a few despicable mechanics headed by base-born people, booksellers, and broken tradesmen' and of securing signatures for their petitions from 'the scum of the earth, the refuse of the people, unworthy to enter the gates of his Majesty's palace.'[36] John Wesley was outraged that 'every cobbler, tinker, porter and hackney-coachman' believed he was qualified to advise or censure the government.[37]

When the American colonists rebelled they were charged by conservative opinion in Britain with insolence and base ingratitude and with undermining the empire's economic prosperity and the whole legal basis of government.[38] The Church of England was left in no doubt that it was its duty to support the efforts to defeat the American rebellion. The authorised *Form of Prayer* in the General Fasts proclaimed by the crown in December 1776 looked forward to 'defeating the unjust attempt of their fellow-subjects against the right of our Sovereign and the lawful authority of the legislature of these kingdoms'. It went on to request God to 'bless the arms of our gracious Sovereign, in the maintenance of his government and lawful rights, and prosper his endeavours to restore tranquillity among his unhappy subjects in *America*, now in open rebellion against his crown, and in defiance of all subordination and legal government.'[39]

The threat to the British constitution posed by domestic radicals and foreign revolutionaries reached an alarming peak in the 1790s. The consequence was a veritable flood of conservative and loyalist propaganda. British radicals were condemned as men of weak heads and bad hearts. They were depicted as traitors to their own country and as dupes of a foreign enemy. Frequently portrayed as dangerous and ambitious demagogues, they were accused of being jealous of the deserved honours of the governing elite and of the merited wealth of their social superiors. To scare off potential recruits to the radical cause the aims of these reformers were deliberately misrepresented and the consequences of adopting their principles were grossly exaggerated. The British people were repeatedly warned that the radicals would destroy the monarchy, overturn the Church, ruin the aristocracy, reinstate primitive equality and level all the natural social and economic distinctions in civilised society. The only beneficiaries of radical change would be the idle and the dissolute, the thieves, cheats, drunkards and propertyless beggars at the very bottom of society. Central to the conservative case was the claim that the radicals were encouraging the poor to seize the property of their social superiors. At the same time conservative propaganda, much of it reprehensible in tone, created a hideous caricature of the rapacious and bloodthirsty French. Appealing to the rampant xenophobia and the virulent anti-gallicanism that had long been a feature of British society, it accused the French of spreading carnage, oppression and desolation across large areas of Europe. In order to defend her trade, her constitution and the balance of power in Europe, Britain was being compelled to make enormous sacrifices and forced to fight a veritable crusade against the terror, anarchy and immorality that stemmed from French principles. Whereas the French lurched from mob rule to military dictatorship, the British must make every effort to preserve a constitution which secured the greatest degree of individual liberty consonant with the preservation of law and order.[40]

II DEMONSTRATIONS OF POPULAR CONSERVATISM

Research on popular radicalism has revealed its success in producing and disseminating a wide range of political propaganda to large numbers of people. It has also shown how the reformers enlisted public support behind their petitioning campaigns and their crowd demonstrations and how they recruited significant numbers of the middling and lower orders to their political clubs and associations. What has not been sufficiently revealed, however, is the extent to which popular conservatism adopted the same tactics and how it achieved an even greater measure of success.

The variety, the sheer volume and the social and geographical distribution of conservative propaganda was certainly much greater than that written or disseminated by radical forces at any time in the eighteenth century. Much recent research has emphasised that the influence of John Locke and of other radical Whigs in the decades after the Glorious Revolution was very much less than was once thought. Far from being the central strand in the dominant Whig ideology the radical doctrines of natural rights, the original contract and popular sovereignty had only limited appeal for the Whigs and a negligible impact on the nation at large.[41] Most Whigs preferred to advance relatively conservative views, but even these never achieved the circulation reached by such high Tory works as *The Memorial of the Church of England* (1705), Dr Henry Sacheverell's famous sermon, *In Peril among False Brethren* (1709), Charles Leslie's *The Rehearsal* and Nathaniel Mist's *Weekly Journal.* When the Whigs impeached Dr Sacheverell in 1710 they created a political storm that drove them out of office and when Bishop Hoadly's words threatened to undermine the privileges of the Church of England in 1716–17 he provoked over a thousand responses and forced an embarrassed government to prorogue Convocation.[42] No Whig government dared to face the assembled clergy in Convocation again during the rest of the eighteenth century.

During their long period of political supremacy under the early Hanoverians the Whigs made no effort to revive radical notions of natural rights or popular sovereignty. On the contrary, long years of power led to a consolidation of those conservative tendencies which had been developing in Whig ideology since the Glorious Revolution. Whig propaganda explicitly rejected the claim that the people were the sovereign authority in the state and that they had the right to resist any government which did not serve their interests. Even opposition propaganda, which criticised the undue political influence of patronage and corruption, did not seek to remodel the constitution on radical lines. Most opposition spokesmen defended monarchy, the Church of England, the balanced constitution and the existing social order. Although they put forward proposals to purify the existing constitution, they did not desire to overhaul it by advocating radical reforms designed to give greater power to a wider section of the population.[43]

During the later eighteenth century, when a great deal of radical propaganda poured from the press, the variety, volume and distribution of conservative propaganda remained much more substantial. The Wilkes affair and the American crisis certainly stimulated radical demands for reform, but there are good grounds for thinking that the array of printed propaganda and other expressions of public opinion indicated majority support for the government's policies. In London the conservative case was put forward in the *General Evening Post,* *Lloyd's Evening Post,* and later by the high-selling *Morning Post,* the *Morning Chronicle,* the newly established *Morning Herald,* and throughout by the government's own highly-influential *London Gazette.*[44] In the provinces too there were numerous conservative newspapers such as the *Manchester Mercury,* the *Bath Chronicle,* the *Hampshire Chronicle,* the *Nottingham and Newark Journal,* the *Newcastle Courant,* the *Chester Chronicle,* and *Aris's Birmingham Gazette.*[45] Although Wilkes won considerable support and the government's military failures in the American war aroused much criticism, it seems very likely that the majority of Britons were not committed either to radical reform or American independence.[46]

During the political crisis of the 1790s there is more certain evidence that conservative propaganda was more substantial than that disseminated by the radicals. Conservative newspapers and periodicals undoubtedly outnumbered and outsold those produced by the radicals and they remained active for much longer periods. In London loyalist views were propagated by the *Star,* the *Sun,* the *True Briton* and the *Observer,* whilst in the provinces they were disseminated in such newspapers as the *York Courant,* the *Liverpool Phoenix,* the *Manchester Mercury,* the *Leicester Journal,* the *Caledonian Mercury* and the *Edinburgh Herald.* Radical newspapers were never in the majority and at no time in the 1790s were more than eight in existence. In towns where there were both radical and conservative newspapers, such as Manchester, Leicester and Newcastle, it was the latter that survived the political contest. The triumph of conservative periodicals was even more pronounced with the success of such journals as the weekly *Anti-Jacobin,* the monthly *Anti-Jacobin Review and Magazine* and the *British Critic.* Although numerous individual radical pamphlets were published and some, most notably Thomas Paine's *Rights of Man,* had huge circulations, there were more contributions on the conservative side and the distribution of the *Cheap Repository Tracts* between 1795 and 1798 far exceeded anything achieved earlier by Paine. Throughout the 1790s a whole range of other publications capable of carrying a political message, including verse, popular ballads, novels, broadsheets and caricatures, was heavily weighted on the conservative side. Religious groups and organised loyalist associations also produced and distributed much more conservative propaganda aimed at a mass readership than was ever achieved by the radical societies of the decade. A vast and successful propaganda campaign was clearly waged to convince the majority of the people to defend the existing political and social order from domestic radicals and French revolutionaries.[47]

Rivalling the importance of all the newspapers, periodicals and pamphlets disseminating conservative political views were the many thousands of sermons delivered (and often printed) by the clergy of the various Christian churches in Britain. The clergy of all denominations serviced the most widespread, popular and influential institutions in the state and the vast majority of them were united in defence of the established order and in outspoken criticism of those who demanded radical change. High-Church Anglicans were the most staunchly conservative and throughout the whole eighteenth century they continued to preach non-resistance and passive obedience, though at first their loyalty was narrowly focused on the crown whereas later they were prepared to preach submission to the whole political establishment. Many Low Churchmen too, despite their closer association with the Whigs, remained conservative on political matters, while the Evangelicals of the later eighteenth century consistently urged the people to submit to the existing political and social order. Although the leading Rational Dissenters, such as Richard Price and Joseph Priestley, were active in radical causes, the majority of Dissenting ministers insisted that they had no wish to overthrow the constitution and, during the political crises provoked by the American and French revolutions, they frequently voiced their sincere attachment to crown and parliament. In 1790, for example, the delegates of Dissenters in several midland counties declared that the constitution was their pride and glory, while, at national level, the Committee of the Dissenting Deputies and the General Body of Protestant Dissenting Ministers of the Three Denominations issued a succession of loyalist declarations. The General Assembly of the Church of Scotland issued similar declarations of loyalty and never supported any radical cause. John Wesley, while he lived, and the Methodist Conference, after his death, also proclaimed loyalty to the constitution and preached the doctrines of non-resistance and passive obedience.[48]

Clergymen and ministers of religion played a major role as political propagandists. Besides being the authors of a large number of more secular tracts, they also delivered thousands of sermons which contained a clear political message. The most important political sermons were preached on state-inspired occasions. There were a whole number of dates in the calendar when such sermons could be delivered: the monarch's birthday, accession day and coronation day, 4 November to celebrate the Glorious Revolution, 5 November to mark the Gunpowder Plot, 29 May to commemorate the restoration of Charles II, and, most important of all, 30 January, the anniversary of the martyrdom of Charles I. On 30 January each year Anglican clergymen preached before the sovereign, the House of Lords, the House of Commons, the Lord Mayor and Corporation of London, Oxford and Cambridge Universities, the House of Convocation if sitting, town corporations throughout the country and many humble parish congregations. Most of these sermons delivered a conservative political message.[49] As Archbishop Sharp reminded the House of Lords on 30 January 1700: 'You all know what kind of argument this day calls for: for by the design of keeping it, the business that the preacher hath to do, is to press obedience and subjection to the government we live under, and to preach against faction and rebellion.'[50] Throughout most of the wars and rebellions of the eighteenth century the crown also proclaimed special Fast Days or Thanksgiving Days when sermons with a political message were preached. Research on these has revealed that many preachers argued that Britain enjoyed a special relationship with God, that God had given her the finest constitution in the world and England the most perfectly reformed church, but that the people were sometimes guilty of black ingratitude. Despite the crying sins of the nation, however, it seemed inconceivable to most preachers that God would allow Catholic and absolutist France or ungrateful rebels to bring down the established order in church and state. Repentance and a renewed dedication to God and his providential order were seen as the means of averting defeat or suppressing rebellion.[51] Even those sermons which were not overtly political, those for example by the evangelical clergy that emphasised spiritual and moral regeneration, could also be effective in combating political radicalism because they urged the need for all classes to bind together in a common pursuit of salvation.[52]

It cannot be known for certain what the people at large made of the veritable flood of conservative propaganda pouring from press and pulpit throughout the eighteenth century. Much of this propaganda was clearly directed at the middling orders, but we cannot be absolutely sure that the message was received, understood and acted upon. The same caveat, however, must apply to any attempt to measure the political impact of radical propaganda. What can be claimed is that conservative propaganda was greater in volume, range, reach and duration than that produced by the radicals. Moreover, there are clear indications in the support for loyal addresses, the number of crowd demonstrations and the recruits to more formal political organisations that a higher proportion of the middling and lower orders defended rather than attacked the existing order in church and state.

Over the century as a whole the number of loyalist addresses, and the number of signatures attached to them, outnumbered those petitions and petitioners who advocated reform. In 1710, for example, well over a hundred addresses proclaimed loyalty to the Queen, the constitution and the established church and protested about those factious spirits who encouraged schism and rebellion.[53] Evidence that the tide of public opinion had swung towards the Tories was clearly demonstrated by their massive victory in the general election later that year. In late 1745, during the Jacobite rebellion, over 200 places in Britain sent in loyal addresses to George II, over 50 armed associations were established, subscriptions were raised across the nation, and some London tradesmen formed the Laudable Association of Anti-Gallicans.[54] During the constitutional crisis over the Middlesex election affair in 1769–70, when Wilkite radicalism appeared to demonstrate considerable hostility to the governing elite, there was, in fact, a great deal of loyalist activity. Loyal addresses were raised by five counties and 12 boroughs in England, by 26 counties and 33 burghs in Scotland, by the clergy of the province of Canterbury, by eight groups of Presbyterian ministers and by universities in both England and Scotland.[55] During the American crisis of 1775–6 the number of loyal addresses critical of American action and supportive of a policy of

coercion actually outnumbered the petitions urging conciliation, though they did not attract as many signatures. Loyal
addresses came in from nine counties and nearly seventy towns
in England, from nearly all the counties and parliamentary
burghs in Scotland, from Oxford and Cambridge universities,
and from such associations as militia regiments. Many of these
were signed by the local elite, such as town corporations, JPs,
and the Anglican clergy, but over 6500 people signed the loyal
address from Lancashire, nearly 2000 signed that organised by
the merchants and livery of London, over 1200 signed the
address from the unrepresented town of Bolton, and hundreds
of signatures were attached to at least eight other addresses.[56]

Loyalist addresses reached massive proportions in the late
eighteenth century. In the first three months of 1784 over 200
addresses were printed in the *London Gazette* in support of the
royal prerogative in general and George III's right to dismiss
the leaders of the Fox-North coalition in particular. Some 7000
people attended a public meeting in York that endorsed a loyal
address by a majority of 5 to 1, while over 2700 signatures were
attached to the addresses from Westminster, Bristol, Leicester,
Glasgow and Devon. The petitions against the Fox-North
coalition were signed by 53500 Englishmen in a 'massive
demonstration of public disapproval'.[57] In 1789 more than 750
addresses congratulated George III on his recovery from
serious illness. In 1795–6 and in 1800 there were hundreds of
addresses of loyalty after attempts had been made on the king's
person.[58] On all these occasions the addresses emanated from
the local elites in towns and counties across the whole kingdom, from the clergy of every denomination, from all the
universities, from groups of merchants and manufacturers,
from clubs and societies, from militia and Volunteer companies and from ordinary citizens. On several other occasions
there were equally impressive demonstrations of popular
support for the existing constitution in church and state. The
response to the two royal proclamations, in May and December
1792, against the spread of seditious writings and radical
activities, produced nearly 500 loyal addresses. Many of these
secured the support of very large numbers of local people. The
loyal address from Liverpool was supported by 11 000 people,
that from London by over 8000, the one from Bath by over
5000, while in many smaller towns well over a thousand

inhabitants attached their names. In remote Cromarty some 280 out of 300 heads of families signed and, it was confidently asserted, had a little more time been given, all but three men would have demonstrated their loyalty in this way.[59]

On many occasions during the eighteenth century there were more militant demonstrations of popular support for existing institutions and traditional practices and hostility towards those who favoured change and innovations. Most of these involved religion, thus revealing the depth of popular prejudices in favour of the established church, but very often religious motives overlapped with political, social and economic causes of resentment. Popular fears that the privileged position of the Church of England was in danger sparked off some of the worst outbreaks of violence in the eighteenth century, but the hostility was also directed at minority groups who were outside the mainstream of society and who appeared to be a threat to its traditional dominance.

Protestant Dissenters, and especially their meeting houses, were the victims of numerous riots and crowd demonstrations. These included the numerous Sacheverell disturbances of 1710; the widespread rioting, mainly in London, Lancashire and the West Midlands, in 1715–16; and many outbreaks of violence, most notably in Birmingham and Manchester, in the early 1790s.[60] The Dissenters were seen as a particularly dangerous threat to the privileged position of the Church of England because they often mounted protests against the Test and Corporation Acts, they themselves were a highly organised and very effective pressure group, and they could always count upon a measure of support from the more liberal element among the Whigs. Popular resentment against them, however, fed off other motives. Many prosperous Dissenters were unpopular because they were influential financiers and stock-jobbers associated in the public mind with the growing burden of the national debt, high taxes, the spread of political corruption, and a readiness to wage expensive foreign wars. Other wealthy Dissenters were actively involved in commerce and manufacturing and, as employers, they became the targets for popular resentment during periods of economic depression. In political terms the Dissenters were always associated in the popular mind with the threat of upheaval and radical change. They were seen as enemies of hereditary monarchy, as constant critics of the existing constitution in church and state, and as the shock troops of radical change in both the earlier and the later eighteenth century. Although this was not a balanced assessment of the political views of the Dissenters as a whole, it was a popular prejudice reinforced by the activities of a minority of Dissenting intellectuals who played a major role in most campaigns for political reform during the eighteenth century.

Anti-Catholicism had even deeper roots in the popular consciousness and, at times in the eighteenth century, it surfaced in explosions of popular rage.[61] The Catholic religion itself was widely associated with superstition, idolatry, persecution and intolerance, but it was the wider aspects of Catholicism that generated the most virulent prejudice. In the popular mind it was identified with absolutist regimes and dire poverty. It was the religion of Irish rebels, of Irish immigrants competing for low-paid jobs, of the Jacobite Pretender and, most of all, of major foreign enemies such as France and Spain. A hatred of Catholics was displayed in endemic sectarian conflict in Ireland, against Irish labourers in London in 1736, 1742 and 1763, during the 1745 Jacobite rebellion and whenever the country was at war.[62] The worst outbreak of militant anti-Catholicism, leading to the most alarming riot of the whole century, occurred after parliament had passed the Catholic Relief Act in 1778 and at a time when there was serious tension in Ireland and the country was waging a losing war against both France and Spain. The relief offered to Roman Catholics was actually very modest. They were allowed to purchase and inherit land and their clergy were no longer subject to severe punishment, but these concessions were only open to Catholics who took the oath of allegiance. The other disabilities imposed on Catholics remained as before and even this concession did not extend to Scotland. None the less, serious rioting broke out in Glasgow and Edinburgh in 1779, followed by the notorious Gordon riots in London in early June 1780. The rioting in London resulted in massive damage to property, very heavy casualties and hundreds of arrests.[63]

Hatred of other religious minorities also incited protests out of all proportion to the threat posed to the established church. Jews, who were always a despised minority, were disliked for their religion, but were also resented on economic grounds whether they were identified in the popular mind with rich financiers or impoverished street traders and tinkers. This hostility, although widespread, only surfaced in a major way in 1753 when the Pelham administration was persuaded to pass the Jewish Naturalisation Act designed to make it easier for Jews to secure British citizenship. Within months this action provoked hostile petitions and public protests, virulent pamphlets, critical newspaper accounts and blatantly anti-Semitic caricatures. The clamour was so great that one of the most secure administrations of the century retreated before an enraged public opinion. The offending act was repealed before the year was out.[64] The early Methodists also suffered considerable hostility in the middle decades of the eighteenth century. Large crowds assaulted worshippers in Exeter in 1745 and Norwich in 1752. New meeting houses were pulled down in many towns, including Sheffield, Wolverhampton, St Ives and Chester, and a number of itinerant preachers, including John Wesley himself, met abuse and even physical violence. Clearly, the early Methodists were not seen as the counter-revolutionary force they were to become by the end of the century, but as a threat to established order and authority. Methodism was feared as a highly articulate and nationwide organisation that appealed to the poor. Its leaders were often seen as men of unknown origins who appeared to act without formal authorisation and outside the control of the local squire and parson. They posed a threat to the status, authority and livelihood of the parish clergy and they were resented as intruders who incited near hysteria and who unleashed unwanted social and religious innovations. They were accused of being both crypto-papists and subversive fanatics and they became the scapegoats for many vague and half-formulated charges. Although they were eventually tolerated, for some years they were the whipping-boys for those who felt a compelling need to demonstrate in aggressive fashion their loyalty to established authority and traditional values.[65]

In times of severe political crisis militant loyalism was more organised and better coordinated by the creation of more formal associations designed to mount sustained campaigns in defence of the established order. In 1715 the Duke of Newcastle established loyalist societies of hired toughs in London who were employed to defend the Hanoverian succession by launching physical assaults on local Jacobite activities.[66] The Jacobite rebellion of 1745 also motivated some English loyalists to set up armed associations and to raise public subscriptions in order to combat the invading army from Scotland.[67] Widespread opposition to the Catholic Relief Act of 1778 enabled Lord George Gordon to build up a nation-wide Protestant Association which recruited tens of thousands of members dedicated to repealing the act. He was able to draw on a very wide constituency, enlisting the support of leading politicians, prominent preachers, JPs and members of town corporations, parish officials of all kinds, and even illiterate sections of the urban population. Petitions from across the country were sent in to Parliament requesting the repeal of the Catholic Relief Act. The petition from Newcastle upon Tyne was supported by 7661 people in the area, that from Glasgow had over 20 000 subscribers, while the one from the London area claimed to have over 120 000 supporters.[68]

It was not until the 1790s, however, that militant loyalism was organised on such a scale that it could effectively outnumber and outmanoeuvre the burgeoning radical movement. As early as 1790 the Dissenters' campaign to repeal the Test and Corporation Acts had provoked such resentment that Church and King Clubs, dedicated to the defence of the existing constitution in church and state, were established in several provincial towns, including Manchester and Birmingham. By late 1792 conservative opinion in Britain was thoroughly alarmed at the revolutionary violence in France and by the outbreak of a war which threatened to involve Britain herself. On 20 November 1792 John Reeves convened a meeting at the Crown and Anchor tavern in London that led to the founding of the militantly loyalist Association for the Preservation of Liberty and Property against Republicans and Levellers. Within days of this being announced in the London press Reeves was inundated by a flood of letters from sympathisers from all parts of the country. Many correspondents offered to set up similar loyalist associations in their areas, advised on how the lower orders might be reached with effective propaganda, and offered to write or to distribute loyalist tracts. Loyalist associations soon spread across the whole country. These associations were not closely directed by the government, but reflected opinion in the localities. Their total number certainly ran into the hundreds and may well have been as high as the 2000 societies which Reeves himself claimed to have fostered. Active membership may well have been confined to local men of wealth and status, but they also enlisted the enthusiastic support of many thousands of humbler men. Although JPs, members of town corporations, Anglican clergy, parish officials and men of property bulked large in the organising committees, the initial meetings and the subsequent loyalist addresses and demonstrations attracted widespread support from the lower orders of society.[69]

In most places where these associations were established the loyalists easily outnumbered the local radicals. Even in places where the radicals were quite strong, such as London, Birmingham and Manchester, the militant loyalists appear to have gained the upper hand. Only in Sheffield do the loyalists appear to have been forced onto the defensive, though even here they made a respectable showing. These loyalist associations flooded their localities with conservative propaganda, but also adopted various forms of intimidation. In many places they initiated prosecutions of those printers and booksellers who distributed radical publications. In several places the magistrates were persuaded to refuse licences to the owners of inns and alehouses if they allowed their premises to be used for radical meetings and the innkeepers usually caved in to such threats. Other forms of intimidation included the refusal to employ radicals, the threat to dismiss them from employment, the withdrawal of custom from radical tradesmen and shopkeepers, and the expulsion of radicals from benefit clubs and friendly societies. Perhaps most insidious of all were the efforts of several associations to pressurise every local householder into signing loyalist addresses and resolutions. A refusal to sign, especially when these abstainers were in a minority in their community, obviously required considerable moral courage. In many places there were also symbolic or actual physical assaults on leading radicals. In the winter of 1792–3, in particular, effigies of Thomas Paine were burned in hundreds of towns and villages across the whole country. Large crowds were assembled, stimulated and excited by the processions, bands, songs, banners, cockades, fireworks and bonfires, as well as by the considerable drinking and public merriment. On many occasions loyalist crowds were prepared to go much further. There were dozens of physical assaults on the persons and the property of prominent local radicals in the years from 1791 to 1795.[70]

The government's repressive legislation, much commented upon by the later historians of radicalism, was, in fact, much less effective in suppressing the movement for reform than were the widespread demonstrations of popular loyalism. Militant conservatism swamped rural radical groups so effectively in most areas that loyalist associations lost focus and direction within a year or so of their creation. The threat of invasion from France, however, enabled the loyalists to find renewed purpose in the armed Volunteer force which the government authorised in March 1794. Considerable sums of money were raised and large numbers of men were recruited to create the largest organisation in the country and one dedicated to resisting a French invasion and preserving order. The creation of Volunteer corps all over the country demonstrated the readiness of men of property to defend their privileges, by force if necessary, but every effort was made to enlist as many humble men as could be trusted to defend the existing political and social order. By the end of the 1790s well over 300 000 men had been enlisted in the Volunteers (in addition to those serving in the militia) and even more were recruited in 1803–4. At first these Volunteer corps were raised by the propertied elite in the counties, but by the late 1790s about two-thirds of the Volunteer corps were recruited in urban and manufacturing areas where the middle classes sought to play a conspicuous part in public life in these years of grave national crisis. They acted as officers in the town corps, but the rank-and-file Volunteers were small shopkeepers, craftsmen, artisans and even some humble labourers.[71] The willingness to serve was used by the propertied elite as a test of loyalty to the existing constitution. The government wanted to recruit huge numbers of men to intimidate the radicals and to promote a patriotic resistance to the French. It was hoped that the Volunteers would render disloyalty unfashionable, sedition dangerous and insurrection almost impossible.[72] Some Volunteer corps were in fact unenthusiastic about suppressing food riots and many men served for reasons other than loyalty to political ideals. They were coerced by employers, influenced by economic pressures and enjoyed the comradeship and excitement. None the less, most were also ready to resist a French invasion and many wished to preserve the existing social order and what they considered to be the rights and privileges of free-born Britons.[73] Thus, the eighteenth century closed with the radicals demoralised and in disarray and with the forces of militant loyalism clearly in the ascendant.

III   CONCLUSION

Although radical critics of the existing constitution in church and state existed in the earlier eighteenth century, it was not until later in the century that an organised radical movement with substantial support appeared on the political stage. It was only from the later 1760s that radical critics developed a coherent ideology, spread their propaganda far and wide, established a range of clubs and societies, and employed a variety of techniques designed to bring pressure to bear upon the governing elite. The size and nature of the radical challenge determined the degree of organisation needed to rally popular support in defence of the prevailing constitution. In the earlier eighteenth century radicalism was so weak and conservative views were so pervasive that popular support for traditional institutions and established values did not need to be organised in a formal or sustained way. The occasional eruption of popular prejudices, as in 1710 and 1715, was sufficient to warn the Whigs that power and stability could only be achieved by rejecting the demands of their radical supporters and by moving to command the centre ground. Only in the later eighteenth century, when the threats from domestic radicals and foreign revolutionaries were serious, did the majority who accepted and admired the existing political order seek to create the sophisticated propaganda machine, the more permanent associations and the range of tactics deemed necessary to combat those who demanded change. In mounting a more sustained response to the radical challenge, the conservative defenders of the existing constitution in church and state matched every action taken by the radicals and usually did so on a larger and more impressive scale. In its strategy and its tactics militant loyalism copied and improved upon those adopted by its radical opponents.

In one respect, however, there was a major distinction between popular radicalism and popular conservatism. Earlier radical critics of the existing constitution either belonged to the propertied elite or established close links with them. By the later eighteenth century radicalism was increasingly divorcing itself from the governing classes and was creating a movement independent of elite patronage and leadership. The more extreme were their political demands, the more the radicals had to create a movement distinct from the existing political institutions in the state. Popular conservatism never had to face such a difficult challenge. Since its prime purpose was to defend the political privileges of the governing elite or, at least, to defend institutions such as the Church of England, which were powerful and popular in their own right, conservatism did not need to establish an identity distinct and separate from the existing power structure. On most occasions when popular conservatism made its presence felt it was originally aroused and motivated by men who belonged to the governing classes and it secured legitimation for its actions through the measure of approval expressed, at least implicitly, by these social superiors. Once tapped, the wells of popular prejudice could spill over and flow further than the elite had planned or anticipated. Popular conservatism could then appear to take on a life of its own and achieve a measure of spontaneity and a degree of independence, but there are few signs that it ever became as autonomous a political movement as did popular radicalism.

Conservative ideology, apart from such simple prejudices as a hatred of foreigners and a dislike of any change, was largely developed by those attached to the governing elite. Much conservative propaganda, from press or pulpit, was produced on government orders or with subsidies and approval from the ruling elite. The great waves of loyalist addresses, in 1710, 1775–6 and 1792, all received direct encouragement from men with political influence at court and they were mainly organised by the ruling oligarchies in the counties and towns whence they came.[74] Local elites also frequently encouraged crowd demonstrations, even acts of violence, against those who were regarded as enemies of church and state. Those historians, who have examined the Sacheverell riots, the widespread disturbances of 1715, the popular clamour against the

Jewish Naturalisation Act, the hostility to the early Methodists, the Gordon riots of 1780 and the Priestley and other riots against Dissenters and radicals in the early 1790s, have all acknowledged that local gentlemen, magistrates and parsons did much to incite or at least to legitimate the prejudices of those who took to the streets.[75] While it is evident that there was widespread popular support for such action and it is clear that the crowds often got out of control and did far more damage than their social superiors had intended, it was in these riots rather than in most other crowd disturbances during the eighteenth century that it is possible to detect involvement at least in the initial stages by men in positions of authority. In most other popular disturbances they were strongly opposed to the demands of the demonstrators.

In the more formal loyalist organisations too there are clear indications of government involvement or at least evidence of approval being expressed by the local ruling elite. The Church and King clubs established in 1790 were led by parish priests and local magistrates. The loyalist associations set up in 1792–3 were founded in the first instance by John Reeves, who was in government employment, were publicised by government-subsidised newspapers, and were largely organised by the ruling oligarchies in the localities where they were created. The Volunteers, the largest loyalist force, were directly authorised by the government and were commanded by the propertied classes in the localities. All of these loyalist organisations depended heavily on the urban middle classes and recruited considerable popular support, but the initiatives in establishing them and the direction they took were largely dictated by men of wealth, status and power.

It must be emphasised that popular conservatism was never simply the creation or subsequently the servile creature of the government or the local elites. Although encouraged, motivated and legitimated by men of authority, the widespread manifestations of popular conservatism were the result of deep-rooted prejudices and widely-held opinions in favour of the existing constitution in church and state. The desire to preserve traditional institutions and established values was not restricted to the propertied elite, but was shared by a majority of the middling and lower orders. What an examination of popular conservatism clearly proves moreover is that the governing elite themselves did not always believe that political opinions and public action should be restricted to a narrow, propertied oligarchy. They were quite prepared to countenance, even to encourage, mass involvement in political questions so long as these buttressed rather than challenged the existing constitution in church and state. While they abhorred and feared the activities of radical critics, they welcomed demonstrations of popular support for the existing power structure. In doing so, they had to accept that at times popular prejudices would get out of control and occasionally they would be exploited by rival groups of the propertied elite as in the violent disturbances of 1715 when both Whigs and Tories unleashed the mob on their political rivals.

List of Abbreviations

Add. MSS.	Additional Manuscripts
AHR	*American Historical Review*
BHJ	*Birmingham Historical Journal*
BIHR	*Bulletin of the Institute of Historical Research*
BJECS	*British Journal of Eighteenth-Century Studies*
BL	British Library
CHJ	*Cambridge Historical Journal*
CJEPS	*Canadian Journal of Economics and Political Science*
DUJ	*Durham University Journal*
EcH	*Economic History*
EcHR	*Economic History Review*
ECS	*Eighteenth-Century Studies*
ED	*Enlightenment and Dissent*
EHR	*English Historical Review*
H	*History*
H&A	*History and Anthropology*
HJ	*Historical Journal*
HLQ	*Huntington Library Quarterly*
HMC	Historical Manuscripts Commission
HT	*History Today*
IRSH	*International Review of Social History*
JBS	*Journal of British Studies*
JCAS	*Journal of the Chester Archaeological Society*
JEcH	*Journal of Economic History*
JEH	*Journal of Ecclesiastical History*
JHI	*Journal of the History of Ideas*
JMH	*Journal of Modern History*
JSH	*Journal of Social History*
LH	*Literature and History*
LJ	*London Journal*
MH	*Midland History*
NH	*Northern History*
Parl Hist	William Cobbett, *Parliamentary History of England*
PER	*Parliament, Estates and Representation*
PH	*Parliament History*
P&P	*Past & Present*
P-PN	*Price-Priestley Newsletter*

PRO	Public Record Office
PSQ	*Political Science Quarterly*
PT	*Political Theory*
RHR	*Radical History Review*
RO	Record Office
SBT	*Studies in Burke and His Time*
SHR	*Scottish Historical Review*
SocH	*Social History*
SPD	State Papers Domestic
THAS	*Transactions of the Hunter Archaeological Society*
THSLC	*Transactions of the Historic Society of Lancashire and Cheshire*
TLCAS	*Transactions of the Lancashire and Cheshire Antiquarian Society*
TLMAS	*Transactions of the London and Middlesex Archaeological Society*
TM	*Thoresby Miscellany*
TRHS	*Transactions of the Royal Historical Society*
TTS	*Transactions of the Thoroton Society*
WHR	*Welsh Historical Review*
WMQ	*William and Mary Quarterly*

Notes

Unless otherwise stated the place of publication is London.

INTRODUCTION

1. See Romney Sedgwick (ed.), *The House of Commons 1715–1754* (2 vols, 1970); L.B. Namier and John Brooke (eds), *The House of Commons 1754–1790* (3 vols, 1964); and R.G. Thorne (ed), *The House of Commons 1790–1820* (5 vols, 1986). The volumes for 1690–1714 have not yet appeared.

2. See, in particular, Geoffrey Holmes, *British Politics in the Age of Anne* (1967); J.H. Plumb, *The Growth of Political Stability in England 1675–1725* (1967); W.A. Speck, *Tory and Whig: The Struggle in the Constituencies 1701–1715* (1970); Linda Colley, *In Defiance of Oligarchy: The Tory Party 1714–60* (Cambridge, 1982); Frank O'Gorman, *The Whig Party and the French Revolution* (1967); and Frank O'Gorman, *The Rise of Party in England: The Rockingham Whigs 1760–82* (1975).

3. See, for example, E.P. Thompson, *The Making of the English Working Class* (1963), E.P. Thompson, *Whigs and Hunters* (1975); E.P. Thompson, 'The Moral Economy of the English Crowd in the Eighteenth Century', *P&P*, 50 (1971), 76–136; George Rudé, *Wilkes and Liberty* (Oxford, 1962); George Rudé, *The Crowd in History 1730–1848* (New York, 1964); George Rudé, *Paris and London in the Eighteenth Century* (1970); John Cannon, *Parliamentary Reform 1640–1832* (Cambridge, 1973); and Albert Goodwin, *The Friends of Liberty: The English Democratic Movement in the Age of the French Revolution* (1979).

4. Among many relevant works see J.G.A. Pocock, *Politics, Language and Time* (New York, 1971); J.G.A. Pocock, *Virtue, Commerce and History* (Cambridge, 1985); J.G.A. Pocock, *The Machiavellian Moment* (Princeton, 1975); J.P. Kenyon, *Revolution Principles: The Politics of Party 1689–1720* (Cambridge, 1985); John Brewer, *Party Ideology and Popular Politics at the Accession of George III* (Cambridge, 1976); Isaac Kramnick, *Bolingbroke and His Circle* (Cambridge, Mass., 1968); Isaac Kramnick's collected essays in *Republicanism and Bourgeois Radicalism* (Ithaca, 1990); and H.T. Dickinson, *Liberty and Property: Political Ideology in Eighteenth-Century Britain* (1977).

5. See J.C.D. Clark, *English Society 1688–1832. Ideology, Social Structure and Political Practice during the Ancien Regime* (Cambridge, 1985); J.C.D. Clark, *Revolution and Rebellion: State and Society in England in the Seventeenth and Eighteenth Centuries* (Cambridge, 1986); Eveline Cruickshanks, *Political Untouchables: The Tories and the '45*; and Eveline Cruickshanks (ed.), *Ideology and Conspiracy: Aspects of Jacobitism 1689–1759* (Edinburgh, 1982).

6.   John Cannon, *Aristocratic Century: The Peerage of Eighteenth-Century England* (Cambridge, 1984) and Ian R. Christie, *Stress and Stability in Late Eighteenth-Century Britain* (Oxford, 1984).
7.   H.T. Dickinson, 'Whiggism in the eighteenth century', in John Cannon (ed.), *The Whig Ascendancy* (1981), pp. 28–44.
8.   Paul Langford, *A Polite and Commercial People: England 1727–1783* (Oxford, 1989), chs 6 and 7.
9.   Ibid., chs 3, 4 and 9; Joanna Innes, 'Jonathan Clark, Social History and England's "Ancien Regime"', *P&P,* 115 (1987), 165–200; John Rule, *Albion's People: English Society, 1714–1815* (1992), chs 1 and 3; and John Rule, *The Vital Century: England's Developing Economy 1714–1815* (1992), ch. 2.

CHAPTER 1:   THE PEOPLE AND PARLIAMENTARY ELECTIONS

1.   This traditional interpretation of parliamentary elections, emphasised by Sir Lewis Namier and many of his disciples, has been challenged in recent years by a number of historians who have paid more attention to the role of the electorate in parliamentary constituencies. My own conclusions have been very much influenced by such publications as W.A. Speck, *Tory and Whig, The Struggle in the Constituencies 1701–1715* (1970); John A. Phillips, *Electoral Behavior in Unreformed England: Plumpers. Splitters and Straights* (Princeton 1982); John A. Phillips, 'Popular Politics in Unreformed England', *JMH,* 52 (1980), 599–625; John A. Phillips, 'The Structure of Electoral Politics in Unreformed England', *JBS,* 19 (1979), 76–100; Frank O'Gorman, 'Electoral Deference in "Unreformed" England: 1760–1832', *JMH,* 56 (1984), 391–429; Frank O'Gorman, 'Campaign rituals and ceremonies: The Social Meaning of Elections in England, 1780–1860', *P&P,* 135 (1992), 79–115; Ronald M. Sunter, *Patronage and Politics in Scotland, 1707–1832* (Edinburgh, 1986); and, most significantly, Frank O'Gorman, *Voters, Patrons and Parties. The Unreformed Electorate of Hanoverian England, 1734–1832* (Oxford, 1989).
2.   See J.H. Plumb, *The Growth of Political Stability in England 1675–1725* (1967), ch. 6 and John Cannon, *Parliamentary Reform 1640–1832* (Cambridge, 1973) ch. 2. In Shrewsbury, for example, there had been about 1900 voters in 1715, but the number was reduced to about 300 voters by 1747 because, in the 1730s, the House of Commons had restructured the franchise by excluding the liberties and most of the suburbs. James E. Bradley, 'Nonconformity and the Electorate in Eighteenth-Century England', *PH,* 6 (1987), 241.
3.   Frank O'Gorman, *Voters, Patrons and Parties,* pp. 61, 148.
4.   W.A. Speck, '"The Most Corrupt Council in Christendom": decisions on controverted elections, 1702–42', in Clyve Jones (ed.), *Party and Management in Parliament 1660–1784* (Leicester 1984), pp. 107–21.
5.   Frank O'Gorman, *Voters, Patrons and Parties,* pp. 19–20.

6. Ibid., pp. 28–31, 66–67.
7. J.V. Beckett, 'The Making of a Pocket Borough: Cockermouth 1722–1756', *JBS*, 20 (1980), 140–57. For a similar competition for control of Appleby, see Brian Bonsall, *Sir James Lowther and Cumberland and Westmorland Elections 1754–1775* (Manchester, 1960), pp. 17–34.
8. Frank O'Gorman, *Voters, Patrons and Parties*, pp. 31–8.
9. James E. Bradley, 'Nonconformity and the Electorate in Eighteenth-Century England', *PH*, 6 (1987), 250, and John Phillips, *Electoral Behavior in Unreformed England*, pp. 47–51.
10. Frank O'Gorman, *Voters, Patrons and Parties*, pp. 38–43.
11. Ibid., p. 39.
12. Ibid., p. 67, and L.B. Namier and John Brooke (eds), *The House of Commons 1754–1790*, i, 261.
13. Ronald M. Sunter, *Patronage and Politics in Scotland, 1707–1832*, pp. 199–232; W.L. Burn, 'The General Election of 1761 at Ayr', *EHR*, 52 (1937), 103–9; and W.R. Ferguson, 'Dingwall Burgh Politics and the Parliamentary Franchise', *SHR*, 38 (1959), 100–7.
14. Frank O'Gorman, *Voters, Patrons and Parties*, pp. 43–55.
15. Ibid., pp. 19–21.
16. Romney Sedgwick (ed.), *The House of Commons 1715–1754*, i, 203. For a later challenge to the Grosvenor interest in Chester, see Frank O'Gorman, 'The General Election of 1784 in Chester', *JCAS*, 57 (1970–1), 41–50.
17. Frank O'Gorman, *Voters, Patrons and Parties*, pp. 61–2; and Ronald M. Sunter, *Patronage and Politics in Scotland, 1707–1832*, pp. 2–3.
18. L.B. Namier and John Brooke (eds), *The House of Commons 1754–1790*, i, 3 and Bedfordshire RO, Whitbread MSS. R3/505. Butler to Wynne, 29 Sept. 1767.
19. Frank O'Gorman, *Voters, Patrons and Parties*, p. 64.
20. For both quotations, see C. Collyer, 'The Rockinghams and Yorkshire Politics 1743–1761', *TM*, 41 (1954), 365.
21. John Phillips, *Electoral Behavior in Unreformed England*, pp. 67–70.
22. Frank O'Gorman, *Voters, Patrons and Parties*, pp. 55–8.
23. Frank O'Gorman, 'The Unreformed Electorate of Hanoverian England: the mid-eighteenth century to the Reform Act of 1832', *SocH*, 11 (1986), 39; and R.G. Thorne (ed.), *The House of Commons 1790–1820*, i, 21–42.
24. Paul Langford, *The Excise Crisis* (Oxford, 1975), pp. 127–9.
25. Romney Sedgwick (ed.), *The House of Commons 1715–1754*, i, 201.
26. Frank O'Gorman, *Voters, Patrons and Parties*, pp. 52–3, 55.
27. John Broad, 'Sir John Verney and Buckinghamshire Elections, 1696–1715', *BIHR*, 56 (1983), 201.
28. E.A. Smith, 'The election agent in English politics, 1734–1832', *EHR*, 84 (1969), 26.
29. J.G.A. Pocock, 'The Classical Theory of Deference', *AHR*, 81 (1976), 516–23; and Frank O'Gorman, 'Electoral Deference in Unreformed England: 1760–1832', *JMH*, 56 (1984), 394–9.
30. Frank O'Gorman, *Voters, Patrons and Parties*. pp. 50–5; Frank O'Gorman, 'The unreformed electorate of Hanoverian England',

SocH, 11 (1986) 47–8; Ronald M. Sunter, *Patronage and Politics in Scotland. 1707–1832*, pp. 3–7; Stephen W. Baskerville, Peter Adman and Katherine F. Beedham, 'The Dynamics of Landlord Influence in English County Elections, 1701–1734: The Evidence of Cheshire', *PH*, 12 (1993), 126–42; and Paul Langford, '*Property* and "Virtual Representation" in Eighteenth-Century England', *HJ*, 31 (1988), 90–3.

31. L.B. Namier, *The Structure of Politics at the Accession of George III* (2nd edn, 1961), p. 358.
32. John M. Triffitt, 'Politics and the Urban Community. Parliamentary Boroughs in the South West of England 1710–1730', unpublished D. Phil. thesis (Oxford University, 1985), pp. 203–22.
33. J.F. Quinn, 'York Elections in the Age of Walpole', *NH*, 22 (1986), 176.
34. Ronald M. Sunter, *Patronage and Politics in Scotland*, 1707–1832, pp. 113–30.
35. Ibid., pp. 134–46.
36. J.W.F. Hill, *Georgian Lincoln* (Cambridge, 1966), p. 86.
37. P.T. Underdown, 'Bristol and Burke' in Patrick McGrath (ed.), *Bristol in the Eighteenth Century* (Newton Abbot, 1972), pp. 41–62; and P.T. Underdown, 'Edmund Burke, the Commissary of his Bristol Constituents, 1774–1780', *EHR*, 73 (1958), 252–69. See also Lucy S. Sutherland, 'Edmund Burke and the Relations between Members of Parliament and their constituents', *SBT*, 10 (1968), 1005–21.
38. P.T. Underdown, 'The Parliamentary History of the City of Bristol, 1750–1790', unpublished MA thesis (Bristol University, 1948), p. 258.
39. T.W. Copeland et al (eds), *The Correspondence of Edmund Burke*, iii, 356. Burke to R. Champion, 26 June 1777.
40. P.T. Underdown, 'The Parliamentary History of the City of Bristol, 1750–1790', pp. 244–53, 260–2, 291–8.
41. W.A. Speck, *Tory and Whig*, p. 26.
42. L.B. Namier and John Brooke (eds), *The House of Commons 1754–1790*, i, 3; and W.A. Speck, *Tory and Whig*, pp. 26–7.
43. Ibid., p. 26.
44. Ibid.
45. Brian Bonsall, *Sir James Lowther and Cumberland and Westmorland Elections 1754–1775* (Manchester, 1960), p. 21.
46. Donald R. McAdams, 'Electioneering Techniques in Populous Constituencies, 1784–96', *SBT*, 14 (1972), 30.
47. E.A. Smith, 'The election agent in English politics, 1734–1832', *EHR*, 84 (1969), 13.
48. Romney Sedgwick (ed.), *The House of Commons 1715–1754*, i, 264.
49. E.A. Smith, 'The election agent in English politics, 1734–1832', *EHR*, 84 (1969), 16, 26.
50. Ibid., pp. 32–3.
51. W.A. Speck, *Tory and Whig*, pp. 40–1.
52. Ibid., pp. 58–9.
53. J.F. Quinn, 'York Elections in the Age of Walpole', *NH*, 22 (1986), 194.
54. W.A. Speck, *Tory and Whig*, p. 57.
55. E.A. Smith, 'The election agent in English politics, 1734–1832', *EHR*, 84 (1969), 15.

56. Eric G. Forrester, *Northamptonshire County Elections and Electioneering 1695–1832* (Oxford, 1941), pp. 29–30.

57. BL. Add. MSS.. 32689, f. 7. 3 Nov. 1733.

58. J.H. Plumb, 'The Growth of the Electorate in England from 1600 to 1715', *P&P*, 45 (1969), 90–116.

59. Frank O'Gorman, *Voters, Patrons and Parties*, pp. 178–80. These figures may be a little exaggerated because of the existence of plural voting. The existence of plural voting is disputed in Derek Beales, 'The Electorate Before and After 1832: The Right to Vote, and the Opportunity', *PH*, 11 (1992), 144–5 and Frank O'Gorman, 'The Electorate Before and After 1832', ibid., 12 (1993), 176.

60. Ibid., p. 181; and John A. Phillips, *Electoral Behavior in Unreformed England*, p. 42.

61. Frank O'Gorman, 'The unreformed electorate of Hanoverian England', *SocH*, 11 (1986), 37–9.

62. John A. Phillips, *Electoral Behavior in Unreformed England*, pp. 88–9.

63. Frank O'Gorman, *Voters, Patrons and Parties*, pp. 201–16.

64. John A. Phillips, *Electoral Behavior in Unreformed England*, pp. 176–93.

65. Frank O'Gorman, *Voters, Patrons and Parties*, p. 237.

66. Ibid., p. 239.

67. Ibid., pp. 246–7.

68. Ibid., pp. 249–51.

69. Ibid., pp. 368–81.

70. J.F. Quinn, 'Yorkshiremen go to the Polls: County Contests in the Early Eighteenth Century', *NH*, 21 (1985), 168.

71. Frank O'Gorman, *Voters, Patrons and Parties*, pp. 49–50, 53, 272; Romney Sedgwick (ed.), *The House of Commons 1715–1754*, i, 203; and J.W.F. Hall, *Georgian Lincoln*, p. 86.

72. Linda Colley, *In Defiance of Oligarchy: The Tory Party in 1714–1760*, pp. 162–3.

73. Romney Sedgwick (ed.), *The House of Commons 1715–1754*, i, 195–6; and L.B. Namier and John Brooke (eds), *The House of Commons 1754–1790*, i, 213, 355.

74. Ibid., i, 207.

75. Ibid., i, 79.

76. Philip Jenkins, *The Making of a Ruling Class: The Glamorgan gentry 1640–1790* (Cambridge, 1983), p. 187.

77. I.G. Doolittle, 'The Half Moon Tavern, Cheapside and City Politics', *TLMAS*, 28 (1977), 328–32; and Nicholas Rogers, 'Resistance to Oligarchy: the City Opposition to Walpole and his Successors, 1725–47', in John Stevenson (ed.), *London in the Age of Reform* (Oxford, 1977), p. 13.

78. Nicholas Rogers, 'Aristocratic Clientage, Trade and Independency: Popular Politics in Pre-Radical Westminster', *P&P*, 63 (1973) 75, 94–6.

79. Romney Sedgwick (ed.), *The House of Commons 1715–1754*, i, 244–5.

80. Linda Colley, 'Eighteenth-Century English Radicalism before Wilkes', *TRHS*, 5th series, 31 (1981), 7–9.

81. Frank O'Gorman, *Voters, Patrons and Parties*, p. 330.

82. Ibid., pp. 290, 330–1, 355.

83. Thomas R. Knox, 'Wilkism and the Newcastle Election of 1774', *DUJ,* 72 (1979), 27.
84. L.B. Namier and John Brooke (eds), *The House of Commons 1754–1790,* i, 283–9.
85. Michael Weinzierl, 'The Norwich Elections of 1794, 1796 and 1802: Conflict and Consensus', *PER,* 6 (1986), 168–74.
86. Lucy S. Sutherland, 'Edmund Burke and the Relations between Members of Parliament and their Constituents', *SBT,* 10 (1968), 1006.
87. Ibid., pp. 1005–21; and Paul Kelly, 'Constituents' Instructions to Members of Parliament in the Eighteenth Century', in Clyve Jones (ed.), *Party and Management in Parliament 1660–1784,* pp. 169–89.
88. Lucy Sutherland, 'Edmund Burke and the Relations between Members of Parliament and their Constituents', *SBT,* 10 (1968), 1005–21; P.T. Underdown, 'Edmund Burke, the Commissary of his Bristol Constituents 1774–1780', *EHR,* 73 (1958), 252–69; and P.T. Underdown, 'Bristol and Burke', in Patrick McGrath (ed.), *Bristol in the Eighteenth Century,* pp. 41–62.
89. *Bristol Journal,* 5 Nov. 1774.
90. W.A. Speck, *Tory and Whig,* pp. 20–30.
91. Paul Langford, *The Excise Crisis,* p. 47.
92. Ibid., p. 113.
93. H.T. Dickinson, 'Popular Politics in the Age of Walpole', in Jeremy Black (ed.), *Britain in the Age of Walpole* (1984), pp. 56–7.
94. Linda Colley, *In Defiance of Oligarchy,* p. 167.
95. Ibid., p. 168.
96. Ibid., p. 165.
97. Ibid., p. 166.
98. Paul Kelly, 'Constituents' Instructions to Members of Parliament in the Eighteenth Century', in Clyve Jones (ed.), *Party and Management in Parliament 1660–1784,* p. 175.
99. L.B. Namier and John Brooke (eds), *The House of Commons 1754–1790,* i, 17; and Thomas R. Knox, 'Wilkism and the Newcastle Election of 1774', *DUJ,* 72 (1979), 24.
100. Ronald M. Sunter, *Patronage and Politics in Scotland, 1707–1832,* p. 193.
101. Frank O'Gorman, *Voters, Patrons and Parties,* p. 269.
102. Ibid., p. 268.
103. L.B. Namier and John Brooke (eds), *The House of Commons 1754–1790,* i, 18.
104. Ibid., i, 351; and Thomas Knox, '"Peace for Ages to come": The Newcastle Elections of 1780 and 1784', *DUJ,* 84 (1992), 3–19.
105. R.G. Thorne (ed.), *The House of Commons 1790–1820,* ii, 396.
106. Frank O'Gorman, 'The General Election of 1784 in Chester', *JCAS,* 57 (1970–1), 45.
107. L.B. Namier and John Brooke (eds), *The House of Commons 1754–1790,* i, 16; R.G. Thorne (ed.), *The House of Commons 1790–1820,* ii, 218, 301; and Frank O'Gorman, *Voters, Patrons and Parties,* pp. 259–85.
108. H.T. Dickinson, 'Radicals and Reformers in the Age of Wilkes and Wyvill', in Jeremy Black (ed.), *British Politics and Society from Walpole to Pitt 1742–1789* (1990), pp. 139–40.

109. Philip Jenkins, *The Making of a Ruling Class*, p. 178; and Frank O'Gorman, *Voters, Patrons and Parties*, pp. 271, 281.
110. W.A. Speck, *Tory and Whig*, pp. 17–18.
111. Frank O'Gorman, *Voters, Patrons and Parties*, p. 111.
112. R.W. Smith, 'Political Organization and Canvassing: Yorkshire Elections before the Reform Bill', *AHR*, 74 (1969), 1543–6; and Donald R. McAdams, 'Electioneering Techniques in Populous Constituencies, 1784–96', *SBT*, 14 (1972), 23–53.
113. Frank O'Gorman, *Voters, Patrons and Parties*, pp. 158–63.
114. Romney Sedgwick (ed.), *The House of Commons 1715–1754*, i, 191.
115. Donald R. McAdams, 'Electioneering Techniques', *SBT*, 14 (1972), 37.
116. Frank O'Gorman, *Voters, Patrons and Parties*, pp. 68–105.
117. Stephen W. Baskerville, Peter Adman and Katharine F. Beedham, 'Manuscript Poll Books and English County Elections in the First Age of Party: A Reconsideration of their Provenance and Purpose', *Archives*, 19 (1991), 400–3.
118. John Brewer, *Party Ideology and Popular Politics at the Accession of George III* (Cambridge, 1976), p. 147.
119. On the conduct of elections and popular participation in them, see Frank O'Gorman, 'Campaign rituals and ceremonies: The social meaning of elections in England 1780–1860', *P&P*, 135 (1992), 79–115.
120. James E. Bradley, 'Nonconformity and the Electorate in Eighteenth-Century England', *PH*, 6 (1987), 247–8; and Donald R. McAdams, 'Electioneering Techniques', *SBT*, 14 (1972), 36.
121. John Brewer, *Party Ideology and Popular Politics*, p. 181.
122. Donald R. McAdams, 'Electioneering Techniques', *SBT*, 14 (1972), 35.
123. J.F. Quinn, 'York Elections in the Age of Walpole', *NH*, 22 (1986), 194–5.
124. B.D. Hayes, 'Politics in Norfolk 1750–1832', unpublished PhD thesis (Cambridge University, 1958), pp. 432–3.
125. Donald R. McAdams, 'Electioneering Techniques', *SBT*, 14 (1972), 40.
126. John Brewer, 'Theatre and Counter-Theatre in Georgian Politics: the Mock Elections at Garrat', in *RHR*, 22 (1979–80), 7–40 and in *HT*, 33 (1983), 15–23.
127. John Brewer, *Party Ideology and Popular Politics*, p. 186.
128. Donald R. McAdams, 'Electioneering Techniques', *SBT*, 14 (1972), 43.
129. Romney Sedgwick (ed.), *The House of Commons 1715–1754*, i, 340.
130. Frank O'Gorman, *Voters, Patrons and Parties*, p. 256.
131. J.W.F. Hill, *Georgian Lincoln*, p. 90.
132. Frank O'Gorman, *Voters, Patrons and Parties*, pp. 225–44.
133. W.A. Speck, *Tory and Whig*, *passim*; and Norma Landau, 'Independence, Deference and Voter Participation: The Behaviour of the Electorate in Early-Eighteenth-Century Kent', *HJ*, 22 (1979), 561–83. See also Stephen W. Baskerville, Peter Adman and Katharine F. Beedham, 'The Dynamics of Landlord Influence in English County Elections, 1701–34: The Evidence of Cheshire', *PH*, 12 (1993), 126–42.
134. R. Hopkinson, 'The Electorate of Cumberland and Westmorland in the Late Seventeenth and Early Eighteenth Century', *NH*, 15 (1979), 102.

135. W.A. Speck, *Tory and Whig*, pp. 98–109; Norman Sykes, 'The Cathedral Chapter of Exeter and the General Election of 1705', *EHR*, 45 (1930), 260–72; Catherine E. Langford, 'The British General Election of 1713', in J.J. Murray (ed.), *Essays in Modern European History* (Indiana 1951), pp. 29–47, and W.A. Speck, 'The General Election of 1715', *EHR*, 90 (1975), 507–22.

136. Geoffrey Holmes, *The Trial of Doctor Sacheverell* (1973), pp. 233–55; W.T. Morgan, 'An Eighteenth Century Election in England', *PSQ*, 37 (1922), 585–604; Mary Ransome, 'The Press in the General Election of 1710', *CHJ*, 6 (1939), 209–21; and Mary Ransome, 'Church and Dissent in the Election of 1710', *EHR*, 56 (1941), 76–89.

137. W.A. Speck, *Tory and Whig*, p. 114.

138. Paul Langford, *The Excise Crisis*, pp. 124–50.

139. C. Collyer, 'The Rockinghams and Yorkshire Politics 1742–1761', *TM*, 41 (1954), 364.

140. Thomas W. Perry, *Public Opinion. Propaganda and Politics in Eighteenth-Century England* (Cambridge, Mass., 1962), ch. 7; Linda Colley, *In Defence of Oligarchy*, pp. 131, 168; and R.J. Robson, *The Oxfordshire Election of 1754* (Oxford, 1949), pp. 31, 82–3, 86–99, 103.

141. Frank O'Gorman, *Voters, Patrons and Parties*, pp. 323–58.

142. *Anecdotes of the Life of Richard Watson, Bishop of Llandaff* (1817), p. 128.

143. Mrs Eric George, 'Fox's Martyrs; The General Election of 1784', *TRHS*, 4th series, 21 (1939), 133–68.

144. John A. Phillips, *Electoral Behavior in Unreformed England*, pp. 253–305.

145. Frank O'Gorman, *Voters, Patrons and Parties*, pp. 361–2.

146. James E. Bradley, 'Nonconformity and the Electorate in Eighteenth-Century England', *PH*, 6 (1987), 236–7, 244.

147. W.A. Speck, *Tory and Whig*, pp. 24–5; S.W. Baskerville, 'The Political Behaviour of the Cheshire Clergy, 1705–1752', *NH*, 23 (1987), 74–97; and Nancy Uhlar Murray, 'The Influence of the French Revolution on the Church of England and its Rivals, 1789–1802', unpublished D. Phil. thesis (Oxford University, 1975), pp. 44–79.

148. L.B. Namier, *The Structure of Politics at the Accession of George III*, p. 299.

149. Ibid., pp. 156–7.

CHAPTER 2:   VESTED INTERESTS AND PRESSURE GROUPS

1. E.P. Thompson, 'Patrician Society, Plebeian Culture', *JSH*, 7 (1974), 382–405; and E.P. Thompson, 'Eighteenth-Century English Society: class struggle without class', *SocH*, 3 (1978), 133–65.

2. Sheila Lambert (ed.), *House of Commons Sessional Papers of the Eighteenth Century* (2 vols, Wilmington, Delaware, 1975–6); and Frederick H. Spencer, *Municipal Origins An Account of English Private Bill Legislation relating to Local Government, 1740–1835* (1911), pp. 38–41, 65–9.

3. Peter Fraser, 'Public Petitioning and Parliament before 1832', *H*, 46 (1961), 195–211.

4. J.R. Pole, *Political Representation in England and the Origins of the American Republic* (1966), pp. 442–57.

5. H.T. Dickinson, *Liberty and Property*, pp. 86–7, 115–18, 279–90.

6. Patrick K. O'Brien, 'The political economy of British taxation, 1660–1815', *EcHR*, 2nd series, 41 (1988), 1–32.

7. D.G. Barnes, *A History of the English Corn Laws 1660–1846* (1930), pp. 23–116; and G.E. Mingay, *English Landed Society in the Eighteenth Century* (1963), chs 3 and 7.

8. Barnes, pp. 42–4; Michael Kammen, *Empire and Interest* (Philadelphia, 1970); and H.T. Dickinson, *Walpole and the Whig Supremacy* (1973), pp. 93–5.

9. Michael Kammen, *Empire and Interest*, pp. 10–11, 66, 88–91, 113–14.

10. W. Pittis, *History of the First Session of the Present Parliament* (1714), p. 99.

11. *The Craftsman*, 28 December 1728.

12. David Hume, *Essays Moral Political and Literary* (Oxford, 1963), pp. 58, 64–5.

13. Edmund Burke, 'Thoughts on the Cause of the Present Discontents', in *The Works of Edmund Burke* (Bohn edn, 6 vols, 1854–6), i, 367. See also *Parl Hist*, xvi (1813), 920–1.

14. 'Speech to the Electors of Bristol, 1774', in *The Works of Edmund Burke*, i, 448.

15. Quoted in Michael Kammen, *Empire and Interest*, p. 88.

16. Adam Smith, *An Inquiry into the Nature and Causes of the Wealth of Nations*, eds R.A. Campbell and A.S. Skinner (2 vols, Oxford, 1976), i, 493; and Michael Kammen, *Empire and Interest*, p. 114.

17. James Burgh, *Political Disquisitions* (3 vols, 1774–5), i, 54.

18. *Parl Hist*, xxiii (1814), 853.

19. William Paley, 'The Principles of Moral and Political Philosophy (1785)', in *The Works of William Paley*, ed. Edmund Paley (7 vols, 1825), iv, 392–3; and *Parl Hist*, xxx (1817), 811–14.

20. James Mackintosh, *A Disclosure of the Study of the Laws of Nature and Nations* (1797), p. 47.

21. Details on the social composition of the House of Commons is provided in Romney Sedgwick (ed.), *The House of Commons 1715–1754* and in L.B. Namier and John Brooke (eds), *The House of Commons 1754–1790*.

22. P.G.M. Dickson, *The Financial Revolution in England* (1967), pp. 15–35; and W.A. Speck, 'The Conflict in Society', in Geoffrey Holmes (ed.), *Britain after the Glorious Revolution 1689–1714* (1969), pp. 135–54.

23. Michael Kammen, *Empire and Interest*, p. 99; John Brooke, *The House of Commons 1754–1790* (Oxford, 1964), pp. 220–30; J.M. Holzman, *The Nabobs in England* (New York, 1926), pp. 15–16; Lucy Sutherland, *The East India Company in Eighteenth Century Politics* (Oxford, 1952), pp. 58, 147, 219, 279–80 ; and H.V. Bowen, '"The Pests of Human Society": Stockbrokers, Jobbers and Speculators in mid-eighteenth-century Britain', *H*, 78 (1993), 38–53.

24. Lucy Sutherland, 'The City of London in Eighteenth-Century Politics', in Richard Pares and A.J.P. Taylor (eds), *Essays presented to Sir Lewis Namier* (1956), pp. 49–74; and P.G.M. Dickson, *The Financial Revolution in England*, ch. 1.

25. B.W. Hill, 'The Change of Government and the "Loss of the City", 1710–1711', *EcHR*, 2nd series, 24 (1971), 395–413.

26. P.G.M. Dickson, *The Financial Revolution in England*, chs 5–6; Lucy Sutherland, 'The City of London and the Devonshire-Pitt Administration 1756–7', in *Proceedings of the British Academy*, 46 (1960), 147–93; and C.H. Philips, 'The East India Company "Interest" and the English Government, 1783–4', *TRHS*, 4th series, 20 (1937), 85–91.

27. P.G.M. Dickson, *The Financial Revolution in England*, chs 5–8.

28. Lucy Sutherland, *The East India Company in Eighteenth Century Politics*.

29. P.G.M. Dickson, *The Financial Revolution in England*, chs 5–7.

30. Lucy Sutherland, 'The City of London in Eighteenth-Century Politics', in Richard Pares and A. J. P. Taylor (eds), *Essays presented to Sir Lewis Namier*, p. 52; and P.G.M. Dickson, *The Financial Revolution in England*, ch. 10.

31. John G. Sperling, *The South Sea Company* (Boston, 1962), ch. 6; Jean O. McLachlan, *Trade and Peace with Old Spain 1667–1750* (Cambridge, 1940), ch. 4; Gerald B. Hertz, *British Imperialism in the Eighteenth Century* (1908), ch. 2; and Harold W.V. Temperley, 'The Causes of the War of Jenkins' Ear, 1739', *TRHS*, 3rd series, 3 (1909), 197–236.

32. Lucy Sutherland, *The East India Company in Eighteenth Century Politics*, pp. 27–30; and Henry Horwitz, 'The East India Trade, the Politicians, and the Constitution: 1689–1702', *JBS*, 17 (1978), 1–18.

33. Gerald B. Hertz, 'England and the Ostend Company', *EHR*, 22 (1907), 255–79.

34. Michael Kammen, *Empire and Interest*, p. 100.

35. C.H. Philips, 'The East India Company "Interest" and the English Government, 1783–4', *TRHS*, 4th series, 20 (1937), 83–101.

36. N.C. Hunt, 'The Russia Company and the Government, 1730–42', *Oxford Slavonic Papers*, 7 (1957), 27–65; Douglas K. Reading, *The Anglo-Russian Commercial Treaty of 1734* (New Haven, 1938); and Alfred C. Wood, *A History of the Levant Company* (Oxford, 1935), pp. 146–7.

37. Glyndwr Williams, 'The Hudson's Bay Company and its Critics in the Eighteenth Century', *TRHS*, 5th series, 20 (1970), 149–71; and Michael Kammen, *Empire and Interest*, pp. 78, 101, 139.

38. A.C. Wood, *A History of the Levant Company*, pp. 153–4, 156–7.

39. *Journals of the House of Commons*, xxv, 777.

40. Glyndwr Williams, 'The Hudson's Bay Company...', *TRHS*, 5th series, 20 (1970), 159–60, 164; and Michael Kammen, *Empire and Interest*, pp. 78–9, 102–3.

41. Lillian M. Penson, 'The London West India Interest in the Eighteenth Century', *EHR*, 36 (1921), 373–92. See also Lillian M. Penson, *The Colonial Agents of the British West Indies* (1924).

42. Richard B. Sheridan, 'The Molasses Act and the Market Strategy of the British Sugar Planters', *JEcH*, 17 (1957), 62–83.

43. Quoted in Lillian M. Penson, 'The London West India Interest', *EHR*, 36 (1921), 380.

44. Ibid., pp. 381–3.
45. Jacob M. Price, 'Glasgow, the Tobacco Trade, and the Scottish Customs, 1707–1730: Some Commercial, Administrative and Political Implications of the Union', *SHR*, 63 (1984), 1–36.
46. Paul Langford, *The Excise Crisis* (Oxford, 1975); and E.R. Turner, 'The Excise Scheme of 1733', *EHR*, 42 (1927), 34–57.
47. Peter Clarke, 'The "Mother Gin" controversy in the early eighteenth century', *TRHS*, 5th series, 38 (1988), 63–84. See also Lee Davison, 'Experiments in the Social Regulation of Industry: Gin Legislation, 1729–1751', in Lee Davison et al. (eds), *Stilling the Grumbling Hive. The Response to Social and Economic Problems in England, 1689–1750* (Stroud, 1992), pp. 25–48.
48. See the references in note 30.
49. Michael W. McCahill, 'Peers, Patronage, and the Industrial Revolution', *JBS*, 16 (1976), 84–107.
50. Adam Smith, *An Inquiry into the Nature and Causes of the Wealth of Nations*, eds R.A. Campbell and A.S. Skinner, ii, 647.
51. Michael Jubb, 'Economic Policy and Economic Development', in Jeremy Black (ed.), *Britain in the Age of Walpole*, pp. 125–7.
52. Patrick O'Brien, Trevor Griffiths and Philip Hunt, 'Political components of the industrial revolution: Parliament and the English cotton textile industry, 1660–1774', *EcHR*, 44 (1991), 395–423; N. Rothstein, 'The calico campaign of 1719–21', *East London Papers*, 7 (1964), 3–21; and Tim Keirn, 'Parliament, Legislation and the Regulation of English Textile Industries, 1689–1714', in Lee Davison et al (eds), *Stilling the Grumbling Hive*, pp. 1–24.
53. R.G. Wilson, *Gentlemen Merchants* (Manchester, 1971), p. 167.
54. Richard Wilson, 'Newspapers and Industry: The Export of Wool Controversy in the 1780s', in Michael Harris and Alan Lee (eds), *The Press in English Society from the Seventeenth to the Nineteenth Centuries* (1986), pp. 87–98.
55. Michael Jubb, 'Economic Policy and Economic Development' in Jeremy Black (ed.), *Britain in the Age of Walpole*, pp. 129–30.
56. Michael Kammen, *Empire and Interest*, pp. 80–1.
57. Patrick Woodland, 'Extra-Parliamentary Political Organization in the making: Benjamin Heath and the Opposition to the 1763 Cider Excise', *PH*, 4 (1985), 115–36. See also Patrick Woodland, 'Political Atomization and Regional Interests in the 1761 Parliament: The Impact of the Cider Debates, 1763–1766', ibid., 8 (1989), 63–89; and Patrick Woodland, 'The House of Lords, the City of London and Political Controversy in the mid-1760s: the Opposition to the Cider Excise further considered', ibid., 11 (1992), 57–87.
58. John Money, 'Birmingham and the West Midlands, 1760–1793: Politics and Regional Identity in the English Provinces in the Later Eighteenth Century', *MH*, 1 (1971), 2–4.
59. Eric Robinson, 'Matthew Boulton and the Art of Parliamentary Lobbying', *HJ*, 7 (1964), 209–29; and B.D. Bargar, 'Matthew Boulton and the Birmingham Petition of 1775', *WMQ*, 3rd series, 13 (1956), 26–39.
60. Michael Kammen, *Empire and Interest*, p. 110.

61. J.M. Norris, 'Samuel Garbett and the Early Development of Industrial Lobbying in Great Britain', *EcHR*, 2nd series, 10 (1957–8), 450–60; Witt Bowden, 'The Influence of the Manufacturers on some of the Early Policies of William Pitt', *AHR*, 29 (1924), 655–74; and Witt Bowden, *Industrial Society in England Towards the End of the Eighteenth Century* (New York, 1925), pp. 169–81.

62. Robert John Auckland (ed.), *The Journal and Correspondence of William, Lord Auckland* (4 vols, 1862), i, 90.

63. *Parl Hist*, xxvi (1816), 382, 390, 392.

64. Witt Bowden, 'The English Manufacturers and the Commercial Treaty of 1786 with France', *AHR*, 25 (1919–20), 18–35; and Witt Bowden, *Industrial Society in England Towards the End of the Eighteenth Century*, pp. 181–93.

65. *Parl Hist*, xxiv (1815), 988.

66. Paul Langford, 'Property and "virtual Representation" in Eighteenth-Century England', *HJ*, 31 (1988), 115.

67. Albert Goodwin, 'Wood's Halfpence', *EHR*, 51 (1936), 647–74.

68. Francis G. James, 'The Irish Lobby in the Early Eighteenth Century', *EHR*, 81 (1966), 543–57; Michael Kammen, *Empire and Interest*, p. 83.

69. W.E. Minchinton (ed.), *Politics and the Port of Bristol in the Eighteenth Century* (Bristol, 1963), pp. xxiv, xxxii–xxxiii; Leon S. Marshall, *The Development of Public Opinion in Manchester 1780–1820* (Syracuse, New York), pp. 185–6; and Witt Bowden, 'The Influence of the Manufacturers on Some of the Early Policies of William Pitt', *AHR*, 29 (1924), 655–74.

70. Alison Gilbert Olson, 'Parliament, Empire and Parliamentary Law, 1776', in J.G.A. Pocock (ed.), *Three British Revolutions* (Princeton, 1980), pp. 289–322.

71. Michael Kammen, *A Rope of Sand: The Colonial Agents, British Politics and the American Revolution* (Ithaca, 1968); and P.D.G. Thomas, *British Politics and the Stamp Act Crisis* (Oxford, 1975), ch. 2.

72. Michael Kammen, *Empire and Interest*, pp. 59–60, 80–1, 130–1.

73. *Parl Hist*, xvii (1813), 1195.

74. James E. Bradley, *Popular Politics and the American Revolution* (Macon, Georgia, 1986); and John Sainsbury, *Disaffected Patriots: London Supporters of Revolutionary America 1769–1782* (Gloucester, 1983).

75. Michael Kammen, *Empire and Interest*, pp. 125–35.

76. Paul Langford, 'Property and "Virtual Representation" in Eighteenth-Century England', *HJ*, 31 (1988), 107.

77. J.R. Harris, 'Early Liverpool Canal Controversies', in J.R. Harris (ed.), *Liverpool and Merseyside* (1969), pp. 88–92.

78. R.C. Gwilliam, 'The Chester Tanners and Parliament 1711–1717', *JCAS*, 44 (1957), 41–9.

79. H.T. Dickinson, *Radical Politics in the North-East of England in the Later Eighteenth Century* (Durham, 1979), p. 8.

80. J. De L. Mann, 'Clothiers and Weavers in Wiltshire during the Eighteenth Century', in L.S. Pressnell (ed.), *Studies in the Industrial Revolution* (1960), pp. 66–96; M. Dorothy George, 'The London Coal-Heavers: Attempts to Regulate Waterside Labour in the Eighteenth and

Nineteenth Centuries', *EcH*, 1 (1926–9), 229–48; C.R. Dobson, *Masters and Journeymen* (1980), pp. 88–9; Arthur G. Rose, 'Early Cotton Riots in Lancashire, 1769–1779', *TLCAS*, 73–4 (1963–4), 72–4; and A.F.J. Brown, 'Colchester in the eighteenth century' in Lionel M. Munby (ed.), *East Anglian Studies* (Cambridge, 1968), pp. 148–9.

81. J.M. Fewster, 'The Keelmen of Tyneside in the Eighteenth Century', *DUJ*, 50 (1957–8), 28–9, 120–1.

82. D.G.D. Isaac, 'A Study of Popular Disturbances in Britain 1714–1754', unpublished PhD thesis (Edinburgh University, 1953), pp. 92–103; and N. Rothstein, 'The calico campaign of 1719–1721', *East London Papers*, 7 (1964), 3–21.

83. Geoffrey Holmes, *The Trial of Doctor Sacheverell* (1973); Nicholas Rogers, 'Popular Protest in Early Hanoverian London', *P&P*, 79 (1978), 70–100; and G.V. Bennett, *The Tory Crisis in Church and State 1688–1730* (Oxford, 1975), pp. 213–15.

84. Thomas W. Perry, *Public Opinion, Propaganda and Politics in Eighteenth-Century England* (Cambridge, Mass., 1962).

85. E.C. Black, *The Association* (Cambridge, Mass., 1963), pp. 131–73; T.C. Hansard, *Parl Hist*, xx (1814), 322–7; ibid., xxi (1814), 386, 533, 654–60, 702–3; and Northumberland County RO, Ridley (Blagden) MSS. ZRI 25/11. Letters to and from Jasper Harrison on the Newcastle petition.

86. N.C. Hunt, *Two Early Political Associations* (Oxford, 1961), chs 1–6.

87. G.M. Ditchfield, 'Parliament, the Quakers and the Tithe question 1750–1835', *PH*, 4 (1985), 87–114.

88. N.C. Hunt, *Two Early Political Associations*, chs 7–9; and J. Steven Watson, 'Dissent and Toleration', in Alex Natan, *Silver Renaissance* (1961), pp. 1–19.

89. Russell E. Richey, 'The Origins of British Radicalism: The Changing Rationale for Dissent', *ECS*, 7 (1973–4), 179–92; and Richard Burgess Barlow, *Citizenship and Conscience* (Philadelphia, 1962), chs 5–6.

90. G.M. Ditchfield, 'The parliamentary struggle over the repeal of the Test and Corporation Acts, 1787–1790', *EHR*, 89 (1970), 551–77; and Thomas W. Davis, *Committees for Repeal of the Test and Corporation Acts: Minutes 1786–90 and 1827–8* (London Record Society, 1978), pp. vii–xvii.

91. G.M. Ditchfield, 'The campaign in Lancashire and Cheshire for the Repeal of the Test and Corporation Acts, 1787–1790', *THSLC*, 126 (1977), 109–38.

92. T.C. Curtis and W.A. Speck, 'The Societies for the Reformation of Manners: A Case Study in the Theory and Practice of Moral Reform', *LH*, 3 (1976), 45–64; Tina Isaacs, 'The Anglican Hierarchy and the Reformation of Manners 1688–1738', *JEH*, 33 (1982), 391–411; Robert B. Shoemaker, 'Reforming the City: The Reformation of Manners Campaign in London, 1690–1738', in Lee Davison et al (eds), *Stilling the Grumbling Hive*, pp. 99–120; and Mary E. Fissell, 'Charity Universal? Institutions and Moral Reform in Eighteenth-Century Bristol', in ibid., pp. 121–44.

93. Joanna Innes, 'Politics and Morals: the Reformation of Manners movement in later eighteenth-century England', in Eckhart Hellmuth (ed.),

The Transformation of Political Culture in Britain and Germany in the Later Eighteenth Century (Oxford, 1980), pp. 57–118.

94. J.R. Poynter, *Society and Pauperism. English Ideas on Poor Relief, 1795–1834* (1969), pp. 91–8.

95. James E. Bradley, *Popular Politics and the American Revolution* in England (Macon, Georgia, 1986), *passim*; and John Sainsbury, *Disaffected Patriots. London supporters of Revolutionary America* (Gloucester, 1987), *passim.*

96. J.E. Cookson, *The Friends of Peace. Anti-war liberalism in England, 1793–1815* (Cambridge, 1982), chs 1–6.

97. This account of the campaign against the slave trade is based on Roger Anstey, *The Atlantic Slave Trade and British Abolition 1760–1810* (1975); Seymour Drescher, *Capitalism and Anti-Slavery: British Mobilisation in Comparative Perspective* (1986); James Walvin, *England, Slaves and Freedom, 1776–1838* (1986); James Walvin (ed.), *Slavery and British Society 1776–1846* (1982), especially the editor's introduction, his essay on 'The Propaganda of Anti-Slavery' and Seymour Drescher's essay on 'Public Opinion and the Destruction of British Colonial Slavery'; James Walvin, 'The Public Campaign in England against Slavery, 1787–1834', in David Eltis and James Walvin (eds), *The Abolition of the Atlantic Slave Trade* (Madison, 1981), pp. 63–79; James Walvin, 'Abolishing the Slave Trade: Anti-Slavery and Popular Radicalism, 1776–1807', in Clive Emsley and James Walvin (eds), *Artisans, Peasants and Proletarians 1760–1860* (1985), pp. 32–56; Peter Marshall, 'The Anti-Slave Trade Movement in Bristol', in Peter McGrath (ed.), *Bristol in the Eighteenth Century* (Newton Abbot, 1972), pp. 182–208; G.M. Ditchfield, 'Repeal, Abolition and Reform: A Study in the Interaction of Reforming Movements in the Parliament of 1790–6', in Christine Bolt and Seymour Drescher (eds), *Anti-Slavery, Religion and Reform* (Folkestone, 1980), pp. 101–18; J.R. Oldfield, 'The London Committee and Mobilization of Public Opinion against the Slave Trade', *HJ*, 35 (1992), 331–43; and E.M. Hunt, 'North of England Agitation for the Abolition of the Slave Trade 1780–1800', unpublished MA thesis (Manchester University, 1959).

98. Anstey, *The Atlantic Slave Trade*, pp. 260–4; Hunt, 'North of England Agitation', pp. 15–26.

99. Drescher, *Capitalism and Anti-Slavery*, pp. 1–12, 123–31; Drescher, 'Public Opinion', pp. 23–5, 35–8; Walvin, 'The Public Campaign', pp. 63–5; Walvin, *Slavery and British Society*, pp. 14, 19; and Walvin, 'Abolishing the Slave Trade', pp. 45–6, 49–52.

100. Anstey, *The Atlantic Slave Trade*, pp. 269–75; Walvin, 'The Public Campaign', p. 66; Hunt, 'North of England Agitation', pp. 83, 109, 135–6, 148–9, 200, 215–7, 255; Walvin, 'Abolishing the Slave Trade', pp. 42–3, 46, 49; J.R. Oldfield, 'The London Committee', pp. 339–40; and Drescher, *Capitalism and Anti-Slavery*, pp. 67–88.

101. Anstey, *The Atlantic Slave Trade*, pp. 286–98; Peter Marshall, 'The Anti-Slave Trade Movement', pp. 199–201; and Walvin, 'Abolishing the Slave Trade', p. 52.

102. Walvin, 'Abolishing the Slave Trade', pp. 46–7, 49, 51.

103. Anstey, *The Atlantic Slave Trade*, pp. 273, 279–82, 321–31.

104. Anstey, *The Atlantic Slave Trade*, pp. 276–8, 317–18; Drescher, *Capitalism*

and Anti-Slavery, pp. 142–4; J.R. Oldfield, 'The London Committee', pp. 339–41; and Walvin, 'Abolishing the Slave Trade', pp. 47–52.
105. Anstey, *The Atlantic Slave Trade*, chs 13–16; and Walvin, 'Abolishing the Slave Trade', pp. 52–4.

CHAPTER 3: POLITICS IN THE URBAN COMMUNITY

1. On the growth of towns see Angus McInnes, *The English Town, 1660–1760* (1980), pp. 1–6; P.J Corfield, *The Impact of English Towns 1700–1800* (Oxford, 1982), pp. 2–10, 15, 146–7; and P.J Corfield, 'The Industrial Towns before the Factory, 1680–1780', in P.J. Corfield, *The Rise of the New Urban Society* (Milton Keynes, 1977), p. 80.
2. Peter Borsay, 'The English urban renaissance: the development of provincial urban culture c. 1680–c. 1760', *SocH*, 5 (1977), 581–603; Peter Borsay, 'Culture, Status, and the English Urban Landscape', *H*, 67 (1982), 1–12; P.J. Corfield, *The Impact of English Towns 1700–1800*, pp. 124–33; and M.J. Daunton, 'Towns and Economic Growth in Eighteenth-Century England', in Philip Abrams and E.A. Wrigley (eds), *Towns in Societies* (Cambridge, 1978), pp. 245–77.
3. P.J Corfield, *The Impact of English Towns 1700–1800*, pp. 125–30, 133–8; Peter Borsay, '"All the town's a stage": urban ritual and ceremony 1660–1800', in Peter Clark (ed.), *The Transformation of English Provincial Towns 1600–1800* (1984), pp. 228–58; Joyce Ellis, 'A dynamic society: social relations in Newcastle upon Tyne 1660–1760', in ibid., pp. 205–12; and John M. Triffitt, 'Politics and the Urban Community Parliamentary Boroughs in the South West of England 1710–1730', unpublished D. Phil. thesis (Oxford University, 1985), pp. 58–80.
4. Ibid., pp. 91–130; Sidney and Beatrice Webb, *English Local Government from the Revolution to the Municipal Corporations Act: The Manor and the Borough* (2 vols, 1908), ii, 390, 438–9, 476–7, 490, 549; Arthur Redford, *The History of Local Government in Manchester* (2 vols, 1939), i, 194–8; R.W. Greaves, *The Corporation of Leicester 1689–1836* (Oxford, 1939), pp. 92–8, 108–9; P.J. Corfield, *The Impact of English Towns 1700–1800*, pp. 139–41; Robert Newton, *Eighteenth Century Exeter* (Exeter, 1984), pp. 11, 15, 51–2; and Helen Cam, '*Quo Warranto* Proceedings at Cambridge 1780–1790', *CHJ*, 8 (1946), 148.
5. Kathleen Wilson, 'The Rejection of Deference: Urban Political Culture in England, 1715–1785', unpublished PhD thesis (Yale University, 1986), pp. 286–8, 382.
6. John Brewer, 'Commercialization and Politics', in Neil McKendrick, John Brewer and J.H. Plumb, *The Birth of a Consumer Society* (1982), pp. 217–62; and Trevor Fawcett, 'Eighteenth Century Debating Societies', *BJECS*, 3 (1980), 217–29; and Peter Clark, 'Sociability and Urbanity: Clubs and Societies in the Eighteenth-Century City' (The H.J. Dyos Memorial Lecture, University of Leicester, 1986), pp. 1–23.
7. John Brewer, 'Commercialization and Politics', pp. 238–40; Peter Borsay, '"All the town's a stage": urban ritual and ceremony 1660–

1800', in Peter Clark (ed.), *The Transformation of English Provincial Towns 1600–1800*, pp. 228–40; Joyce Ellis, 'A dynamic society: social relations in Newcastle upon Tyne 1660–1760', in ibid., p. 200; George A. Tressider, 'Coronation day celebrations in English towns, 1685–1821: elite hegemony and local relations on a ceremonial occasion', *BJECS*, 15 (1992), 1–16. Kathleen Wilson, 'The Rejection of Deference', pp. 28–43, 85–102; Kathleen Wilson, 'Admiral Vernon and Popular Politics in Mid–Hanoverian Britain', *P&P*, 121 (1988), 74–109; and Gerald Jordan and Nicholas Rogers, 'Admirals as Heroes: Patriotism and Liberty in Hanoverian England', *JBS*, 28 (1989), 201–24.

8. Sidney and Beatrice Webb, *English Local Government ... The Manor and the Borough* (2 vols) and *English Local Government: Statutory Authorities for Special Purposes* (London, 1922).

9. Edward Gillett, *A History of Grimsby* (Oxford, 1970), pp. 151–3; and Henry W. Meikle, *Scotland and the French Revolution* (Glasgow, 1912), p. 22.

10. Sidney and Beatrice Webb, *English Local Government ... The Manor and the Borough*, i, 368–9.

11. Ibid., ii, 433–41, 448–70, 482–90; P.J. Corfield, *The Impact of English Towns 1700–1800*, pp. 150–2; R.G. Wilson, *Gentlemen Merchants: The merchant community in Leeds 1700–1830* (Manchester, 1971), pp. 162–5; Robert Newton, *Eighteenth Century Exeter*, pp. 34–50; and F.E. Sanderson, 'The Structure of Politics in Liverpool 1780–1807', *THSLC*, 127 (1978), 65.

12. P.J. Corfield, *The Impact of English Towns 1700–1800*, p. 152: and P.J. Corfield, 'The Industrial Towns before the Factory, 1680–1780', in *The Rise of the New Urban Society*, p. 99.

13. George Rudé, *Hanoverian London 1714–1808* (1971), pp. 127–8.

14. R.W. Greaves, *The Corporation of Leicester 1689–1836*, p. 5.

15. John A. Phillips, 'From Municipal Matters to Parliamentary Principles: Eighteenth-Century Borough Politics in Maidstone', *JBS*, 27 (1988), 334–5.

16. Kathleen Wilson, 'The Rejection of Deference', pp. 187–8.

17. Malcolm I. Thomis, *Politics and Society in Nottingham 1785–1835* (Oxford, 1969), pp. 114, 117.

18. Nicholas Rogers, *Whigs and Cities. Popular Politics in the Age of Walpole and Pitt* (Oxford, 1989), ch. 9; D.S. O'Sullivan, 'Politics in Norwich, 1701–1835', unpublished M.Phil. thesis (University of East Anglia, 1975), pp. 1–56; Kathleen Wilson, 'The Rejection of Deference', pp. 391–3.

19. George Rudé, *Hanoverian London 1714–1808*, pp. 120–5; Gary S. De Krey, 'Political Radicalism in London after the Glorious Revolution', *JMH*, 55 (1983), 587–9; Gary S. De Krey, *A Fractured Society: The Politics of London in the First Age of Party, 1688–1715* (Oxford, 1985), pp. 39–44.

20. J.M. Triffitt, 'Politics and the Urban Community', abstract and pp. 23–5, 149–53, 157, 263; and P.J Corfield, *The Impact of English Towns 1700–1800*, pp. 146, 152, 161–2.

21. J.M. Triffitt, 'Politics and the Urban Community', pp. 24, 133–4, 137–42; and P.J. Corfield, *The Impact of English Towns*, pp. 157–8.

22. Paul Langford, *Public Life and the Propertied Englishman 1689–1798* (Oxford, 1991), pp. 267–8.
23. J.M Triffitt, 'Politics and the Urban Community', pp. 137–8; and Sidney and Beatrice Webb, *English Local Government: Statutory Authorities for Special Purposes*, pp. 371–2, 376.
24. George Rudé, *Hanoverian London 1714–1808*, pp. 127–8; and F.H.W. Sheppard, *Local Government in St. Marylebone 1688–1835* (1958), p. 8.
25. Sidney and Beatrice Webb, *English Local Government: Statutory Authorities*, p. 371; and Sue Farrant, *Georgian Brighton 1740–1820* (University of Sussex, Occasional Papers, no. 13 (1980)), p. 49.
26. George Rudé, *Hanoverian London 1714–1808*, pp. 131–3.
27. J.W.F. Hill, *Georgian Lincoln* (Cambridge, 1966), pp. 241–6.
28. M.J. Smith, 'Politics in Newark in the 1790s', *TTS*, 84 (1980), 61, 63, 65.
29. J. Ramsay Muir and Edith M. Platt, *A History of Municipal Government in Liverpool* (Liverpool, 1906), p. 122; and Frederick H. Spencer, *Municipal Origins: An Account of English Private Bill Legislation relating to Local Government, 1740–1835* (1911), p. 41.
30. Arthur Redford, *The History of Local Government in Manchester*, i, 43, 47, 63; and François Vigier, *Change and Apathy: Liverpool and Manchester during the Industrial Revolution* (Cambridge, Mass., 1970), pp. 83, 106.
31. P.J. Corfield, *The Impact of English Towns 1700–1800*, p. 152.
32. Ibid., pp. 157–8; Sidney and Beatrice Webb, *English Local Government: Statutory Authorities*, pp. 2–3, 235; Frederick H. Spencer, *Municipal Origins*, pp. 4–5.
33. François Vigier, *Change and Apathy*, p. 108.
34. Robert Newton, *Eighteenth Century Exeter*, pp. 30–1.
35. Frederick H. Spencer, *Municipal Origins*, pp. 117–28.
36. Kathleen Wilson, 'Urban Culture and Political Activism in Hanoverian England: The Example of Voluntary Hospitals', in Eckhart Hellmuth (ed.), *The Transformation of Political Culture*, pp. 165–84; Kathleen Wilson, 'The Rejection of Deference', pp. 470–2; J.V. Pickstone and S.V.F. Butler, 'The Politics of Medicine in Manchester, 1788–1792: Hospital Reform and Public Health Services in the Early Industrial City', *MH*, 28 (1984), 227–49; and John Morey, *Experience and Identity: Birmingham and the West Midlands 1760–1800* (Manchester, 1977), pp. 9–10.
37. E.L. Jones and M.E. Falkus, 'Urban Improvement and the English Economy in the Seventeenth and Eighteenth Centuries', *Research in Economic History*, 4 (1979), 214.
38. Ibid., p. 213.
39. Frederick H. Spencer, *Municipal Origins*, p. 149.
40. Paul Langford, *Public Life and the Propertied Englishman 1689–1798*, pp. 228–36.
41. Ibid., p. 230.
42. Frederick H. Spencer, *Municipal Origins*, pp. 134–7.
43. Paul Langford, *Public Life and the Propertied Englishman 1689–1798*, p. 171.
44. Frederick H. Spencer, *Municipal Origins*, pp. 7–8, 65–9.
45. Lucy Sutherland, 'The City of London in Eighteenth-Century Politics', in Richard Pares and A.J.P. Taylor (eds), *Essays presented to Sir Lewis*

Namier, pp. 49–74; A.J. Henderson, London and the National Government 1721–1742 (Durham, N. Carolina, 1945), pp. 3–24, 74–115; George Rudé, *Hanoverian London 1714–1808*, ch. 7; I.G. Doolittle, 'Walpole's Election Act (1725)', *EHR*, 97 (1982), 504–29; and Nicholas Rogers, 'The City Elections Act (1725) reconsidered', ibid., 100 (1985), 604–17.

46. D.S. O'Sullivan, 'Politics in Norwich, 1701–1835', pp. 57–76, and Sidney and Beatrice Webb, *English Local Government ... The Manor and the Borough*, ii, 531–48.

47. Ramsay Muir, *A History of Liverpool* (1907), pp. 168–70; and J. Ramsay Muir and Edith M. Platt, *A History of Municipal Government in Liverpool*, pp. 125–8.

48. Ibid., pp. 128–9; Joseph Clegg, *To the Gentlemen, Members of the Common-Council of the Corporation of Liverpool* (Liverpool, 1757); Joseph Clegg, *To the Worshipful the Mayor, Bailiffs, and Burgesses of the Corporation of Liverpool* (Liverpool, 1757); Joseph Clegg, *To the Worshipful Richard Hughes, Esquire, Mayor of Liverpool* (Liverpool, 1757); Joseph Clegg, *A Letter to the Free Burgesses of Liverpool*, etc. (Liverpool, 1757); and Joseph Clegg, *A Narrative: containing a vindication of Alderman Clegg's Conduct* (Liverpool, 1757).

49. Sylvia McIntyre, 'The Scarborough Corporation Quarrel, 1736–1760', *NH*, 14 (1978), 208–26.

50. P. Morant, *The History and Antiquities of Colchester* (1748), pp. 70–1.

51. B. Howard Cunnington, *Rural Mayors in Devizes in the Reign of Queen Anne* (Devizes, 1934), pp. 1–21; J.R. Burton, *A History of Bewdley* (1883), p. 45; and Romney Sedgwick (ed.), *The House of Commons 1715–1754*, i, 209–12 (Grampound).

52. Helen Cam, '*Quo Warranto* Proceedings at Cambridge 1780–1790', *CHJ*, 8 (1946), 145–65.

53. John M. Triffitt, 'Politics and the Urban Community', pp. 242–50.

54. Deborah G. Jenkins, 'County Administration in the reign of George II: the example of Surrey', unpublished PhD thesis (Warwick University, 1986) pp. 121–2.

55. F.H.W. Sheppard, *Local Government in St. Marylebone 1688–1835*, pp. 102–21.

56. George Rudé, *Hanoverian London 1714–1808*, p. 133.

57. Deborah G. Jenkins, 'County Administration in the reign of George II', pp. 123–5.

58. Frederick H. Spencer, *Municipal Origins*, pp. 9–11.

59. Ibid., p. 41; and J. Ramsay Muir and Edith M. Platt, *A History of Municipal Government in Liverpool*, p. 122.

60. John M. Triffitt, 'Politics and the Urban Community', pp. 274–5.

61. Sidney and Beatrice Webb, *English Local Government ... The Manor and the Borough*, ii, 458–9; and Robert Newton, *Eighteenth Century Exeter*, pp. 30–1.

62. Sidney and Beatrice Webb, *English Local Government ... The Manor and the Borough*, ii, 456–7.

63. Paul Langford, *Public Life and the Propertied Englishman 1689–1798*, pp. 224–6.

64. Sidney and Beatrice Webb, *English Local Government ... The Manor and the Borough*, ii, 433–4, 463; A. Temple Patterson, *A History of Southampton 1700– 1914. Vol. One: An Oligarchy in Decline 1700–1835* (Southampton, 1966), pp. 46–7; R.W. Greaves, *The Corporation of Leicester 1689–1836*, pp. 32–3; Frederick H. Spencer, *Municipal Origins*, pp. 39–42; Malcolm I. Thomis, *Old Nottingham* (Newton Abbot, 1968), p. 45; and Sylvia McIntyre, 'Towns as health and pleasure resorts: Bath, Scarborough and Weymouth, 1700– 1815', unpublished D.Phil thesis (Oxford University, 1973), p. 92.

65. Frederick H. Spencer, *Municipal Origins*, pp. 38–9; and Conrad Gill, 'Birmingham under the Street Commissioners, 1769–1851', 1 (1947–8), 255–87.

66. Romney Sedgwick (ed.), *The House of Commons 1715–1754*, i, 203.

67. A. Temple Patterson, *A History of Southampton*, i, 78–83.

68 Sylvia McIntyre, 'Towns as health and pleasure resorts', pp. 65–6, 73, 76–7; François Vigier, *Change and Apathy*, pp. 45–6; J. Ramsay Muir and Edith M. Platt, *A History of Municipal Government in Liverpool*, pp. 120–1; and A. Temple Patterson, *A History of Southampton 1700–1914*, i, 23–5.

69. John M. Triffitt, 'Politics and the Urban Community', p. 235; and P.J. Corfield, *The Impact of English Towns 1700–1800*, p. 155.

70. F.E. Sanderson, 'The Structure of Politics in Liverpool 1780–1807', in *THSLC*, 127 (1978), 69.

71. P.J. Corfield, *The Impact of English Towns 1700–1800*, p.155; R.W. Greaves, *The Corporation of Leicester 1689–1836*, p. 102; Kathleen Wilson, 'The Rejection of Deference', p. 326; Nicholas Rogers, *Whigs and Cities*, p. 287; and John A Phillips, *Electoral Behavior in Unreformed England*, p. 75.

72. Romney Sedgwick (ed.), *The House of Commons 1715–1754*, i, 203.

73. Sidney and Beatrice Webb, *English Local Government ... The Manor and the Borough*, ii, 439.

74. George Rudé, *Hanoverian London 1714–1808*, p. 133.

75. Joseph Clegg, *A Letter to the Free Burgesses of Liverpool*, etc. (Liverpool, 1757), p. 17. For Clegg's other tracts, see note 48.

76. Kathleen Wilson, 'The Rejection of Deference', p. 335; Robert Newton, *Eighteenth Century Exeter*, p. 82; John Money, *Experience and Identity*, pp. 15–20; Sylvia McIntyre, 'Towns as health and pleasure resorts', p. 74; Helen Cam, '*Quo Warranto* Proceedings at Cambridge 1780– 1790', *CHJ*, 8 (1948), 145–65; A. Temple Patterson, *A History of Southampton 1700–1914*, i, 78–89; and Leon S. Marshall, *The Development of Public Opinion in Manchester 1780–1820*, pp. 80–91.

77. R.W. Greaves, *The Corporation of Leicester 1689–1836*, pp. 78–82.

78. Kathleen Wilson, 'The Rejection of Deference', pp. 312–17; and H.T. Dickinson, *Radical Politics in the North-East of England in the Later Eighteenth Century* (Durham, 1979), p. 8.

79. Malcolm I. Thomis, *Politics and Society in Nottingham 1785–1835*, p. 123; and Malcolm I. Thomas, *Old Nottingham*, pp. 52–6.

80. Gary S. De Krey, 'Political Radicalism in London after the Glorious Revolution', *JMH*, 55 (1983), 585–617.

81. Nicholas Rogers, 'Resistance to Oligarchy: The City Opposition to Walpole and his Successors, 1725–47 ', in John Stevenson (ed.), *London in the Age of Reform*, pp. 1–29.

82. Joseph Clegg, *To the Worshipful Richard Hughes, Esquire, Mayor of Liverpool* (Liverpool, 1757), p. 2.
83. Ramsay Muir, *A History of Liverpool*, pp. 168–71; and J. Ramsay Muir and Edith M. Platt, *A History of Municipal Government in Liverpool*, pp. 125–9.
84. Nicholas Rogers, *Whigs and Cities*, pp. 290–1; and Sidney and Beatrice Webb, *English Local Government ... The Manor and the Borough*, ii, 456–7.
85. *Parl Hist*, xv (1813), 470–507.
86. Alexander J. Murdoch, 'Politics and the People in the Burgh of Dumfries, 1758–60', *SHR*, 70 (1991), 151–71.
87. Alexander Murdoch, 'The Importance of being Edinburgh. Management and Opposition in Edinburgh Politics, 1746–1784', *SHR*, 62 (1983), 1–16. William Brydon, 'Politics, government and society in Edinburgh, 1780–1833', unpublished PhD thesis (University of Wales, Bangor, 1989), pp. 89–91; and Richard B. Sher, 'Moderates, managers and popular politics in mid–eighteenth century Edinburgh', in J. Dwyer, R. Mason and A. Murdoch (eds), *New Perspectives on the Politics and Culture of Early Modern Scotland* (Edinburgh, 1988), pp. 179–209.
88. Quoted in John A. Phillips, 'From Municipal Matters to Parliamentary Principles: Eighteenth-Century Borough Politics in Maidstone', *JBS*, 27 (1988), 336.
89. Ibid., pp. 327–51, and John A. Phillips, 'Municipal Politics in Later Eighteenth Century Maidstone: Electoral Polarization in the Reign of George III', in Eckhart Hellmuth (ed.), *The Transformation of Political Culture*, pp. 185–203.
90. *The Contest* (Newcastle upon Tyne, 1774), p. 8.
91. Kathleen Wilson, 'The Rejection of Deference', pp. 337–8; and Thomas R. Knox, 'Popular Politics and Provincial Radicalism: Newcastle upon Tyne, 1769–1785', *Albion*, 2 (1979), 231–4.
92. Malcolm I. Thomis, *Politics and Society in Nottingham 1785–1835*, pp. 114–17.
93. Robert Newton, *Eighteenth Century Exeter*, p. 82.
94. Helen Cam, '*Quo Warranto* Proceedings at Cambridge 1780–1790', *CHJ*, 8 (1946), 160.
95. Sylvia McIntyre, 'Towns as health and pleasure resorts', p. 232.
96. Ibid., pp. 74–7, 92–3.
97. P.J. Corfield, *The Impact of English Towns 1700–1800*, p. 151.
98. A. Temple Patterson, *A History of Southampton 1700–1914*, i, 78–81.
99. Ibid., i, 81.
100. John Money, *Experience and Identity*, pp. 8–22; and Conrad Gill, 'Birmingham under the Street Commissioners, 1769–1851', *BHJ*, 1 (1947–8), 265–6.
101. François Vigier, *Change and Apathy*, pp. 113–17.
102. Leon S. Marshall, *The Development of Public Opinion in Manchester 1780–1820*, p. 90.
103. Ibid., p. 91.
104. François Vigier, *Change and Apathy*, p. 71.
105. Ibid., pp. 71–2; Richard Brook, *Liverpool as it was during the last quarter of the eighteenth century* (Liverpool, 1853), pp. 204–30; and J. Ramsay Muir and Edith M. Platt, *A History of Municipal Government in Liverpool*, pp. 129–32.

106. Quoted in John Cannon, *Parliamentary Reform 1640–1832* (Cambridge, 1973), pp. 112–13.
107. Ibid., pp. 110–4; and Henry W. Meikle, *Scotland and the French Revolution* (1969), pp. 18–24, 76–7.

CHAPTER 4: THE POLITICS OF THE CROWD

1. Robert J. Holton, 'The crowd in history: some problems of theory and method', *SocH*, 3 (1978), 219–33; and Mark Harrison, *Crowds and History. Mass Phenomena in English Towns, 1790–1835* (Cambridge, 1988), pp. 10–12.
2. George Rudé, *The Crowd in History 1730–1848*; George Rudé, *Paris and London in the Eighteenth Century: Studies in Popular Protest*; George Rudé, *Wilkes and Liberty*; E.P. Thompson, 'The Moral Economy of the English Crowd in the Eighteenth Century', *P&P*, 50 (1971), 76–136; E.P. Thompson, 'Patrician society, Plebeian Culture', *JSH*, 7 (1974), 382–405; and Edward Thompson, *Whigs and Hunters. The Origins of the Black Act* (1975).
3. Adrian J. Randall, 'The Gloucestershire Food Riots of 1766', *MH*, 10 (1985), 74.
4. R. Wells, 'Counting Riots in Eighteenth-Century England', *Bull. of Soc. for Study of Labour History*, 38 (1978), 68–72; and Roger Wells, *Wretched Faces, Famine in Wartime England 1763–1803* (Gloucester, 1988), pp. 90–4.
5. Robert B. Shoemaker, 'The London "Mob" in the Early Eighteenth Century', *JBS*, 26 (1987), 276.
6. C.R. Dobson, *Masters and Journeyman. A Prehistory of Industrial Relations 1717–1800* (1980), p. 22.
7. John Bohstedt, *Riots and Community Politics in England and Wales 1790–1810* (Cambridge, Mass., 1983), p. 5.
8. George Rudé, *The Crowd in History*, pp. 36–8; and A.J. Randall, 'Gloucestershire Food Riots of 1766', *MH*, 10 (1985), 72.
9. George Rudé, *The Crowd in History*, pp. 35–6.
10. Roger Wells, *Wretched Faces*, pp. 420–9. See also John Stevenson, 'Food Riots in England, 1792–1818', in R. Quinault and J. Stevenson (eds), *Popular Protest and Public Order* (1974), pp. 33–74.
11. John Bohstedt, *Riots and Community Politics*, p. 14.
12. Roger Wells, *Wretched Faces*, p. 95.
13. Ibid., p. 94.
14. John Bohstedt, *Riots and Community Politics*, p. 4.
15. PRO. SPD. 36/4, ff. 22–3.
16. Ibid., 36/51, f. 92.
17. Alfred Plummer, *The London Weavers' Company* (Boston, 1972), pp. 292–314.
18. R.B. Rose, 'A Liverpool Sailors' Strike in the Eighteenth Century', *TLCAS*, 68 (1958), 85–92.
19. H.T. Dickinson, 'The Hexham Militia Riot of 1761', *Bull. Durham County Local Hist. Soc.*, 22 (1978), 2–6.

20. R.B. Rose, 'The Priestley Riots of 1791', *P&P,* 18 (1960), 68–88; G.M. Ditchfield, 'The Priestley Riots in Historical Perspective', *Trans. Unitarian Hist. Soc.,* 20 (1991), 3–16; David L. Wyles, '"The Spirit of Persecutors exemplified": The Priestley Riots and the victims of the Church and King mobs', ibid., pp. 17–39; and Martin Smith, 'Conflict and Society in Late Eighteenth-Century Birmingham', unpublished PhD thesis (Cambridge University, 1977), 1–56.

21. Geoffrey Holmes, 'The Sacheverell Riots: the Crowd and the Church in early eighteenth-century London', *P&P,* 72 (1976), 55–85.

22. Christopher Hibbert, *King Mob* (1959); George Rudé, 'The Gordon Riots: A Study of the Rioters and their Victims', in Rudé, *Paris and London,* pp. 268–92; Nicholas Rogers, 'The Gordon Riots Revisited', in *Historical Papers/Communications historiques* (Windsor, 1988), pp. 16–34; and Nicholas Rogers, 'Crowd and People in the Gordon Riots', in Eckhart Hellmuth (ed.), *The Transformation of Political Culture,* pp. 39–55.

23. John Stevenson, *Popular Disturbances in England 1700–1870* (1979), p. 47.

24. Ibid., pp. 47, 49.

25. Sidney and Beatrice Webb, 'The Assize of Bread', *The Economic Journal,* 14 (1904), 196–218.

26. John Stevenson, *Popular Disturbances,* pp. 93–7.

27. Edward Thompson, 'Patrician Society, Plebeian Culture', *JSH,* 7 (1974), 385–7; R.B. Shoemaker, 'The London "Mob"', *JBS,* 26 (1987), 279–80; John Bohstedt, *Riots and Community Politics,* p. 23; and Andrew Charlesworth and Adrian J. Randall, 'Morals, Markets and the English Crowd in 1766', *P&P,* 114 (1987), 206.

28. R.B. Shoemaker, 'The London "Mob"', *JBS,* 26 (1987), 287–94.

29. See the sources cited in notes 20–22 and John Walsh, 'Methodism and the Mob in the Eighteenth Century', in G.J. Cuming and D. Baker (eds), *Studies in Church History* (Cambridge, 1972), viii, 213–27.

30. George Rudé, *Paris and London,* pp. 311–17; Nicholas Rogers, 'Popular Disaffection in London during the Forty-Five', *LJ,* 1 (1975), 21–5.

31. George Rudé, *Paris and London,* p. 311.

32. PRO. SPD. 37/4, ff. 202–3.

33. John Brewer and John Styles (eds), *An Ungovernable People. The English and their law in the seventeenth and eighteenth centuries* (1980), pp. 15–16.

34. George Rudé, 'The London "Mob" of the Eighteenth Century', in Rudé, *Paris and London,* pp. 293–318; and R.W. Malcolmson, *Life and Labour in England 1700–1780* (1981), pp. 109–10.

35. John Bohstedt, *Riots and Community Politics,* pp. 52–4.

36. Ibid., pp. 69–83.

37. A. Charlesworth and A.J. Randall, 'Morals, Markets and the English Crowd in 1766', *P&P,* 114 (1987), 205–8; M. Dorothy George, 'The London Coal-Heavers: Attempts to Regulate Waterside Labour in the Eighteenth and Nineteenth Centuries', *EcH* (a supplement to *The Economic Journal*), 1 (1926–9), 229–48; Adrian Randall, 'The Industrial Moral Economy of the Gloucestershire Weavers in the Eighteenth Century', in John Rule (ed.), *British Trade Unionism 1750–1850: The Formative Years* (1988), pp. 29–51; Robert W. Malcomson, 'Workers'

Combinations in Eighteenth-Century England', in Margaret Jacob and James Jacob (eds), *The Origins of Anglo-American Radicalism* (1984), pp. 149–61; J.M. Fewster, 'The Keelmen of Tyneside in the Eighteenth Century', *DUJ,* 50 (1957–8), 24–33, 66–75, 111–23; John Stevenson, *Popular Disturbances,* pp. 113–27: J. De L. Mann, 'Clothiers and Weavers in Wiltshire during the Eighteenth Century', in L.S. Presswell (ed.), *Studies in the Industrial Revolution,* pp. 69–96; and Arthur G. Rose, 'Early Cotton Riots in Lancashire, 1769–1779', *TLCAS,* 73–4 (1963–4), 60–100.

38. Robert W. Malcolmson, '"A set of ungovernable people": the Kingswood colliers in the eighteenth century', in John Brewer and John Styles (eds), *An Ungovernable People,* pp. 85–127.

39. E.P. Thompson, 'The Moral Economy of the English Crowd', *P&P,* 50 (1971), 76–8.

40. Ibid., p. 78.

41. The main criticisms or refinements are in Dale Edward Williams, 'Morals, Markets and the English Crowd in 1766', *P&P,* 104 (1984), 56–73; John Bohstedt, *Riots and Community Politics,* pp. 27–68, 211–12; and J. Stevenson, 'The "Moral Economy" of the English Crowd: Myth and Reality', in Anthony Fletcher and John Stevenson (eds), *Order and Disorder in Early Modern England* (Cambridge, 1985), pp. 218–38.

42. See, for example, Walter J. Shelton, *English Hunger and Industrial Disorders* (1973), pp. 51–93; Alan Booth, 'Food Riots in the North-West of England 1790–1801', *P&P,* 77 (1977), 84–107; Roger Wells, 'The revolt of the south-west, 1800–1801: a study in English popular protest', *SocH,* 6 (1977), 713–44; Roger Wells, *Dearth and Distress in Yorkshire 1793–1802* (York, 1977); Roger Wells, *Wretched Faces*; A.J. Randall, 'The Gloucestershire Food Riots of 1766', *MH,* 10 (1985), 72–93; Kenneth J. Logue, *Popular Disturbances in Scotland 1780–1815* (Edinburgh, 1979), pp. 18–53; John Stevenson, *Popular Disturbances,* pp. 91–112.; and A. Charlesworth and A.J. Randall, 'Morals, Markets and the English Crowd in 1766', *P&P,* 114 (1987), 200–13. Dale Edward Williams was more sympathetic to Thompson's views in 'Midland Hunger Riots in 1766', *MH,* 3 (1976), 256–97. Some of the views Thompson expressed can be found in work which pre-dated his. See R.B. Rose, 'Eighteenth Century Price Riots and Public Policy in England', *IRSH,* 6 (1961), 276–92; Walter M. Stern, 'The Bread Crisis in Britain, 1795–96', *Economica,* new series, 31 (1964), 168–87; D.J.V. Jones, 'The Corn Riots in Wales, 1793–1801', *WHR,* 2 (1964), 322–50; and S.G.E. Lythe, 'The Tayside meal mobs 1772–3', *SHR,* 46 (1967), 26–36.

43. E.P. Thompson, 'The Moral Economy of the English Crowd', *P&P,* 50 (1971), 79.

44. See note 41.

45. PRO. SPD. 36/51. William Price to Andrew Stone, 13 June 1740; and PRO. Home Office Papers, 42/53. Letter from James Hartley dated Nov. 1800. (Cited in Alan Booth, 'Food Riots in the North-West', *P&P,* 77 (1977), 91.

46. George Rudé, *The Crowd in History,* p. 35; John Stevenson, *Popular Disturbances,* pp. 40–3; John Leopold, 'The Levellers' Revolt in Galloway in 1724', *Journal of the Scottish Labour Hist. Soc.,* 14 (1980),

4–29; J.M. Neeson, 'The Opponents of Enclosure in Eighteenth-Century Northamptonshire', *P&P,* 105 (1984), 114–39; R.W. Greaves, *The Corporation of Leicester 1689–1836,* pp. 78–82; H.T. Dickinson, *Radical Politics in the North-East of England in the Later Eighteenth Century,* p. 8; and Malcolm I. Thomis, *Old Nottingham,* pp. 52–6.

47. Edward Thompson, *Whigs and Hunters,* pp. 119–41.
48. Ibid., pp. 55–115, 142–66; P.B. Munsche, *Gentlemen and Poachers. The English Game Laws 1671–1831* (Cambridge, 1981); and Douglas Hay, 'Poaching and the Game Laws on Cannock Chase', in Douglas Hay et al (eds), *Albion's Fatal Tree. Crime and Society in Eighteenth-Century England* (1975), pp. 189–253.
49. John Stevenson, *Popular Disturbances,* pp. 43–5, D.G.D. Isaac, 'A Study of Popular Disturbances in Britain 1714–1754', unpublished PhD thesis (Edinburgh University, 1953), pp. 104–21; Philip D. Jones, 'The Bristol Bridge Riot and its Antecedents: Eighteenth-Century Perception of the Crowd', *JBS,* 19 (1980), 74–92; and Mark Harrison, '"To Rise and Dare Dissent": The Bristol Bridge Riot of 1793 Re-examined', *HJ,* 26 (1983), 557–85.
50. D.G.D. Isaac, 'Popular Disturbances in Britain', pp. 122–9; George Rudé, '"Mother Gin" and the London riots of 1736', in Rudé, *Paris and London,* pp. 53–63; and Peter Clark, 'The "Mother Gin" controversy in the early eighteenth century', *TRHS,* 5th series, 38 (1988), 63–84.
51. J.R. Western, *The English Militia in the Eighteenth Century* (1965), pp. 290–302; John Stevenson, *Popular Disturbances,* pp. 35–40; John Stevenson, 'The London "Crimp" Riots of 1794', *IRSH,* 16 (1971), 40–58; Kenneth J. Logue, *Popular Disturbances in Scotland 1780–1815,* pp. 75–127; K.J. Logue, 'The Tranent Militia Riot of 17197', *Trans. East Lothian Antiquarian and Field Naturalists' Soc.,* 14 (1974), 37–61; Sandy Mullay, *Scotland's Forgotten Massacre* (Edinburgh, 1979); and H.T. Dickinson, 'The Hexham Militia Riot of 1761', *Bull. Durham County Local Hist. Soc.,* 22 (1978), 2–6.
52. John Rule, 'Labour Consciousness and Industrial Conflict in Eighteenth-Century Exeter', in Barry Stapleton (ed.), *Conflict and Community in Southern England* (Stroud, 1992), pp. 92–109.
53. See notes 18 and 37; Norman McCord and David E. Brewster, 'Some Labour Troubles of the 1790s in North East England', *IRSH,* 13 (1968), 366–83, George Rudé, 'Wilkes and Liberty, 1768–9', in Rudé, *Paris and London,* pp. 222–67; and Walter J. Shelton, *English Hunger and Industrial Disorders,* pp. 165–202.
54. Michael Duffy, *The Englishman and the Foreigner* (Cambridge, 1986), pp. 13–52; and Colin Haydon, *Anti-Catholicism in Eighteenth-Century England* (Manchester, 1992).
55. See note 22.
56. George Rudé, *Paris and London,* pp. 288–91.
57. See the essays by Nicholas Rogers in note 22; and Colin Haydon, 'The Gordon Riots in the English Provinces', *Historical Research,* 63 (1990), 354–9.
58. Thomas W. Perry, *Public Opinion, Propaganda, and Politics in Eighteenth-Century England* (Cambridge, Mass., 1962), pp. 72–122.

59. See notes 20–21; Nicholas Rogers, 'Popular Protest in Early Hanoverian London', *P&P*, 79 (1978), 70–100; and Nicholas Rogers, 'Riot and Popular Jacobitism in Early Hanoverian England', in Eveline Cruickshanks (ed.), *Ideology and Conspiracy: Aspects of Jacobitism, 1689–1759*, pp. 70–88.

60. John Walsh, 'Methodism and the Mob in the Eighteenth Century', in G.J. Cuming and Derek Baker (eds), *Studies in Church History*, viii, 213–27.

61. R.B. Shoemaker, 'The London "Mob"', *JBS*, 26 (1987), 303; and Nicholas Rogers, 'Popular Protest in Early Hanoverian London', *P&P*, 79 (1978), 99–100.

62. K.J. Logue, *Popular Disturbances in Scotland*, pp. 3–5; H.T. Dickinson, 'Popular Conservatism and Militant Loyalism 1789–1815', in H.T. Dickinson (ed.), *Britain and the French Revolution 1789–1815* (1989), pp. 118–19; Alan Booth, 'Popular Loyalism and public violence in the north-west of England 1790–1800', *SocH*, 8 (1983), 295–313; and note 20.

63. A.J. Randall, 'The Gloucestershire Food Riots of 1766', *MH*, 10 (1985), 85.

64. On the Porteous riot see H.T. Dickinson and K.J. Logue, 'The Porteous Riot', *HT*, 22 (1972), 272–81; and idem, 'The Porteous Riot: A Study of the Breakdown of Law and Order in Edinburgh, 1736–1737', *Journal of the Scottish Labour Hist. Soc.*, 10 (1976), 21–40.

65. See notes 18, 19, 22, 49 (by Harrison and Jones), 51 (by Logue and Mullay); and Joyce Ellis, 'Urban Conflict and Popular Violence. The Guildhall Riots of 1740 in Newcastle upon Tyne', *IRSH*, 25 (1980), 332–49.

66. George Rudé, *The Crowd in History*, pp. 247–50.

67. Ibid., pp. 250–2; and R.B. Rose, 'Eighteenth Century Price Riots', *IRSH*, 6 (1961), 292.

68. R.B. Shoemaker, 'The London "Mob"', *JBS*, 26 (1987), 281.

69. George Rudé, *The Crowd in History*, pp. 60–1, 198–210; and Rudé, *Paris and London*, pp. 21–2.

70. J. Stevenson, 'The "Moral Economy" of the English Crowd,' in A. Fletcher and J. Stevenson (eds), *Order and Disorder in Early Modern England*, p. 236.

71. J. Stevenson, 'Food Riots in England', in R. Quinault and J. Stevenson (eds), *Popular Protest and Public Order*, pp. 48–9; E.P. Thompson, 'The Moral Economy of the English Crowd', *P&P*, 50 (1971), 119; John Bohstedt, *Riots and Community Politics*, pp. 166–72; and A.J. Randall, 'The Gloucestershire Food Riots', *MH*, 10 (1985), 82–3.

72. All the recent work on riots supports this assertion.

73. E.P. Thompson, 'The Moral Economy of the English Crowd', *P&P*, 50 (1971), 115–17; Kenneth J. Logue, *Popular Disturbances in Scotland*, pp. 199–203; R.B. Shoemaker, 'The London "Mob"', *JBS*, 26 (1987), 285; and A.J. Randall, 'The Gloucestershire Food Riots', *MH*, 10 (1985), 83.

74. R.W. Malcolmson, *Life and Labour in England 1700–1780*, pp. 108–9.

75. John Bohstedt, *Riots and Community Politics*, p. 26.

76. E.P. Thompson, *Whigs and Hungers*, p. 262.
77. W. Nippel, '"Reading the Riot Act": The discourse of law-enforcement in 18th century England', *H&A*, 1 (1985), 402–4.
78. Ibid., pp. 404, 411.
79. D.G.D. Isaac, 'A Study of Popular Disturbances in Britain 1714–1754', pp. 128–9; and H.T. Dickinson and K.J. Logue, 'The Porteous Riot', *HT*, 22 (1972), 281.
80. W. Nippel, '"Reading the Riot Act"', *H&A*, 1 (1985), 405–6.
81. D.G.D. Isaac, 'A Study of Popular Disturbances in Britain 1714–1754', pp. 287–92.
82. Roger Wells, *Wretched Faces*, pp. 269–73.
83. Tony Hayter, *The Army and the Crowd in Mid-Georgian England* (1978); and Max Beloff, *Public Order and Popular Disturbances 1660–1714* (1963), pp. 107–10.
84. W. Nippel, '"Reading the Riot Act"', *H&A*, 1 (1985), 406–7.
85. Ibid., pp. 407–9; and Tony Hayter, *The Army and the Crowd*, p. 17.
86. Mark Harrison, '"To Raise and Dare Resentment"', *HJ*, 26 (1983), 574–7.
87. Tony Hayter, *The Army and the Crowd*, p. 52; and PRO. SPD. 36/43, ff. 120, 136, 255–7.
88. W. Nippel, '"Reading the Riot Act"', *H&A*, 1 (1985), 406–7.
89. H.T. Dickinson and K.J. Logue, 'The Porteous Riot', *HT*, 22 (1972), 277.
90. PRO. SPD. 35/16, f. 1.
91. W. Nippel, '"Reading the Riot Act"', *H&A*, 1 (1985), 407–9.
92. Ibid., pp. 410–13.
93. R.B. Shoemaker, 'The London "Mob"', *JBS*, 26 (1987), 296.
94. Ibid., p. 294; and W. Nippel, '"Reading the Riot Act"'; *H&A*, 1 (1985), 417.
95. Ibid.
96. R.B. Shoemaker, 'The London "Mob"', *JBS*, 26 (1987), 296–7.
97. PRO. SPD. 36/46, f.247.
98. Ibid., 36/50, f.431.
99. R.B. Shoemaker, 'The London "Mob"', *JBS*, 26 (1987), 295.
100. Ibid., pp. 295–6.
101. Joyce Ellis, 'Urban Conflict and Popular Violence', *IRSH*, 25 (1980), 347–8.
102. R.B. Rose, 'A Liverpool Sailors' Strike', *TLCAS*, 68 (1958), 91.
103. Roger Wells, *Dearth and Distress in Yorkshire 1793–1802*, p. 32.
104. H.T. Dickinson, 'The Hexham Militia Riot of 1761', *Bull. Durham County Local Hist. Soc.*, 22 (1976), 6.
105. A.J. Randall, 'The Gloucestershire Food Riots of 1766', *MH*, 10 (1985), 72, 88.
106. George Rudé, *Paris and London*, p. 275.
107. PRO. SPD. 35/63. Cr. Earl to Duke of Newcastle, 26 Dec. 1726.
108. J. De L. Mann, 'Clothiers and Weavers in Wiltshire during the Eighteenth Century', in L.S. Pressnell (ed.), *Studies in the Industrial Revolution*, pp. 70–1.
109. Donald Grove Barnes, *A History of the English Corn Laws (1660–1846)* (1930), pp. 37–44; and R.B. Rose, 'Eighteenth Century Price Riots', *IRSH*, 6 (1961), 290.

110. Joyce Ellis, 'Urban Conflict and Popular Violence', *IRSH*, 25 (1980), 348; and PRO. SPD. 36/51, f.87v. William Price to Andrew Stone, 13 June 1740.
111. Roger Wells, *Wretched Faces*, pp. 202–6.
112. PRO. SPD. 36/51, f.183.
113. A.J. Randall, 'The Gloucestershire Food Riots of 1766', *MH*, 10 (1985), 75.
114. Roger Wells, *Wretched Faces*, p. 230.
115. Ibid., p. 83.
116. Walter J. Shelton, 'The Role of Local Authorities in the Provincial Hunger Riots of 1766', *Albion*, 5 (1973), 51–4.
117. Roger Wells, *Wretched Faces*, pp. 82–3.
118. Ibid., pp. 184–201; and Walter M. Stern, 'The Bread Crisis in Britain, 1795–96', *Economica*, new series, 31 (1964), 176–9.
119. Roger Wells, *Wretched Faces*, p. 83; A.J. Randall, 'The Gloucestershire Food Riots of 1766', *MH*, 10 (1985), 82; and John Bohstedt, *Riots and Community Politics*, p. 61.
120. Martin Smith, 'Conflict and Society in Late Eighteenth-Century Birmingham', pp. 265–76; Roger Wells, *Wretched Faces*, pp. 290–302; Roger Wells, *Dearth and Distress in Yorkshire 1793–1802*, pp. 18–22; and John Bohstedt, *Riots and Community Politics*, p. 19.
121. R.W. Malcolmson, *Life and Labour in England 1700–1780*, p. 109.
122. Nicholas Rogers, 'Popular Protest in Early Hanoverian London', *P&P*, 79 (1978), 74–5.
123. BL. Add. MSS. 32690, f. 84.
124. PRO. SPD. 36/51, f. 1.
125. R.W. Malcolmson, 'Workers' Combinations in Eighteenth-Century England', in M. Jacob and J. Jacob (eds), *The Origins of Anglo-American Radicalism*, p. 157.
126. PRO. Home Office Papers. 42/22. T. Powditch to H. Dundas, 2 Nov. 1792.
127. John Bohstedt, *Riots and Community Politics*, p. 5.
128. A.J. Randall, 'The Gloucestershire Food Riots of 1766', *MH*, 10 (1985), 86, 89; E.P. Thompson, 'The Moral Economy of the English Crowd', *P&P*, 50 (1971), 126–8; D.J.V. Jones, 'The Corn Riots in Wales, 1793–1801', *WHR*, 2 (1964), 336–7; E.P. Thompson, 'Eighteenth-Century English Society: class struggle without class?', *SocH*, 3 (1978), 154–62; J. Brewer and J. Styles (eds), *An Ungovernable People*, pp. 15–16; John Bohstedt, *Riots and Community Politics*, pp. 24–6; and R.W. Malcolmson, *Life and Labour in England 1700–1780*, pp. 130–4.

CHAPTER 5:   THE DEBATE ON ENGLISH LIBERTIES AND NATURAL RIGHTS

1. On different concepts of liberty, see Isaiah Berlin, *Two Concepts of Liberty* (Oxford, 1958); H.T. Dickinson, 'The Rights of Man: From John Locke to Tom Paine', in O.D. Edwards and George Shepperson (eds),

Scotland, Europe and the American Revolution (Edinburgh, 1976), pp. 38–48 ; and H.T. Dickinson, 'The rights of man in Britain: From the Levellers to the Utopian Socialists', in Günter Birtsch (ed.), *Grund-und Freiheitsrechte von der ständischen zur spätbürgerlichen Gesellschaft* (Göttingen, 1987), pp. 67–87.

2. Christopher Hill, 'The Norman Yoke', in Christopher Hill, *Puritanism and Revolution* (1958), pp. 50–122.

3. John Plamenatz, *Man and Society* (2 vols, 1963), ii, ch. 1; William Thomas, The Philosophic Radicals (Oxford, 1979), ch. 3; and Elie Halévy, *Growth of Philosophic Radicalism* (new edn, 1972), Part I, ch. 3; Part II, chs 1 and 3.

4. *Parl Hist,* xxiv (1815), 988.

5. John Locke, *Second Treatise,* paras. 25–51, 87, 124, 134, 138–40, 193, 222; C.B. Macpherson, *The Political Theory of Possessive Individualism* (Oxford, 1962), pp. 149–262; J.W. Gough, *John Locke's Political Philosophy* (Oxford, 1950), pp. 64–92; and John Dunn, *The Political Thought of John Locke* (Cambridge, 1969), pp. 120–47.

6. For example Thomas Burnet, *An Essay upon Government* (Dublin, 1716), pp. 17–19; John Jackson, *The Grounds of Civil and Ecclesiastical Government Briefly Consider'd* (1718), p. 8; Richard Cumberland, *A Treatise of the Laws of Nature* (1727), pp. 64–6, 314, 322–5; *London Journal,* 6 Mar. 1731 and 9 Sept. 1732; Henry Kames, *Essays upon several subjects in Law* (Edinburgh, 1732), pp. 100–1; David Hume, *A Treatise of Human Nature* (1740), Book III, pt.2, sect. ii; Francis Hutcheson, *A System of Moral Philosophy* (2 vols, 1755), i, 323; Adam Smith, *Lectures on Justice, Police, Revenue and Arms,* ed. Edwin Cannan (Oxford, 1896), p.15; and Adam Smith, Wealth of Nations (2 vols, Everyman edn, 1910), ii, 199.

7. William Blackstone, *Commentaries upon the Laws of England* (7th edn, 4 vols, Oxford, 1775), i, 139. See also Daniel Boorstin, *The Mysterious Science of the Law* (Cambridge, Mass., 1941), ch. 9.

8. Thomas Walker, *A Review of Some of the Political Events which have occurred in Manchester during the Last Five Years* (1794), pp. 46n–7n.

9. William Paley, *Principles of Moral and Political Philosophy* (1785), in Edmund Paley (ed.), *The Works of William Paley* (4 vols, 1825), iv, 450–76.

10. Thomas Copeland et al (eds), *Correspondence of Edmund Burke,* iii, 111–12.

11. Richard Burgess Barlow, *Citizens and Conscience* (Philadelphia, 1962), ch. 6; and Russell E. Richey, 'The Origins of British Radicalism: The Changing Rationale for Dissent', *ECS,* 7 (1973–4), 179–92.

12. David Williams, *A Letter to the Body of Protestant Dissenters and to the Protestant Ministers of all Denominations* (1777), pp. 23–4.

13. Joshua Toulmin, *Two Letters on the Late Application to Parliament by the Protestant Dissenting Ministers* (1774), p. 8. See also Andrew Kippis, *A Vindication of the Protestant Dissenting Ministers* (1772), p. 26; Richard Price, *Observations on the Nature of Civil Liberty* (1776), pp. 21–2; and Richard Price, *Additional Observations on the Nature and Value of Civil Liberty and the War in America* (1777), p. 4.

14. On the defence of a free press, see the *London Journal*, 4 Feb. 1721; the Introduction to the collected edition of *Common Sense* (1738); David Hume, 'On the Liberty of the Press', in *Essays, Moral, Political and Literary* (Edinburgh, 1741); Horace Walpole, *A Letter to the Whigs* (1747), *passim*; Thomas Hayter, *Essays on the Liberty of the Press* (1755); *A Letter concerning Libels, Warrants and the Seizure of Papers, etc.* (1764); Junius, *A Dedication to the English Nation* (Nov. 1771); William Bollan, *An Essay on the Right of Every Man in a Free State to Speak and Write Freely in order to Defend the Public Rights and Promote the Public Welfare* (1772); *The Speech of Thomas Erskine at a Meeting of the Friends of the Liberty of the Press* (1792); Thomas Erskine, *Declaration of the Friends of the Liberty of the Press* (1793); G.S. Adam, 'The Press and its Liberty: Myth and Ideology in Eighteenth Century Politics', unpublished PhD thesis (Queen's University, Montreal, 1978), pp. 219–302; and Eckhart Hellmuth, '"The Palladium of all other English Liberties": Reflections on the Liberty of the Press in England during the 1760s and 1770s', in Eckhart Hellmuth (ed.), *The Transformation of Political Culture*, pp. 467–501.

15. William Blackstone, *Commentaries upon the Laws of England*, iv, 151–2.

16. *Parl Hist*, xxviii (1815), 29.

17. William Blackstone, *Commentaries upon the Laws of England*, i, 129.

18. Edmund Burke, *Reflections on the Revolution in France* (Penguin edn, Harmondsworth, 1969), p. 149.

19. For example, James Tyrrell, *Bibliotheca Politica* (1694), p. 808; and Benjamin Hoadley, *The Original and Institution of Civil Government Discuss'd* (1710), p. 150.

20. John Locke, *Second Treatise*, paras 208, 225, 230; Joseph Priestley, *Letters to the Right Honorable Edmund Burke* (Birmingham, 1791), p. 23; William Belsham, *Examination of An Appeal from the New to the Old Whigs* (1792) in his *Essays Philosophical and Moral, Historical and Literary* (2 vols, 1799), ii, 244–5, 298–9, 308–9, 342–3; George Rous, *Thoughts on Government* (1791), pp. 30–2; Capel Lofft, *Remarks on the Letter to the Right Hon Edmund Burke* (1790), p. 39; Robert Hall, *An Apology for the Freedom of the Press* (1793), pp. 57–8; and William Cuninghame, *The Rights of Kings* (1791), pp. 43–4.

21. David Hume, *A Treatise of Human Nature*, ed., P. Ardal (1979), p. 276; Adam Smith, *Lectures on Justice, Police, Revenue and Arms*, ed. Edwin Cannan, p. 68; William Blackstone, *Commentaries upon the Laws of England*, i, 126–7, 138–40; and Edmund Burke, *An Appeal from the New to the Old Whigs* (1791), in *The Works of Edmund Burke* (Bohn edn, 6 vols, 1854–61), iii, 45.

22. On the debate about standing armies and citizen militias, see Lois Schwoerer, *No Standing Armies! The Anti-army Ideology in Seventeenth-Century England* (Baltimore, 1974), pp. 155–87; J.R. Western, *The English Militia in the Eighteenth Century* (1965), pp. 77–126; H.T. Dickinson, *Liberty and Property*, pp. 104–6, 184–7; and John Robertson, *The Scottish Enlightenment and the Militia Issue* (Edinburgh, 1985).

23. William Jones, *Principles of Government* (1782), p. 8.

24. Richard Price, *Observations on the Nature of Civil Liberty* (7th edn, 1776), pp. 15–16. Similar statements can be found in Francis Hutcheson, *A*

Short Introduction to Moral Philosophy (2 vols, Glasgow, 1764), ii, 327–40; [Obadiah Hulme,] *An Historical Essay on the English Constitution* (1771), pp. 4–7; *Resistance no Rebellion* (1775), pp. 12–13; Richard Watson, *The Principles of the Revolution Vindicated* (Cambridge, 1776), p. 11; James Mackintosh, *Vindiciae Gallicae* (1791), p. 294; Thomas Paine, *Rights of Man* (1791–2; Penguin edn, Harmondsworth, 1969), pp. 111, 142, 146, 150–2, 165–6, 213; *The Birthright of Britons* (1792), pp. 120–3; and John Thelwall, *The Natural and Constitutional Rights of Britons* (1795), *passim*.

25. H.T. Dickinson, 'The Eighteenth-Century Debate on the Sovereignty of Parliament', *TRHS*, 5th series, 26 (1976), 189–210.

26. Thomas Paine, *Rights of Man*, p. 92. See also pp. 87–95, 207–31; Earl Stanhope, *A Letter from Earl Stanhope to the Rt. Hon. Edmund Burke* (1790), p. 26; George Rous, *A Letter to the Rt. Hon. Edmund Burke* (Dublin, 1791), p. 44; Robert Hall, *An Apology for the Freedom of the Press* (1793), p. 9; and Benjamin Flower, *The French Revolution* (1792), pp. 123–4.

27. Richard Price, *A Discourse on the Love of Our Country* (1790), pp. 28–9.

28. H.T. Dickinson, *Liberty and Property*, pp. 121–62, 270–318.

29. *Parl Hist*, viii (1811), 1325.

30. H.T. Dickinson, *Liberty and Property*, pp. 102–18, 181–92.

31. James Tully, *A Discourse on Property* (Cambridge, 1980), p. 173; Richard Ashcroft, *Revolutionary Politics and Locke's 'Two Treatises of Government'* (Princeton, 1986), ch. 11; Richard Ashcroft, *Locke's Two Treatises of Government* (1987), chs 4–5; and Ruth W. Grant, *John Locke's Liberalism* (Chicago, 1987), *passim*.

32. Ibid., chs 5–7; Judith Richards, Lotte Mulligan and J. Graham, '"Property" and "People": Political Usages of Locke and Some Contemporaries', *JHI*, 42 (1981), 29–51; Richard Ashcraft, 'Revolutionary Politics and Locke's *Two Treatises of Government*: Radicalism and Lockean Political Theory', *PT*, 8 (1980), 429–86; and Richard Ashcraft, *Revolution Politics and Locke's 'Two Treatises of Government'*, pp. 578–84.

33. Algernon Sidney, *Discourses Concerning Government* (3rd edn, 1751), pp. 75, 149, 423; James Tyrrell, *Bibliotheca Politica* (1694), advertisement; James Tyrrell, *A Brief Enquiry into the Ancient Constitution and Government of England* (1695), p. 4; John Toland, *The Militia Reform'd* (1698), p. 19; and [John Trenchard,] *An Argument, shewing that a Standing Army is inconsistent with a Free Government* (1697), p. 4.

34. *The Claims of the People of England, Essayed* (1701), p. 106.

35. e.g. *London Journal*, 30 Dec. 1721.

36. *Bibliotheca Politica*, 9 Sept. 1732.

37. *The Livery-Man: or Plain Thoughts of Public Affairs* (1740), pp. 7, 56; [J. Campbell,] *The Case of the Opposition Partially Stated* (1742), pp. 51–2; and Linda Colley, *In Defiance of Oligarchy*, p. 170.

38. Carla H. Hay, *James Burgh: Spokesmen for Reform in Hanoverian England* (Washington DC, 1979), pp. 60–8, 95, 97, 107; and *Reflexions on Representation in Parliament* (1766), p. 6.

39. John Cartwright, *Take Your Choice!* (1776), pp. 2–3.

40. Joseph Priestley, *An Essay on the First Principles of Government* (1768), pp. 54–5; and Richard Price, *Observation on the Nature of Civil Liberty* (1776), pp. 21–2.

41. John Cartwright, *Take Your Choice!*, p. 47; John W. Osborne, *John Cartwright* (Cambridge, 1972), pp. 22, 61, 63, 72–3, 147–9; [Obadiah Hulme,] *An Historical Essay on the English Constitution* (1771), *passim*; Christopher Hill, 'The Norman Yoke', in Christopher Hill, *Puritanism and Revolution*, pp. 50–122; Bridget and Christopher Hill, 'Catharine Macaulay and the Seventeenth Century', *WHR*, 3 (1967), 381–402; and Lynne E. Withey, 'Catharine Macaulay and the Uses of History: Ancient History, Perfectionism and Propaganda', *JBS*, 16 (1976), 59–83.

42. Isaac Kramnick, 'Republican Revisionism Revisited', *AHR*, 87 (1982), 629–44. For favourable contemporary references to Locke, see, e.g., Joseph Towers, *A Vindication of the Political Principles of Mr. Locke* (1782); George Rous, *Thoughts on Government* (1790), pp. 22–3; William Hall, *An Apology for the Freedom of the Press* (1793), pp. 9–10, 56–7; and Henry Redhead Yorke, *The Spirit of John Locke* (1794).

43. Richard Price, *A Review of the Principal Questions and Difficulties in Morals* (2nd edn, 1769), p. 345; and Richard Price, *Observations on Reversionary Payments* (1771), p. 275.

44. Thomas Paine, *Rights of Man*, pp. 63–7, 94, 113, 215. See also James Mackintosh, *Vindiciae Gallicae*, pp. 294, 306, 313–22, 330–2, 346–7.

45. Lois Whitney, *Primitivism and the Idea of Progress in English Popular Literature in the Eighteenth Century* (Baltimore, 1934).

46. Margaret Canovan, 'Two Concepts of Liberty – Eighteenth-Century Style', *P-PN*, 2 (1978), 27–43; Margaret Canovan, 'Paternalistic Liberalism: Joseph Priestley on Rank and Inequality', *ED*, 2 (1983), 29; James J. Hoecker, 'Joseph Priestley as a Historian and the Idea of Progress', *P-PN*, 3 (1979), 29–40; and Clarke Garrett, 'Joseph Priestley, the Millennium and the French Revolution', *JHI*, 34 (1973), 51–66.

47. Richard Price, *A Discourse on the Love of Our Country*, pp. 41–2. See also *The Cabinet* (3 vols, Norwich, 1795), i, 178; Mary Wollstonecraft, *A Vindication of the Rights of Men* (1790), pp. 67, 72; and James Mackintosh, *Vindiciae Gallicae*, pp. 48–9.

48. William Godwin, *Enquiry Concerning Political Justice* (1793; 3rd edn, 2 vols, 1798), ii, 114–20.

49. Mary P. Mack, *Jeremy Bentham: An Odyssey of Ideas 1748–1792* (1962), pp. 409–66.

50. [Obadiah Hulme,] *An Historical Essay on the English Constitution*, pp. 76, 153–4; and James Burgh, *Political Disquisitions* (3 vols, 1774), pp. 26–8, 36–8, 51–4, 87–94, 106–27.

51. Richard Price, *A Collection of Letters which have been Addressed to the Volunteers of Ireland on the Subject of Parliamentary Reform* (1783), pp. 83–4; and Catharine Macaulay, *Observation on the Reflections of the Right Hon. Edmund Burke* (1790), p. 79.

52. Joseph Priestley, *Lectures on History and General Policy* (3rd edn, Philadelphia, 1803), pp. 116–18.

53. Christopher Wyvill, *Political Papers* (6 vols, York, 1794–1804), v, 262. See also Christopher Wyvill, *A State of the Representation of the People of England on the Principles of Mr. Pitt in 1785* (York, 1793), pp. 33–46.

54. William Belsham, *Remarks on Parliamentary Reform* (1791), in his *Essays Philosophical and Moral, Historical and Literary*, ii, 372. See also Vicesimus

Knox, *The Essence of the Calm Observer* (2nd edn, 1793), pp. 49–50.

55. John Cartwright, *Take Your Choice!*, pp. 19, 21–2. See also John Cartwright, *The People's Barrier against Undue Influence and Corruption* (1780), pp. 21–8, 56, 109; and John Cartwright, *Give us our Rights* (1782), pp. 4–6.

56. Francis Stone, *An Examination of the Right Hon. Edmund Burke's Reflections on the Revolution in France* (1792), p. 44. See also Joseph Towers, *Thoughts on the Commencement of a New Parliament* (1790), p. 154.

57. Thomas Paine, *Dissertation on the First Principles of Government* (1795), in Philip S. Foner (ed.), *The Complete Writings of Thomas Paine* (2 vols, New York, 1945), ii, 579.

58. Isaac Kramnick, 'Republican Revisionism Revisited', *AHR*, 87 (1982), 629–44; and Isaac Kramnick, 'English Middle-Class Radicalism in the Eighteenth Century', *Literature of Liberty*, 3 (1980), 5–48.

59. Margaret Canovan 'Paternalistic Liberalism: Joseph Priestley on Rank and Equality', *ED*, 2 (1983), 23–37.

60. D.O. Thomas, 'Neither republican nor democrat', *P-PN*, 1 (1977), 49–60.

61. James Burgh, *Political Disquisitions*, ii, 62.

62. James Mackintosh, *Vindiciae Gallicae*, pp. 365–6.

63. John Cartwright, *The Commonwealth in Danger* (1795), p. 163.

64. John Thelwall, *The Natural and Constitutional Rights of Britons to Annual Parliaments, Universal Suffrage and the Freedom of Popular Association* (1795), pp. 46–8.

65. PRO. Treasury Solicitor's Papers. TS.11957/3502(1). Thelwall's 'Lecture Notes'.

66. John Cartwright, *An Appeal, Civil and Military, on the Subject of the English Constitution* (1799), p. 17.

67. John Longley, *An Essay toward forming a more complete Representation of the Commons of Great Britain* (1795), pp. 4, 6.

68. Mary Wollstonecraft, *A Vindication of the Rights of Woman*, ed. Miriam Brody (Penguin edn, 1985), p. 260.

69. H.T. Dickinson (ed.), *The Political Works of Thomas Spence* (Newcastle upon Tyne, 1982), pp. xiv–xv, 62–3, 107.

70. George Phillips, *The Necessity of a Speedy and Effectual Reform of Parliament* (Manchester, 1792), p. 12n; H.M. Ellis, 'Thomas Cooper – A Survey of his Life: Part 1 – England, 1759–1794', *South Atlantic Quarterly*, 19 (1927), 38; and *The Cabinet*, i, 178–84 and ii, 42–8.

71. James Burgh, *Political Disquisitions*, i, 9, 11, 18; D.O. Thomas, 'Neither republican nor democrat', *P-PN*, 1 (1977), 49–60 (for Price); and John Cartwright, *The Commonwealth in Danger* (1795), pp. xxxv, ci–cii.

72. John Oswald, *Review of the Constitution of Great Britain* (3rd edn, 1793), p. 12.

73. Thomas Paine, *Rights of Man*, pp. 102–6, 144–5, 148, 152–3, 162–6, 186–7, 200, 206, 209, 220–4.

74. Thomas Paine, *Dissertation on the First Principles of Government*, in Philip S. Foner (ed.), *The Complete Writings of Thomas Paine*, ii, 578–83.

75. William Godwin, *Enquiry Concerning Political Justice* (3rd ed.n, 1798), i, 165–6. See also, i, 144–7, 167–70, 186, 214–16, 256–7; and ii, 86–96.

76. *Parl Hist*, xxxi (1815), 738.

77. Liverpool University Library. Rathbone Papers. Scrapbook, p. 50. For a similar view expressed by Manchester radicals, see Thomas Walker, *A Review of Some of the Political Events which have occurred in Manchester during the Last Five Years* (1794), pp. 46n–7n.

78. William Godwin, *Enquiry Concerning Political Justice*, ii, 240–53, 296–304.

79. Margaret Canovan, 'Paternalistic Liberalism: Joseph Priestley on Rank and Inequality', *ED*, 2 (1983), 32–3.

80. Thomas Cooper, *A Reply to Mr. Burke's Invective* (1792), pp. 31–2, 64–7. Other advocates of state education include John Thelwall, *The Rights of Nature* (1796), ii, 81; [Thomas Bentley], *The Poor Man's Answer to the Rich Associators* (1793), p. 2; and Daniel Isaac Eaton, *Hog's Wash or Politics for the People* (1793–4), 9 November 1793.

81. George Dyer, *The Complaints of the Poor People of England* (2nd edn, 1793), p. 18.

82. Thomas Paine, *Rights of Man*, pp. 262–81; and *Agrarian Justice*, in Philip S. Foner (ed.), *The Complete Works of Thomas Paine*, i, 611–19.

83. John Oswald, *Review of the Constitution of Great Britain* (3rd edn, 1793), p. 59; William Ogilvie, *An Essay on the Right of Property in Land* (1782), pp. 74, 87; and anonymous contributors to *The Cabinet*, ii, 215–9 and iii, 281–95.

84. H.T. Dickinson (ed.), *The Political Works of Thomas Spence, passim*; Malcolm Chase, *The People's Farm: English Radical Agrarianism 1775–1840* (Oxford, 1988), pp. 18–77; and James Eayrs, 'The Political Ideas of the English Agrarians, 1775–1815', *CJEPS*, 18 (1952), 287–302.

CHAPTER 6: RADICAL IDEAS AND POPULAR POLITICS BEFORE WILKES

1. See in particular H.T. Dickinson, 'The Precursors of Political Radicalism in Augustan Britain', in Clyve Jones (ed.), *Britain in the First Age of Party 1680–1750* (1987), pp. 63–84; H.T. Dickinson, 'Popular Politics in the Age of Walpole', in Jeremy Black (ed.), *Britain in the Age of Walpole*, pp. 45–68; Caroline Robbins, *The Eighteenth-Century Commonwealthman* (Cambridge, Mass., 1959); J.G.A. Pocock, 'Radical Criticism of the Whig Order in the Age between Revolutions', in Margaret Jacob and James Jacob (eds), *The Origins of Anglo-American Radicalism*, pp. 35–57; Nicholas Rogers, 'The Urban Opposition to Whig Oligarchy, 1720–60', in ibid., pp. 132–48; Nicholas Rogers, *Whigs and Cities*; Nicholas Rogers, 'Aristocratic Clientage, Trade and Independency: Popular Politics in Pre-Radical Westminster', *P&P*, 61 (1973), 70–106; Nicholas Rogers, 'Resistance to Oligarchy: The City Opposition to Walpole and his Successors, 1725–47', in John Stevenson (ed.), *London in the Age of Revolution*, pp. 1–29; Gary S. De Krey, 'Political Radicalism in London after the Glorious Revolution', *JMH*, 65 (1983), 585–617; Gary S. De Krey, *A Fractured Society*; Linda Colley, 'Eighteenth-Century English Radicalism before Wilkes', *TRHS*, 5th series, 31 (1981), 1–19; and N.C. Hunt, *Two Early Political Associations*.

2. H.T. Dickinson, *Liberty and Property*, chs 2 and 4.
3. See M.C. Jacob, *The Newtonians and the English revolution 1688–1720* (Hassocks, 1976), ch. 6; Caroline Robbins, *The Eighteenth-Century Commonwealthman*, pp. 115–33; and J.M. Bulloch, *Thomas Gordon: The 'Independent Whig'* (Aberdeen, 1918).
4. J.C.D. Clark, *English Society 1688–1832*, pp. 277–307.
5. See Algernon Sidney, *Discourses upon Government* (3rd edn, 1751), pp. 75, 423; James Tyrrell, *Bibliotheca Politica* (1694), advertisement; James Tyrrell, *A Brief Enquiry into the Ancient Constitution and Government of England* (1695), p. 4; John Toland, *The Militia reform'd* (1698), p. 19; John Trenchard, *An Argument, Shewing that a Standing Army is inconsistent with a Free Government* (1697), p. 4; and *The Claims of the People of England, essayed* (1701), p. 106.
6. J.H. Franklin, *John Locke and the Theory of Sovereignty* (Cambridge, 1978), ch. 4.
7. See James Tyrrell, *Bibliotheca Politica*, p. 808; and Benjamin Hoadly, *The Original and Institution of Civil Government Discuss'd* (1710), p. 150.
8. See, for example, C.B. Macpherson, 'The Social Bearing of Locke's Political Theory', *Western Political Theory*, 7 (1954), 1–22.
9. James Tully, *A Discourse on Property*, p. 173. See also Richard Ashcraft, *Revolutionary Politics and Locke's 'Two Treatises of Government'*, ch. 11; Richard Ashcraft, *Locke's Two Treatises of Government*, chs 4–5; and Ruth W. Grant, *John Locke's Liberalism, passim*.
10. James Tully, *A Discourse on Property*, chs 5–7.
11. Judith Richards, Lotte Mulligan and John Graham, '"Property" and "People": Political Usages of Locke and some contemporaries', *JHI*, 42 (1981), 29–51; Richard Ashcraft, 'Revolutionary Politics and Locke's *Two Treatises of Government*: Radicalism and Lockean Political Theory', *PT*, 8 (1980), 429–86; and Richard Ashcraft, 'The *Two Treatises* and the Exclusion Crisis: The Problem of Lockean Political Theory as Bourgeois Ideology', in J.G.A. Pocock and Richard Ashcraft, *John Locke* (Los Angeles, 1980), pp. 25–114.
12. John Dunn, 'The politics of Locke in England and America in the eighteenth century', in John Yolton (ed.), *John Locke: Problems and Perspectives*, ch. 4; Martyn P. Thompson, 'The Reception of Locke's Two Treatises of Government 1690–1705', *Political Studies*, 24 (1976), 184–91; J.P. Kenyon, 'The Revolution of 1688: Resistance and Contract', in Neil McKendrick (ed.), *Historical Perspectives* (1974), pp. 43–69; J.P. Kenyon, *Revolution Principles*, ch. 2; and H.T. Dickinson, *Liberty and Property*, pp. 125–34.
13. Richard Ashcraft and M.M. Goldsmith, 'Locke, Revolution Principles, and the Formation of Whig Ideology', *HJ*, 26 (1983), 773–800.
14. Lois G. Schwoerer, *The Declaration of Rights 1689* (Baltimore, 1981), p. 159; and Mark Goldie, 'The Revolution of 1689 and the Structure of Political Argument. An Essay and an Annotated Bibliography of Pamphlets on the Allegiance Controversy', *Bull. Research in the Humanities*, 83 (1980), 473–564.
15. On Locke's impact on later eighteenth-century radicals, see Isaac Kramnick, 'Republican Revisionism Revisited', *AHR*, 87 (1982), 629–64.

16. Lois G. Schwoerer, *The Declaration of Rights 1689*, pp. 22–33, 159–67; Mark Goldie, 'The Roots of True Whiggism 1688–1694', *History of Political Thought*, 1 (1980), 195–236; *Edmund Ludlow: A Voyce from the Watch Tower: Part Five, 1660–1662*, ed. A.B. Worden, *Camden Society*, fourth series, 21 (1978), introduction; and Caroline Robbins, *The Eighteenth-Century Commonwealthman*, ch. 4.

17. David Hayton, 'The "Country" interest and the party system, 1689–c.1720', in Clyve Jones (ed.), *Party Management in Parliament 1660–1784*, pp. 37–85. See also H.T. Dickinson, 'The October Club', *HLQ*, 33 (1970), 155–73; and Linda Colley, 'The Loyal brotherhood and the Cocoa-Tree: The London Organization of the Tory Party, 1727–1760', *HJ*, 20 (1977), 77–95.

18. H.T. Dickinson, *Liberty and Property*, chs 3 and 5; H.T. Dickinson, *Bolingbroke* (1970), chs 11–12; J.G.A. Pocock, 'Radical Criticisms of the Whig Order in the Age between Revolutions', in M. Jacob and J. Jacob (eds), *The Origins of Anglo-American Radicalism*, pp. 33–57; and Geoffrey S. Holmes, 'The Attack on "the influence of the Crown" 1702–1716', *BIHR*, 39 (1966), 47–68.

19. Daniel Defoe, *Considerations upon Corrupt Elections of Members of Parliament* (1701); Daniel Defoe, *The Freeholders Plea against Stockjobbing Elections of Parliament* (1701); and John Toland, *The Danger of Mercenary Parliaments* (1698).

20. Daniel Defoe, *The Original Power of the Collective Body of the People of England, Examined and Asserted* (1702), p. 23; *The Electors Right Asserted* (1701), p. 1; *Some Reasons for an Annual Parliament* (1693), pp. 4, 8; *Questions of Common Right* (c. 1695), p. 3; Earl of Marchmont, *A Serious Exhortation to the Electors of Great Britain* (1740), pp. 16–17; *Common Sense*, 20 Oct. 1739; *The Works of Lord Bolingbroke* (4 vols, 1844), ii, 150–1; *London Magazine* (1742), ii, 101, 128; and *A Letter to a Member of this New Parliament from a true lover of the liberties of the People* (1742), p. 6.

21. *Some Remarks upon Government* (1689), pp. 25–6; *The Representation of London and Westminster in parliament, examin'd and consider'd* (1702); John Toland, *The Art of Governing by Partys* (1701), pp. 75–7; and Daniel Defoe, *The Freeholder's Plea against Stockjobbing Elections of Parliament Men* (1701), pp. 16–19.

22. *The Craftsman*, 27 July 1734; *Gentleman's Magazine*, 4 (1734), 381 and ibid., 11 (1741), 378; *Jopson's Coventry Mercury*, 26 March and 23 April 1759; and Marie Peters, 'The "Monitor" on the Constitution, 1755–65; new light on the ideological origins of English radicalism', *EHR*, 86 (1971), 706–25.

23. *Common Sense*, 15 April 1738, 6 Oct. 1739, and 10 Jan. 1741.

24. *Westminster Journal*, quoted in the *Gentleman's Magazine*, 17 (1747), 329 *et seq.*

25. *Some Remarks upon Government* (1689), pp. 25–6. See also Walter Moyle, *An Essay upon the Constitution of the Roman Republic*, in Caroline Robbins (ed.), *Two English Republican Tracts* (Cambridge, 1969), pp. 238, 240–1; and *Some Observations concerning the regulating of Elections* (1689), p. 17.

26. *Fog's Journal*, 20 April 1734; and *Liberty and Right: Or an Essay Historical and Political on the Constitution and Administration of Great Britain* (1747), pp. 43–51.

27.   *Some Remarks upon Government*, pp. 24–6; and *Some Observations concerning the regulating of elections for Parliament*, pp. 9–12.

28.   See, for example, *London Journal*, 30 Dec. 1721.

29.   *Letters to Parliament-Men, in reference to some proceedings in the House of Commons* (1701), pp. 9–10.

30.   *London Journal*, 9 Sept. 1732.

31.   *The Livery-Man: or Plain Thoughts on Public Affairs* (1740), pp. 7, 56; [John Campbell], *The Case of the Opposition Impartially Stated* (1742), pp. 51–2. The connection between taxation and representation was advanced by the *Westminster Journal* in 1747, the *Monitor* in the 1750s and *Jopson's Coventry Mercury* in 1759: see Linda Colley, *In Defiance of Oligarchy*, p. 170.

32.   Carla H. Hay, *James Burgh: Spokesman for Reform in Hanoverian England* (Washington DC, 1979), pp. 60–8, 95, 97, 107; and *Reflexions on Representation in Parliament* (1766), p. 6.

33.   *An Essay on Government* (1743), pp. 132–5.

34.   *A Letter to a Member of Parliament, on the Importance of Liberty* (1745), pp. 4, 6–7, 19–25; and *Proposals for carrying on the War with Vigour, raising the Supplies within the Year and Forming a National Militia* (1757), pp. 12, 44–50.

35.   G.A. Cranfield, 'The *London Evening Post*, 1727–1744: A study in the development of the political press', *HJ*, 6 (1963), 20–37.

36.   Michael Harris, *London Newspapers in the Age of Walpole* (1987), p. 122. See also Michael Harris, 'Press and Politics in the Age of Walpole', in Jeremy Black (ed.), *Britain in the Age of Walpole*, pp. 189–210.

37.   Lawrence Hanson, *Government and the Press 1695–1763* (Oxford, 1936), pp. 64, 67–9, 108–12; and F.S. Siebert, *Freedom of the Press in England 1476–1776* (Urbana, 1965), pp. 318–20, 340–4, 382–3.

38.   For the political role of the provincial press, see G.A. Cranfield, *The Development of the Provincial Newspaper 1700–1760* (Oxford, 1962), chs 6–7.

39.   BL. Add. MSS. 32695, vol. ii, f. 391. 11 Nov. 1740.

40.   Gary S. De Krey, *A Fractured Society*, pp. 197, 262–3, 267–9; H. Horwitz, 'Minutes of a Whig Club 1714–1717', in *London Politics 1713–1717*, London Record Society publication, 17 (1981), 1–61; I.G. Doolittle, 'The Half Moon Tavern, Cheapside and City Politics', *TLMAS*, 28 (1977), 328–32.

41.   Linda Colley, *In Defiance of Oligarchy*, p. 163.

42.   Lillian M. Penson, 'The London West India Interest in the Eighteenth Century', *EHR*, 36 (1921), 373–92; and Richard B. Sheridan, 'The Molasses Act and the market strategy of the British Sugar Planters', *JEcH*, 17 (1957), 62–83.

43.   For the Dissenting pressure groups in the age of Walpole, see N.C. Hunt, *Two Early Political Associations*.

44.   *Parl Hist*, viii (1813), 1305–6.

45.   See especially Lucy S. Sutherland, 'Edmund Burke and the Relations between Members of Parliament and their Constituents', *SBT*, 10 (1968), 1005–8. This view has been challenged by Paul Langford, *The Excise Crisis* (Oxford, 1975), ch. 4; Linda Colley, 'The Tory Party, 1727–1760', unpublished PhD thesis (Cambridge University, 1976), pp. 110–1,

156–8, 163–4; Thomas W. Perry, *Public Opinion, Propaganda and Politics in Eighteenth-Century England*; and Marie Peters, *Pitt and Popularity* (Oxford, 1980), pp. 46–57.

46. Paul Langford, *The Excise Crisis*, appendix A.
47. Ibid., ch. 4; and Nicholas Rogers, 'Resistance to Oligarchy', in John Stevenson (ed.), *London in the Age of Reform*, p. 6.
48. These details are from Paul Langford, *The Excise Crisis*, ch. 8 and especially pp. 52–3.
49. Nicholas Rogers, 'Resistance to Oligarchy', pp. 7–13.
50. Ibid., p. 12.
51. Linda Colley, *In Defiance of Oligarchy*, p. 166.
52. Ibid., p. 168.
53. *Gentleman's Magazine*, 12 (1742), 159–61, 217, 274.
54. *The Several Addresses of the Merchant company and corporations of Edinburgh, to the Magistrates and Town Council thereof* (Edinburgh, 1739).
55. *Common Sense*, 20 Oct. 1739.
56. BL. Add. MSS. 35406, f. 159. Quoted by Nicholas Rogers, 'Resistance to Oligarchy', p. 9.
57. Quoted by Romney Sedgwick (ed.), *The House of Commons 1715–1754*, i, 282.
58. Thomas W. Perry, *Public Opinion, Propaganda and Politics*, chs 5, 6 and 8.
59. Quoted in ibid., p. 160.
60. *Parl Hist*, xv (1813), 102.
61. This paragraph is based on Marie Peters, *Pitt and Popularity*, pp. 46–79.
62. Peter Borsay, 'The English urban renaissance: the development of provincial urban culture c.1680–c.1760', *SocH*, 5 (1977), 581–603; and Peter Borsay, 'Culture, status, and the English urban landscape', *H*, 67 (1982), 1–12.
63. For this account of London politics see Nicholas Rogers, 'Resistance to Oligarchy', pp. 2–7; and Alfred James Henderson, *London and the National Government 1721–1742*.
64. I.G. Doolittle, 'Walpole's City Elections Act (1725)', *EHR*, 97 (1982), 504–29.
65. Nicholas Rogers, 'Aristocratic Clientage, Trade and Independency: Popular Politics in Pre-Radical Westminster', *P&P*, 61 (1973), 73–5, 78–83.
66. See the relevant borough entries in Romney Sedgwick (ed.), *The House of Commons 1715–1754*, vol. i.
67. PRO. SPD. 35/32. S. Legge to Townsend, 30 Aug. 1722.
68. Romney Sedgwick (ed.) *The House of Commons 1715–1754*, i, 203; and John Stevenson, *Popular Disturbances in England 1700–1870*, p. 24.
69. See especially ibid.; D.G.D. Isaac, 'A Study of Popular Disturbances in Britain 1714–1754', unpublished PhD thesis (Edinburgh University, 1953); and George Rudé, *Paris and London in the Eighteenth Century* (1970).
70. Nicholas Rogers, 'Riot and Popular Jacobitism in Early Hanoverian England', in Eveline Cruickshanks (ed.), *Ideology and Conspiracy*, p. 83.
71. PRO. SPD. 35/27, item 15.
72. Ibid., 35/54, items 54–8.

73.   Nicholas Rogers, 'Popular Protest in Early Hanoverian England', *P&P,*
      79 (1978), 70–100.
74.   Nicholas Rogers, 'Riot and Popular Jacobitism', pp. 81–5.
75.   George Rudé, *Paris and London,* pp. 218–20.
76.   BL. Add. MSS. 32690, f.84. To Newcastle, 28 Sept. 1735.
77.   Pat Rogers, 'The Waltham Blacks and the Black Act', *HJ,* 17 (1974),
      465–86; and E.P. Thompson, *Whigs and Hunters* (1975).
78.   D.G.D. Isaac, 'Popular disturbances', pp. 104–21.
79.   H.T. Dickinson and K.J. Logue, 'The Porteous Riot', *HT,* 22 (1972),
      272–81.
80.   C.R. Dobson, *Masters and Journeymen,* pp. 61–2; D.G.D. Isaac, 'Popular
      disturbances', pp. 51–78; and John Stevenson, *Popular Disturbances in
      England,* p. 114.
81.   D.G.D. Isaac, 'Popular Disturbances', pp. 92–103; and John Stevenson,
      Popular Disturbances in England, pp. 120–1.
82.   D.G.D. Isaac, 'Popular Disturbances', pp. 51–78; and J. De L. Mann,
      'Clothiers and Weavers in Wiltshire during the Eighteenth Century', in
      L.S. Pressnell (ed.), *Studies in the Industrial Revolution* (1960), pp. 66–96.

CHAPTER 7:   RADICALS AND REFORMERS IN THE LATER EIGHTEENTH CENTURY

1.   Much of this chapter is based on H.T. Dickinson, 'Radicals and
      Reformers in the Age of Wilkes and Wyvill', in Jeremy Black (ed.),
      British Politics and Society from Walpole to Pitt 1742–1789 (London, 1990),
      pp. 123–46 and H.T. Dickinson, *British Radicals and the French Revolution
      1789–1815,* ch. 1 and 3, though more recent research has also been
      incorporated into it.
2.   For this section see H.T. Dickinson, *Liberty and Property,* ch. 6.
3.   *Public Advertiser,* 8 Feb. 1769.
4.   On the impact of the American issue on British extra-parliamentary
      politics, see, in particular, Colin C. Bonwick, *English Radicals and the
      American Revolution* (Chapel Hill, 1977); James E. Bradley, *Popular
      Politics and the American Revolution in England* (Macon, Georgia, 1986);
      James E. Bradley, *Religion, Revolution and English Radicalism*
      (Cambridge, 1990), chs 6, 9–10; John Sainsbury, *Disaffected Patriots;*
      Paul Langford, 'London and the American Revolution', in John
      Stevenson (ed.), *London in the Age of Reform,* pp. 55–78; John Brewer,
      Party Ideology and Popular Politics at the Accession of George III, pp. 201–16;
      and John Brewer, 'English Radicalism in the Age of George III', in
      J.G.A. Pocock (ed.), *Three British Revolutions: 1641, 1688, 1766*
      (Princeton, 1980), pp. 323–67.
5.   On the impact of the French Revolution on British extra-parliamentary
      politics, see, in particular, Albert Goodwin, *The Friends of Liberty,* chs 1,
      4–10; E.P. Thompson, *The Making of the English Working Class,* chs 1, 4–5;
      G.S. Veitch, *The Genesis of Parliamentary Reform* (London, 1965 ed.),

chs 5–14; Carl B. Cone, *The English Jacobins* (New York, 1968), chs 4–10; Gwyn A. Williams, *Artisans and Sans-Culottes* (1968), chs 4, 6; and John Stevenson, 'Popular Radicalism and Popular Protest 1789–1815', in H.T. Dickinson (ed.), *Britain and the French Revolution*, pp. 61–84.

6. Isaac Kramnick, *Republicanism and Bourgeois Radicalism*, ch. 1.
7. Jack Fruchtman, Jr, *The Apocalyptic Politics of Richard Price and Joseph Priestley: A Study in Late Eighteenth-Century English Republican Millennialism* (Philadelphia, 1983); C. Garrett, 'Joseph Priestley, the Millennium and the French Revolution', *JHI*, 34 (1973), 51–66; and Isaac Kramnick, 'Religion and Radicalism: English Political Theory in the Age of Revolution', *PT*, 5 (1977), 505–34.
8. On this ideological debate, see H.T. Dickinson, *Liberty and Property*, ch. 6; Colin C. Bonwick, *English Radicals and the American Revolution*, chs 1–5; J.C.D. Clark, *English Society 1688–1932*, pp. 307–23; J.G.A. Pocock, 'Radical Criticism of the Whig Order in the Age between Revolutions', in Margaret Jacob and James Jacob (eds), *Origins of Anglo-American Radicalism*, pp. 35–57; Isaac Kramnick, 'Republican Revisionism Revisited', *AHR*, 87 (1982), 629–64; D.O. Thomas, *The Honest Mind: The Thought and Work of Richard Price* (Oxford, 1977), chs 8–10; and Anthony Lincoln, *Some Political and Social Ideas of English Dissent 1763–1800* (Cambridge, 1938), chs 4–5.
9. Christopher Wyvill, *Political Papers*, ii, 20–1; iii, 66, 69. On Wyvill's campaigns see Ian R. Christie, Wilkes, *Wyvill and Reform* (1962), chs 3–6.
10. *Parl Hist*, xviii (1813), 1287–97.
11. H.T. Dickinson, *Liberty and Property*, pp. 219–29; Christopher Wyvill, *Political Papers*, i, 228–43; and *The Report of the Sub-Committee of Westminster* (1780), pp. 3–8.
12. H.T. Dickinson, *Liberty and Property*, pp. 248–54. See also Chapter 5, notes 68–70, above.
13. Ibid., pp. 254–8.
14. John Brewer, *Party Ideology and Popular Politics*, pp. 163–77.
15. Ian R. Christie, Wilkes, *Wyvill and Reform*, pp. 71–2.
16. 'Thomas Hardy' in J.O. Baylen and N.J. Gossman (eds), *A Biographical Dictionary of British Radicals* (2 vols, Hassocks, 1979), i, 206–10.
17. John Brewer, 'English Radicalism in the Age of George III, in J.G.A. Pocock (ed.), *Three British Revolutions*, pp. 331–4; John Brewer, 'Commercialization and Politics', in Neil McKendrick, John Brewer and J.H. Plumb, *The Birth of a Consumer Society* (1982), pp. 254–8; John Brewer, *Party Ideology and Popular Politics*, ch. 8; Caroline Robbins, *The Eighteenth-Century Commonwealthman*, ch. 9; and C.C. Bonwick, 'An English Audience for American Revolutionary Pamphlets', *HJ*, 19 (1976), 355–74.
18. George Rudé, *Wilkes and Liberty*, chs 5, 8, 10; and John Brewer, 'Commercialization and Politics', in McKendrick et al, *The Birth of a Consumer Society*, pp. 203–16.
19. Ibid., pp. 241–60.
20. James E. Bradley, *Religion, Revolution and English Radicalism*, chs 4–5; Robert Hole, 'English sermons and tracts as media of debate on the French Revolution 1789–99', in Mark Philp (ed.), *The French*

Revolution and British Popular Politics (Cambridge, 1991), pp. 23–4; and especially Martin Fitzpatrick, 'Heretical Religion and Radical Political Ideas in Late Eighteenth-Century England', in Eckhart Hellmuth (ed.), *The Transformation of Political Culture*, pp. 339–72.

21. J.C.D. Clark, *English Society 1688–1832*, pp. 307–24; C.C. Bonwick, 'English Dissenters and the American Revolution', in H.C. Allen and Roger Thompson (eds), *Contrast and Connection* (1976), pp 88–112; Russell E. Richey, 'The Origins of British Radicalism: The Changing Rationale for Dissent', *ECS*, 7 (1973–4), 179–92; James E. Bradley, 'Whigs and Nonconformists: "Slumbering Radicalism" in English Politics, 1739–1789', *ECS*, 9 (1975–6), 1–27; James E. Bradley, 'Religion and Reform at the Polls. Nonconformity in Cambridge Politics, 1774– 1784', *JBS*, 23 (1984), 55–78; James E. Bradley, *Religion, Revolution and English Radicalism*, chs 1, 3–5; and John Seed, 'Gentlemen Dissenters: The Social and Political Meanings of Rational Dissent in the 1770s and 1780s', *HJ*, 28 (1985), 299–325.

22. Mary Thale (ed.), *Selections from the Papers of the London Corresponding Society 1792–1799* (Cambridge, 1983), pp. xxiii–xxiv.

23. Ibid., p. xix; and Günther Lottes, *Politische Aufklärung und plebejisches Publikum* (Munich, 1979), pp. 360–73.

24. A.W.L. Seaman, 'Radical Politics at Sheffield, 1791–1797', *THAS*, 7 (1957), 215–28; and John Stevenson, *Artisans and Democrats. Sheffield and the French Revolution, 1789–1797* (Sheffield, 1989), pp. 15–17.

25. John Dinwiddy, 'Interpretation of anti-Jacobinism', in Mark Philp, ed., *The French Revolution and British Popular Politics*, p. 48.

26. John Brewer, 'Commercialization and Politics', in McKendrick et al, *The Birth of a Consumer Society*, pp. 217–36; and Verner W. Crane, 'The Club of Honest Whigs: Friends of Science and Liberty', *WMQ*, 3rd series, 23 (1966), 210–33.

27. John Brewer, 'English Radicalism in the Age of George III', in J.G.A. Pocock (ed.), *Three British Revolutions*, pp. 331–2, 342, 357–8; and John Brewer, *Party Ideology and Popular Politics*, pp. 180, 194–9, 206.

28. Ian R. Christie, Wilkes, *Wyvill and Reform*, chs 3–4.

29. E.C. Black, *The Association: British Extraparliamentary Political Organ- ization, 1769–1793* (Cambridge, Mass., 1963), pp. 71–5, 86–9; Carl B. Cone, *The English Jacobins*, pp. 61–2, 65–70; Edward Royle and James Walvin, *English Radicals and Reformers 1760–1848* (1982), pp. 29–32; and Günther Lottes, *Politische Aufklärung und plebejisches Publikum*, pp. 29– 52.

30. Henry Collins, 'The London Corresponding Society', in John Saville (ed.), *Democracy and the Labour Movement* (1954), pp. 103–34.

31. Mary Thale, 'London debating societies in the 1790s', *HJ*, 32 (1989), 57–86.

32. See note 24.

33. P. Handforth, 'Manchester radical politics, 1789–94', in *TLCAS*, 66 (1956), 87–106; C.B. Jewson, *The Jacobin City* (1975); and Albert Goodwin, *The Friends of Liberty*, ch. 5.

34. John Brewer, 'The Wilkites and the law, 1763–1774', in J. Brewer and J. Styles (eds), *An Ungovernable People* (1980), pp. 128–71; and John

Brewer, 'English Radicalism in the Age of George III', in J.G.A. Pocock (ed.), *Three British Revolutions*, pp. 344–8.

35. Peter D.G. Thomas, 'John Wilkes and the Freedom of the Press (1771)', *BIHR*, 33 (1960), 86–98.
36. Günther Lottes, *Politische Aufklärung*, pp. 208–14.
37. John Brewer, *Party Ideological and Popular Politics*, pp. 139–60; John Brewer, 'Commercialization and Politics', in Neil McKendrick et al, *The Birth of a Consumer Society*, pp. 254–8; Solomon Lutnick, *The American Revolution and the British Press 1775–1783* (Columbia, Mo., 1967), passim; and John Money, *Experience and Identity: Birmingham and the West Midlands 1760–1800* (Manchester, 1977), ch. 6.
38. C.C. Bonwick, 'An English Audience for American Revolutionary Pamphlets', *HJ*, 19 (1976), 355.
39. John Brewer, *Party Ideology and Popular Politics*, pp. 146, 154–5.
40. John Sainsbury, *Disaffected Patriots*, p. 29.
41. John Brewer, *Party Ideology and Popular Politics*, pp. 171–4; and Horace Breackley, *The Life of John Wilkes* (1917), pp. 189–90.
42. Edward Royle and James Walvin, *English Radicals and Reformers*, p. 30.
43. Mary Thale (ed.), *Selections from the Papers of the London Corresponding Society 1792–1799*, preface.
44. Donald Clare, 'The Local Newspaper Press and Local Politics in Manchester and Liverpool, 1780–1800', *TLCAS*, 73–4 (1963–4), 104–8, 111–13.
45. A.W.L. Seaman, 'Reform Politics at Sheffield, 1791–1797', *THAS*, 7 (1957), 220–3.
46. C.B. Jewson, *The Jacobin City*, pp. 58–61.
47. H.T. Dickinson, *British Radicalism and the French Revolution 1789–1815*, p. 20.
48. Gregory Claeys, *Thomas Paine, Social and Political Thought* (1989), pp. 111–13; and E.P. Thompson, *The Making of the English Working Class*, p. 117.
49. Harry Hayden Clark (ed.), *Thomas Paine: Representative Selections* (revised edn, New York, 1961), pp. cviii–cxciii.
50. George Rudé, *Wilkes and Liberty*, chs 7–8; John Cannon, *Parliamentary Reform 1640–1832*, pp. 62–3; and John A. Phillips, 'Popular Politics in Unreformed England', *JMH*, 52 (1980), 601–5.
51. James E. Bradley, *Popular Politics and the American Revolution*, pp. 121–49; and James E. Bradley, *Religion, Revolution and English Radicalism*, chs 9–10.
52. Ian R. Christie, *Wilkes, Wyvill and Reform*, chs 3–6; John Cannon, *Parliamentary Reform 1640–1832*, ch. 4; E.C. Black, *The Association*, chs 2–3; G.S. Veitch, *The Genesis of Parliamentary Reform*, chs 3–4.
53. Albert Goodwin, *The Friends of Liberty*, pp. 277–80.
54. Ibid., p. 391.
55. H.T. Dickinson, *Liberty and Property*, pp. 224, 263.
56. Edward Royle and James Walvin, *English Radicals and Reformers*, pp. 65–6; and Albert Goodwin, *The Friends of Liberty*, pp. 284–8.
57. Ibid., pp. 292–306.
58. John Brewer, *Party Ideology and Popular Politics*, pp. 178–90; and John Brewer, 'Commercialization and Politics', in Neil McKendrick et al, *The Birth of a Consumer Society*, pp. 238–41.

59. John Brewer, 'The Number 45: A Wilkite Political Symbol', in Stephen Baxter (ed.), *England's Rise to Greatness* (Los Angeles, 1983), pp. 349–80.

60. H.T. Dickinson, *Radical Politics in the North-East of England in the Later Eighteenth Century*, p. 6.

61. George Rudé, *Wilkes and Liberty*, chs 2–3, 5–6, 10; and George Rudé, 'Wilkes and Liberty, 1768–9', *Guildhall Miscellany*, 1 (1952), 3–24.

62. H.T. Dickinson, *Liberty and Property*, pp. 265–9.

63. N. McCord and D.E. Brewster, 'Some Labour Troubles of the 1790s in North-East England', *IRSH*, 13 (1968), 366–83; and Roger Wells, *Dearth and Distress in Yorkshire 1793–1802*, Borthwick Institute Papers, no. 52 (York, 1977).

64. John Salisbury, *Disaffected Patriots*, p. 91.

65. Albert Goodwin, *The Friends of Liberty*, pp. 391–8.

66. H.T. Dickinson, *Liberty and Property*, pp. 263–4; and John Dinwiddy, 'Conceptions of Revolution in the English Radicalism of the 1790s', in Eckhart Hellmuth (ed.), *The Transformation of Political Culture*, pp. 535–60.

67. G.S. Veitch, *The Genesis of Parliamentary Reform*, chs 7–8, 12–14; John Cannon, *Parliamentary Reform*, ch. 6; John Cannon, *Aristocratic Century*, pp. 164–5; M.I. Thomis and P. Holt, *Threats of Revolution in Britain 1789–1848*, ch. 1; and Ian R. Christie, *Stress and Stability in Late Eighteenth-Century Britain*, pp. 46–53.

68. E.P. Thompson, *The Making of the English Working Class*, ch. 5; Roger Wells, *Insurrection: The British Experience 1795–1803* (Gloucester, 1983), chs 3–8; and Roger Wells, 'English society and revolutionary politics in the 1790s: the case for insurrection', in Mark Philp (ed.), *The French Revolution and British Popular Politics*, ch. 9.

69. Albert Goodwin, *The Friends of Liberty*, ch. 11; J. Ann Hone, *For the Cause of Truth: Radicalism in London 1796–1821* (Oxford, 1982), ch. 2; and John Dinwiddy, 'Conceptions of Revolution in the English Radicalism of the 1790s', in Eckhart Hellmuth (ed.), *The Transformation of Political Culture*, pp. 535–60.

70. On the United Irishmen, see Marianne Elliott, *Partners in Revolution: The United Irishmen and France* (1977) and David Dickson, Dáire Keogh and Kevin Whelan (eds), *The United Irishmen: Republicanism, Radicalism and Rebellion* (Dublin, 1993).

71. See the works cited in notes 67 and 68.

72. David Eastwood, 'Patriotism and the English state in the 1790s', in Mark Philp (ed.), *The French Revolution and British Popular Politics*, pp. 162–7.

73. Conrad Gill, *The Naval Mutinies of 1797* (Manchester, 1913); E.P. Thompson, *The Making of the English Working Class*, pp. 183–5; and Roger Wells, *Insurrection*, ch. 5.

74. H.T. Dickinson, *British Radicalism and the French Revolution 1789–1815*, ch. 2; H.T. Dickinson, 'Popular loyalism in Britain in the 1790s', in Eckhart Hellmuth (ed.), *The Transformation of Political Culture*, pp. 503–33; and H.T. Dickinson, 'Popular Conservatism and Militant Loyalism 1789–1815', in H.T. Dickinson (ed.), *Britain and the French Revolution 1789–1815*, pp. 103–25.

CHAPTER 8:   POPULAR CONSERVATISM AND MILITANT
LOYALISM

1.   Ian R. Christie, *Stress and Stability in Late Eighteenth-Century Britain.*
2.   J.C.D. Clark, *English Society 1688–1832*, pp. 42–276; J.A.W. Gunn, *Beyond Liberty and Property* (Kingston and Montreal, 1983), pp. 164–93; H.T. Dickinson, *Liberty and Property*, pp. 13–56, 121–62, 270–318; and Thomas Philip Schofield, 'Conservative Political Thought in Britain in Response to the French Revolution', *HJ*, 29 (1986), 601–22.
3.   An attempt has been made to examine the dissemination of conservative propaganda to the lower orders in the late eighteenth century by Robert Hole, 'British counter-revolutionary popular propaganda in the 1790s', in Colin Jones (ed.), *Britain and Revolutionary France: Conflict, Subversion and Propaganda* (Exeter, 1983), pp. 53–69; Susan Pederson, 'Hannah More meets Simple Simon: Tracts, Chapbooks, and Popular Culture in Late Eighteenth-Century England', *JBS*, 25 (1986) 84–113; and Herbert M. Atherton, 'The British Defend their Constitution in Political Cartoons and Literature', in Harry C. Payne (ed.), *Studies in Eighteenth Century Culture* (Madison, 1982), ii, 3–31. I have examined conservative propaganda and loyalist activity at the end of the eighteenth century in 'Popular Conservatism and Militant Loyalism 1789–1815', in H.T. Dickinson (ed.), *Britain and the French Revolution 1718–1815*, pp.103–25, 266–8; and 'Popular Loyalism in Britain in the 1790s', in Eckhart Hellmuth (ed.), *The Transformation of Political Culture*, pp. 503–33. See also Michael Weinzierl, *Freiheit, Eigentum und keine Gleichheit. Die Transformation der englischen politischen Kultur und die Anfänge des modernen Konservatismus 1791–1812* (Munich, 1993), chs 2, 3, and 5.
4.   See works listed in note 2, above.
5.   J.C.D. Clark, *English Society 1688–1832*, p. 132; and W.A. Speck, *Tory and Whig*, pp. 110–14.
6.   Leicester RO. Finch Mss. Box vi, bundle 22. Lord Normanby to the Earl of Nottingham, 10 Mar. 1702.
7.   *The Examiner*, 5 April 1711.
8.   G.V. Bennett, *White Kennett* (1957), pp. 86–7.
9.   *A Collection of the Addresses which have been presented to the Queen, since the impeachment of the Reverend Dr. Henry Sacheverell* (2 vols,1711), i, 1.
10.   Ibid., i, 6.
11.   HMC, *Bath MSS*, i, 199. Shrewsbury to Harley, 20 Oct. 1710.
12.   J.C.D. Clark, *English Society 1688–1832*, pp. 132, 142–7; and Nicholas Rogers, 'Popular Jacobitism in Provincial Context', in Eveline Cruickshanks and Jeremy Black (eds), *The Jacobite Challenge* (Edinburgh, 1988), pp. 123–37.
13.   *Parl Hist*, xii (1812), 615.
14.   Linda Colley, *Britons. Forging the Nation 1707–1837* (1992), pp. 201–3.
15.   J.C.D. Clark, *English Society 1688–1832*, pp. 126–8.
16.   Bangor University College Library. Baron Hill Ms.6776. 8 Oct. 1714.
17.   *The Works of Lord Bolingbroke*, ii, 378.

18. Nicholas Rogers, 'Popular Disaffection in London during the Forty-Five', *LJ*, 1 (1975), 5–27; Nicholas Rogers, 'Resistance to Oligarchy: The City Opposition to Walpole and his Successors, 1725–47', in John Stevenson (ed.), *London in the Age of Reform* (Oxford, 1977), pp. 14–20, and Linda Colley, *Britons*, pp. 81–5.

19. J.C.D. Clark, *English Society 1688–1832*, pp. 174–8, 194.

20. *London Gazette*, March–June 1789.

21. Linda Colley, 'The Apotheosis of George III: Loyalty, Royalty and the British Nation 1760–1820', *P&P*, 102 (1984), 94–129; and Linda Colley, *Britons*, pp. 206–22.

22. J.C.D. Clark, *English Society 1688–1832*, pp. 230–4; Robert Hole, *Pulpits, Politics and Public Order in England 1760–1832* (Cambridge, 1989), pp. 18–21, 51–3; J.A.W. Gunn, *Beyond Liberty and Property*, pp. 167–75; and James E. Bradley, 'The Anglican Pulpit, the Social Order, and the Resurgence of Toryism during the American Revolution', *Albion*, 21 (1989), 368–73.

23. Michael Weinzeirl, 'John Reeves and the Controversy over the Constitutional Role of Parliament in England during the French Revolution', *PER*, 5 (1985), 71–77.

24. J.C.D. Clark, *English Society 1688–1832*, pp. 216–76.

25. Robert Lowth, *A Sermon preached before the Lords Spiritual and Temporal, ... January 30*, 1767 (1767), pp. 7, 10.

26. J.A.W. Gunn, *Beyond Liberty and Property*, pp. 164–84; and Tina Isaacs, 'The Anglican Hierarchy and the Reformation of Manners, 1688–1738', *JEH*, 33 (1982), 397–411.

27. H.T. Dickinson, 'The Eighteenth Century Debate on the Sovereignty of Parliament', *TRHS*, 5th series, 26 (1976), 189–210.

28. H.T. Dickinson, *Liberty and Property*, pp. 121–62, 270–318.

30. Michael Duffy, *The Englishman and the Foreigner*, pp. 13–52; Gerald Newman, *The Rise of English Nationalism* (New York, 1987), *passim*; John Dinwiddy, 'England', in Otto Dann and John Dinwiddy (eds), *Nationalism in the Age of the French Revolution* (1988), pp. 57–70; Linda Colley, 'Whose Nation? Class and National Consciousness in Britain 1750–1830', *P&P*, 113 (1986), 97–117; H.T. Dickinson, 'The Tory Party's Attitude to Foreigners': a Note on Party Principles in the Age of Anne', *BIHR*, 40 (1967), 153–65; and H.T. Dickinson, 'The Poor Palatines and the parties', *EHR*, 82 (1967), 464–85.

31. Samuel Clarke, *A Discourse concerning the Unalterable Obligation of Natural Religion* (1706) in Richard Watson (ed.), *A Collection of Theological Tracts* (6 vols, Cambridge, 1785), iv, 189.

32. See, e.g., Offspring Blackall, *The Lord Bishop of Exeter's Answer to Mr Hoadly's Letter* (1709), pp. 15–18; David Hume, *Essays Moral, Political and Literary*, (eds), T.H. Green and T.H. Grose (2 vols, 1875), i, 446–7; and Samuel Johnson, *Taxation No Tyranny* (3rd edn, 1775), p. 34.

33. See, e.g., Francis Atterbury, *The Voice of the People, No Voice of God* (1710), p. 6.

34. *A Collection of Addresses*, ii, 7.

35. *Parl Hist*, ix (1811), 474. See also Francis Hare, *A Sermon preached before the House of Commons ... January 31, 1731* (1731), *passim*; and *The Freeholder's Alarm to his Brethren* (1734), p. 5.

36. *Parl Hist*, xvi (1813), 695–6.

37. J.C.D. Clark, *English Society 1688–1832*, p. 237.

38. Samuel Johnson, *Taxation No Tyranny*, John Wesley, *Calm Address to our American Colonies* (1775); and Anti-Sejanus in the *London Chronicle*, 28 Jan. and 13 Feb. 1776.

39. *Gentleman's Magazine*, xlvi (1776), 505. See also Paul Langford, 'The English Clergy and the American Revolution', in Eckhart Hellmuth (ed.), *The Transformation of Political Culture*, pp. 275–307.

40. H.T. Dickinson, 'Popular Conservatism and Militant Loyalism 1789–1815', in H.T. Dickinson (ed.), *Britain and the French Revolution 1789–1815*, pp. 104–9; Robert Hole, 'British counter-revolutionary popular propaganda in the 1790s', in Colin Jones (ed.), *Britain and Revolutionary France*, pp. 53–69; Gregory Claeys, 'The French Revolution Debate and British Political Thought', *History of Political Thought*, 11 (1990), 59–80; Emily Lorraine de Montluzin, *The Anti-Jacobins 1798–1800* (1988), pp. 1–52; and Emma Vincent, '"The Real Grounds of the Present War": John Bowles and the French Revolutionary Wars, 1792–1802', *H*, 78 (1993), 393–420.

41. Martyn P. Thompson, 'The Reception of Locke's Two Treatises of Government 1690–1705', *Political Studies*, 24 (1976), 184–91; J.P. Kenyon, 'The Revolution of 1688: Resistance and Contract', in Neil McKendrick (ed.), *Historical Perspectives*, pp. 43–69; Richard Ashcraft, *Revolutionary Politics and Locke's 'Two Treatises of Government'*, pp. 521–601; Mark Goldie, 'The Revolution of 1689 and the Structure of Political Argument', *Bull. Research in the Humanities*, 83 (1980), 473–564; John Dunn, 'The politics of John Locke in England and America in the eighteenth century', in John W. Yolton (ed.), *John Locke Problems and Perspectives*, pp.45–80; H.V.S. Ogden, 'The State of Nature and the Decline of Lockian Political Theory in England, 1760–1800', *AHR*, 46 (1940), 21–44; and H.T. Dickinson, *Liberty and Property*, pp. 125–34, 306–10.

42. Geoffrey Holmes, *The Trial of Doctor Sacheverell*, pp. 233–55; and G.V. Bennett, *The Tory Crisis in Church and State 1688–1730*, pp. 214–15.

43. H.T. Dickinson, *Liberty and Property*, pp. 163–94.

44. Solomon Lutnick, *The American Revolution and the British Press 1775–1783*, pp. 12–34.

45. James E. Bradley, *Popular Politics and the American Revolution*, ch.4; and John Money, *Experience and Identity*, ch. 8.

46. Ian R. Christie, *Wilkes, Wyvill and Reform*, pp. 67, 116–7, 182, 184; Paul Langford, 'London and the American Revolution', in John Stevenson (ed.), *London in the Age of Reform*, pp. 55–76; Paul Langford, 'Old Whigs, Old Tories, and the American Revolution', *Journal of Imperial and Commonwealth History*, 8 (1980), 112, 120–1, 125, 127–8; and John Sainsbury, *Disaffected Patriots*, pp. 114, 125, 129–32.

47. Gayle Trusdel Pendleton, 'English Conservative Propaganda during the French Revolution, 1789–1802', unpublished PhD thesis (Emory University, 1976), *passim*; H.T. Dickinson, 'Popular Conservatism and Militant Loyalism 1789–1815', in H.T. Dickinson (ed.), *Britain and the French Revolution 1789–1815*, pp. 110–12; Susan Pederson,

'Hannah More meets Simple Simon: Tracts, Chapbooks, and Popular Culture in Late Eighteenth-Century England', *JBS*, 25 (1986), 84–113; Marilyn Butler, *Jane Austen and the War of Ideas* (Oxford, 1975), pp. 88–123; Betty T. Bennett, *British War Poetry in the Age of Romanticism 1793–1815* (New York, 1974), *passim;* Herbert M. Atherton, 'The British Defend their Constitution in Political Cartoons and Literature', in Harry C. Payne (ed.), *Studies in Eighteenth Century Culture*, ii, 3–31; J.A.W. Gunn, *Beyond Liberty and Property*, pp. 176–93; and Martin John Smith, 'English Radical Newspapers in the French Revolutionary Era, 1790–1803', unpublished PhD thesis (London University, 1979), pp. 5–19.

48. J.C.D. Clark, *English Society 1688–1832*, pp. 126–7, 137–40, 216–40, 244–7; Nancy Uhlar Murray, 'The Influence of the French Revolution on the Church of England and its Rivals, 1789–1802', unpublished D. Phil. thesis (Oxford University, 1975), pp. 44–79, 212–307; Deryck Lovegrove, 'English Evangelical Dissent and the European Conflict 1789–1815', in W.J. Shiels (ed.), *Studies in Church History* (Oxford, 1983), xx, 266; John Walsh, 'Methodism at the End of the Eighteenth Century', in Rupert Davies and Gordon Rupp (eds), *A History of the Methodist Church in Great Britain* (1965), i, 303–8; John Sainsbury, *Disaffected Patriots*, pp. 80–1; Paul Langford, 'The English Clergy and the American Revolution', in Eckhart Hellmuth (ed.), *The Transformation of Political Culture*, pp. 275–307; James E. Bradley, 'The Anglican Pulpit, the Social Order, and the Resurgence of Toryism during the American Revolution', *Albion*, 21 (1989), 361–88; Robert Hole, *Pulpits, Politics and Public Order in England 1760–1832*, pp. 95–159; and Robert Hole, 'English sermons and tracts as media of debate on the French Revolution 1789–99', in Mark Philp (ed.), *The French Revolution and British Politics*, pp. 18–37.

49. J.A.W. Gunn, *Beyond Liberty and Property*, pp.150–5; and J.C.D. Clark, *English Society 1688–1832*, pp. 158–60.

50. John Sharp, *The Duty of Subjection to the Higher Powers* (1700), quoted by J.C.D. Clark, *English Society 1688–1832*, p. 159.

51. D. Napthine and W.A. Speck, 'Clergymen and Conflict 1660–1763', in W.J. Shiels (ed.), *Studies in Church History* (Oxford, 1983), xx, 231–51; Henry P. Ippel, 'Blow the Trumpet, Sanctify the Fast', *HLQ*, 44 (1980), 43–60; and Henry P. Ippel, 'British Sermons and the American Revolution', *Journal of Religious History*, 12 (1982), 191–205.

52. John Dinwiddy, 'Interpretations of anti-Jacobinism', in Mark Philp (ed.), *The French Revolution and British Popular Politics*, pp. 44–6.

53. *A Collection of the Addresses which have been presented to the Queen* (2 vols, 1710), *passim.*

54. Linda Colley, *Britons*, pp. 81–4.

55. James E. Bradley, *Popular Politics and the American Revolution*, pp. 123–4.

56. Ibid., pp. 22, 52n, 61, 65, 67, 69, 77, 79; and Linda Colley, *Britons*, pp. 137–8.

57. Donald R. McAdam, 'Addresses to the King and the Fox-North Coalition', *HLQ*, 35 (1972), 381–5; and John Cannon, *The Fox-North Coalition* (Cambridge, 1969), p. 188.

58. These addresses were all printed in the *London Gazette*. See also Linda Colley, 'The Apotheosis of George III: Loyalty, Royalty and the British Nation 1760–1820', *P&P*, 102 (1984), 94–129.

59. Robert Dozier, *For King, Constitution and Country: The English Loyalists and the French Revolution* (Lexington, 1983), p. 63; and H.T. Dickinson, 'Popular Conservatism and Militant Loyalism 1789–1815', in H.T. Dickinson (ed.), *Britain and the French Revolution 1789–1815*, p. 113.

60. Geoffrey Holmes, 'The Sacheverell Riots: The Crowd and the Church in Early Eighteenth-Century London', *P&P*, 72 (1976), 55–85; Nicholas Rogers, 'Popular Protest in Early Hanoverian London', *P&P*, 79 (1978), 70–100; Nicholas Rogers, 'Riot and Popular Jacobitism in Early Hanoverian England', in Eveline Cruickshanks (ed.), *Ideology and Conspiracy*, pp. 70–88; R.B. Rose, 'The Priestley Riots of 1791', *P&P*, 18 (1960), 68–88; and Martin Smith, 'Conflict and Society in Late Eighteenth-Century Birmingham', unpublished PhD thesis (Cambridge University, 1977), pp. 1–56.

61. On anti-Catholicism see Linda Colley, *Britons*, ch. 1; and Colin Haydon, *Anti-Catholicism in Eighteenth-Century England*.

62. Michael Duffy, *The Englishman and the Foreigner*, pp. 22, 32–4; and Nicholas Rogers, 'Popular Disaffection in London during the Forty-Five', *LJ*, 1 (1975), 5–27.

63. George Rudé, *Paris and London*, pp. 268–92; Christopher Hibbert, *King Mob* (1959), pp. 27, 43–140; and Nicholas Rogers, 'Crowd and People in the Gordon Riots', in Eckhart Hellmuth (ed.), *The Transformation of Political Culture*, pp. 31–55.

64. Thomas W. Perry, *Public Opinion, Propaganda and Politics in Eighteenth-Century England*, *passim*.

65. John Walsh, 'Methodism and the Mob in the Eighteenth Century', in G.J. Cuming and Derek Baker (eds), *Studies in Church History* (Cambridge, 1972), vii, 213–27.

66. James L. Fitts, 'Newcastle's Mob', *Albion*, 5 (1975), 41–9.

67. Nicholas Rogers, 'Popular Disaffection in London during the Forty-Five', *LJ*, 1 (1975), 5–27; and Nicholas Rogers, 'Resistance to Oligarchy: The City Opposition to Walpole and his Successors', in John Stevenson (ed.), *London in the Age of Reform*, pp. 1–29.

68. Nicholas Rogers, 'Crowd an People in the Gordon Riots', in Eckhart Hellmuth (ed.), *The Transformation of Political Culture*, pp. 39–55; *Parl Hist*, xxi (1814), 386, 533, 654–60; and *Journals of the House of Commons*, xxxvii (1803), 723–4, 779, 791, 806, 812, 839, 840, 848, 889, 893, 900, 901.

69. For the loyalist associations see Robert Dozier, *For King, Constitution and Country*, pp. 55–79; Austin Mitchell, 'The Association Movement of 1792–3', *HJ*, 4 (1961), 56–77; Donald E. Ginter, 'The Loyalist Association Movement of 1792–93 and British Public Opinion', *HJ*, 9 (1966), 179–90; E.C. Black, *The Association*, ch. 7; H.T. Dickinson, 'Popular Conservatism and Militant Loyalism 1789–1815', in H.T. Dickinson (ed.), *Britain and the French Revolution 1789–1815*, pp. 114–16; and H.T. Dickinson, 'Popular Loyalism in Britain in the 1790s', in Eckhart Hellmuth (ed.), *The Transformation of Political Culture*, pp. 503–33;

Michael Weinzierl, *Freiheit, Eigentum und keine Gleichheit,* chs 2, 3 and 5; and the Reeves papers which are in the British Library, Add. MSS. 16919–28.

70.   H.T. Dickinson, 'Popular Conservatism', pp. 118–19; Alan Booth, 'Popular Loyalism and public violence in the north-west of England, 1790–1800', *SocH,* 8 (1983), 295–313; and Alan Booth, 'Reform, Repression and Revolution: Radicalism and Loyalism in the North-West of England, 1789–1803', unpublished PhD thesis (Lancaster University, 1979), pp. 144–53.

71.   J.E. Cookson, 'The English Volunteer Movement of the French Wars, 1793–1815: Some Contexts', *HJ,* 32 (1989), 867–91.

72.   H.T. Dickinson, 'Popular Conservatism' in H.T. Dickinson (ed.), *Britain and the French Revolution 1789–1815,* pp. 116–17, 122–3; Robert Dozier, *For King, Constitution and Country,* pp. 141–9; and J.R. Western, 'The Volunteer Movement as an Anti-Revolutionary Force, 1793–1802', *EHR,* 71 (1956), 603–14.

73.   Linda Colley, *Britons,* pp. 288–318, 378–81.

74.   Geoffrey Holmes, *The Trial of Doctor Sacheverell,* p. 239; James E. Bradley, *Popular Politics and the American Revolution* in England, pp. 22–4, 43–6, 48–51, 58, 108–13, 175–8; B.D. Bargar, 'Matthew Boulton and the Birmingham Petition of 1775', *WMQ,* 3rd series, 13 (1956), 32–3; *London Gazette,* May–Dec. 1792; and Robert Dozier, *For King, Constitution and Country,* pp. 21, 33.

75.   See the works on riots and disorder listed in notes 60–8.

Index